Development, Democracy

Critical Essays with Insights
and Wider Africa Contexts

Yusuf Bangura

Sierra Leonean Writers Series

Development, Democracy and Cohesion:
Critical Essays with Insights on Sierra Leone and Wider Africa Contexts

Copyright © 2015 by Yusuf Bangura

ISBN: 978-99910-54-36-0

First published 2015

Sierra Leonean Writers Series (SLWS)
Warima/Freetown/Accra
120 Kissy Road, Freetown, Sierra Leone
Publisher: Prof. Osman Sankoh (Mallam O.)
publisher@sl-writers-series.org

To my grandson,
Kemokai,
whose big, lovely smile fills me with joy

Yusuf Bangura

Contents

Part II: Democratic Politics

Part III: Cohesion and Security

Foreword

This rich collection brings together in one volume, 45 essays on politics, economy and society in Africa written during a period of immense and continuing change both on the continent and in the wider international system in which it is evolving. Produced between 1993 and 2015, they offer carefully considered insights on some of the key political, economic and social policies and processes that have combined to shape contemporary Africa as we know and experience it. On the continent itself, these policies and processes, as well as the political economy underpinning them have, most notably, included the ubiquitous one-size-fits-all International Monetary Fund and World Bank structural adjustment programmes that defined socio-economic policy making across Africa from the early 1980s through to the end of the 1990s and beyond, the popular pressures which built up for politico-governance reform that spread throughout the continent from the early 1990s, the end of official apartheid in South Africa, and the breakdown of central governmental authority in several countries that translated into devastating intra-state wars, some with genocidal dimensions. Globally, it was also the period when the old East-West Cold War came to an end along with the demise of the Soviet Union and Soviet communism, the collapse of the Berlin Wall, and the dissolution of the Eastern Bloc of countries allied to the Soviet Union in the defunct Warsaw Pact. Much policy attention was also beginning to be focused on the new phase of globalisation which a fast-paced revolution in information and communication technologies was helping to underwrite on the back of major drives towards rapid global trade, investment and financial liberalisation.

The range, dimensions and speed of the changes that were witnessed in virtually all spheres of life in Africa and globally during the 1990s into the new millennium, and the complex inter-connections linking them to one another, were daunting enough in their own right to be easily or fully digested by scholars and citizens interested in making sense of them. They were made even more difficult to grasp for many because they challenged most of our inherited frames of analyses and defied much of what the theories we had learnt to use taught us to expect. In Gramscian terms, we were witnesses to a period in which old certainties and paradigms were being rapidly eroded even as new ones were yet to be fully forged and tested. For many a commentator looking at the African world during the 1990s, it was easy either simply to adopt an "Afro-pessimist" frame of mind, slip into a conscience-soothing charity-making role, take refuge behind arguments for a recolonisation of the continent, or opt for easy, formulaic or omnibus academic explanations that sacrificed nuance and, therefore, became too simplistic to be of any use.

Yusuf Bangura was one of the leading scholars whose academic writings enabled at least two generations of Africans and Africanists to gain the kinds of robust analytic insights that were required for a proper understanding of the complex interplay of politics and economy on a continent and in a world that was undergoing rapid change. We were all to become the richer for it following his decision to carry his interventions beyond the confines of the academy into the broader public sphere through the kinds of short essays he subsequently took to producing and which now mostly comprise this volume. Deliberately written in an accessible, non-academic language and style, they were published in outlets that brought his perspectives on different topical subjects to a much broader audience with an intention to inform, educate and propel towards action.

The essays that make up this book represent some of the most authoritative commentaries produced on the political economy of Africa over a period spanning more than two decades. I had the privilege of reading most of them as they were published in the heat of discussions and debates about different events or concerns unfolding in and around Africa. Re-reading them as one collection, I am struck by their currency, the lucidity of the thinking underpinning them, and the coherence of the arguments advanced. The essays are nuanced without being riddled with and cancelled out by an excess of caveats and alibis. They are rigorously argued without being suffused with the kinds of jargons that all too often reduce the effectiveness of many an aspiring public intellectual coming from a rich scholarly background. In their magisterial breadth, we see the demolition of some popular myths about African politics and society and, simultaneously, a robust repudiation of some of the fetishes that have been projected as foundational to the African world. In their sheer depth of knowledge and experience, we are shown how to function within a clear world view without being hostage to a paradigm.

The reader is left in no doubt whatsoever about the deep and enduring pan-African commitments of the author but is spared the blind ideological sloganeering that is sometimes deployed as a substitute for proper argumentation. Yusuf Bangura also shows himself to be passionate about certain core values that he believes are indispensable to successful public service and leadership but he conveys his position without being hostage to narrow, doctrinaire views about Africa's problems and prospects, including the country of his birth, Sierra Leone. These strengths, together with the skilful blend of balanced interpretation and the clear vision of an Africa that is democratic, developmental, united, dignified and free which Bangura projects serve as powerful commendation of the essays both as a valuable educational resource and a tool for engaged political action towards the progressive transformation of the continent.

Adebayo Olukoshi,
Director, UN African Institute for Economic Development and Planning,
Dakar, Senegal.

Endorsements

"This book confirms Yusuf Bangura's reputation as one of the most incisive contemporary commentators on African development. In it, he accomplishes the difficult task of making deep and detailed analysis of Africa's development challenges accessible to a wide audience. Unlike many books of this type, Bangura does not achieve accessibility at the cost of over-simplification. On the contrary, he demonstrates a dizzying breadth and depth of knowledge regarding the struggles of development and democracy in contemporary Africa. In addition to cases from his native Sierra Leone, the book ranges across the length and breadth of the continent, from the Arab Spring to Zimbabwe, and covers issues of employment generation, elections, ethnicity, social cohesion and security. Whether speaking of the continent as a whole, or of particular countries and issues, Bangura's analysis is always grounded in a deep understanding of local realities rather than a drop-down menu of random African examples. Amid his engagement with complexity, Bangura's writing has a remarkable clarity and insight which makes this a book that can be read by anyone, but should be read by policy makers".
Kate Meagher, Associate professor of Development Studies,
London School of Economics.

"*Development, Democracy and Cohesion*, is a tour de force in Sierra Leonean studies by one of the great minds in contemporary African Studies. In this collection of essays, Bangura has put down a marker for all those involved in Sierra Leone's and by implication Africa's development. This is compulsory reading for academics, administrators and those who seek political offices in Africa".
Alfred Zack-Williams, Professor Emeritus in Sociology,
University of Central Lancashire.

"Notwithstanding its head-start at independence, Sierra Leone now finds itself among the stragglers of the world, unable to deal with any shock, and slipping dangerously back to pre-conflict status in some spheres of life. Yusuf Bangura's essays are a collection of brilliant articles covering social, political, cultural and economic challenges confronting the

country, but with equal relevance to many African countries. Sierra Leoneans and other Africans are invited to revisit known orthodoxies, eschew platitudes, and boldly but openly accept to understand the root causes of the current predicament. Getting democracy to deliver development and national cohesion, when divisive politics is the preferred route to political power in the guise of democratic elections, and where such politics manipulate development dividends selectively, is at the core of the collection. The essays also point to options for using the results of rigorous analysis to move the country towards resilient, inclusive and sustained growth. This book is a must read for anyone who seeks to understand the underlying political, social and economic forces at play in Sierra Leone, and the reasons for the consistent failure to break out of the low income trap the country seems to now find itself in".
Herbert P. M'cleod, Country Director,
International Growth Centre, Sierra Leone.

"What is remarkable about the essays in this book is the clarity of thought which Yusuf Bangura has brought to bear on the challenges and prospects for consolidating development, democracy, and social cohesion in Sierra Leone and Africa in general. Bangura's study of the inter-connectedness of these three existential issues is unassailable, but he also raises serious questions about how national priorities are set when, for example, funding for development projects is made to the countries of the South by the rich countries of the North whose political agendas may not cohere with those of the South. Bangura argues that most African countries are still susceptible to the dictates of the World Bank and the IMF, and local and transnational interests have had a deleterious effect on the structures of power and social divisions in many states despite more than 50 years of independence. Drawing on his vast knowledge as a research coordinator at UNRISD, he contends that social cohesion and security are often undermined by socio-economic inequalities, racism, ethno-regional electoral politics, military adventurism, and intra-state wars. He states with unusual candour and eloquence that consolidating the gains in democratisation must involve a rights-based approach to development, social cohesion, accountability, capacity-building, poverty eradication, effective use of state resources, and sensitivity to ethnic cleavages among others. In 45 essays, he has given us a rare insight into his thoughts on a wide range of issues

touching on the very existence of the post-colonial African and has done so in a coherent manner and a level of critical analysis that will make this book a must read not only for development experts but also for the general reader who is interested in issues of development, democracy, and social cohesion in contemporary Africa".
Peter A. Dumbuya, Professor of History,
Fort Valley State University, USA.

"Yusuf Bangura, one of Sierra Leone's finest thinkers and Africa's leading public intellectuals, provides a compendium of incisive and thought-provoking essays on many of the political and developmental issues facing the continent in the last two decades. Drawing from serious research and astute observations, he offers compelling analyses of the continent's challenges as well as sound recommendations for laws, policies and actions to help Africans chart a future that will be peaceful, productive and enriching. With its wide range of engaging topics and depth of wisdom, this book is an indispensable gem for scholars, policy makers, and all those who want to get their fingers on the pulse of the continent and contribute to its positive transformation".
Ismail Rashid, Professor of History,
Vassar College, USA.

"Yusuf Bangura, one of Africa's leading intellectuals, has made a significant contribution to our understanding of Africa's weighty challenges. This collection of essays covers over two decades and engages a diversity of concerns ranging from constitutional reforms, rebuilding of post-conflict societies to responses to the current Ebola crisis. The major strength of the book lies in its ability to combine deeply insightful socio-political analysis with innovative policy alternatives and presenting these in a highly accessible manner. *Development, Democracy and Cohesion* is crucial for anyone seeking to understand contemporary African realities".
Zenebework Tadesse, Former President of Council for the Development of Social Science Research in Africa, Dakar, Senegal.

"In this compelling and highly readable collection of 45 essays written over a period of 25 years of his professional life, Yusuf Bangura – a first class scholar and fearless policy advocate – has comprehensively tackled

the major challenge of nation-building and transformation in Africa under three essential themes: development, democracy and social cohesion. The collection, which is "a reflection on some of the momentous economic, political and social changes" in the continent in the post-independence era, is dazzling in its punchy narrative, critical analysis and powerful arguments. This book is so good and useful in many ways: it is a must read for anyone interested in developing societies and the challenge of sustainable development; a reference book on development for libraries in the global South and North; and a development policy maker's guide on key issues and topics. It should be purchased forthwith as you are unlikely to find a more thorough, comprehensive and open-minded account of Africa's development challenge".
Franklyn Lisk, Professorial Research Fellow,
Centre for the Study of Globalisation and Regionalisation, University of Warwick.

"This is an excellent collection not only on Yusuf Bangura's thought but on radical UN thinking as manifested in the UNRISD research programme. It is also a highly valuable contribution to the Sierra Leone debate in a period of particular agony. Many of the pieces were known to me as I was privileged to be on the list when they were first distributed. I was also present both in Kano and in Abuja when Yusuf Bangura presented the UNRISD flagship report, *Combatting Poverty and Inequality*, which he so masterly had produced. Although developments in Sierra Leone are addressed in particular detail, these essays cover much more, including Nigeria, where both of us taught political economy in the 1980s. But the coverage is wider still. I want to congratulate both the author and the publisher for this exceptionally brilliant book of essays".
Bjorn Beckman, Emeritus Professor, Department of Political Science, Stockholm University.

"Yusuf Bangura's book is a magnificent collection on the travails of the African state, but more importantly, an exposition on analytical perspectives leading to policy choices for state reconstruction. The three challenges he examines, development, democracy and cohesion, are indeed the entry points for policies that can place Africa on the path to building a better society. The 45 essays are written in clear, easy-to-read prose and devoid of academic jargon. It is a gift to the general reader of

over three decades of solid political economy academic research rooted in a tradition of progressive reform. Two key arguments strike me in the book. First, there is sufficient evidence that authoritarianism is bad for development while democracy is better. Second, democratic regimes in Africa have not done as much as they could to promote development and combat poverty. The progressive agenda that flows from the logic, therefore, is the imperative of improving the quality of democracy and social cohesion on a platform that addresses the core problems of poverty and growing inequality by more effective use of the continent's resource wealth. For this to happen, the political process, he argues, must become more rooted in Africa's pro-poor social movements. One controversial issue he places on the agenda is that of the future of female genital mutilation, or clitorectomy, within the context of socialisation of women in African society. By refusing to use the terms that have governed this debate in feminist literature and advocacy, he appears to take a more understanding "Africanist" approach that would deservedly invite criticism. All the same, the issues of social reality he raises are a good contribution to a complex debate".
Jibrin Ibrahim, Professor of Political Science,
Babcock University, Ilishan, Nigeria; and former Executive Director, Centre for Democracy and Development, Abuja, Nigeria.

"In this collection of insightful essays Yusuf Bangura sheds light on the challenges, both old and new, that confront Sierra Leone and other African countries in building state-society configurations that are developmental, democratic and socially cohesive in a globalised world that reinforces underdevelopment and inequality. The chapters written in a very accessible style, expose the multiple constraints that have to be overcome – from narrowly conceived macroeconomic blueprints imposed by global financial institutions, to processes of de-industrialisation, labour informalisation and resource plunder ('land grabs'), fiscally constrained policies that have left the social infrastructure threadbare, to weak democratic institutions that are not up to the task of managing the continent's ethnic diversity. But the book is not a story of 'doom and gloom': the analysis of existing challenges is laced with rich historical and comparative insights from the African continent to East Asia and Northern Europe, pointing to alternative pathways that can create more inclusive and developmental democracies that work for the benefit of all".

Shahra Razavi, Chief, Research and Data Section,
UN Women, New York.

Acknowledgements

The 45 essays in this volume were written between 1993 and 2015, covering largely the period when I coordinated research projects at the United Nations Research Institute for Social Development (UNRISD). When I set out to prepare the volume, it became clear that there is a close connection between the popular essays I have written on Sierra Leone and other African countries and the research work I directed at UNRISD, much of which focused on the inter-connections of development, democracy and cohesion. Over the years, I have been able to draw on research insights from my UNRISD work to inform my general commentaries on economic, social and political developments in Africa.

I am grateful to UNRISD and colleagues at the Institute for providing an environment for collaborative, stimulating and serious work. The Institute's multi-disciplinary approach to the study of social development--which required understanding of the basic principles of economics, political science and sociology--suited my academic training and interests. At the London School of Economics and Political Science, where I did my undergraduate degree in the early 1970s, economics, political theory and international history were compulsory three-year subjects for all students irrespective of fields of specialisation. My doctoral thesis, which I also wrote at the LSE in 1978, was on international political economy—it analysed the economic and political bargains which British policy makers struck with African leaders in the context of decolonisation to defend the pound sterling's role as an international currency around issues of monetary policy, trade, and investment and aid relations. Before joining UNRISD, the Department of Political Science at Ahmadu Bello University in Nigeria offered me an opportunity to teach courses in political economy for eight years and to conduct research on the politics of structural adjustment policies. The essays in this volume benefited substantially from this long engagement with political economy in which issues of social justice feature prominently.

Simplifying research findings for the general public and linking research to policy issues were important demands at UNRISD. Developing these skills at the Institute helped tremendously in writing these essays. Most of the essays have been published in journals, magazines, bulletins, on-line discussion forums and newspapers. Except for a few essays extracted from some of my academic publications, which may help readers with conceptual and thematic issues, I have excluded my longer, fully referenced and more complex academic articles.

I would like to thank the publishers of the following journals, magazines, bulletins and newspapers where these essays were first published:

- CODESRIA Bulletin (Dakar)
- Southern African Political and Economic Monthly (Harare)
- UNRISD Research and Policy Brief (Geneva)
- UNRISD eBulletin (Geneva)
- Review of African Political Economy (London)
- European Journal of Development Research (London)
- African Journal of Political Science (Harare)
- South Letter (South Centre, Geneva)
- AAPS Newsletter (African Association of Political Science, Harare)
- Social Development Review (London)
- Africa Renewal (New York)
- Africa Demos (Carter Center, Atlanta)
- West Africa (London)
- Open Democracy (London)
- Financial Times Africa (London)
- Association of Concerned Africa Scholars Special Bulletin in the USA
- Sierra Express Media (Freetown)
- Sewa News (London)
- The Sewa Chronicle (London)
- Patriotic Vanguard (Vancouver)
- Cocorioko (New York)
- Awoko (Freetown)
- Global Times (Freetown)

- APC Times (All Peoples Communication, Online Sierra Leone News)
- New Citizen (Freetown)
- This is Sierra Leone
- The Salone Monitor
- Daily Trust (Kaduna)
- Premium Times (Abuja)
- Sierra Leone Signposts (Freetown)
- People's Daily (Abuja)
- Think Media (Nassau, Bahamas)
- The Nation (Nairobi)
- The Herald (Harare)
- The Monitor (Kampala)
- La Tribune (Algiers)
- AfrikNews (Paris)
- Momagri (Paris)
- Public Agenda (Accra)
- Cameroon Post (Yaounde)
- Leonenet Discussion Forum

I would also like to thank Bangali, my son, for his great help in compiling the essays, which were scattered in various files, into a single volume. Thanks are also due to the other members of Team Bangura, my wife, Kadie, and my daughter, Mariama Schaeffer. Writing has been really exciting with these two wonderful women in my life.

Marie Ndiaye of CODESRIA helped to retrieve and scan from CODESRIA's archive two missing essays from my files; and Suroor Alikhan of UNRISD converted these scanned pdf picture files into standard word files. I thank them very much for their effort.

I should end these acknowledgements with a note of thanks to Osman Sankoh (who we all call Mallam O), publisher of the Sierra Leonean Writers Series (SLWS) and Executive Director of INDEPTH Network, for commissioning this volume and having it reviewed by an SLWS referee. I thank the anonymous reviewer for his useful comments. Mallam O's offer to publish my popular essays gave me an opportunity to retrace a good party of my intellectual life. I very much enjoyed re-

reading and editing the essays, as well as writing the introduction, which places the essays in context and throws light on the inter-connections of development, democracy and cohesion. Without his initiative, many of these essays would have been lost in difficult-to-retrieve newspapers and magazines.

Nyon, Switzerland
July 2015

About the Author

Yusuf Bangura teaches international political economy at the Department of Political Science, Fourah Bay College, University of Sierra Leone. He previously coordinated research at the United Nations Research Institute for Social Development (1990-2012), and was the lead author of the Institute's flagship report *Combating Poverty and Inequality: Structural Change, Social Policy and Politics* (2010). He is the Editor of the Series *Developmental Pathways to Poverty Reduction* (Palgrave and UNRISD) and *Ethnicity, Inequality and Public Sector Governance* (Palgrave and UNRISD). He received his undergraduate and doctoral degrees from the London School of Economics and Political Science in 1974 and 1978. Before joining UNRISD, he taught political science at Dalhousie University in Canada in 1979-1980, and political economy at the Department of Political Science, Ahmadu Bello University in Nigeria from 1980-1988. He served as Chief Examiner of the national examination for the papers on Government organised by the Interim Joint Matriculation Board for first year admission into Ahmadu Bello University (1985 - 87), and as Vice President of the Nigerian Political Science Association (1984-1986). He was also a Visiting Research Fellow at the Departments of Political Science at Stockholm and Uppsala Universities in Sweden in 1988-1989. During his research fellowship in Sweden, he worked closely with the Working Group for the Study of Alternative Development Strategies (AKUT) and the Nordic Africa Institute, helping the latter to develop its research project on the political and social consequences of structural adjustment programmes in Africa.

His publications include, *Developmental Pathways to Poverty Reduction* (edited, Palgrave Macmillan, 2015); "Combating Poverty in Africa: 2015 and Beyond", in R. Wilkinson and D. Hulme (eds.) *The Millennium Development Goals and Beyond: Global Development After 2015* (Routledge 2012); "Inequality and the Politics of Redistribution", *European Journal of Development Research*. No. 23, Issue 4, 2011; *Democracy and Social Policy* (edited, Palgrave Macmillan, 2007); *Ethnic Inequalities and Public Sector Governance* (edited, Palgrave and UNRISD, 2006); *Public Sector Reform in Developing Countries: Capacity Challenges to Improve Services* (co-edited, Palgrave Macmillan, 2006); "Ethnic Inequalities in the Public Sector: A Comparative Analysis", *Development and Change* (Vol. 37, No. 2, 2006); *Racism and Public Policy* (co-edited, Palgrave Macmillan, 2005); "Strategic

Policy Failure and Governance in Sierra Leone", *Journal of Modern African Studies,* Vol. 38, Issue No. 4, 2000; *Youth Culture and Political Violence: The Sierra Leone Civil War, Special Issue of Africa Development,* 1997. Vol. XXII, Nos. 3-4 (co-edited); "Economic Restructuring, Coping Strategies and Social Change: Implications for Institutional Development in Africa", *Development and Change,* Vol. 25, Issue 4, 1994; *Intellectuals, Economic Reform and Social Change: Constraints and Opportunities in the Formation of a Nigerian Technocracy* (CODESRIA, 1994); *Authoritarianism, Adjustment and Democracy: The Politics of Economic Reform in Africa* (co-edited, The Scandinavian Institute of African Studies, 1992); and *Britain and Commonwealth Africa: The Politics of Economic Relations Between 1951 and 1975* (Manchester University Press, 1983).

List of Acronyms

ADFL	Alliance of Democratic Forces for the Liberation of Congo
AFL	Armed Forces of Liberia
AFRC	Armed Forces Revolutionary Council
ANC	African National Congress
APC	All People's Congress
AU	African Union
CDF	Civil Defence Force
CODESRIA	Council for the Development of Social Science Research in Africa
DDR	Disarmament, Demobilization and Reintegration
ECOMOG	Economic Community of West African States Monitoring Group
ECOWAS	Economic Community of West African States
GAD	Gender and Development
GDI	Gender Development Indicator
GEM	Gender Empowerment Measure
GST	Goods and Services Tax
IMF	International Monetary Fund
INEC	Interim National Electoral Commission
LSE	London School of Economics
MDC	Movement for Democratic Change
MDG	Millennium Development Goals
MPLA	Popular Movement for the Liberation of Angola
MRU	Mano River Union
NAC	National Advisory Council
NATO	North Atlantic Treaty Organization
NCD	National Commission for Democracy
NDA	National Democratic Alliance
NDMC	National Diamond Mining Company
NEPU	Northern Elements Progressives Union
NEC	National Electoral Commission
NLC	Nigeria Labour Congress
NLP	National Liberation Party
NPFL	National Patriotic Front of Liberia
NPN	National Party of Nigeria

NPRC	National Provisional Ruling Council
NPC	Northern People's Congress
OAU	Organization of African Unity
ODA	Overseas Development Administration
OECD	Organization for Economic Cooperation and Development
PDP	People's Democratic Party
PMDC	People's Movement for Democratic Change
PNDC	Provisional National Defence Council
PNP	People's National Party
PRSP	Poverty Reduction Strategy Papers
RSLMF	Republic of Sierra Leone Military Force
RUF	Revolutionary United Party
SADC	Southern African Development Cooperation
SLPP	Sierra Leone People's Party
TBA	Traditional Birth Attendants
TNCs	Transnational Corporations
TRC	Truth and Reconciliation Commission
ULIMO	United Liberation Movement of Liberia
UNAMSIL	United Nations Mission in Sierra Leone
UNDP	United Nations Development Programme
UN-IDEP	United Nations Institute for Development and Economic Planning
UNIP	United National Independence Party
UNPP	United National People's Party
UNITA	National Union for the Total Independence of Angola
UNRISD	United Nations Research Institute for Social Development
UPP	United People's Party
USA	United States of America
WHO	World Health Organization
WID	Women in Development
WTO	World Trade Organization
ZANU-PF	Zimbabwe African National Union-Patriotic Front
ZAPU	Zimbabwe African People's Union

Introduction

The Challenge of Building Developmental, Democratic and Cohesive States and Societies

Sierra Leone and other African countries face huge challenges in overcoming underdevelopment and building democratic and cohesive societies that will enhance the well-being of their citizens. Even after more than 50 years of independence, poverty levels remain high, the structure of their economies is undiversified and dependent on the production of raw materials, civic and democratic rights are still heavily contested in many countries, fledgling democratic institutions do not respond robustly to citizens' needs, and government policies and institutions are not always inclusive of all segments of society.

This book is a collection of essays that address the challenge of building developmental, democratic and cohesive societies. Written in accessible prose, it targets the general reader and draws on a rich body of development research and policy analysis spanning almost forty years. The essays were written between 1993 and 2015, covering largely the period when I was involved in applied social development research at the United Nations Research Institute for Social Development. They were meant to provoke debate and reflection on some of the momentous economic, social and political changes that were occurring in Africa and elsewhere during that period. Most of the essays have been published in journals, bulletins, online forums, magazines and newspapers.

Development, democracy and cohesion are inter-connected. Development theory and policy has moved substantially beyond basic concerns about the maximisation of GDP growth to issues related to changes in the structures of economies, environmental sustainability, expansion of incomes and employment, access to social services and social protection, and improvements in social relations and institutions that expand individual freedoms. Development is not just an economic issue; it is also about how power and social differences are organised and managed for the benefit of all. Indeed, Amartya Sen sees "development as freedom", or improving human capabilities or the choices of

1

individuals to live the type of lives they have reason to value. This suggests that economic, social and political processes and relations should be treated in tandem. Seen from this perspective, to talk meaningfully about development is to talk about democracy and social cohesion.

For much of the 1980s and 1990s, economic development was elusive in Africa as countries experienced economic crises and civil wars and adopted deflationary stabilisation policies that further compounded the problem. Improvements in global commodity prices between 2000 and 2014 ushered in a period of high GDP growth especially in mineral-rich countries. During this period, nine of the world's 20 fastest growing economies were in Africa, with Sierra Leone touted as having the third fastest growth in 2013. Most countries used the upswing in revenues to rehabilitate and expand their infrastructure, such as the construction of roads and improvements in electricity generation. However, the structures of their economies could not be transformed beyond the production of raw materials. Especially in Sierra Leone and other small least developed countries, economic growth could not meaningfully reverse the process of de-industrialisation associated with the crisis of the 1980s and 1990s.

Despite the rhetoric of transformation, there was very little manufacturing activity, agricultural productivity and diversification remained low, and the mining sector could not provide enough jobs for the large number of young people that eke out a miserable living in the overcrowded informal sector. Even though social expenditures improved from a very low base, they could not match the investments in infrastructure and fell far short of what was required to build human capital for economic transformation and well-being. Lack of effective industrial policies, weak governance of the extractive sector, deep-seated corruption, excessive trade openness and the huge influence of the international financial institutions on economic policy making made it difficult to translate high growth into structural transformation or changes in sectoral output and employment that would improve the well-being of the majority of citizens.

Democratic change and its effects on economic development and well-being have also been uneven. Economic development has occurred in both authoritarian and democratic settings. Indeed, the East Asian developmental states' impressive development is often used to justify authoritarian practices in advancing development. However, the empirical evidence shows that democracies can also deliver growth and are more resilient than authoritarian regimes in handling systemic shocks and protecting gains by the poor over the long run. Besides, it is possible to disentangle the strategies that produced the growth miracles in the East Asian economies from the authoritarian practices of those states. And given the elevation of democracy as a norm in international development, as well as the widespread construction of democratic institutions in many countries today, the real challenge is how to ensure that those democracies are developmental and made to work for everyone. Instructively, most authoritarian regimes, especially those in Africa, have been highly anti-developmental. The evidence in Sierra Leone, for instance, suggests that some development, however limited, is always achieved when the country's politics is democratic; the economy regresses when the country is governed by a single party, the military or warlords.

However, making democracy deliver development and work for the poor remains a big challenge. It is clearly not enough to rely on the four or five-yearly vote alone to transform leaders into active and accountable agents of economic and social development. It is important to build additional sets of institutions, policies and strategies to direct development and democracy for the benefit of all. This requires the institutionalisation of rights that will allow citizens to exercise political choice and hold leaders to account; and ensuring that pro-poor advocacy groups and production-based interest organisations develop capacity for independent organisation and establish links for effective bargaining with those involved in policy making. The formation of broad coalitions that involve critical groups in the economy may create encompassing interests or national visions beyond the specific interests of each group, and help to ensure that economic growth and redistribution are pursued in tandem instead of subordinating one to the other in the bargaining process. It is also important to make electoral politics competitive as the fear of losing office can serve as an incentive for economic performance and redistribution. Democracy is unlikely to support economic development or work for the poor where democratic institutions, such as the courts and parliament, are weak and elections are rigged; political parties are embedded in patronage politics that prioritise the accumulation of power and sectional interests over concerns for the public good; and leaders enjoy enormous powers to do as they wish and are in the habit of manipulating national constitutions.

As an ethnically diverse region with high levels of inequalities, Africa faces an additional challenge of building cohesive societies. Especially in polarised settings, and where inequalities mirror group differences, ethnicity may shape choices and can be used as a tool to mobilise individuals for divisive collective action. High levels of inequalities may make it difficult to sustain growth and fight poverty as growth may be concentrated in sectors that are not within the reach of the poor. And if ethnic groups are geographically segregated, development may bypass groups that are not located in dynamic zones. Such outcomes may fuel ethnic animosity and weaken the bonds of citizenship. Exclusion, in turn, may lower the potential for growth, by weakening the productive capacity of the excluded groups and thus their potential contribution to growth.

Promoting social cohesion has, therefore, become a central objective of development policy. However, how ethnic diversity and inequalities are managed will vary depending on whether governments adopt a development focus in their strategies. Policies that focus only on cohesion often privilege elite bargains, or social integration at the top, which may not address the problems of the poor or development more broadly. Citizens may find it difficult to hold privileged elites to account or get them to deliver developmentally uplifting outcomes. An alternative approach is one that places development squarely at the centre of strategies for generating social cohesion. It focuses not only on providing incentives for the emergence of moderate leaders and inclusion of disadvantaged groups in governance institutions, but also on the need for leaders to be developmental in formulating and implementing public policies. It is concerned not only with elite pacts, but also with development pacts that reflect the interests of the poor. Such an approach has implications for the construction of party systems, the kinds of bargains struck at different levels of society, the development strategies pursued, and the social policies embraced by governments.

A note on the essays

The 45 essays in this volume cover a wide range of issues under the themes of development, democracy and cohesion. The three themes have over the years been central to my research interests, professional work and advocacy on public policy. About half of the essays are think pieces on Sierra Leone, written to provoke debate at critical points in the political, economic and social development of that country; and twelve essays focus on wider Africa experiences. I have included about 12 essays of a general conceptual and thematic character, some of which are overviews of research findings on aspects of the three themes based on work carried out at the UN Research Institute for Social Development. While preparing the essays for this volume, it became clear that there is a close link between the popular essays on Sierra Leone/Africa and my research work on development, democracy and cohesion at UNRISD. Insights from my research work impacted strongly on the popular essays. Each of the three parts of the volume starts with essays that help the reader to understand some of the important research findings, theoretical ideas and policy underpinnings of the subject.

The development challenge

The volume opens with an essay on North-South collaboration in advancing research agendas in the South. This was a speech delivered in 1996 at an international conference in Berne, Switzerland, on scientific research partnerships for sustainable development. Poorly performing economies, public expenditure cuts, and lack of priority given to research by African governments have led to high levels of rich country penetration of Southern research agendas. This has implications for the kinds of research conducted in such countries and ability of Southern-based researchers to influence national development agendas.

The next six essays, Chapters 2-9, throw light on the dynamics of economic growth, the employment challenge, redistributive strategies, financing development, social policy and the kinds of politics that are conducive to good social outcomes. They are based on findings from four research projects conducted at UNRISD between 2000 and 2012: *Public Sector Reform in Developing Countries, Democracy and Social Policy, Poverty Reduction and Policy Regimes*, and the Institute's flagship report *Combating Poverty and Inequality: Structural Change, Social Policy and Politics*.

Chapter two discusses the conditions under which democratic politics can deliver growth and redistribution. It highlights the importance of social rights, active citizenship, independent group organisation, group coalitions that are structured around issues of growth and employment, collective bargaining, and competitive elections. Chapter three provides insights on the experiences of Nordic social democratic countries and welfare democracies in the global South in tackling poverty and inequality. Chapter four interrogates the potential and limits of policy regime approaches in the study of poverty. Chapter five highlights the importance of jobs and equity in overcoming poverty in Africa. Chapter six underscores the need to take inequality seriously, which has risen substantially within and across countries, making it harder to incorporate the poor in the development process. Chapter seven provides an overview of state reforms, emphasising three kinds of capacity for achieving economic development and well-being: political capacity, resource mobilisation capacity, and allocative and enforcement capacity. Chapter eight discusses the potential benefits of revenue bargains in financing of Africa's development in a context of less-robust aid commitments and decline in resource-based revenues. And Chapter nine examines a variety of policy dialogue frameworks for achieving gendered development.

Chapters 10-12 use the theoretical insights and findings of the previous essays to explain the development challenge in Nigeria and Sierra Leone. Chapter 10 argues that democracy does not work for the Nigerian poor because of the problems of conducting credible elections that offer possibilities to vote out under-performing incumbents, the failure to embed political parties in broad social movements that reflect the interests of the poor, and the failure of the project of developmentalism, which would compel the state to engage constructively with production-based business interests and popular sector groups. In that essay, which I wrote in 2011, one of the questions I asked was whether the elections chief, Attahiru Jega, a person of unquestioned integrity, would be allowed much space and authority to conduct free and fair elections. The results of the 2015 elections confirm that having individuals with a sense of professionalism, fairness and autonomy to head public offices is crucial in building institutions. The defeat of the incumbent president Jonathan Goodluck may have relaxed the electoral constraint in the politics of development, but the other two constraints remain potent and may frustrate the ambitions of the new president. The state will have to engage value-creating entrepreneurs and subaltern groups around issues of growth, structural change and redistribution if the gains in electoral democracy are to translate into meaningful gains for the economy and the poor.

Chapters 11 and 12 are reflections on Sierra Leone's 50 years of independence based on a keynote speech I delivered at a policy dialogue organised by the UN African Institute for Economic Development and Planning and Sierra Leone's Ministry of Finance and Economic Development. It addresses issues related to the governance of natural resources and economic development, human capital formation, the politics of inclusion and climate change. Lost revenue due to ridiculously high tax concessions, the downturn of global commodity prices, collapse of iron ore mining (the key driver of growth in the last few years), corruption and weak governmental commitment to institutional development may make it harder to revive Sierra Leone's economy and achieve the government's Agenda for Prosperity even after the Ebola crisis.

Underdevelopment is associated with a large informal sector as excluded groups struggle to eke out a living in very difficult environments. This often leads to overcrowded, disorganised and filthy cities. Perhaps there are very few cities in the world that are comparable to Sierra Leone's capital city, Freetown, in terms of congestion and poor planning. Chapter 13 examines the conflictual relations between street traders and state power in the use of Freetown's streets. It argues that the Sierra Leone state will be unable to rid the streets of traders if it fails in its duty of social provision, such as providing mega markets that can accommodate the majority of traders, and solving the long term problem of underemployment among the youth population. Chapter 14, on the Ebola crisis, brings out in bold relief the problems of mass-scale informalisation and state failure to engage productively with citizens in advancing the development project. Governments are hardly present in the lives of most people for the most fundamental things, such as jobs, social services and social security. Because people invariably fend for themselves, they have learned to not depend on, or trust, the word of government, making it harder to change risky behaviour and curb the high rates of ebola infection.

Development is also about cultural change. Chapters 15 and 16 take a close look at Sierra Leone's traditional Bondo female society, which has come under attack especially from international bodies, for the harmful effects of circumcision or genital mutilation on the health of young girls. The two essays, written in 1996 and discussed extensively on Leonenet (an online discussion forum on Sierra Leone issues), situate the Bondo society within a broader context than circumcision. It addresses issues related to traditional conceptions of womanhood, the power which the institution traditionally confers on women, and the society's entertainment value to show why a simple ban is unlikely to be effective. The state can undertake reforms to protect non-adults from being initiated into the society, urge and ultimately enforce adoption of alternative initiation ceremonies that do not involve circumcision, and ensure that in the transition period initiation ceremonies are safe for consenting adults.

Democratic politics

The opening essay, Chapter 17, in Part II on democratic politics, discusses the research findings of a project I directed at UNRISD on the choices democracies face in globalising economies. Despite the global spread of democracy, the power of international finance is changing the parameters of democratic politics by limiting economic policy making to a limited set of objectives that prioritise fiscal stabilisation, privatisation and liberalisation over other public policy objectives, such as employment and social investments. In order to support this policy bias, governments try to insulate key institutions, such as central banks and finance ministries, from public scrutiny and restrict policy making to experts. Such a technocratic style of governance distorts the structure of accountability, making governments more answerable to the multilateral agencies and investors than to representative institutions and the public at large. UNRISD's research shows that countries have managed the tensions between technocracy and democratic accountability differently. Exposure to different types of financial pressure, the economic situation before democratic transition, elite consensus, party behaviour, the balance of power in the legislative branch, technical skills of legislators, and civic activism may determine the extent to which policy making may reflect democratic choices.

Chapter 18, which also draws on the research findings of another UNRISD project on economic crisis, coping strategies and social change, tackles a different problem. The 1990s were a period of momentous change in Africa and elsewhere as countries experienced long-running economic crisis, ethnic conflicts, civil wars and democratisation. Understanding the inter-connections and dynamics of these developments taxed the minds of many researchers. A recurring theme was the rapid informalisation of the public sector and economic activities in general, including the multiple coping strategies adopted by households to make ends meet. Such strategies had implications for the performance of public sector institutions and democratic politics. Insights from this research constituted the basis for the assessment of different patterns of political development in Africa in the 1990s.

Organising credible elections, ensuring that democratic institutions, such as parliaments and the courts, defend the public interest and hold the executive to account, promoting internal party democracy, and making leaders respect limits on executive authority and the supremacy of constitutions have been important issues in the politics of Sierra Leone and other African countries. They deal with the rules of the democratic game, which all mature democracies now take for granted, but which are still strongly contested in many countries in Africa. Democracy cannot promote development and work for the poor if the basic rules of the game have not been consolidated. Chapters 19-30 address these issues.

Chapter 19 interrogates the role of elections and the transition in Ghana in 1992 from military to civil rule. The Council for the Development of Social Science Research in Africa (CODESRIA) nominated me to join the Carter Center's team that monitored the Ghana presidential elections in November 1992. My participation in that observer mission gave me first-hand experience of the problems of conducting elections in poor countries experiencing democratic change. The elections highlighted three main problems: the impartiality of the electoral system, including the roles of elections officers, party polling agents, the reliability of the electoral register and voter identification system; the advantages of incumbency in use of state resources and personnel; and the role of parastatal forces in constraining the activities of opposition parties and choices of voters. It is a big relief that Ghana has gone a long way in consolidating its democracy since the controversial elections of 1992, which the main opposition party strongly contested by refusing to participate in the parliamentary election that came after the presidential vote. Chapter 20 uses insights from the monitoring of Ghana's elections to review the founding document of the

9

Swedish Foreign Ministry's Independent Electoral Institute Commission for the creation of a global institute for the monitoring of elections in countries that are in transition to democratic rule, which led to the establishment of the now-popular Institute for Democracy and Electoral Assistance in Stockholm.

Chapters 21-28 turn the spotlight on Sierra Leone. After more than 25 years of single party rule and military dictatorship, and in the middle of a brutal civil war, Sierra Leone was thrown into a difficult democratic transition in 1996. There were strong calls from the military to postpone the elections and focus resources on the war. However, Sierra Leoneans were tired of both the war and military rule, and accused the military of collaborating with the rebels in committing atrocities in villages. Chapter 21 reviews the arguments for and against the conduct of the elections and suggests policies for ensuring the safety of citizens, the credibility of the vote and the cohesion of society.

The 1996 elections were won by the Sierra Leone's People Party (SLPP), which was however unable to end the war or control the military. The government was overthrown by the military in May 1997 and the rebel movement, the Revolutionary United Front (RUF), joined the military leaders in the new government. World leaders condemned the coup, the UN imposed sanctions on the military leaders, and the Nigerian military under ECOMOG helped the ousted civilian government to regain power in 1998 after a violent and costly war. But the government could not protect its grip on power. The rebels and the ousted military struck for a second time in 1999, causing a large number of deaths, untold brutality on civilians and destruction of property on a massive scale. British military forces, the UN and the Nigerian military eventually overwhelmed the rebels after a period of joint civilian-rebel government brokered by a peace treaty in Lomé.

Following the successful conclusion of the war, the SLPP government was given a resounding mandate (it obtained more than 70% of the votes for the presidency) in 2002. However, the government was unable to translate this mandate into effective governance that would benefit the majority of citizens. It lost the 2007 elections to a revitalised All People's Congress (APC), which had a terrible track record of violence, rigging of elections, corruption and poor governance when it was in power between 1968 and 1992. The SLPP responded to the APC's return to power by fielding for the 2012 elections a former military leader, Julius Maada Bio, whose NPRC (National Provisional Ruling Council) government was also associated with gross human rights violations and large scale corruption. Chapters 22 and 23 interrogate the folly of choosing such a leader at a time when the APC had rebranded itself as a New APC and much of the public held a favourable view of the government's development programme.

After my retirement from UNRISD in 2012, I spent three months in Sierra Leone to observe the dynamics of electoral politics and gauge public opinion in the run-up to the 2012 elections--the focus of Chapters 24 and 25. I was struck by the supreme confidence of both the APC and SLPP in winning the elections. I knew both parties could not be right and tried to evaluate their chances of winning. Predicting elections in the absence of credible polls is a difficult exercise even for a political scientist.

Chapter 24 used data from the biometric electoral register, past voting behaviour and insights from random interactions with a wide range of potential voters to predict the outcome of the elections. Some SLPP partisans did not like my prognosis and called me names, including the absurd view that I am an APC partisan, because their party did not fare well in the analysis. Others used the essay to alert the party to the difficult tasks of regaining power. A leading member of the SLPP is still in awe of my analysis and we often joke about how closely my numbers reflected the outcome. My interest in Sierra Leone's politics is to advance the project of building democratic institutions and values, defend the public interest, and make democracy work for everyone—not just for politicians and parties. The job of a social scientist is to listen, observe and examine all evidence dispassionately. Chapter 25 provides an overview of why the SLPP lost the elections: the changed electoral demographics brought about by the biometric voter registration system, the fielding of a candidate that could appeal largely to only one half of the electorate, the high level of popularity of the incumbent president, and the public's perception that the government's Agenda for Change brought improvements in the country.

Chapters 26-28 discuss three problems that are often faced by African democracies: the inability of opposition parties to respond effectively to governments even when they have a record of executive governance; the lack of democratic accountability of parties to their membership; and the tendency of leaders to side-step constitutional procedures by claiming supreme executive authority.

Most African parties cannot articulate sound public policies on a consistent basis without the help of the state bureaucracy. Three additional problems in Sierra Leone are: the leader of the main opposition party does not hold an elected national office, the party's presidential candidate is expected to relinquish leadership of the party after a failed election, and the leader of the party in parliament lacks sufficient clout within the party to provide effective national leadership. As Chapter 26 argues, these developments tend to create a power vacuum and may lead to dangerous outcomes: unelected party leaders may try to usurp the powers of parliamentary leaders; popular but failed flag bearers may attempt to cling to power or undermine the work of uncooperative party and parliamentary leaders; and the parliamentary caucus may fragment and be rendered ineffective. In Chapter 27, a case is made for parties to grant the vote to all registered party members in primary elections rather than having only a small number of delegates choose party representatives in national elections. This will check the biases of party leaders, ensure a level playing field for all candidates, improve party organisation at local levels and connect parliamentarians more effectively to party members. Such an approach may also help to discipline party leaders and minimise the tendency for parties to fragment and become easy prey to the executive branch of government.

Chapter 28 discusses the controversial decision by Sierra Leone's President, Ernest Bai Koroma, to sack his Vice President, Sam Sumana, without following the constitutional provisions that require the involvement of parliament and the courts on such an issue. The essay highlights the danger of the idea, advanced by the President, of continuous membership of a political party for the posts of VP and President. The reason is simple. Such a requirement will give a small bunch of unelected party officials the power to decide whether a VP or President with a popular mandate can continue in office. In addition, if the president can use "supreme executive authority" to sack the VP without following constitutional procedures, what will stop him from ignoring other provisions of the constitution in exercising his will? This crisis has laid bare the hollowness of the claim that the governing party is a New APC, as it seems to be reverting to the old style of arbitrary governance. Development is not sustainable when governments are not committed to the growing of institutions and leaders see themselves as all-powerful.

The last two essays in democratic politics, Chapters 29 and 30, focus on the Arab Spring and Qaddafi's fall from power. Sierra Leone's Truth and Reconciliation Commission (TRC) implicated Qaddafi in the country's brutal war and asked the government to demand reparations from Qaddafi's government. David Crane, former prosecutor at the Sierra Leone Special Court, announced that he named and shamed Qaddafi in his indictment, but could not proceed with the indictment because of pressure from Western powers. Sierra Leone's governments preferred instead to settle privately with Qaddafi by soliciting puny gifts, such as buses, garbage collection trucks and bags of rice; and, astonishingly, in 2009 parliament through cross-party support conferred on Qaddafi the status of an honorary member of parliament. It took the courage of the Libyan people through mass action during the Arab Spring to expose the folly of the appeasement policy towards Qaddafi. The Arab Spring itself held much promise in advancing the cause of open, competitive and accountable government in the Arab world. However, it needs to be democratically anchored in the right institutions and made to serve the interests of the broad mass of the people for it to be sustainable. Unfortunately, most countries have not been successful in achieving this.

Cohesion and security

Much of my research work also dealt with issues of social cohesion, with a strong focus on ways of managing ethnic and racial diversity and inequality. The first two essays, Chapters 31 and 32, in Part III on cohesion and security, draw on some of the research findings and policy recommendations of that work. Chapter 31 situates the management of ethnic diversity and inequality within a development context. This was a keynote speech I delivered in Colombo, Sri Lanka, in 2010 in a conference organized by the Government of Sri Lanka, the German aid agency, GTZ, and the European Union Office in Sri Lanka. It underscores the point that ethnic diversity is not pathological. In a 15-country UNRISD study on ethnic inequalities and the public sector, we found that a high level of ethnic fragmentation—in which no group is large enough to dominate the public sphere—leads to less inequality and encourages good inter-group cooperation. The difficult cases are countries with polarised ethnic structures in which two or three groups compete for dominance, or ethnic fragmentation is interspersed with a few large and relatively equal groups that may form selective ethnic coalitions. Managing such types of diversity requires trust among ethnic groups. Trust can be achieved by tackling inequalities in the cultural, governmental and socioeconomic domains. However, for the poor to benefit and development advanced, elite bargains need to be combined with development pacts that involve the participation of the poor. Chapter 32, which further elaborates on these issues, provides an overview of ideas generated by high level scholars from around the world for an UNRISD conference I organized on racism and public policy in Durban, South Africa in 2001, to coincide with the World Conference Against Racism, Racial Discrimination and Related Intolerance. It focuses on how the construction of race and racism affects social solidarity and citizenship; and the promotion of social justice in societies with deep racial divisions.

The next three essays, Chapters 33-35, use some of the ideas of Chapters 29 and 30 to tackle the problem of ethnic diversity in Sierra Leone. Chapter 33 provides a snapshot of the configuration of Sierra Leone's ethnic groups, the ethno-regional bifurcation of the country, and structural pressures for cohesion. Instructively, the composition, leadership and electoral base of the two main parties, the APC and the SLPP, tend to be ethno-regional, making it difficult to maximise the country's development potential and build trust in governance institutions. Chapters 34 and 35 address ways of bridging the ethno-regional divide, by advancing five proposals for constitutional reform: having an inclusive cabinet with representation from all districts and without any two regions accounting for more than 60 percent of the appointments; making it mandatory that each registered party member should participate in primary elections and be entitled to one vote; preventing political parties from choosing their presidential candidates from the same region or ethnic group in more than two consecutive elections; setting time limits for settling electoral disputes, and ensuring that winners are not sworn in or inaugurated before electoral disputes have been resolved by the courts; and establishing a fixed date for holding presidential and parliamentary elections.

The research findings on ethnic diversity and inequality provided the basis for two interventions, Chapters 36 and 37, on debates dealing with power sharing in Zimbabwe and the rebuilding of ethnically fractured and war-torn Cote d'Ivoire. Zimbabwe experienced a protracted crisis after its presidential election of 2002, as the opposition party, backed by Western governments, refused to recognise the results, and embarked on mass action to unseat the government. Many international and local commentators and policy advisers called for a government of national unity to end the crisis. Chapter 36 offers a different take on the issue. Zimbabwe did not need a government of national unity since it was not at war; and the elections had signalled a decentring of ethnicity in politics. Even though the Shona and the Ndebele constitute the two main ethnic groups, with the Shona accounting for more than 60% and the Ndebele 15%, the Shona vote had fragmented in terms of its support for the two main parties; and although much of the Ndebele vote went to the opposition party, a sizeable proportion was also cast for the governing party. The major dividing line was rural-urban. The governing party failed to connect with urban workers and the middle class, whereas the opposition won most of the votes in the cities, but offered no credible message to the land-hungry peasantry. Building on the opposition's strong representation in parliament, solving the land question and disentangling it from the politics of organising credible elections, and de-linking the opposition from Western strategies of reversing land reform offered better prospects of advancing the democratisation project.

Cote d'Ivoire's ethnic structure is more fragmented than Sierra Leone's and Zimbabwe's. However, the influx of migrants from neighbouring countries in search of work during the boom of the 1960s and 1970s changed the country's ethnic distribution and created a bifurcated society based on religion and region. As demands for competitive elections grew, a xenophobic discourse of Ivoirité or indigeneity emerged that elevated the Muslim-Christian/North-South divide over other cleavages. Chapter 37 calls for bold and creative efforts to drain the poison of Ivoirité from the body politic, manage the North-South schism, and develop a culture of shared citizenship. It interrogates the Sierra Leone experience on security, inclusive government and development to suggest ways of helping Cote d'Ivoire to rebuild its fractured society.

Much of Africa was engulfed in civil war during the 1990s. Although I did not direct a research programme that addressed war and security issues at UNRISD, I stayed engaged with the literature and debates on the subject, and often intervened in those debates through think pieces and a few academic articles. The remaining eight essays, Chapters 38-45, are some of the products of that engagement at the popular or advocacy level. They cover the wars in Sierra Leone, Liberia, Congo and the wider Great Lakes region, and address issues related to regional military interventions, security sector reform and state building. Chapter 38 makes a strong case for a Nigerian-led ECOMOG intervention force in the Sierra Leone war; Chapter 39 is a critique of the Lomé peace agreement that rewarded Sierra Leone's rebel movement with a share of state power and control of the country's mineral resources; and Chapter 40 provides a policy framework for the democratisation of military security, involving the participation of citizens in productive work. It argues that it is citizen involvement in national security--not professionalisation of the military per se--that will check the chronic tendency of the military to threaten security through coups. A citizen-based army may help to heal ethnic divisions, break rigidities in the political system, and serve as a basis for shared citizenship and nation-building.

The Sierra Leone and Liberian wars were closely intertwined, and most Sierra Leonean scholars and popular commentators followed events in Liberia keenly. When Sierra Leone seemed to be making headway in containing the rebel incursion and organising free and fair elections in 1996, there were calls from many influential policy circles to replicate the Sierra Leone "model of conflict management" in Liberia. Chapter 41 highlights key differences between the two countries and the dynamics of their conflicts. It suggests ways of ending the Liberian conflict, which in the 1990s seemed to be similar to the Somalia conflict in terms of multiple warlords, large scale banditry and collapse of a rule-based state system. It is remarkable that Liberia was ultimately able to end its war, eliminate the power of its warlords, and change its political trajectory by embracing democratic institutions.

Chapter 42 provides a critique of demands in the 1990s for a recolonisation of Africa, a period when many African countries were mired in conflict and a Pax Africana seemed out of reach as a conflict resolution mechanism. It interrogates the exchange between Ali Mazrui and Archie Mafeje, two prominent African scholars, by calling for a reform of Africa's state systems that will provide the basis for building an effective regional body to police the African space and advance the continent's elusive development project. Chapter 43 makes a case for a Pan-African intervention force, as opposed to a Western-led force that was proposed in some Western policy circles, as a mechanism to restore order in the Great Lakes region, which was thrown into intractable conflict in the mid-1990s. At the core of the Great Lakes crisis was the war in Congo, which like the Liberia war, had regional spill-over effects and threatened to destabilise large parts of Central, Eastern and Southern Africa. It was even dubbed Africa's First World War. Chapter 44 discusses the regional security implications of that war, the strategies of the key regional players, and ways of ending the war.

The last essay of the volume, Chapter 45, provides an overview of key issues involved in security sector reform, a subject that has gained prominence in research and policy circles. Security sector reform deals with disarmament, demobilisation and reintegration of ex-combatants into society; and right-sizing and professionalisation of the military and police. The essay argues that security sector reform has tended to ignore or treat very casually the development dimension in peacebuilding, and has reduced inclusive government to quick fix power-sharing deals between warring factions without effective citizen participation. To achieve sustainable peace, security sector reform needs to be grounded in inclusive government and growth strategies that deliver jobs to the poor. This underscores the importance of understanding the inter-connections of development, democracy, cohesion and security.

Part I: The Development Challenge

1

Who Defines, Who Pushes, and Who Funds Research Agendas in the South?[1]

Introduction

The capacity to define, implement and fund research agendas in many countries of the South has experienced rapid decline in recent years. The reasons for this decline are complex and many. They include questions relating to reduced government revenues; the low priority given to research issues in economic restructuring programmes and university budgets; the failure of the emerging private sector to engage itself in national research activities; the collapse of official incomes in universities and research institutes; and the massive flight of experienced academics to the private economy, the parastatal sector and overseas institutions.

Not surprisingly, foreign organisations, scholars, and donors have attempted to fill the void in the South's capacity to control its research agenda. Northern interests in promoting research in the South are varied, depending on the institution, researcher and funding agency that one deals with. Four broad types of objectives in North-South research collaboration appear to be important. First, there are research programmes that largely reflect the self-interests of the funding agencies -- viz. those that channel resources to issues and countries that are likely to support their cultural, economic, political or strategic interests. The second type deals with those research activities that are driven by an age-old missionary instinct for discovery, conversion, and creation of a native clientele. The third relates to researchers who simply follow the flow of global research funds, most of which emanate from the North, in order to enhance their careers and livelihoods. And the fourth type deals with institutions and researchers who may be driven by an interest in

---

[1] Published in *South Letter* (South Centre, Geneva), Vol. 25, Nos. 1&2. 1996; and in *AAPS Newsletter* (African Association of Political Science), September-December 1996. Speech delivered at the International Conference on "Scientific Research Partnership for Sustainable Development: North-South and South-South Dimensions", Organised by the Swiss Commission for Research Partnerships with Developing Countries. Berne, Switzerland. 5-7 March 1996.

conducting or supporting research that is likely to be beneficial to the people and governments of the South. Under this fourth type are also researchers and agencies who may strive to ensure that Southern researchers and institutions regain the initiative in national research activities through mutually respectable and transparent partnerships.

Based on the background document that has been prepared for this conference, I assume that the organisers are mainly interested in the fourth type of North-South collaboration in Southern-based research activities. It is important, however, to keep in mind the other three as they sometimes inadvertently influence the fourth. What are the main issues in the debate? Perhaps it will be useful if we can divide the discussion around a set of problems that traces the research process from the point of conception to the final product. What kinds of problems do Southern and Northern researchers, institutions and funding agencies often face, or are likely to face, in their attempts to collaborate in the definition, implementation and funding of Southern research, as well as in the publication and application of research results?

Defining the research agenda

The question of who defines research agendas in the South depends upon funding situations, the influence of global ideas on national research communities, and the knowledge base, technical competence and motivation of Southern researchers. Radically reduced local funding possibilities have meant that Southern researchers now heavily rely on Northern sources of funding. In most cases, these funds are driven by the big issues or ideas that are produced in the North for global consumption: human rights, NGO-led civil society, democratisation, environmental sustainability, gender equality, population control, globalisation, post-modernity, market liberalisation, etc. It is not that these issues do not have local or national relevance in the South. They do.

However, there are two main problems with such types of externally-driven agendas. First, Southern researchers sometimes tend to engage these issues largely from the perspectives of those who first defined them as important -- posing the same questions, quoting the same authors, and using the same methodology and analytical categories even when local realities demand a search for new categories and new questions. Second, reliance on globally-produced research agendas often prevents national researchers and their foreign collaborators from working on issues that do not quite fit the global fads, even though such issues might be relevant for understanding and assisting local and national development. In the field of structural adjustment, for instance, there are more studies on the economics of liberalisation than on coping strategies and social change; and studies on democratisation pay scant attention to political arrangements that reflect the plurality of local social cleavages.

An additional problem relates to the erosion of the scientific base of Southern research. As official incomes, research facilities and resources become inadequate for sustaining basic needs and respectable academic careers, researchers tend to abandon primary research and opt instead for administrative work or the production of consultancy reports. This trend has been supported in recent years by the massive invasion of Southern countries by bilateral donor agencies, multilateral institutions and NGOs, striving to influence economic and social development in those countries. These institutions often require experts of some sort to help them prepare feasibility or appraisal reports on their projects. As they tend to pay very large amounts of money for such reports, sometimes in excess of officially earned incomes, they often succeed in attracting the best scholars who should have been engaged in defining the research frontiers in their countries.

In some countries there is a very real possibility that the normal cycle of endogenous social scientific knowledge production and its articulation has been severely disrupted. Under normal conditions, primary research should be entrusted with the responsibility of feeding applied and other types of intellectual work with new data and new findings. If a national scientific community stops doing fundamental research, the national scientific knowledge base will either atrophy or such a community will have to depend upon the outside world for understanding its own society. However, if in addition to the absence of a flourishing local scientific culture, the stock of available foreign knowledge about a country is limited or unsuitable, the work of national scholars may fail to rise above the insights and offerings of informed journalists or project evaluators. They may thus become incapable of defining a national research agenda.

Panellists may wish, therefore, to consider three main questions: how to stop the downward spiral of scientific research in the South, which has partly been induced by a proliferation of monetary and other types of incentives to produce consultancy reports; how to help national researchers to take the initiative in defining research agendas that reflect national needs and that are also sensitive to developments in the world at large; and how to encourage foreign researchers and funding institutions to think collectively and constructively with Southern researchers in defining research problems. The latter may require patience, humility, and readiness to spend more time with national researchers in local settings. Such a process can be very expensive. Is it not necessary, therefore, to set up special funds to nurture egalitarian and confidence-building relationships when North-South collaborative research programmes are being drawn up?

Research implementation

A second important dimension of research collaboration relates to the problems of implementing a research project. Who takes responsibility for what? Who does the primary data collection and who does the interpretation? Who handles theoretical issues and who supplies case study data? How often and where should the two sets of partners meet in order to ensure that the work gets done within a prescribed time frame? These are very sensitive issues which, when not properly handled, can strain relations between Southern and Northern researchers.

It is important to appreciate the problems on both sides of the relationship if progress is to be made in devising more mutually-supportive and equal relationships. A Northern researcher participating in a Northern-funded programme may come to the project with a sense of power and intellectual superiority: he or she is very close to the sources of funds and, compared to a Southern research counterpart, may be more familiar with the global discourse, literature and analytical techniques that are likely to be adopted for the project. Such a researcher often wants to supervise rather collaborate in the implementation of the project; he or she may also opt for the more intellectually challenging aspects of the research, such as interpretation and theory construction; and would prefer to make only occasional visits to the research sites, especially if living conditions in the local area are extremely hazardous.

National researchers are generally aware that they do not control the funding source and, perhaps, may not be as fully conversant as their foreign counterparts are likely to be, with the global discourse, literature and methodology for the study. They very often feel, however, that they are much closer than their foreign counterparts, to the problem under investigation and, therefore, should take primary responsibility for the study. As local residents, such researchers may enjoy doing field work and preparing case studies, but they may also feel that their intellectual abilities are being held up or questioned if they are not allowed to participate in the overall process of interpretation and theory formulation. There are a number of cases where Northern intellectual hegemony in collaborative research programmes has undermined effective Southern participation, and has encouraged Southern researchers to be less committed to the project than, perhaps, they would have liked to be.

However, it is important to note that there are increasing problems of getting Southern researchers to devote sufficient time to scientific research projects even when Northern researchers seek to collaborate with them as equals. Part of the problem is related, as we have already seen, to the survival strategy of allocating more time to consultancy reports. A related problem is a tendency to take on many more research projects or non-academic tasks than they can handle at any given point, because of the need to sustain threatened livelihoods and to maximise opportunities in multiple international research networks.

What can be done to solve the problem of patron-client relations in North-South research collaboration, and unsustainable commitments to multiple programmes by Southern researchers? How can Northern researchers be made to recognise and uphold the need to work with their Southern counterparts as equals at all levels and dimensions of a research project? What special schemes may be needed to get Northern researchers to spend more time with local researchers in the field in order for the former to be socially sensitive to a research problem and the practical demands of a research project? What can be done to protect the incomes of Southern researchers and encourage them to allocate their research time more efficiently? How can Southern researchers be assisted to upgrade their knowledge of current discourses, methodologies and literature in situations of under-funded libraries and laboratories?

And what kinds of programmes would be needed to ensure that such upgrading of national scientific knowledge does not lead to a detachment of such researchers from the national research scene?

Research results: publication and application

Problems may also emerge in North-South collaboration over questions that relate to the publication and application of the findings of a research project. In many countries of the South, the infrastructure for the publication and dissemination of academic manuscripts is still very weak. In such countries, even though efforts are often made to publish manuscripts locally, the dominant trend is to publish high quality work in the North and distribute some copies of the product in the South. Where the local distribution of such a publication is not subsidised by an external funding agency, only a handful of researchers and general readers may get to see it because of its very high local cost. Thus, rather than the research product improving research capacity in the South, it may enrich instead the knowledge base of Northern researchers and institutions, as well as their power to perform leadership roles in defining research agendas in Southern countries. What can be done to improve the capacity of the South to handle publication and distribution of high quality research work that has been conducted in the South?

An additional problem is the question of preparing parts of the research data for publication in refereed journals -- a faster and simpler way of reaching the research community than books. However, most of the best journals are located in the North, and are run or edited by researchers based in that region. Even when the orientation of such journals is to support articles that deal with South issues, the editors tend to be largely Northern, who may have a preference for certain types of ideas, styles of presentation and modes of analysis. As publishing in such journals enhances international contacts and professional careers, a Southern researcher may end up adopting the hidden values and world views of those who control such journals. Unfortunately, many Southern journals are published intermittently or fail to attract the kinds of analytical or empirically-based manuscripts that could enhance their reputation and global standing. How can Southern journals and editors be supported to ensure that their journals are able to attract high quality work from Southern and Northern researchers?

The question of what to do with research findings is equally important. Should research findings be the preserve of only the scientific community or should policy makers and ordinary citizens also benefit from them? At present, many donor agencies and multilateral institutions are able to benefit from research in the South and elsewhere either because they funded it, or because of their increasing technical capacity to relate with the development research community. The same cannot be said for many Southern governments and citizen organisations. It is not surprising, therefore, that Northern governments, international NGOs, and multilateral agencies are often on the frontline in pushing new ideas in the South, whereas their local counterparts are reduced to performing supportive or reactive roles. Panellists may wish, therefore, to consider the question of how to ensure that scientific research findings are packaged in ways that would make them accessible to a wide audience. What resources, personnel and structures should be put in place in the South to ensure that researchers are able to talk to the public through their research?

Research funds

Perhaps at the core of the problem of North-South research co-operation is the question of funding. Southern-based institutions are increasingly finding it difficult to fund basic research. Unlike in the North where the private sector, including research foundations, plays an active role in the funding of research programmes, in many countries of the South an overwhelming proportion of the limited funds that are allocated to research comes from governments. When government budgets are in bad shape, as they are in most crisis economies today, research is often among the first casualties in programmes of expenditure rationalisation. Southern researchers will continue to find it difficult to take the initiative in defining the research agenda for their countries and the global community if they are not assured of an autonomous funding base. How can the private sector that has benefited from economic liberalisation programmes be made to fund research programmes in the places where they operate? And what needs to be done to get governments and universities to protect the research components of academic life from the types of savage cuts that they have experienced in the last decade and half?

Since an increasingly high proportion of the funds for Southern research now comes from the North, it is important to consider the kinds of problems which this type of dependency sometimes generate. Some of the problems have already been covered in previous sections. They include the tendency for Northern funding institutions to determine national research agendas; and the tendency for Northern funds to empower Northern researchers in North-South research relations. Some of the funding agencies seem to be aware of this problem and have adopted a policy of allowing research institutions in the South to draw up their own research programmes without much input or pressure from the North. This works mainly in situations where donors decide to fund institutional capacity, often over a three year period, rather than specific projects.

However, problems may arise at the end of a three year period when donors send Northern researchers to evaluate the work programme of an institution. As the Northern evaluator combs through the publications of the institution in the presence of his or her colleagues, all the problems of patronage and imperial arrogance that are associated with North-South relations may crop up. A Northern evaluator who may be sensitive to this problem may produce a report which glosses over some very important shortcomings of the institution. On the other hand, a Southern institution which receives a bad report from a Northern evaluator may attempt to mobilise the standard argument of neo-colonial bias as a strategy of self-defence. Panellists may wish to consider whether such evaluations should not be done by multi-regional teams of researchers, especially in situations where a funding agency is involved in supporting research in more than one region.

Let me conclude by stressing that social scientific research is important in efforts to overcome underdevelopment in the South. Southern countries can only ignore it at their own peril.

2

When do Democracies Deliver Economic Growth and Redistribution?[2]

Introduction

Economic growth and redistribution have been central to the strategies of countries that have drastically reduced poverty. Especially when driven by sectors that provide employment to the poor, growth improves incomes and public revenues, and makes the pursuit of redistributive policies less burdensome on governments and tax payers. Similarly, when redistributive policies are progressive or universal, they may improve the incomes and well-being of the poor and reduce social hierarchies and divisions.

Not all countries have adopted growth and redistributive strategies simultaneously in tackling poverty. For some, such as the developmental states of East Asia, the primary focus was on manufacturing-led growth strategies that provided ample employment and protection to workers. Redistributive strategies focused more on land reform and affordable quality education for all, than on social risks related to unemployment, old age and sickness. For former socialist countries, the aim was to equalise opportunities and outcomes through socialisation of the economy. Poor growth in subsequent years rendered this highly redistributive model untenable. The historical record suggests that countries that consistently pursued both growth and redistribution tended to be few.

This piece examines the political drivers for growth and redistribution that can lead to less poverty and inequality. Growth and redistributive outcomes have occurred in both authoritarian and democratic societies. Indeed, some scholars and policy makers often point to the impressive economic transformation and low levels of inequality of East Asian developmental states as evidence of the necessity of authoritarian practices in fighting poverty.

---

[2] Extracted from Y. Bangura, "Politics of Growth and Redistribution in a Development Context", in Y. Bangura (ed.) *Developmental Pathways to Poverty Reduction*. Basingstoke: Palgrave Macmillan and UNRISD. 2015.

The focus here is on how growth and redistribution can be pursued in democratic contexts. Surely, the empirical evidence suggests that democracies can also deliver growth, even if not at the level and quality of East Asian-type miracles, and are more resilient than authoritarian regimes in handling systemic shocks and protecting gains by the poor over the long run. Besides, as Amartya Sen has observed, it is possible to disentangle the strategies that produced the growth miracles in the East Asian economies from the authoritarian practices of those states. And given the widespread acceptance of democracy in many poor countries today, the real challenge for policy is how to ensure that those democracies deliver pro-poor and pro-growth outcomes. The point ought also to be stressed that most authoritarian regimes have been anti-developmental, especially those in low-income countries.

Like authoritarian regimes that show wide variations in outcomes, not all democracies can deliver pro-growth and pro-poor outcomes. Indeed, many new democracies today are finding it difficult to achieve both outcomes. The question then is: under what conditions can democracies deliver socially-inclusive growth outcomes?

We argue that democracies can deliver growth that is beneficial to the poor when rights are institutionalised, allowing the poor to exercise political choice, build alliances with others, and hold leaders to account; and groups with strong ties to the poor develop capacity for independent organisation and establish structural links for bargaining with actors involved in policy making, which may sometimes lead to social pacts. The formation of broad coalitions that involve critical groups in the economy may lead to encompassing or non-sectional interests, which may ensure that growth and redistribution are pursued in tandem instead of subordinating one to the other in the bargaining process. Some success can be achieved without formal group ties to state actors, but this usually requires high levels of contestation and continuous mobilisation to sustain gains. Competitive elections, in which governments may lose office, can also serve as an incentive for economic performance and redistribution. However, electoral competitiveness without effective group organisation and contestation may produce weak redistributive outcomes. The poor suffer when interest groups and social movements are weak and the electoral system is not sufficiently competitive.

Growth, redistribution and democracy

The link between growth and inequality has been extensively debated by economists, but without any clear consensus. Some countries with high growth enjoy low levels of inequality, whereas other high growth economies are associated with high levels of inequality. Similarly, some relatively egalitarian countries have not done well on the growth front, whereas others have been able to combine high growth and low levels of inequality.

Despite the variety of outcomes in the growth-inequality relationship, economic policy for much of the post-war period downplayed the importance of inequality and redistributive policies in the development process. Following Simon Kuznets, it was assumed that inequality was a transient phenomenon, which was bound to fall as economies grew or developed. If growth ultimately drives inequality downwards, then a focus on redistribution in the short-run will have adverse effects on growth, which will make it harder to help the poor and achieve egalitarian outcomes.

However, two developments have helped to bring back the issue of inequality and redistribution on the policy agenda. The first is the co-existence of high growth and high inequality in many poor countries and the failure of growth to improve the lives of most people. The second relates to the high levels of inequality in the last two decades in developed countries that had previously enjoyed low levels of inequality. Indeed, one of the key points in Thomas Picketty's ground breaking book, *Capital in the Twenty First Century,* is that the drop in inequality that Kuznets observed was not driven by the dynamics of development but owed much to exogenous factors such as the two world wars of the 20th century and explicitly redistributive policies pursued in the 1950s and 1960s; these policies were reversed by financial globalisation and regressive taxation in the 1980s and 1990s.

The two developments of high inequality in both poor and rich countries are perceived as threatening to social stability and the legitimacy of democratic institutions. Therefore, in current academic and policy discourse, redistribution is not only seen as necessary for the survival of the capitalist economy, it also does not necessarily impact negatively on growth. Indeed, certain types of redistributive policies, such as those that improve the incomes of the poor, enhance equity in

29

quality education, and improve participation and returns to women and marginalised groups in labour markets, may actually be good for growth. Low levels of inequality are also highlighted as an advantage in converting growth into pro-poor outcomes.

If redistribution and growth are now increasingly seen as not antithetical in the development process, the way the two relate to democratic politics is still hotly contested. Two contrasting views inform the debate on growth and democracy. In the first, democracy is believed to impact positively on growth because of the freedoms and guarantees it offers for individual choices; the periodic renewal of leaders through elections, which may check predatory rule and abuse of power; the protection of contract and property rights; and the overall predictability of policy making that democracy offers. The second view is sceptical of the growth-enhancing powers of democracy. It argues that the electoral cycle, which may not exceed four or five years, encourages policy makers to engage in rent-seeking behaviour or yield to public pressure for expenditures that may enhance consumption at the expense of savings and investments.

The debate on inequality, redistribution and democracy is equally contentious. One view, based on the median voter theorem, posits a positive link between democracy and redistribution. It argues that in highly unequal economies where the median voter's income is less than the mean income, most voters will demand higher taxes and redistributive policies to improve their share of national income. Others contend that high inequality is itself incompatible with democracy since rulers, who are afraid of redistribution, will repress their subjects, and the poor may lack the resources to sustain demands for democratisation and redistribution. Democracy and redistribution become mutually supportive only at moderate or "middling" levels of inequality, when the cost of redistribution outweighs the cost of repression, and elites and the poor agree on a social compromise. Views on the impact of globalisation on the link between democracy and redistribution are mixed. One view highlights its negative effects on social expenditures as governments respond to financial firms with mobile assets that are averse to taxation; another view underscores the imperative of governments to increase social expenditure in order to compensate for the social dislocations caused by globalisation.

Many quantitative studies on growth, inequality and democracy suffer from a number of problems associated with cross-country studies. These include subjective selection of control variables (a large number of variables may be significant in explaining growth); problems of collinearity in which control and explanatory variables may be correlated; difficulties of separating democratic processes from growth or development processes; and differences in the quality of democracy across countries.

Similarly, much of the conceptualisation of democracy and redistribution, which relies on the abstract notion of a median voter, is devoid of group influences. It assumes that all voters earning incomes below the average are a homogenous group that will automatically vote for redistribution. However, behaviour is influenced by numerous factors, including relationships at the workplace, by social and cultural settings, and by the political environment. Voting itself is a collective action mediated by organised groups with competing preferences and requires concerted effort for effective outcomes. It needs to be combined with other modes of organisation to affect redistributive outcomes.

Group organisation may take three broad forms: as social movements, as interest-based associations and networks, and as political parties. Social movements emerge when protests against specific issues are linked to other efforts to address similar concerns; these may be sustained over time across different locations in a polity. They are often diffuse and may not always be formally organised. Interest-based associations, which may emerge from, or support, social movements, include trade unions, farmers associations, professional and business organisations, neighbourhood groups, women's organisations and advocacy groups. The politics of production-based interest associations have, in some contexts, created a bargaining regime that places them firmly within the institutions of policy making rather than as lobbyists operating from outside. Groups may combine voting power, bargaining and direct action to improve welfare.

How individuals organise into groups and affect public policy is important in understanding the politics of redistribution and growth. In advanced industrialised democracies, movements, associations and parties tended to cluster according to the basic capital-labour cleavage associated with industrialisation. Indeed, many political parties and interest associations were a product of social movements. In developing country contexts, the three forms of organisation do not cluster according to the basic industrial cleavage, although social movements and interest-based associations have provided a foundational base for parties that have embraced redistributive policies.

Three issues are important in explaining the political dynamics that drive democracies to deliver growth and redistribution. The first is institutionalisation of rights, which is necessary for political organisation, alliance building and contestation of public policies. Most countries today are classified as democratic, but not all have been able to institutionalise rights. Indeed, one of the problems that cross-country empirical studies on democracy and development face is the quality of the data on democratic countries. In this work, greater prominence is given to countries with a long history of democracy where issues of institutionalisation have been more or less settled.

The second theme is group formation, group links to political parties and participation in policy making. An important point here is the ability of groups to develop a national outlook beyond the members they represent or coalesce into large formations that will cover most sectors of society. Mancur Olson refers to this as encompassment, which allows leaders to strike deals at the policy level that will reflect the interests of all and ensure minimum resistance from members. In the absence of encompassment, growth may only be internalised in the strategies of subaltern groups when governments provide considerable autonomy to central banks to pursue deflationary monetary policies, which may have negative distributional effects.

The third factor is the quality of the electoral process, which should be sufficiently credible and fair so that governing parties may be thrown out of office if they lose the confidence of voters.

3

The Politics of Poverty Eradication Strategies[3]

Poverty reduction has become a central objective of the world community. This can partly be traced to the failure of the stabilisation policies of the 1980s and 1990s to generate or sustain growth in many poor countries and the worsening of poverty in some regions. The elevation of social or human development in international development policy is perhaps one of the major contributions of the Millennium Development Goals, in which governments commit to halve poverty and hunger by 2015. Development assistance is now strongly oriented towards poverty reduction and other MDG targets. This has led to a shift in aid allocation in favour of social services. The public expenditures of poor countries have also tended to reflect this shift, with increased spending on basic services used by the poor. There has also been a proliferation of social assistance schemes, such as free health care for children, pregnant women, lactating mothers, and the aged; pensions for the elderly; income transfers for child care; employment guarantee schemes; and school feeding programmes. In some poor countries, donors play a crucial role in funding these programmes.

Sustained progress in many of these initiatives and lifting the vision of human development to the level where it addresses broader issues of productive capacities that provide decent jobs, social protection and services to all depends substantially on politics. This refers to processes of cooperation, conflict and negotiation that influence decisions about how resources are produced, distributed and used. Outcomes in the political process further depend on the distribution of power, the types of relationships governments establish with different

[3] Extracted from Y. Bangura, "Politics of Growth and Redistribution in a Development Context", in Y. Bangura (ed.), *Developmental Pathways to Poverty Reduction*. Basingstoke: Palgrave Macmillan 2015 and UNRISD; and "Democracy and the Politics of Poverty Reduction", in UNRISD, *Combating Poverty and Inequality: Structural Change, Social Policy and Politics.* Geneva: UNRISD. 2010. Background paper for speech at the Expert Group Meeting on Poverty Eradication, Organised by UNDESA and UNECA. Addis Ababa, Ethiopia. 15-17 September 2010.

groups in society, and the institutions that mediate conflicts among competing interests.

Unfortunately, the politics of poverty reduction is still top-down in many countries and lessons have not been drawn from the types of politics that have made significant and sustained dents into poverty in democratic countries. This contribution draws on the UNRISD Report *Combating Poverty and Inequality: Structural Change, Social policy and Politics* to shed light on the conditions under which democracies deliver outcomes that are beneficial to the poor.

Shortcomings of the participatory framework of PRSPs

Most low-income countries have relied on the participatory frameworks of the Poverty Reduction Strategy Papers (PRSPs) to involve citizens in designing and implementing anti-poverty strategies. However, the PRSPs have adopted a consultative process that does not give citizen groups the power to effect real change or get policy makers to deliver on agreed-upon goals. Many groups that participate in the process typically feel that real decisions on important policies lie elsewhere. Participation is often limited to NGOs without the active involvement of associations of informal and formal workers, farmers or artisans, whose livelihoods are directly affected by development policies. Research in many countries shows that important issues are often left out of discussions. One common omission or area that is ring-fenced is the macroeconomic framework of PRSPs, which is largely based on the IMF's Poverty Reduction and Growth Facility and negotiated between governments and the IMF. The type of participation associated with the social pacts that produced rapid poverty reduction in the past differs substantially from the bargaining regime of the PRSPs.

When democracies deliver outcomes that benefit the poor

The UNRISD Report *Combating Poverty and Inequality* argues that poverty reduction requires effective and accountable states, the institutionalisation of rights, sustained public engagement, expansion of the bargaining power of the poor and those who represent them, and pacts that are structured around issues of employment, welfare and growth. The report shows that democracies have been able to deliver outcomes that are beneficial to the poor when:

- rights are institutionalised, which allows the poor to exercise political choice, build alliances with others and hold leaders to account;
- groups with strong ties to the poor develop capacity for independent organisation and mobilisation;
- and when groups establish structural links for bargaining with actors involved in policy making;
- electoral competitiveness can also serve as an incentive for economic performance and redistribution. However, electoral competitiveness without effective group organisation and contestation may produce weak redistributive outcomes;
- the poor suffer when interest groups and social movements are weak and the electoral system is not sufficiently competitive.

My contribution will focus on the institutional arrangements and political dynamics of Nordic social democracies and social democracies in the South in tackling poverty.

Nordic social democracies

In high-income democracies, contestation by organised interest groups produced institutional regimes that allowed groups to bargain with employers and state authorities and influence the direction of public policies. Union density (the percentage of the workforce that is unionised) in Sweden, Denmark, Finland and Norway was higher historically than in other OECD countries. In 1990, it ranged from 58% in Norway to 72% in Finland, 75% in Denmark, and 81% in Sweden. The European Union average was 33%. In the Nordic countries, unions did not only enjoy autonomy to bargain with employers and the state; they were also linked institutionally to social democratic parties, which were committed to growth and redistributive policies.

In these countries, as the literature on welfare regimes has observed, democracy and welfare development were driven by similar processes in which trade unions, acting through social democratic parties, played a substantial role. For unions, democracy, including the freedoms

35

and rights it provides, was not just an end in itself; it was also an instrument to improve the bargaining power of workers in the distribution of the national product. Socialist/labour voting in the early period of democratisation correlated highly with welfare programme consolidation (meaning that countries adopted at least three of the four main social insurance programmes relating to work accidents, health, pension and unemployment). However, as John Stephens has observed in his studies on welfare democracies, labour needed allies, since working-class parties could not obtain electoral majorities. Socialist parties' share of the vote averaged 30 per cent.

In the Nordic countries, workers collaborated with segments of the middle class and small farmers, who defended their interests through agrarian parties. Initially, unions preferred a welfare regime that was based on individual contributions and benefits, which would have disadvantaged small farmers. Ultimately, it was the preferences of agrarian parties for flat-rate, universal, tax-financed benefits that came to define the welfare policies of social democratic regimes. As Stephens noted, despite the importance of small farmers in democratisation and social policy development, early agrarian democracies or those with no strong labour participation (such as Canada, France, New Zealand, Norway, Switzerland and northern and western parts of the United States) were laggards in welfare development. In Belgium and the Netherlands, unions and working-class organisations worked through clerical parties, which were critical of free-market capitalism. However, while social democratic parties provided platforms for women's groups to mobilise for the incorporation of gender issues in welfare policies, clerical parties were not so accommodating to gender interests. In the Netherlands, for instance, women perform poorly on labour force participation, unpaid care work and the provision of childcare.

The bargaining regime of countries with superior social outcomes took the form of social pacts. The key features of such pacts included the recognition granted to representatives of labour and employers in negotiations over wages, employment, working conditions and welfare; the ability of group representatives to ensure members' compliance when decisions were reached; and the mutual recognition of each actor's importance in achieving goals, including the relative capacity of parties to obstruct outcomes that were not based on consensus. Social pacts were not confined to the industrial sector. Agrarian pacts were also constructed in many countries. These improved farm incomes and narrowed rural-urban inequalities in many countries where farmers' votes were important.

High levels of unionisation and coverage rates in social democratic regimes encouraged unions to support policies that reconciled wage and welfare demands with the goals of profitability and growth. Unions supported policies of wage compression and equal pay for equal work across sectors, which spurred employers to raise labour productivity and avoid the option of cheap labour and segmentation. Unions were able to restrain the short-term interests of their members because of their encompassing position in the economy: union density was high, deals that arose from bargaining had wide worker coverage, and bargaining took place at the national, not industry, level. Redistribution and growth were thus pursued in tandem. This institutional arrangement may explain why the growth rates of social democratic countries were comparable to, and in some cases even better than, countries, such as the US, Canada and the UK, that pursued more liberal policies or adopted pluralistic institutions in managing state-union relations. During Sweden's so-called "golden years" (1870-1970), which included the high point of the welfare state, the country's productivity increased 17 times to become, by 1970, the fourth richest country in the world.

The data on social transfers and poverty for Organisation for Economic Cooperation and Development (OECD) states show that although social transfers have reduced poverty in all high-income democracies, countries classified as social democratic have been more effective in reducing poverty, followed by countries classified as Christian democratic. Those characterised as liberal regimes, which have weak labour movements and pluralistic institutions of interest representation in policy making, are the least effective.

Welfare democracies in the South

As Richard Sandbrook and his co-authors have observed in *Social Democracy in the Global South*, in a few established democracies in developing countries, subaltern interest groups are fairly well organised and are part of broad social movements that have influenced the policies of political parties. The most well-known cases are Costa Rica, the Indian states of Kerala and West Bengal, and Mauritius. Because these were largely agrarian societies when democratic politics were introduced, peasant movements and organizations, as well as small and medium-sized business groups and the middle class, were much more active in the construction of the alliances that produced welfare-enhancing policies. In Costa Rica and Mauritius, smallholders displayed remarkable organisational abilities because of the absence of powerful landowning elites. In Kerala and West Bengal, revolutionary parties implemented land reforms during the early stages of democratisation.

In Costa Rica, although the dominant coffee elite owned a few large farms, the bulk of its income was derived from processing and external trade, and not from the exploitation of farm labour. There were many unions representing landless peasants and defending land invasions between 1970 and 1990. In Mauritius, although agriculture was dominated by merchant capital and an agrarian bourgeoisie, there was also a large class of small landholders and rural farm workers. In Kerala, highly unequal agrarian landownership, discriminatory caste structures, and growth of a rural proletariat that followed land commercialisation in the south spawned a range of peasant movements for land reform, wage increases and social reforms, which enhanced the role of smallholders and the rural proletariat in the political economy.

In these societies, subaltern groups were sufficiently organised to influence the orientation of politicians without reliance on intermediaries. In Costa Rica, farmers formed the National Association of Coffee Producers to defend smallholders' interests on prices, taxes, credit and welfare. In Mauritius, the peasantry collaborated with the growing agricultural labour force, which had formed the Mauritius Agricultural Labourers' Association, and urban trade unions, such as the Engineering and Technical Workers' Union, which waged active campaigns for labour rights, wage increases and improved working conditions. These organisations played a role in the formation of the first nationalist party, the Mauritius Labour Party, which spearheaded social reforms. Significantly, these interest-based organisations and parties bridged the Indian–Creole ethnic divide that threatened to undermine social peace. In Kerala, because of the twin problems of land alienation and social discrimination, the main social movements were the anti-caste reformist movements in the south, and the land reform movements in the more feudalistic north. All three cases involved a dense network of civil society organisations. In Kerala, unionisation often extended to informal sector workers. Social pacts involving the participation of government, labour and business were constructed in Kerala and Mauritius. This helped to reduce strikes and improve wages and working conditions.

In these societies, the main political parties embraced a discourse of social rights and equity. In Kerala and West Bengal, the main parties of reform were communist parties, which embraced a parliamentary route to transformation and established strong ties with the peasantry and, especially in Kerala, a small working class. In Costa Rica, although the main parties were not strongly linked to social movements, the elite adopted a social democratic orientation. According to Martinez Franzoni and Sanchez-Ancochea, a coalition of small and medium-sized businesses and urban professionals clustered around the main party of reform, the National Liberation Party (NLP). This new elite and the NLP, which were influenced by international progressive ideas on social policy, were committed to a "double incorporation" of citizens into the market and the welfare regime. A reformist communist party (later banned), with ties to a small labour force, also helped shape the discourse on social rights when the welfare state was established in the 1940s. In Mauritius, all the major parties define themselves as social democratic and consistently regard social rights as acquired rights by citizens. The deepening of democracy and extension of social rights eroded clientelistic relationships.

In Costa Rica, Kerala and Mauritius, parties routinely alternate in government. No single party accounts for all the votes of subaltern groups. In Kerala, despite its transformative agenda, the Communist Party has never ruled for two consecutive terms, and competes with the Congress Party for the votes of the peasantry and rural workers. This, as many scholars have observed, has forced the Communist Party to retain much of its social movement character – constantly mobilising its base, reaching out to new groups, and making demands that address the interests of its core supporters. Electoral competition and active citizenship have also forced the Congress Party to imitate the strategies of the Communists by responding to the needs of the electorate. The failure to build permanent winning coalitions suggests that competitive elections play a more substantial role in forcing leaders to pursue redistributive policies than in the social democracies of advanced industrialised societies where social democrats governed for long periods through the electoral alliance of workers, small farmers and the middle class. Some have argued that power alternation in Kerala explains its superior social outcomes when compared to West Bengal, where Communists were in power for more than 20 years.

Interest-group politics have tended to be inclusive, rather than sectarian, because groups forged rural–urban alliances that incorporated wide segments of the population. This has been favourable to both growth and redistribution. Although the growth rates of these welfare democracies did not reach the levels of the East Asian developmental states, they were respectable for much of the period of the 1960s–1990s (with growth in Mauritius reaching 6 per cent; in Costa Rica, it averaged 5.3 per cent in 1963–2000, and 7.6 per cent in 1963–1973). This ensured some economic transformation and funding of extensive social programmes, although Kerala relies substantially on overseas remittance income. Rural-urban alliances also facilitated extension of welfare rights to all citizens. Welfare protection in Costa Rica initially covered non-skilled and semi-skilled workers, and later those who were not considered poor. Social insurance coverage in that country was eventually extended to informal sector workers and farmers.

Remarkable strides in social development have been made in all four cases. Costa Rica spends 16 per cent of its GDP on the social sector. And, unlike countries with highly regressive welfare policies, social expenditure is shared almost equally among education (31 per cent), health care (31 per cent) and pensions (28 per cent). Social policy is oriented towards increased coverage of the population under a unified system. Similarly, in Kerala, a large proportion of the population enjoys social protection and has access to food subsidies; the coverage of health care and primary education is universal. In Mauritius, there is a universal basic retirement pension, free primary and secondary education, comprehensive free medical care and subsidised basic foodstuffs. The overall effect is that poverty rates have been drastically reduced in these cases, and literacy and life expectancy rates are comparable to those of industrialised countries.

4

Understanding Poverty from a Perspective of Policy Regimes[4]

This essay examines the potential and limits of policy regimes in the study of poverty. There have been many studies on poverty, ranging from those that measure income poverty, to those that highlight poverty's multiple dimensions. Other approaches, which are sociological, include those that address social exclusion, marginality and the underclass. Strategies to combat poverty range from those that emphasise economic growth and targeted assistance to the 'deserving' poor, to those that support extensive state provision through universal policies. In addition, there are approaches that are critical of both state and market provision and privilege community-based and NGO interventions. Part of this literature includes "post-modernist" approaches that reject grand development strategies or narratives and locate solutions in the hands of the poor, unfettered by large structures and interlocutors.

Most current approaches to poverty reduction do not systematically address the complex interactions of institutions, policies and politics or the causes and dynamics of poverty; and when they try to analyse these issues, as in the World Bank's 2006 Report, *Equity and Development*, they do not draw out their implications for redefining macro-economic policies and power configurations to achieve the desired change. The Millennium Development Goals set targets on poverty reduction that countries should meet by a certain date, but are silent on causes, institutional arrangements and means. The key poverty reduction instrument (Poverty Reduction Strategy Papers) for developing countries says nice things about participation and national ownership, but tends towards selectivity in social policy, is weak on redistribution, and stuck on orthodox macro-economic policies that have been unsuccessful in improving the conditions of the poor. Most approaches treat poverty as a category detached from the dynamics of production systems, social

---

[4] Extracted from Y. Bangura, "Poverty Reduction and Policy Regimes: A Background Note". UNRISD. 2007.

41

policies and political processes. They are, in other words, not anchored in a policy regime framework. This may explain the strong faith in the transferability of policies, unconstrained by institutions, and why it has been easy for the international community to agree on targets while solutions have remained elusive.

This essay discusses some of the issues involved in adopting a policy regime approach to the study of poverty, its usefulness in aiding understanding of variations among countries in reducing poverty, and problems that may need to be considered when studying countries with very different economic, social and political institutions.

Why study poverty from a policy regime perspective?

Two sets of literature have spawned interest in policy regime approaches to the study of development, welfare and poverty. The first is Gosta Esping-Andersen's highly influential *Three Worlds of Welfare Capitalism*, which examines variations in welfare provision among advanced industrial societies. According to this work, welfare variations are a product of competing values on social rights, institutional divisions between markets and states, labour market policies and differences in power structures. Aggregate data on indicators that measure decommodification – the extent to which individuals are less dependent on markets for their well-being – stratification, and mix of state-market provision on pensions show that countries cluster into three regimes: liberal, conservative (corporatist) and social democratic. Significantly, these regimes tend to produce different labour market and poverty outcomes.

The second is Peter Hall and David Soskice's *Varieties of Capitalism*, which studies advanced industrial economies on the basis of how firms develop relationships to promote their core competencies in the production and distribution of goods and services. Countries are classified according to whether they are co-ordinated market economies (CME) or liberal market economies (LME) around five core areas of firm activities: industrial relations; training; corporate governance; intra-firm relations; and strategies to prevent adverse selection, moral hazard, and information hoarding by employees. LMEs tend to use market instruments to coordinate activities in financial systems and industrial relations; and CMEs tend to rely on non-market institutions to coordinate activities in both spheres. Significantly, liberal market economies tend to have liberal welfare states and low levels of benefits, underscoring a key finding in the welfare regime literature. Countries classified as social democratic and conservative (corporatist) in the welfare regime literature fall under the CME category, making it difficult to tease out their different social policy configurations in the varieties of capitalism book.

A policy regime framework for studying poverty is important for the following reasons.

First, a policy regime approach aids classification of countries in terms of the dynamics of institutions, policy instruments and political processes; and may help to explain why poverty may persist even when economies experience growth and countries have the resources and capacities to eliminate it. It challenges one-size-fits-all solutions, such as the view in Jeffrey Sachs's UN Report of the Millennium Project that "Whatever one's motivation for attacking the crisis of extreme poverty – human rights, religious values, security, fiscal prudence, ideology – the solutions are the same. All that is needed is action".

Second, a policy regime approach is a useful corrective to policy convergence theories. Even when countries get increasingly integrated into the world economy, they do not necessarily converge on a single neoliberal regime. By highlighting the inter-connections of policies, institutions and politics as historically generated configurations, the approach helps explain why variations in development strategies, welfare outcomes and poverty may persist among countries even under globalisation.

Indeed, certain policy regimes may be good in tackling some problems, but may perform poorly in others. For instance, as the varieties of capitalism literature has shown, a liberal welfare regime and liberal market economy may encourage radical policy change and innovation especially during crisis, and less constraints in moving production activities to developing countries. However, such a regime may also produce high levels of inequality, underdevelopment of skills among the working population, low levels of welfare protection, and high levels of poverty in the home country.

Third, a policy regime approach may facilitate understanding of policies and institutions as mutually reinforcing or interdependent. Effectiveness of one institution or policy in a particular sector may lead to, or require, complementary institutions and policies in other sectors. For instance, it has been shown that companies with high levels of exposure to stock markets tend to have flexible labour market institutions; and companies that depend on banks for capital and non-market forms of coordination require coordinated labour markets. This has implications for current approaches that tend to see poverty reduction as discrete sets of policies. From this perspective, the effects of micro-level interventions in tackling poverty will make sense only when placed within broad institutional and policy contexts.

Fourth, a policy regime approach draws attention to the limitations of quick fixes in much current discussions on poverty reduction. There may be long lags between the enactment of new policies and their effects, especially if the institutional architecture is less conducive to such policies. Calls for rule of law, property rights, participation, good governance, human rights, and public-private partnerships in debates on poverty reduction that are not anchored in a country's institutional infrastructure may fail to produce the desired outcomes.

Problems

However, a policy regime approach is not devoid of problems or challenges. Indeed, scholars question its relevance in developing countries. I highlight a few these problems.

First, the main policy regime approaches -- the welfare regimes and varieties of capitalism literatures – address developed economies with integrated markets for labour, capital and other production factors. In the welfare regime literature, even though regimes differ in decommodification and stratification, they are similar in levels of development and expenditures. Therefore, issues of development and social expenditures do not feature highly in the analysis—suggesting that countries do not have to worry about economic growth, structural change and financing social development; and despite the historical approach that informs the welfare regime literature, the three regimes of welfare capitalism—liberal, conservative (corporatist) and social democratic--appear as end-points in the analysis. Little light is shed on the complex ways regimes were transformed from dualism or fragmentation to attain the highly integrated liberal, conservative or social democratic outcomes.

The same holds for the varieties of capitalism literature, whose unit of analysis is the firm operating in integrated formal settings. Here countries belong either to liberal or co-ordinated market regimes. Again, levels of economic performance are similar for the two regimes, as Hall and Soskice observe, and are therefore not central in the analysis; differences are mainly in technological innovation, income distribution, employment, working hours and welfare policies. As critics have pointed out, there is, indeed, much complementarity between the two policy regime approaches even though welfare regimes and production regimes do not cluster neatly.

On the other hand, developing countries vary in capitalist penetration, industrialisation and labour markets. Low-income countries have large agrarian and informal sectors. Decommodification in social policy may be a positive factor in highly industrialised societies, as Ian Gough and Geof Wood, among others, have pointed out in *Insecurity and Welfare Regimes in Asia, Africa and Latin America*, but in agrarian and informal economies commodification may be a prerequisite for development and enhancing well-being.

Second, the social structure and politics that underpin the policy regime approach in advanced economies may not exist in developing countries. The welfare regime literature is anchored in an analysis of class relations, interest articulation and class conflicts. It addresses the complex ways unions, employers and political parties that can be placed on a left-right axis interact strategically to influence production, macro-economic policies and social provision. Indeed, some analysts believe that the key to understanding welfare regimes is that "countries cluster on policy because they cluster on politics". In many developing countries, however, because the majority of the labour force is in agriculture and levels of unionisation are low, the strategic links between organised groups, political parties and governments tend to be weak. It is, indeed, difficult to place parties on a left-right axis in many countries as there are important non-class variables that determine voting behaviour and interest articulation, as well as party and governmental practices.

Third, a policy regime approach assumes that institutions, policies and their corresponding political values and configurations evolve over time for them to constitute a regime. A regime denotes a distinct pathway of development, which can only be discerned historically. As a set of interrelated rules and organisational features that regulate relations between states, markets, and households, a regime has an element of path dependence: as Paul Pierson as observed in his studies on path dependence, increasing returns and the welfare state, once certain paths of development are taken, they generate self-reinforcing processes or positive feedback and make it difficult to reverse or change them. While social actors may change regime paths, they may be forced to adapt to the prevailing institutional environment.

Critics argue, however, that in the case of developing and transition countries that have experienced rapid policy change and transformation, it is counter-productive to talk about a policy regime. What exists instead is policy fluidity. These countries have not enjoyed stable democratic rule for the same length of time as their economic and social policies; economic policies have changed from import substitution industrialisation to narrow concerns about stabilisation; and social policies have seen major changes from formal, even if stratified, universal provisioning to targeted assistance and, in some cases, a return to selective use of universalism. It may be argued that policy regimes cluster in advanced industrial societies because democracy, economic policies and social policy development have a similar trajectory and have grown in tandem at least for the last 50 years. Similar social forces tend to drive them.

A fourth concern is that most developing countries are pursuing similar economic policies. If convergence has not occurred among advanced industrial societies where national policy regimes are resilient, developing countries may be moving towards policy convergence because of their indebtedness to international capital markets and multilateral financial institutions that have a strong hold on their policy agendas. Most aid-dependent countries, for instance, are pursing PRSPs that have turned out to be very similar. If policies are the same, it may be redundant to talk about regimes, which may evoke expectations of divergent paths in economic development, social policy and politics. A linear approach may be more appropriate as countries move from poverty and underdevelopment to well-being and development. In such an environment, policies and institutions can be transferred from one country to another with limited constraints.

A fifth concern is that a policy regime approach has been useful in the study of advanced industrial societies because the universe of country cases used to construct the regimes is small and countries have similar levels of development. It is relatively easy to develop typologies for 20 or so countries than for more than 180 countries with very different histories, institutions, cultures and values. Esping-Andersen's welfare regimes are based on data generated for 18 OECD countries, with Sweden, Germany and the US as the representative cases for the three regimes of social democracy, conservatism, and liberalism. Hall and Soskice's *Varieties of Capitalism* classifies 17 OECD countries into liberal market economies and coordinated market economies, but uses Germany and the US as case studies to illustrate the arguments. Even with this limited number of countries, questions have been raised about the location of countries in the three welfare regimes, whether in fact there can be two, four, or even a fragmented welfare system, and the inadequate treatment of household relations and a wider range of social programmes to reveal how regimes are gendered.

Developing typologies on policy regimes and poverty reduction

Critics tend to miss a crucial point about policy regimes and the study of poverty and development. Countries do not have to share the same social, economic and political characteristics for a policy regime approach to be useful. Indeed, one of the main insights of the welfare regime and varieties of capitalism literatures is that countries that are assumed to share common characteristics because of their levels of development and practice of capitalism and democracy turn out to be very different societies on closer investigation. Scholars working on Latin American policy regimes, such as in Evelyn Huber's, *Models of Capitalism: Lessons for Latin America*, do not find high levels of convergence among countries even though this region has experienced the longest period of exposure to IMF policy reforms. Even Africa, which is highly aid-dependent and exposed to high levels of conditionality, reveals variations in institutional configurations and outcomes when countries are closely studied. Complaints by the international financial institutions in the 1980s and 1990s about policy slippage among some countries denote some measure of institutional incompatibility with the reforms – thus the increased focus on institutional and governance reforms.

In addition, a policy regime approach does not have to use all the concepts and variables that inform the conceptual apparatuses of those used to analyse OECD countries. In the words of Esping-Andersen, "To talk of a regime is to denote the fact that in the relation between state and economy a complex of legal and organisational features are systematically interwoven". A policy regime approach, as Michael Shalev has observed, teases out "a limited number of qualitatively different configurations with distinctive historical roots". These configurations highlight mutually reinforcing institutions in the economic, social and political domains that may impact, constrain, or facilitate policy makers' interventions in poverty reduction or other public policy objectives. From this angle, it is counterproductive to study poverty reduction as discrete policies unrelated to the production system, macroeconomic regime, welfare policies and political institutions. In short, a policy regime approach is a political economy approach.

All humans irrespective of whether they live in agrarian or industrial societies face social risks such as old age, illness, disability, unemployment/underemployment, and child rearing. The fact that states with large agrarian and informal sectors do not protect their citizens from these risks or are miserly in their efforts should not diminish their significance. A social policy regime in agrarian and informal societies will still face the task of interrogating how these risks have been addressed by states, markets, households, civil society groups and communities over time; whether the policies are redistributive or regressive; whether they cover all or limited sections of the population; whether eligibility criteria are generous or restrictive; whether the various forms of intervention facilitate high or low participation in labour markets; and whether they transform or reproduce women's roles in the care economy. To ignore the roles of states and markets and their various configurations and focus instead on informal coping mechanisms, as in Ian Gough and Geof Wood's *Insecurity and Welfare Regimes in Asia, Africa and Latin America*, is inadequate. Informal coping strategies vary considerably – some highly structured and based on a core labour market activity, others less so – and have to be understood within the context of a country's economic and social system. There are varieties of informal security provision regimes even in poor countries.

Similarly, the fact that the formal business sector is limited in countries with large agrarian and informal sectors does not mean that a policy regime approach that seeks to understand how production systems function in tackling poverty is not helpful. Studying the structure and dynamics of economic systems was indeed the business of development studies before stabilisation and concerns about prices became dominant in the field. Problems of dualism, agrarian change, market segmentation, dependent development, industrialisation and inequalities were the staple of development studies in the 1960s and 1970s. Analysis of production regimes does not have to be limited to typologies of liberal and coordinated market economies, although scholars working on African agriculture have found the typology useful in analysing patterns of change in produce marketing, input supply and extension services.

It may be difficult to read off the economic and welfare regimes of countries from their politics if we adopt the class categories that inform the construction of the welfare state regime in OECD countries. Interestingly, the political regime is not well developed in the varieties of capitalism literature, which tends to be restricted to unions, business actors, and governments. This literature does not examine how business groups and workers relate to different political parties, including the partisan composition of governments that co-ordinate or not co-ordinate the market economies. There is no strong reason why there should be a lack of correspondence between politics and welfare provision or politics and production in developing countries. For instance, the under-provision of welfare in countries with adequate incomes may be linked to low levels of unionisation, weak links between organised interest groups and political parties, and limited or ambiguous tenure of pro-welfare parties in government. A policy regime approach should facilitate analysis of how different actors concerned with development, welfare and poverty, including unions, business groups, agrarian/informal organizations, NGOs and community organizations interact with political parties and governments to produce particular outcomes.

Constructing typologies for selecting countries

Constructing a typology of policy regimes that will reflect the experiences of the more than 180 countries in the world is a daunting challenge. Studies that aim to capture global outcomes on well-being have adopted two methods, which tend to be linear: cross-country regression methods, which allow for listing of countries in terms of how well they perform on the chosen indicators or variables; and classification of countries according to income levels.

However, these approaches tell us nothing about institutional and policy configurations. It is assumed that advances in the chosen indicators or variables are enough to propel a country from one category to another. Another approach is that provided by Alejandro Ramirez, Gustav Ranis and Frances Stewart, in their discussion of economic growth and human development. They examine why the performance of certain countries in human development is consistent over time with their levels of income while other countries periodically emerge as "positive outliers" and "negative outliers" when their income levels are compared to their levels of human development. Countries with economic growth-lopsided strategies are contrasted with those with human development-lopsided strategies. This framework does not systematically treat institutional issues.

Constructing typologies that will reflect institutional configurations in the three domains of production, welfare and politics is challenging. A comparative approach demands use of a conceptual framework that can be applied to all countries. It is unhelpful, for instance, to use a sustainable livelihood framework for developing countries and a welfare regime framework for advanced industrial societies as in Ian Gough and Geof *Wood's Insecurity and Welfare Regimes in Asia, Africa and Latin America.* Even if we assume that levels of development should not preclude adoption of a common framework of analysis for all countries, we will still have to explain how to integrate the different institutional features of economy, welfare and politics in such a framework.

The approaches in the welfare regime and varieties of capitalism literatures provide insights. These two frameworks start by developing a single concept and set of variables that throw light on different dimensions of the concept, against which countries' performances are measured and classified. *The Three Worlds of Welfare Capitalism* uses two key measures -- decommodification and social stratification, as well as an analysis of the mix of state-market provision -- to classify countries. The measures correlate strongly, suggesting that the decommodification index may substitute for the other measures in understanding welfare regimes. The decommodification index uses three variables – pensions, sickness and unemployment benefits – constructed on the basis of coverage, eligibility criteria, personal contributions, comprehensiveness, and income replacement rates. The different scores for the three social programmes are then aggregated to produce a composite index for each country. When these scores are presented, they tend to show three patterns or three worlds, although countries at the margins do not show sharp differences.

Varieties of Capitalism uses the concept of firms' strategic relationships to solve co-ordination problems in five spheres (or variables) that are important in the production and distribution of goods and services: industrial relations; vocational training and education; corporate governance; inter-firm relations; and prevention of adverse selection, moral hazard, and information hoarding by employees. Countries are then classified as liberal market economies or coordinated market economies depending on how they coordinate their activities in these spheres.

Even though both sets of literature adopt an institutional approach, they choose only one entry point to gain understanding of institutional complementarities or dynamics between economic policy, social policy and politics. The welfare regime approach uses institutions in the welfare domain as its entry point to examine the relations between welfare regimes, labour markets and power structures. Evelyn Huber and John Stephens combine this framework with the production regime framework in *Development and Crisis of the Welfare State*, but with the welfare regime providing the foundation for analysing how regimes cluster on welfare, production, politics, gender and poverty. The literature on varieties of capitalism uses the firm as entry point to discuss the links between different market economies, welfare, and interest group politics. It is silent, however, on other dimension of politics, such as partisan government.

It may not be possible to fully adopt the methodology of the welfare regime and varieties of capitalism literatures in studying poverty in developing countries. In both literatures, the entire set of OECD countries is used to classify countries even though detailed discussion of the regimes often revolves around a few representative cases. Especially in the welfare regime literature, the listing of country scores before the classification gives the impression that the regimes were not constructed on the basis of apriori assumptions about countries, but is the product of how they cluster on the key variables that measure welfare and co-ordination. It may be difficult to follow this method, especially if some of the peculiarities of developing countries in welfare provision and production activities are to inform construction of the framework. One approach might be to develop a few set of issues or variables around a key concept on production or welfare policies and select a limited set of countries based on existing knowledge for systematic study.

Should the UNRISD project on "Poverty Reduction and Policy Regimes" develop its typology around institutions on social policy and study how such institutions interact with institutions in the production system and political arena, or should we construct the typology on the foundations of production regimes and examine their links with welfare institutions and power structures? The proposal on "Poverty Reduction and Policy Regimes" highlights four regimes: socialist, Asian developmentalist, Nordic social democratic, and neoliberal adjustment/poverty reduction strategies (PRSPs). These models represent various ways of coordinating economies, with the socialist regime being the most co-ordinated. They suggest the need to open up existing typologies and think in terms of varieties of market co-ordination and varieties of market liberalism, with implications for welfare, labour markets, politics and gender relations. High levels of state co-ordination without markets, as in the socialist model, may produce universal welfare, full employment and relatively equal income distribution, but with repressed labour markets/industrial relations and authoritarian rule. One can trace through the different forms of co-ordination and their implications for welfare, labour markets, employment and politics for the other models. One application of the varieties of capitalism model to the liberalisation of cotton markets in Africa by Poulton, Gibbon, Hanyani-Mlambo et al suggests a variety of co-ordination regimes: concentrated market-based regimes where liberalisation has produced a few dominant actors; concentrated local monopolies, where liberalisation has produced a consortium of actors; and fragmented regimes with numerous small players. Peasants fare differently in these different regimes on such issues as input credit, extension service and produce quality control.

Alternatively, we can develop a typology based on patterns of structural change, such as economies that have made successful transitions to manufacturing; cases where industrialisation is advanced but labour markets are dualistic, with about half of the working population earning a living in the informal economy; cases where the services sector plays a leading role in stimulating economic growth;

economies in which agriculture dominates in terms of employment and output; and mineral-rich economies.

The challenge of combating poverty is likely to be different in each of these patterns of structural change. Research could then focus on the following themes: development strategies, the nature of structural change and poverty outcomes; wealth and income distribution; social protection; social services; and the politics of structural change and redistribution, bringing out how the poor benefits or is disadvantaged in each case. While this may not qualify as a policy regime approach, it may still help us to understand the dynamics of different production systems, welfare policies and politics in analysing poverty outcomes.

5
Jobs and Equity Key to Africa's Poverty Fight[5]

Africa has the highest poverty rate in the world. Even though some countries are on track to meet the MDG target of halving poverty by 2015, most are likely to fall well short. Income inequality is also higher in Africa than in most regions, while gender, ethnic and regional inequalities persist.

Such injustices endure for a variety of reasons, argues a new report by the UN Research Institute for Social Development (UNRISD), *Combating Poverty and Inequality*. The report, which was launched just before the September MDG summit of the UN General Assembly, highlights problems that have not been adequately addressed by the MDG approach. These include poor or unstable growth--which has failed to generate productive employment—and fragmented and underfunded social policies. Moreover, governments have been ineffective and their policies unresponsive to citizens' needs, so the poor lack influence over public policies.

Following Africa's economic contraction of the 1980s and 1990s, growth picked up from 2000 through 2007, thanks to a boom in commodity prices and improvements in the world economy. This helped countries such as Ethiopia, Ghana, Mali and Senegal to reduce poverty. However, even for these countries, poverty levels remain high and growth has not transformed African economies and delivered decent jobs.

Employment and equity

In the world's high-income countries, economic growth fuelled a shift from agriculture to industry and from industry to services. But Africa has

---

[5] Published in *Africa Renewal* (United Nations Department of Public Information, New York), December 2010. Adapted versions were published in *Financial Times Africa* (London) 5 February 2011; *La Tribune* (Algiers), 22 December 2010 (in French); *AfrikNews* (Paris), 11 January 2011; *Momagri* (Paris), 17 January 2011; *Public Agenda* (Accra), 11 February, 2011; and *Cameroon Post*, 4 February 2011.

not been able to follow a similar course. Instead, industrialisation in much of the continent has been stunted or narrow, while productivity in agriculture and services has been low.

As a result, labour markets have been segmented and unequal. There is widespread underemployment, incomes in informal and agricultural activities remain low and even relatively diversified economies such as that of South Africa experience persistent and large-scale unemployment. The terms and conditions of work are particularly poor for women.

Growth with jobs has been elusive for two reasons. First, globalisation has weakened the links between agriculture and industry. Urban people are fed largely by importing food, which undermines domestic agriculture. Countries also import most of their manufactured goods rather than expanding domestic production. So agriculture and industry have stagnated. Second, free-market ideas continue to dominate macroeconomic policies, emphasizing tight spending, privatisation and liberalisation. From that perspective, employment is regarded as a by-product of growth, with no need for specific policies.

But to achieve growth that is equitable and creates jobs, deliberate policies are required. Among other things, African governments could:

- connect agriculture more productively to industry and other sectors,
- expand domestic production and raise the demand for locally made goods and services,
- invest in infrastructure and education to improve skills and the quality of employment for women,
- avoid austerity policies during periods of slow grow,
- promote progressive taxation, and
- demand global reforms that reduce sharp fluctuations in commodity prices and interest rates, phase out agricultural subsidies in rich countries and grant African exports more access to Northern markets.

Universal social protection

Social investments can also drastically reduce poverty levels. During the 1960s and 1970s, public spending on education and health grew rapidly in most African countries. Primary and secondary school enrolment rose and infant mortality rates declined.

But in the 1980s economic crises and extreme pro-market policies led to severe cuts in social expenditures in most countries. The burden of financing shifted to consumers through user fees. In Kenya, government spending on basic services fell from 20% of total expenditure in 1980 to only about 12% in 1997. As a result, low-income groups generally had access only to poor-quality services and could ill afford the fees required for better amenities.

In recent years, popular pressures and shifts in aid allocations towards basic services have led to increased social spending. Social assistance schemes such as free health care for children, pensions for the elderly and cash transfers for the poor have proliferated. Yet Africa spends only about 3.5% of its gross domestic product on social protection, compared to 4.5% in all low-income countries, 10.5% in middle income countries and 20.6% in high income countries.

In countries where targeted social programmes are well funded and reach a large number of people, the results have been positive. This is the case in South Africa, where one in four people receives an income financed out of general taxation. Yet even there, poverty reduction has been seriously constrained by widespread joblessness and the high levels of inequality inherited from the apartheid era. In countries where such programmes are limited, targeting has failed to make significant and sustained inroads into poverty.

Social policies for reducing poverty must be grounded in universal rights. They must aim for redistribution, protect people from risks of unemployment, sickness and old age, and enhance the productive capacities of individuals and communities. They cannot be separated from efforts to create employment.

States and politics matter

Countries that have reduced poverty in relatively short periods had political systems that deliberately promoted growth and enhanced welfare. For the most part, they also built and maintained competent bureaucracies, institutionalised rights and had competitive democratic regimes.

In Mauritius, one of Africa's oldest democracies, small farmers collaborated with agricultural labourers and urban trade unionists to force the state to institutionalise social rights. These organisations contributed to the formation of the first nationalist party, the Mauritius Labour Party, which spearheaded social reforms. Today, all the major parties in Mauritius, which alternate in government, regard social rights as citizens' rights. There is a universal basic pension, free primary and secondary education and comprehensive free medical care.

During the anti-colonial struggles and early independence period, parties in other countries also had strong ties with urban and rural organisations and social movements. But the descent into one-party and military dictatorships, economic crises and adoption of structural adjustment policies in the 1980s loosened the ties between citizens and states.

Today, in the design of anti-poverty strategies, many countries rely on the participatory procedures of the Poverty Reduction Strategy Papers (PRSPs), supported by the World Bank and the International Monetary Fund. But the PRSP consultative process does not give citizen groups the power to effect real change. Participation is often limited to selected non-governmental organisations, without the involvement of associations of informal and formal workers, farmers or artisans, whose livelihoods are directly affected by development policies.

Competitive elections have opened up possibilities for demanding accountability from leaders. Taking advantage of a national election in 1993, the 400,000 farmers' federation in Senegal forced the country's president, who was worried about the rural vote, to discuss agricultural policy. That led to an agreement to cut interest rates on agricultural loans, remove import taxes on agricultural inputs, issue a moratorium on farmers' debts and institute dialogue between the farmers' organisation and the agriculture ministry. In general, however, limited electoral competition and the weakness of social movements in Africa have made it difficult to sustain gains.

Africa's experience so far suggests that anti-poverty measures that are not linked to production systems, broader social policies and politics will have limited results. Economic, social and political processes and institutions need to be consciously coordinated to achieve the maximum impact.

6
Inequality and the Politics of Redistribution[6]

Several thousands of years ago, Aristotle famously argued that "extremes of wealth and poverty are the main sources of evil" in the world. In our time, evil signifies short, miserable and undignified lives; xenophobia; urban crime; and violence. Yet a common point with Aristotle's epoch is that all these phenomena disproportionately impact the poor rather than the rich. Seen from this perspective, it can be argued that to talk meaningfully about poverty inevitably also implies talking about wealth, insofar as it is the processes and institutions that connect people differently that make some poor and others rich. In other words, attacking poverty requires a focus on inequality.

However, inequality has been treated marginally in international development policy. It is as if what matters in creating a more humane world is absolute poverty. In this view, if extreme poverty is falling, governments should not worry about what happens at the other end of the income distribution. This is particularly evident when one considers the Millennium Development Goals (MDGs). Several factors have contributed to the unfortunate divorce of poverty and inequality. In the 1990s, the view gained ground among some economists that high growth rates were sufficient to alleviate poverty, especially if income distribution remained unchanged. Governments were advised that they need not follow equity-based growth strategies, since what mattered most was the income level of the poor, rather than equality, whose pursuit may affect efficiency and ultimately growth itself.

The fixation with growth and absolute poverty coincided with the triumph of free-market ideas and the finance and technology-induced boom of the 1990s. Even low-income countries in Africa started to experience growth in the late 1990s after the regression of the previous decade. On the eve of the new millennium, there was thus a strong belief that the plight of the poor could be improved without questioning macroeconomic policy orthodoxy and income distribution. An increasing body of evidence is however showing that highly unequal societies need

---

[6] Published in *European Journal of Development Research*. No. 23. Issue 4. 2011. pp. 531-36.

higher levels of growth than relatively equal ones to overcome poverty, and that there is no trade-off between equity and growth.

In particular, poverty is closely related to inequalities of class, ethnicity and gender, which are therefore dysfunctional for development. High levels of inequality make it harder for the poor to participate in the growth process; restrict the expansion of the domestic market; may raise crime levels or cause violent conflict; and may create institutions that lock the poor into poverty traps. This clearly implies that there is a real need for specific policies that promote greater equity in society. These are obviously fundamentally political in nature, and this has had a profound influence on the debates surrounding potential measures. It is critical, however, to remember that combating inequality is also important from a human rights perspective, insofar as the international human rights framework commits governments to uphold equality in civil and political rights. Seen from this perspective, some notion of equity is thus central to the construction of socially inclusive states and the realisation of substantive citizenship.

Rising, persistent and interlocking inequalities

Income inequality has risen in most countries in the last three decades. The sharpest increase occurred during the 1980s and 1990s when most countries pursued economic liberalisation policies. Such policies were associated with regressive taxation, a shrinking fiscal base, weak social protection for the poor, decline of the civil service and industrial working class, and labour market interventions that increased casual, informal and unprotected employment. These developments help explain the strong and persistent link between personal and functional income distribution, as the wage share of national income also declined in most countries with data.

Most poor countries are highly unequal because of inegalitarian land tenure systems and dependence on mineral rents that are captured by those at the top. Declining terms of trade and rising interest rates in the 1980s and 1990s also impacted negatively on income distribution. In the case of high income countries, the dominance of financial and technological sectors has reversed a previous trend of falling inequality. Transition economies, such as those of China and the former Soviet Union, that had low inequalities under communism, have also witnessed sharp increases in inequality. The same goes for liberalising East Asian countries that industrialised under conditions of moderate inequality.

Gender, ethnic and regional inequalities also persist. They intersect with vertical or class inequalities and produce multiple disadvantages for many people. A particularly important contributor is the structure of the labour market, which can generate or sustain inequalities along several dimensions - not only in income or class status, but also by region, ethnicity and gender. It is important to address between-group (or horizontal) inequalities because they make up a large component of overall inequality within any country. Some groups may be seriously disadvantaged even when overall vertical inequality is low. Furthermore, if ethnic groups are geographically clustered, industrialisation may bypass groups that are not located in dynamic zones, intensifying poverty in the neglected areas.

Group inequalities often arise as a result of structural shocks that propel countries along specific development trajectories. Three well known shocks are slavery, colonialism, and transitions from communal to feudal land tenure systems in which the ethnicity of landlords is different from those of peasants. The racial inequalities in the United States can be traced to centuries of racial discrimination, with slavery as the structural shock. Latin America's high inequalities have their origins in the iniquitous *latifundia* system that dispossessed indigenous Indian populations of their land. The ethnic inequalities in Malaysia were shaped by the colonial ethnic division of labour, in which Chinese and Indians were mostly employed in the modern sector, while Malays were predominantly found in the low-productivity peasant sector. Similarly, regional inequalities in Ghana and Cote d'Ivoire can be traced to the effects of colonial policies that favoured heavy investment in regions where raw materials were readily produced and cheapest to export, which was in the south of both countries.

In all these examples, groups starting out in advantageous positions accumulate more, inherit higher human capital and have better social connections, while those that are disadvantaged may fall into a vicious cycle of poverty. It may be difficult to improve the positions of poor people in disadvantaged groups without tackling the position of the group. At the same time, gender inequalities are also closely linked to the ways in which women and men are integrated into different sectors of the economy, their representation in political and social institutions, as well as in the way that identities are valued in the cultural sphere. While economic development may enhance women's participation in the labour market, some patterns of growth thrive on, and reinforce, gender inequality. For instance, the successful East Asian model of industrialisation depended on employing young, unmarried women on highly unequal terms. Even by 1990, less than 40 percent of female workers in Korea had regular full time jobs (compared to about 65 percent of male workers) and women earned only half the wages of men.

Redistributive policies

Although the reduction of inequality has been marginal to the international development agenda, several multilateral agency reports have recognised its intrinsic value as well as its relevance for growth and poverty reduction. Perhaps the most influential view is that advanced by the World Bank in its 2006 World Development Report, which privileges equality of *opportunities* over *outcomes*. This justifies unequal outcomes if the processes that generate them are "fair", with only those falling below an absolute threshold of need deemed worthy of some form of protection. This approach however avoids tackling current inequalities of income and wealth, hoping instead that investment in opportunities might produce more equitable outcomes in the future.

Yet it can clearly be argued that redistributive policies and processes that lead to equitable outcomes have both intrinsic and instrumental value. Some notion of equity or fairness informs the values of major religions, ethical debates and many cultures around the world. There is an assumption that people are morally equal and the same value should be assigned to each person. Indeed, social experiments have shown that individuals will choose equality if they are ignorant of where they will fall in the income distribution. Upholding the intrinsic value of equality is not a case for perfect equality, which can undermine effort, personal responsibility and freedom. However, a growing body of evidence posits that a Gini coefficient (a measure of inequality in which 0 represents perfect equality and 1 represents total inequality) of more than 0.4 impacts negatively on economic and social well-being. Objectives of relative equality facilitate rapid poverty reduction, spread the benefits of growth more widely, and contribute to social cohesion.

Such objectives can be achieved through a range of policies, including for example employment-centred growth strategies, progressive taxation, or comprehensive social policies and affirmative action. Many of these obviously require a rethink of free-market ideas that have dominated international development policy in the last three decades. As the recent global financial crisis and its adverse effects on livelihoods have starkly demonstrated, there is a strong case for reworking the balance between markets and states worldwide.

Employment represents a crucial channel through which income derived from growth can be widely shared. If people have adequately remunerated jobs, they can lift themselves out of poverty and improve their well-being. Studies show that income inequalities between African Americans and White Americans tend to fall when employment levels are high. Similarly, the low-levels of inequalities that underpinned East Asian industrialisation have been attributed to adoption of labour-intensive manufacturing strategies, land reforms, and investment in education for all citizens. This suggests the need for agricultural and industrial policies that combine growth and employment generation, avoidance of deflationary macroeconomic policies, as well as improvements in infrastructure and the terms and conditions of work for all categories of individuals.

Progressive taxation is also important. Unfortunately, poor countries have a poor record in fiscal redistribution because of their low tax base, which is due to low incomes and a large untaxed informal sector. Still, tax revenues can be substantially improved if tax administration is strengthened to prevent widespread tax evasion and avoidance, and if efforts are made to reverse the trend of generous tax concessions, especially for mining companies, and lower rates of income and corporate taxes associated with liberalisation.

Social transfers and investments that include the poor can also drastically reduce inequalities, with the most significant reductions occurring in countries with comprehensive social policies that aim at universal coverage. For instance, although social transfers have reduced inequality and poverty in all high-income democracies, countries classified as social democratic, viz. Sweden, Denmark, Norway and Finland (with high levels of universal provision) have been more effective in reducing poverty and inequality, followed by countries classified as Christian democratic (Germany, Belgium, Netherlands,

France and Switzerland). Those characterized as liberal regimes (USA, Australia, Canada, Ireland and United Kingdom), with more targeted or residual approaches to social protection, are the least effective.

In countries with high levels of ethnic and gender inequalities, a strong case can be made for combining affirmative action and universal social policies. Affirmative action includes use of quotas and targets to enhance access to state services, business opportunities, tertiary education, the civil service and the corporate sector. However, evidence suggests that although affirmative action may improve horizontal inequalities, it may worsen intra-group and (overall) vertical inequalities. Policies that target both ends of the distribution may lead to improvements in both inter- and intra-group income distribution. In Malaysia, policies targeted both capital ownership at the top and educational and employment opportunities at the bottom. As a result, intra-group income distribution improved. Policies that focus largely on the upper end of the income distribution may lead to a worsening of intra-group inequality. This appears to be the case in South Africa where affirmative action has largely benefited the black middle class.

Politics of redistribution

Achieving substantial reductions in inequality is a political choice. Three models of redistribution offer insights on the types of politics that are conducive to equity. The first, associated with Kuznets' inverted U curve, posits that inequality first rises and then declines as countries industrialise. This assumes egalitarian societies as starting points and presence of similar forces for equalisation (such as democratisation, union pressure for wage increases, and mass education) in all countries as they develop. However, the existence of high inequalities in many agrarian economies and differences in levels of inequality among industrialised countries suggest the need for more explicit interrogation of country-specific political drivers for redistribution.

The second is the communist model, which recorded some of the lowest levels of inequality the world has seen in recent history. It was based on nationalisation of production assets, full employment, free education, generous social transfers, and wage compression between intellectual and manual labour as well as between skilled and unskilled labour. However, the authoritarian methods used for achieving these outcomes and the stifling of entrepreneurship and efficiency made the model unsustainable.

The third model is social democracy, which combines equity, efficiency, trade openness and democracy. In this model, trade unions, acting through social democratic parties, played a substantial role in the politics of redistribution. However, as the Nordic experience shows, workers could not produce electoral majorities on their own. They collaborated with segments of the middle class and small farmers, who defended their interests through agrarian parties. Women's groups were also able to mobilise and work with social democratic parties in incorporating gender issues in welfare policies. The bargaining regime took the form of social pacts that regulated wages, employment, working conditions and welfare. High levels of unionisation encouraged unions to support policies that reconciled wage and welfare demands with the goals of profitability and growth. Operating in a context of open economies, unions supported policies of wage restraint, as well wage compression and equal pay for equal work across sectors, which spurred employers to raise labour productivity and avoid the option of cheap labour and segmentation. Recent variations in welfare policies and governing coalitions have not radically changed the relatively lower levels of inequality and poverty in these countries when compared to other OECD countries.

A similar pattern of party-interest group ties in reducing inequalities can be found in welfare democracies in agrarian societies. In these countries, subaltern interest groups were part of broad social movements that influenced the policies of political parties. The most well-known cases are Costa Rica, the Indian state of Kerala, and Mauritius. Because these were largely agrarian societies when democratic politics were introduced, peasant organisations were much more active in the construction of the alliances that produced welfare-enhancing policies. In Costa Rica and Mauritius, the absence of powerful land-owning elites allowed small farmers to organise and engage the state strategically. In Kerala, a revolutionary party implemented land reforms during the early stages of democratisation. Elections were highly competitive in all three cases, with parties routinely alternating in government, forcing politicians to stay connected with voters' aspirations.

Groups forged rural-urban alliances that incorporated wide segments of the population. This favoured both growth and redistribution. Although the growth rates of these welfare democracies did not reach the levels of the East Asian developmental states, they were respectable for much of the period of the 1960s–1990s. This ensured funding of extensive social programmes, although Kerala relies substantially on overseas remittance income. The overall effects are moderate levels of inequality, substantial reductions of poverty, and literacy and life expectancy rates that are comparable to those of industrialised countries.

In highly unequal democracies that are leaning towards welfare development, such as Brazil and South Africa, social pacts or governments that emerge from social movements have also been important. In Brazil, Lula's government represented the rise to power of a workers' party that was committed to redistribution in a context of economic liberalisation. The government's *Bolsa Familia* programme provided monthly income transfers to 11 million extremely poor households. Inequality and poverty have fallen in recent years, although income, wealth and other disparities remain high.

In South Africa, despite recurring tensions and differences, the pact between the labour movement and the ANC government that ended apartheid has survived. When combined with electoral pressures, the alliance has tended to push the government in a social democratic direction on social policy. Today, even as the government pursues a strategy of market-conforming growth, one in four South Africans receives a pension or grant financed out of general taxation. However, the very high levels of inequality inherited from the apartheid era and widespread joblessness act as serious constraints on the development of social democracy.

International development policy has failed to draw lessons from these experiences of party-union-social movement ties in articulating a politics of poverty reduction. In the design of anti-poverty strategies, most low-income countries rely on the participatory procedures of the Poverty Reduction Strategy Papers (PRSPs), supported by the World Bank and International Monetary Fund. But the PRSP consultative process does not give citizen groups the power to effect real change. Participation is often limited to selected non-governmental organisations, without the active involvement of associations of informal and formal workers, farmers or artisans, whose livelihoods are directly affected by development policies.

Conclusion

Poverty and wealth are inextricably intertwined. People are poor, not because they lack a certain level of income or material things, but because of the way they are connected with the rich in the production and distribution of goods and services. Poverty and inequality have multiple dimensions and vary widely across countries, even among those that have industrialised. This underscores the importance of understanding the policies, institutions and politics that drive them. Egalitarian outcomes are achieved in democratic settings when groups with strong ties to the poor organise independently and establish links with, as well as hold to account, actors involved in policy making. Countries where governing parties are sensitive to redistribution have produced relatively egalitarian outcomes. Electoral competition in which there is a high probability that governments may lose office can act as an incentive for redistribution. However, electoral competition without effective group organisation and contestation may produce weak redistributive outcomes. The poor suffer when interest groups and social movements are weak and when the electoral system is not sufficiently competitive.

7
State Capacity for Economic Development and Well-being[7]

The public sectors of most countries expanded a great deal between 1945 and 1980 despite differences in their economic systems, levels of development and ideologies. As economies grew and societies became highly differentiated, the state's conventional tasks of regulation, allocation and redistribution became more complex. Public sector growth was also a function of the types of societies various governments sought to promote. For instance, commitments to the welfare state and macro-economic stability in OECD countries encouraged acceptance of the state as a central institution for redistributing wealth, protecting the vulnerable and stimulating aggregate demand. Similarly, nationalism, efforts to create cohesive societies in multi-ethnic settings, and pressures for rapid growth, facilitated expansion of the state in developing countries. A number of enterprises were nationalised, partially or fully. Governments also established parastatals on a wide range of activities because the private sector was perceived as either too slow to respond to incentives or showed little or no interest in investing in preferred sectors. Social services were also expanded as part of efforts to develop national elites and promote citizenship or solidarity in newly independent states.

Issues of efficiency, representation, participation and accountability, though important, were not central to the growth of the state in most countries, except where democratic forms of rule and markets were already well established. The state was seen essentially as an institution that would foster unity or solidarity, promote national development and macro-economic stability, regulate foreign domination, protect domestic markets and, in some cases, redistribute wealth. This vision of the state came under considerable attack during the 1980s and 1990s in practically every region of the world. An alternative vision,

[7] Extracted from Y. Bangura and G. Larbi (eds.), *Public Sector Reform in Developing Countries: Capacity Challenges to Improve Services.* Basingstoke: Palgrave Macmillan and UNRISD. 2006; and Chapter 10, "Building State Capacity for Poverty Reduction", in UNRISD, *Combating Poverty and Inequality: Structural Change, Social Policy and Politics.* Geneva: UNRISD. 2010.

embraced in varying degrees among countries, has sought to create a market-friendly, transnational, lean, decentralised, customer-oriented, managerial and democratic state. The core elements in the vision are sometimes contradictory as different social forces drive them in different national contexts and with varying levels of capabilities. There are tensions between, on the one hand, concerns for efficiency, market-soundness, deregulation, competition and stabilization, and issues of accountability, representation, participation and equity on the other.

Two major initiatives have been important in the process of state restructuring in poor countries: public sector management reform, and the distribution of governmental power among competing interests in society. Public sector management reform deals with issues of fiscal stability, managerial efficiency, capacity building and public accountability; whereas reforms relating to the distribution of power are concerned with the promotion of plurality in the central institutions of government and dispersal of power to lower authorities. The latter is often referred to as decentralisation. Both reforms are being applied in varying degrees across regions and countries. Despite the strong calls for reform, there are fundamental differences between visions and realities or between theory and practice. The content and depth of the reforms vary considerably between countries, including countries within the same region or with similar levels of development. Organisational cultures, social segmentation, power relations and international donor pressures affect choice of reform instruments and explain why some reforms have been difficult to implement than others.

Research suggests that public sector reforms are likely to be unsustainable or ineffective if politicians and citizens have not worked out a framework for managing governmental power that will yield a minimum level of consensus about public policies. The pursuit of reforms under unstable or highly contested political systems may turn such reforms into technocratic or top down exercises. This may invite opposition, non-compliance, indifference or high implementation slippage. A related point is the need to understand the rationale or missions of states in the period when they were seen as legitimate actors in shaping development. Much recent research, including in economics, has demonstrated the folly of basing public policies on assumed perfect competitive markets that will lead to optimal outcomes for most citizens, sectors and countries. Societies have to contend with both market and state failure; and the level of government intervention to correct market failure or promote development cannot be determined apriori. The rush for reforms, especially when driven from outside, has often done havoc on vital institutions that societies had created either to foster national unity, defend disadvantaged groups and regions or support national investments. Reforms that ignore the core developmental missions of states may not only yield poor results but may also undermine political settlements and make it difficult to reconstruct failing states, institutions and economies.

Reforms should also pay attention to the basic needs of employees. The trend in most crisis-ridden states where downsizing has not led to payment of "living wages" exposes public servants to multiple survival strategies that may be detrimental to state capacity and administrative efficiency. Modern bureaucracies are founded on the premise that individuals who work in them will serve the public good as opposed to catering to personal or sectional interests. This presupposes a basic income that will allow public servants to carry out their duties without succumbing to extraneous pressures. However, the real incomes of public servants in low-income countries have fallen sharply over the years. The data suggest that pay declined somewhat as a proportion of GDP per capita in developing countries as a whole between the early 1980s and early 1990s. The average central government wage bill as a percentage of GDP per capita is estimated to have fallen in Africa from 6.1 percent in the early 1980s to 4.8 percent in the early 1990s; in Latin America from 2.7 percent to 2.3 percent; and in OECD countries from 1.7 percent to 1.6 percent. The data for Asia shows an increase from 2.9 percent to 3.8 percent over the same period. The same goes for public employment. The available data suggest that Africa had fewer people working in the public sector than other developing regions: this was 1.9 percent of the population in Africa compared to 4.6 percent in Latin America, 4.9 percent in the Middle East, and 3.1 percent in Asia and the Pacific. One can conclude, on the basis of these data, that Africa today is the most under-governed region in the world. The sharp reductions in expenditure, incomes, and employment affected the incentive structures of African bureaucracies, making public service unattractive or not fully rewarding.

Three types of state capacity

Governments need to build three types of state capacity for development. The first is political capacity for setting and implementing public policy. Governments in poor countries face enormous constraints in defining, adopting and implementing policies. They may experience policy capture by powerful segments of society, sustained opposition by organised interest groups, and intractable ethnic or religious conflicts. Authoritarian developmental states, such as those in East Asia, overcame such constraints by relying on coercion, repression and control, as well as by delivering high and inclusive growth, employment expansion, job security and provision of services. The coercion-repression option of building political capacity is not available to countries that have opted for a democratic path of development. In democratic countries, citizens enjoy basic rights and the freedom to contest, frustrate or block state policies.

Democratic states with good development outcomes engage citizens more actively in efforts to build the necessary consensus and support for public policies. Respect for the right to contest policies, bargaining and redistributive policies are therefore central to the strategies of political capacity building in such regimes. Where authoritarian regimes resolve the wage-productivity problem by repressing workers, democratic regimes are more likely to develop social pacts with the working population using redistributive policies. The participation of subaltern groups is essential in building political capacity and resolving the tension between profits and welfare in democracies. Studies suggest that democracies have been able to regulate distributional conflicts and promote macroeconomic and welfare outcomes when the workforce is highly unionised, collective bargaining agreements cover large sections of the working population, and bargaining takes place at the national level. In democratic Costa Rica, the state of Kerala in India, and Mauritius, political capacities for development were nurtured through active citizenship, the crafting of political parties that were strongly oriented towards equality, the self-organisation of subaltern groups and alliances, strong party-social movement ties and electoral competitiveness that gave value to the votes of the poor. The redistributive social policies of such regimes were often part of political settlements that allowed states to pursue effective growth strategies.

The capacity of states to mobilise resources is a second important measure of the extent to which they can achieve their development objectives. The capacity to mobilise resources improves policy space and the ability to set agendas; it also empowers states to influence the orientation and strategies of civic and business groups. However, resource mobilisation is highly political. Commitment to domestic resource mobilisation does not guarantee that the desired amount of resources will be generated, let alone allocated to preferred programmes, or that the burden of resource extraction will be distributed fairly among different population groups. Issues of trust, solidarity, consensus and reciprocity in state-society relations influence the extent to which governments can succeed in extracting resources from the populace. Studies suggest that even East Asian authoritarian developmental states that demonstrated capacities to generate high savings and tax yields did not rely on coercion alone. Provision of services, job security, and social insurance for workers in key industries helped to build state-citizen relations conducive to high levels of resource mobilisation.

Coercion alone is unlikely to succeed in low-income aid-dependent countries that have experienced democratisation. The reason is simple: democratic politics offers citizens and business opportunities to contest resource extraction strategies and make claims on how resources should be spent. In addition, the weak capacities of low-income states suggest that resource mobilisation strategies may fail or lead to slippage, payment avoidance or capture of state officials by powerful groups if efficacious state-citizen relations are not developed that provide benefits to tax payers and savers. Significantly, the visions of the key actors involved in resource mobilisation– the state, citizens, business, and donors – are often conflictual. They may differ not only on the types of resources to be mobilised, but on who pays for the resources and by how much, as well as on the balance that should be achieved in allocating resources to productive sectors and public services.

The capacity to put resources to effective use (or allocative and enforcement capacity) is the third measure of state power for development. Where the financial system is dominated by capital markets, as in the liberal market economies of the United States and the United Kingdom, the capacity of the state to intervene in the economy and influence the flow of financial resources is limited. Where the financial system is credit-based, states have more leverage in shaping investment outcomes, especially if they control the key banking institutions. The financial systems of the East Asian developmental states were state-led. During the early period of transformation, all banks in the Republic of Korea and Taiwan Province of China were state-owned. This allowed the state to take a lead role in coordinating investment, although Taiwan Province of China had a flourishing informal credit market for small and medium-sized enterprises. The developmental states did not grant banks the kinds of autonomy they enjoyed in the credit-based financial systems of European economies. Credit control in East Asia allowed the state to select beneficiaries and influence their investment decisions. The state combined subsidised credit with other policy instruments, such as tariff and tax exemptions as well as export subsidies, to influence the behaviour of firms and the general growth trajectory.

Allocative and enforcement capacity is enhanced when the state is knowledgeable about the sectors in which it intervenes. This calls for systematic collection, storage and analysis of economic and social data of value not only to government but also to business and citizens. The cost of enforcement is reduced when citizens are provided with accurate information about resource allocation and participate in the monitoring of resource use. The priority areas for business are technological developments, quality standards, raw materials and changing market conditions. It enables governments to identify new opportunities and constraints, and urges firms to act upon them, upgrade their activities and climb up the value chain. Knowledge is enhanced when the state undertakes research in sectors that need upgrading.

The East Asian developmental states invest heavily in industry-based information gathering and research. This activity is often carried out by a lead agency entrusted with directing the industrial transformation—the Ministry of International Trade and Industry in Japan, the Economic Planning Board in the Republic of Korea and the Council for Economic Planning and Development in Taiwan Province of China. The Republic of Korea mandates all industries to report regularly on export and other types of business performance. In Taiwan Province of China, a network of publicly funded research institutes, such as the Industrial Technology Research Institute, the Electronics Research Service Organisation and the Computing and Communications Laboratory, performs the role of knowledge generation.

These nodal agencies, which are insulated from special-interest groups, help to create coherence and direction within the bureaucracy. Such insulation is crucial, since it provides the agencies an encompassing or national character and institutional mission to achieve the state's goals. The nodal agencies decide which industries to support and which to phase out or allowed to disappear, based on their understanding of a country's industrial structures and international competitiveness. They also build support in the private sector for the state's plans and facilitate private sector ties with foreign investors and trading companies. Monitoring and enforcement were effective partly because the nodal agencies eschewed comprehensive state planning or wide-ranging discretionary powers of the type that were prevalent in the former Soviet economies.

There were clearly price distortions and potential for rent-seeking, since government planners, who might not have been infallible in deciding what was best for the economy, favoured certain sectors. However, prices did not deviate substantially from market-clearing levels, and protections and subsidies tended to be time-bound. Bureaucracies for monitoring and enforcement were often not very large, and were staffed by well-paid and trained individuals recruited through highly competitive examinations. The switch to export-oriented industrialisation also strengthened the enforcement capacity of the state. Local firms needed state support to attract foreign capital, break into the US market and maintain standards. The survival of firms came to depend largely on increasing their efficiency and export performance, since they were now competing in a global market, and the state was reluctant to bail out non-performing companies.

Allocative and enforcement capacity can be improved by involving citizen groups in regulating development agents and service providers in discussing the conditions under which business can contribute to progressive social outcomes. This requires that governments make available information required by citizens to hold business groups accountable. The involvement of informed citizens and non-state actors in articulating citizen claims and monitoring resource use reduces the cost to government of allocating resources and enforcing policies. For instance, participatory budgeting (a process involving a range of civil society actors who deliberate with state officials on how government revenues should be spent) and citizen charters can help strengthen state-society relations and improve the capacity to enforce rules, especially in democratic contexts. They have been shown to improve allocative and enforcement capacities and redistributive outcomes in situations in which governing elites resolve to change power structures in favour of the poor and marginalised and where there is a dense network of civil society groups that can engage government authorities in policy making. In Porto Alegre, Brazil, participatory budgeting led to a big increase in the number of households with access to water and sewerage, children in public schools and paved roads, and expansion of local government revenues.

Citizen charters seek to ensure that citizens are consulted and offered adequate information about the quality of public service. Service delivery or user surveys are an important source of information and have been promoted in many countries. With government support, the surveys aim to measure how consumers or citizens feel about a range of services provided by local and central governments. Results are disseminated among civic groups and the media and given to governments for actions. The expectation is that governments will improve their performance based on the survey findings. One of the most well-known and advanced applications of this instruments is the Public Affairs Centre's Report Card, pioneered in the Indian cities of Ahmedabad, Bangalore, Calcutta, Madras and Pune, which solicits citizens' views on services such as telephones, electricity, water, health, the postal system, public transport, the police, public banks and food distribution systems.

8

Revenue Bargains Key to Financing Africa's Development[8]

The Issue

Revenue bargains in which states extract revenues from citizens in exchange for investments that impact positively on well-being are key to financing Africa's development. They can substantially increase revenues, nurture effective state-citizen relations, force companies to pay correct taxes, push inegalitarian and fragmented systems of service provision in the direction of universalism, improve policy space and make aid more effective.

Africa has enjoyed a growth momentum since 2000 after the wasted years of the 1980s and much of the 1990s. In 2014, seven of the ten fastest growing economies were in Africa, and African leaders increasingly talk about structural transformation and lifting their populations out of poverty. This optimism is underpinned by more than 10 years of high global commodity prices, improvements in domestic revenue collection, and growing demands for better services in a context of expanding rights and democratic politics. Many countries have invested heavily in infrastructure and increased social expenditures.

Africa's turn of fortune coincided with the emergence of target-setting strategies in international development policy. These strategies include calls on poor countries to mobilise an additional 4 per cent of their GDP to fight poverty; the social protection floor initiative which requires governments to commit 4.5 per cent of their GDP to basic social protection; the 20 percent of government expenditure target for education; the MDG 1 percent of GDP target for comprehensive access to water; and the African Union's targets on infrastructure and agriculture.

Meeting these targets requires huge resources, which existing funding strategies will be unable to generate. Global commodity prices

---

[8] Prepared for UNRISD's "Think Pieces on Financing for Development: The Road to Addis", as part of its contribution to the Third International Conference on Financing for Development, 13-16 July 2015, Addis Ababa, Ethiopia.

have fallen sharply in the last twelve months; capacity to mobilise domestic revenues is waning; the jury is still out on proposals for improved funding of the newly-minted Sustainable Development Goals after the less than stellar funding of the expiring MDGs; and the anticipated structural change that will diversify economies, expand employment and improve incomes is proving elusive. Revenue bargains may hold the key to breaking out of the vicious circle.

Revenue bargains have a long history and are at the heart of development

African countries need to address two types of bargains: domestic and global, with an emphasis on domestic bargains, which are necessary for global bargains to be effective. The Monterrey Consensus of the 2002 Conference on Financing for Development represented a revenue bargain of sorts at the global level, in which donors pledged to increase aid in return for improved tax efforts by developing countries. More than 10 years after that conference, there are no signs that aid will improve to a level where it can plug poor countries' financing gaps. Although aid has increased by 66 per cent in real terms since 2000, reaching a record high of USD$135 billion in 2014, many donors have failed to honour their pledges, citing fiscal constraints induced by the global financial crisis. Furthermore, only five countries' aid meets the UN's target of 0.7 percent of gross national income, with the average stuck on 0.29 per cent of GNI.

Besides, critics of aid have become vocal, and sections of voters in donor publics are either weary of aid or insist on aid delivering results. A growing body of literature even sees aid as a curse that stifles development and democratic accountability of governments to citizens. From the perspective of African governments, even if aid improves substantially, it often comes with conditions, including ceding considerable space in the policy process to donors.

The second type of revenue bargain, involving mutual accountability of states and citizens in the mobilisation and use of revenues, may substantially increase revenues as well as help to overcome the problems of accountability and mutual mistrust that have plagued the aid relationship. The sources of revenues for constructing such bargains are taxes, savings, social insurance schemes and mineral rents. With growing economies, the tax-to-GDP ratio of African countries has increased in the last 15 years, even though non-resource related taxes have stagnated. Indeed, the boom in global commodity prices and widening of the tax net through value added taxes contributed to a modest decline in aid dependency.

The savings rates of African countries have also risen even though in many countries they are yet to return to pre-structural adjustment levels. Governments have also launched social security schemes to provide old age, invalidity and survivors' benefits to formal sector workers. Because of the youthful age structure of the African workforce and the period it will take for benefits to mature, these schemes have generated huge savings that can finance development.

Revenue bargains may be crucial in maximising yields from these various revenue sources. They were at the heart of state formation, extension of the franchise, and improvements in welfare in Europe. In democratic contexts, they imply negotiation and less coercion in extracting resources from citizens. In bargains over taxation and political representation, for instance, European governments wanted resources to finance wars and citizens wanted representative governments that could deliver public goods.

Similarly, East Asia's extraordinarily high savings rates that financed its development were based on a bargain: state pursuit of growth with jobs, security of tenure and social protection for the employed, universal provision of housing especially in Singapore, and affordable quality education for all.

In Western Nigeria, in the 1950s and 1960s, the Action Group party's development programme was based on a policy of extracting surpluses from cocoa farmers in exchange for universal primary education, and extension and social services that benefited farmers and their children, giving that region the highest literacy rate in the country. The close party-state-citizen relationship that was a hallmark of that bargain ensured the party's dominance in regional elections.

Following Eritrea's independence and resolve to finance its development without dependence on donors, a bargain was struck with its Diaspora citizens to pay two per cent of their income as a tax in exchange for state services. Although a laudable bargain at the time, the persistence of authoritarian rule and lack of accountability to citizens on how the money is spent has undermined the maximisation of revenue from the diaspora tax. Many Eritreans now question its legitimacy and have stopped paying the tax.

Concerns for environmental standards and pressure by mining communities for a fairer share of mineral rents have also produced a variety of bargains in mineral-rich countries. In Sierra Leone, Community Development Agreements allocate about 3 per cent of diamond export tax revenues to local mining communities for services and other benefits. However, most of the bargains are lopsided, and local elites, especially traditional rulers, are the main beneficiaries.

Five potential benefits of revenue bargains

Revenue bargains that are transparent, and in which citizens exercise influence, provide five potential benefits. First, they offer opportunities to build purposeful, mutually supportive and durable state-citizen relations that have been lacking since the structural adjustment period of the 1980s that eschewed planning and dialogue. Despite the spread of democracy, governments are hardly present in most people's lives in terms of jobs, social services and social security. People invariably fend for themselves and very often do not trust the word of government. The Ebola crisis in West Africa demonstrated this problem in bold relief as weak citizen-state ties and lack of trust in government made it difficult to curb the high rates of infection.

Revenue bargains work best when they are crafted around benefits that impact directly on well-being, such as social services and social protection. Unfortunately, trends in aid allocation that have prioritised social sectors because of the MDGs, and Africa's growing dependence on aid to finance its social services, may act as a constraint in building effective revenue bargains. Aid should focus on infrastructure and the productive sectors and African governments should construct viable bargains with their citizens that will fund social programmes as is the case in all countries that have grown out of poverty. In East Asia's industrialisation, aid supported agricultural technology, basic industry and economic infrastructure, not social programmes. Social programmes were the exclusive responsibilities of states and citizens and were central to the construction of effective state capacity in advancing the project of economic transformation.

Second, revenue bargains can deepen accountability by improving citizens' capacity to organise and make claims on public policy. Such activism may be driven by expansion of the tax net to most citizens in productive work, including those in the informal sector. Tax yields are low in Africa partly because tax advocacy groups, such as the Tax Justice Network, are few, lack strong ties with tax payers, and mostly address the extractive sector. When more citizens pay taxes and are brought into bargains with defined benefits, they are likely to develop an interest in how revenues are spent, making it easier for more groups to be formed and for strong links to develop between advocacy groups and tax payers. Activism may also serve as pressure to upgrade the quality of institutions in social provision, which tend to be neglected in economic policies that emphasise tight spending. Since the 1980s, financial institutions, such as central banks and finance ministries, have been better capacitated than social sector institutions in advancing public policies. This needs to change if development is to impact positively on the poor.

Third, revenue bargains that are crafted around citizens' taxes may help governments to increase yields from other revenue sources, such as those in the extractive sector and value added taxes paid by trading enterprises. African countries have been unable to capture a large share of resource rents because of generous concessions in the form of royalties, corporate taxes, value added taxes and import duties, given to mining companies, as well as widespread corruption by regulatory institutions and state officials dealing with such companies. It has been estimated that Sierra Leone lost US$224 million in 2012 largely because of generous tax concessions given to the five largest mining companies. In Guinea, an Israeli company, which bought iron ore mining rights for US$160 million, sold those rights to a Brazilian company for US$2.5 billion. In Zambia, an Indian businessman was caught on video boasting that although he paid only US$25 million for a copper mine, he makes US$500 million every year on the mine. Mining companies get away with these kinds of deals because of lack of transparency in negotiating contracts, the limited number of groups that monitor the extractive sector, and lack of sufficient citizen engagement with revenue issues.

Similarly, many trading companies do not fully pay value added taxes because of collusion between tax collectors and trading companies and consumers' indifference to the culture of demanding receipts. In Sierra Leone, for instance, many trading companies circumvent or exploit value added taxes by issuing illegal receipts to buyers or none at all. As buyers do not often ask for receipts, let alone insist on the official ones, the companies appropriate the taxes that they should pay to the state. Increasing the stake of citizens in revenue bargains may encourage them to police the behaviour of companies in the payment of taxes. It may also help to strengthen regulatory institutions and curb the rampant illicit financial flows (IFFs) from Africa, which the Thabo Mbeki-led African Union-Economic Commission for Africa panel report on IFFs estimates at US$50 billion a year—more than what Africa receives yearly in foreign aid.

Fourth, revenue bargains may help to reverse the perniciously inegalitarian and fragmented system of social provision that has emerged in much of Africa since the 1980s. In the field of education, even though enrolment rates have risen, the quality of education remains poor, and the public schools that offered opportunities for upward mobility to children from poor backgrounds have been seriously degraded. Now rich and middle class parents send their children to well-resourced private schools and children from poor backgrounds are condemned to very poor public schools or none at all. Many in the middle class that have opted for private provision may be tempted to return to public provision, if more people with incomes are brought into revenue bargains and insist on quality services for their taxes. This would further enhance demands for improved services based on the standards of the middle class.

Fifth, revenue bargains may improve state capacity to exercise relative autonomy vis-à-vis donors in policy making, avoid capture by powerful interest groups, and help policy elites to provide leadership in the development process. They may encourage citizens to play active roles in the monitoring of aid and ensuring that such aid reaches the right targets. This may raise the credibility of African governments in the aid relationship. It has been estimated that aid that is linked to domestic revenue mobilisation can lead to a 10-fold increase in revenue yields in Africa. In other words, if aid and domestic revenue mobilisation work in tandem, African governments will be responsive to both citizens and donors, and over time may be weaned of aid dependency.

Conclusion

Constructing revenue bargains is challenging but doable. Success requires a focus on four issues. First, revenue bargains are always imperfect. Some citizens may want to evade taxes while still enjoying services that others have paid for; and governments may under-supply services if bargains are not institutionalised. Second, citizens may support revenue bargains when they are perceived as fair in terms of the level and progressivity of taxes, and when all tax payers honour their commitments. Third, the credibility of governments to deliver their own part of the bargain is important, especially in countries where the track record of governments in supplying services has been poor. How governments signal credibility is crucial in understanding the politics of revenue bargains and their chances of success. Fourth, lessons from participatory budgeting in Brazil, which focuses on the expenditure side of bargains, suggest that revenue bargains may be effective in situations where governing elites are committed to changing power structures in favour of low-income groups and where there is a dense network of groups that can engage the state in bargaining.

9

Policy Dialogue and Gendered Development[9]

The concept of policy dialogue has gained much currency as a mechanism for promoting equitable, violence-free and sustainable development. Yet, for all its wide use in numerous pronouncements by international agencies and governments there has been no systematic attempt to unpack the basic elements of the concept and analyse the conditions under which it is likely to be successfully applied as a framework for development. Historical experience suggests that there are, in fact, a variety of models of policy dialogue with varying degrees of effectiveness and implications for gendered development; and that it is not always clear which model social activists and policy makers have in mind when they invoke the need for dialogue. In this essay, I examine four models of policy dialogue-- corporatism, technocracy, entryism and power sharing--and their implications for gendered development.

Unpacking the concept of policy dialogue

Policy dialogue is defined as organised deliberation between two or more actors on the allocation of values that is likely to result in new policies or modification of existing ones. Implicit in the concept of policy dialogue is the clarification of issues and understanding of the interests and concerns of contending parties. A policy dialogue also presupposes readiness on the part of actors to accept compromise and accommodation, as well as some degree of relative autonomy for all actors. By seeking to avoid confrontations and unilaterally defined outcomes, policy dialogues can be very time consuming and may produce results that may not fully satisfy the wishes of participants.

Several issues are important in discussing policy dialogues and their likely outcomes and gender implications. The first is the question of participation. Is participation restricted to special groups or is it open to

---

[9] Extracted from Y. Bangura, "Policy Dialogue and Gendered Development: Institutional and Ideological Constraints", *African Journal of Political Science*, Vol. 2, No. 2, 1997; and UNRISD Discussion Paper No. 87, 1997.

all interested groups? How are special groups defined for purposes of participation? Participation may be restricted, for instance, to groups that have powerful influence on the functioning of economies, such as employers federations and workers unions; groups with specialised knowledge of public issues such as technocrats and specially chosen intellectuals, journalists and public figures; or groups that are likely to be affected by specific public policies regardless of their technical expertise on the subject or strategic locations in the economy. The nature of group participation has implications for definitions of policy agendas.

The second issue deals with relations between group leaders and followers. To what extent are leaders representative of their followers? Are there structures that allow for the selection of leaders to represent followers in policy dialogues, or do actors assume leadership roles on the basis of their status, activism and knowledge of the issues? Are leaders able to regulate the behaviour of followers to accept binding agreements that may come out of dialogues? Conversely, are followers able to hold leaders accountable if they strike poor deals or are co-opted by dominant actors? Can dialogues regulate the "free-rider" or "principal-agency" problems that leaders often exploit in institutions? Relations between leaders and led are important in explaining the organisational settings of policy dialogues and the way power is likely to be used or not used in the policy process.

A third issue relates to the relative distribution of power in dialogue settings. This can vary tremendously. Its understanding is important in assessing likely policy outcomes. Three main patterns of power distribution can be identified: all actors are equally strong or enjoy recognition of formal equality; one or few actors are stronger than others; and all actors are equally weak and require external stimulus and protection to keep dialogues going. The strong/strong pattern has potential to sustain dialogue if actors can recognise and be made to enjoy win/win outcomes as a result of their participation in the dialogue process. The corporatist model, which distributes benefits to all participating actors, seems to fit this proposition. The strong/weak pattern may result in limited or marginal changes in a policy framework that may be initiated by a strong actor. The technocracy and "entryism" or Women in Development (WID) models may help to illustrate this point. The weak/weak pattern may produce outcomes that are uncertain, unstable and ineffective unless win/win scenarios under generalised weakness can be created and backed by massive infusions of resources and external support. The power sharing model will be instructive in this case.

A fourth issue is the constraining effect of the dominant discourse for dialogue. Is this discourse ideological or is it eclectic? By ideological discourse is meant a discourse that does not allow for a questioning of the fundamentals of a policy framework, where opposing parties can only negotiate change at the margins of the policy. I cite the neoliberal policy framework in the technocracy model as an example. By eclectic is meant a discourse that is sufficiently open to accommodate the competing interests of actors in the fundamentals of a policy framework even if such a framework may have been derived from an ideological reading of society. The Keynesian policy framework in the corporatist model is a good case in point. The nature of dominant discourses is central to an understanding of the essence of dialogue models and is likely to substantially determine the kinds of progress groups in dialogue are likely to make in changing the direction and content of specific policies.

The number of themes that are sanctioned in dialogue is the fifth issue. These can vary from single issues, such as reconciliation and macro-economic stabilisation, as in the power sharing and technocracy models; to a set of strategic issues like wages, productivity, employment and profitability as in the corporatist model; and to multiple sets of issues that cover all major facets of public life as in the Women in Development (WID) or entryism model.

A sixth issue deals with the medium in which dialogue takes place. Does this occur within existing bureaucracies, as in the WID and technocracy models, for instance; or does dialogue require or result in the establishment of special institutions within and outside the bureaucracy, as in the corporatist and power sharing models? Indeed, does the nature of change advocated require the establishment of multiple mediums that transcend national public bureaucracies? The medium of dialogue can influence the extent to which issues can be transformed into policies for effective implementation. It is important to distinguish between open-ended or forum-type dialogues from dialogues that directly impact upon the policy process. Political liberalisation in much of the world has been accompanied by a wide variety of dialogue systems which are not tied to state level decisions. These are often promoted by research centres or institutes and organisations in civil society. They often aim to clarify issues and strengthen the knowledge base of individuals who may seek to influence the policy making process.

A seventh issue deals with the nature and amount of resources that are required to develop and sustain dialogue. This depends upon the resource endowments of respective actors, the nature and speed of change sought, and the distribution of power among groups. Fewer resources for dialogue are required in the corporatist model of formal equality among parties, where even subordinated actors can develop negotiating capacities through autonomous and self-financed technical expertise. More resources are required in the entryism and power sharing models -- the first because of the wide-ranging nature of the changes sought and the relative weakness of the actors that are likely to be the chief beneficiaries of change; and the second because of the generalised weakness of all key actors. A final eighth point deals with the duration of dialogues --whether they are short or long-term, and intermittent or continuous.

Let me briefly discuss these models and their implications for gendered development.

Corporatism

Corporatism refers to a system for managing socioeconomic conflicts in which organised interests are brought into the governmental policy making process to facilitate debate, bargaining and compromise over key issues that affect the performance of the macro economy, the livelihoods of workers, and the process of industrial accumulation. In the liberal democratic settings in which these regimes were nurtured, contending actors enjoyed a high degree of relative autonomy and certain rights of organisation and expression that are fundamental to the functioning of democratic societies.

In the corporatist model of Western Europe, the key actors are organised labour, organised employers and governments. In general, participation is not open to other pressure groups irrespective of whether contested issues and corporatist deals or outcomes affect their interests or life chances. In this model, labour is primarily concerned about gains to be made in wages, employment, social security, working hours and industrial safety. Capital is driven by the need to increase the productivity of labour, maximise profit, expand markets and reduce the burden of taxation and regulation on private enterprise. Governments seek to manage the macro economy to prevent recessions, inflation and balance of payments crises, as well as raise revenue for various socioeconomic programmes.

Much has been written about the powerful roles of gender movements in securing the gains that women made in the corporatist or welfare state models of Western societies. The activities of these movements should not be underestimated. It seems, however, that success owed much to the dynamics and potentially gender-friendly discourse of the corporatist model than to gender activism per se. The corporatist agenda, it seems, helped to make the work of gender activists coherent and effective. A comparison of the gender movements in the USA and those of Scandinavia would show that the movements in Scandinavia were not better organised, vocal or influential than those in the USA. Indeed, it has been observed that the WID initiative owed its origin to the militant work of the US feminist movement.

Yet, in both countries, what the UNDP has defined as Gender Development Indicators (GDI) and Gender Empowerment Measure (GEM), the Scandinavian countries perform much better than the USA in these indicators, especially in the GEM. The USA is ranked second in the Human Development Indicators, but fourth in GDI and ninth in GEM. Indeed, the first four countries in GEM are the three Scandinavian countries plus Finland. These countries also have the most advanced model of corporatism and welfare in Western societies. Unionised labour, a critical condition for corporatism, is also much higher in the Scandinavian countries than in the USA. Whereas unionised labour fell from 23 percent to 16 percent in the USA from 1970 to 1990, it grew from 51 percent to 56 percent in Norway, 51 percent to 71 percent in Finland, 68 percent to 83 percent in Sweden, and 60 percent to 71 percent in Denmark over the same period. The conclusion we may draw from this is that women make gains when labour unions are strong and when the macro-economic discourse for bargaining is sensitive to equity.

Technocracy

The technocratic approach to policy dialogue questions the role of vested interests in policy making. It accords substantial weight to market forces in the allocation of resources. Employment, which is a central feature of the corporatist model, is dethroned from the centre stage of macro-economic policy. In other words, it is no longer the purpose of economic policy to pursue full employment -- this becomes a micro-level concern, to be achieved mainly by launching special work and training programmes for the unemployed. Instead, economic policy should now be concerned with problems of inflation and efficiency. The main actors expected to implement this neoliberal model are not vested interests but technocrats in governments and the international financial institutions. These have specialist knowledge about how the macro-economy operates, and strong loyalty to the values of neoliberalism.

Low-income countries that seek help from the multilateral financial institutions are required to organise policy dialogues with broad groups in society, including women's organizations, in designing and implementing poverty reduction strategies (PRSPs). However, policy dialogue in PRSPs is largely consultative, with limited power by participating groups to effect real change or get policy makers to deliver on agreed-upon goals. Many groups that participate in the process typically feel that real decisions on important policies lie elsewhere. Important issues are often left out of discussions, such as the macro-economic policy, which is largely based on the IMF's Poverty Reduction and Growth Facility, and negotiated between governments and the IMF.

On balance, the effects of this approach to policy making on gender have been uneven, and in many cases negative. Latin America experienced reasonable growth in the late 1980s and early 1990s, only for that growth to falter in a number of countries in the mid-1990s, impacting negatively on various dimensions of gender relations, such as employment, incomes, access to services and social protection. Much of Africa failed to grow, or experienced only marginal growth in the 1980s, although a few countries started to register reasonable growth in the 1990s. The erosion of welfare programmes in the transition to market economies in Eastern Europe undermined gains which women made in child birth grants, child care leave, child nursing benefits, universal child allowances, benefits for single parent and large families, and child care services. Case studies in a number of countries suggest that women have largely been the ones who pick up the burdens of social provisioning, as households resort to traditional methods of social security. Hopefully, the development of the GDI and GEM in the Human Development Reports would encourage governments and statistical agencies to make data on socio-economic development and participation in public institutions more gender sensitive. Such time series data would help us to have a better picture of the extent to which women have gained or lost under the technocratic model of policy dialogue for structural adjustment.

Power sharing

Power sharing is a system of politics that allows leaders of competing groups to share the commanding heights of politics in such institutions as the executive, bureaucratic, legislative and coercive arms of government. It seeks to prevent majority or powerful groups from imposing zero-sum outcomes on minorities, encourage all groups to develop a sense of responsibility towards the political system, minimise conflicts and maintain stability. Power sharing arrangements are underpinned by constitutional, electoral and redistributive rules of political participation. The model is similar to corporatism since its basic working principles are the promotion of compromise and stability. It differs, however, from corporatism in the crucial area of the management of power. Whereas the corporatist model is primarily concerned about the regulation of relations between groups with conflicting claims on the economy, in the power sharing model regulation is mainly about political power.

The power sharing model of conflict resolution is, in general, gender-blind, since the main goal is to end conflicts, restore order, and get the basic institutions of society to function again. Gender issues hardly featured in any of the high level political settlements that have emerged out of recent conflicts, even though women have been among the main victims of such conflicts. For instance, the Sierra Leone Peace Agreement of 30 November 1996 did not contain a single reference to women or gender questions despite the very high costs of the war on women and the major roles they played in campaigns for peace and democracy. However, because of the general breakdown of national institutions and heavy involvement of external actors in the management of peace and reconstruction, considerable scope has been created for the advancement of gender issues in areas such as relief, welfare, education, health, employment programmes, and in campaigns to raise the level of female representation in political institutions.

NGOs, donor agencies and international organisations have tried to push gender issues in their various reconstruction and rehabilitation programmes. A number of national and local level women's organisations have also sprung up to take up the challenge. For instance, the chair of the Council of State of Liberia's interim government of armed factions, Ruth Perry, was an active member of the Liberian Women's Initiative, which sponsored various initiatives to end that country's war. Internally-displaced people's camps in the Western Area of Sierra Leone had camp committees of both male and female representatives for all districts that were affected by the war. NGOs and international agencies were active in the camps. It seems that having women on camp committees was a condition for access to donor support.

Entryism

Entryism is a political strategy employed by marginal activist groups to penetrate, and eventually take over, key institutions of society, or get such institutions to adopt their political agendas. Such groups often seek to introduce radical changes in society, but adopt the strategy of penetration because of their general weakness, and realisation that independent forms of organisation, advocacy and mobilisation would not secure desired objectives. The concept gained currency among Marxist political circles in the post-second world war period as some militant groups, frustrated by what they saw as the conservatism of their societies, felt that the best way to speed up the prospects for socialist transformation was to enter established social democratic parties and work diligently towards the goal of taking them over and implementing their radical agendas.

Efforts to promote the Women In Development/Gender And Development (WID/GAD) agenda in international and national bureaucracies could be likened to the political strategy of entryism. Various international conferences on women have helped to create conceptual clarity to issues of gender inequalities and discrimination, and evolve strategies for overcoming them. Much of the debate has focused on questions of social justice and equity -- improving women's educational and employment opportunities, increasing their access to health and welfare services, and raising their participation levels in social and political institutions. Economic efficiency arguments have also been linked to the pursuit of equity issues, as it is argued that women can immensely contribute to the development process if the barriers to their full participation are eliminated. Central to the WID/GAD initiative is a strategy of "selling" gender issues to policy makers in both international and national bureaucracies through establishment of WID machineries in such institutions. Through a process of entering what are regarded as gender-insensitive bureaucracies, and gradually engaging key decision making actors in a process of dialogue, it is felt that the WID/GAD agenda will not only change major development strategies, but that over time it will become routinised in the daily practices of bureaucratic actors.

WID/GAD units to promote gendered development have been established in several developed and developing countries as well as in key international agencies. The main actors are feminist bureaucrats, or "femocrats" (a concept popularised by Australian feminists), male governmental and bureaucratic allies, and key decision making agents. There are very tenuous links between femocrats and their base constituencies, unlike in the corporatist and power sharing models, in which groups have strong links with their outside membership. Femocrats are expected to behave as "bureaucrats", by upholding the rules and norms of their respective institutions, and by insulating their work from much of the politics of the wider society. They cannot, therefore, actively mobilise their gender constituencies to exert pressure on decision makers when things go wrong. In short, femocrats are not put in bureaucracies by their gender constituencies and, therefore, are not mandated to negotiate on their behalf. Instead, femocrats mainly rely on their skills of persuasion, moral suasion and the goodwill of fellow bureaucrats to get things done, although opportunities for linking up with wider social constituencies could be created when new regimes embrace the rhetoric of popular mobilisation as a strategy for securing legitimacy -- as has happened in Uganda, for instance, under Yoweri Museveni and his National Resistance Movement and government.

WID/GAD units for the promotion of dialogue and gendered development do not have a single institutional home. They have been located in ministries of social welfare, planning, or youth and community development; offices of presidents or prime ministers; or in special ministries of women and children's affairs. WID/GAD units have developed a variety of instruments for influencing public policy, such as gender-sensitive policy guidelines, plans and statements; checklists of critical issues to be monitored; the setting up of inter-ministerial committees; and gender training schemes. Work in these areas is expected to help shape debates on gender issues across the entire spectrum of policy making and implementation.

As UNRISD studies have shown, the technical skills of feminist bureaucrats in the crucial areas of policy and project analysis are generally poor. Gender-inspired statements tend to be couched in very general terms, making it difficult to assess the gender implications of new policies and proposals right through the various stages of the budgetary process. Case studies in Mali, Jamaica, Chile, Uganda, Morocco and Bangladesh suggest that WID/GAD units tend to be marginalised in national bureaucracies even in situations where they receive high profile treatment, as in Uganda, Chile and Jamaica, for instance. Stigmatisation; under-funding; lack of commitment by bureaucrats and, in some cases, even by feminist advocates; and limited rewards to attract ambitious and highly trained personnel to the work of WID were some of the problems highlighted in the UNRISD six-country studies under the Gender and Development programme. Considerable resources are, therefore, required to improve upon the technical competence of femocrats through training workshops, to review and raise the bureaucratic incentive structures in favour of WID, and support the sensitisation and analytical work of femocrats.

10
Why Nigeria's Democracy does not Work for the Poor[10]

Eradicating poverty and promoting more open and democratic forms of politics have been central objectives of development policy in the last two decades. At least in the African context, the elevation of democracy in public policy reflects the fact that authoritarian one-party and military dictatorships have been associated with economic decline. The new development agenda is grounded in the belief that democracy offers prospects for better scrutiny of public policies, holding leaders to account, and launching countries on a trajectory of growth that will improve the welfare of the poor.

However, the driving forces that push democratic regimes to deliver anti-poverty outcomes are complex. Despite the elevation of democracy in public policy, there is little understanding of the types of politics and institutions that enable democracies to achieve growth and human well-being. In the design of anti-poverty strategies, most low-income countries rely on the participatory procedures of the Poverty Reduction Strategy Papers (PRSPs), supported by the International Monetary Fund and World Bank. But the PRSP consultative process does not give citizen groups the power to effect real change. Participation is often limited to selected non-governmental organisations, without the active involvement of associations of informal and formal workers, farmers or artisans, whose livelihoods are directly affected by development policies.

In this essay, I explore the links between democratic politics and poverty eradication. I seek to explain the conditions under which democracies deliver good social outcomes. Why have popular struggles for democracy and welfare development in Nigeria not produced the desired results? My contribution draws on the UNRISD report, *Combating Poverty and Inequality: Structural Change, Social Policy and Policy*, which was launched in September 2010. The report argues that poverty eradication requires effective and accountable states, the

---

[10] Extracted from B. Beckman and Y. Z. Yau (eds.), *Organizing for Democracy*. PODSU: Stockholm University. 2012.

institutionalisation of rights, sustained public engagement, expansion of the bargaining power of the poor and those who represent them, and pacts that are structured around issues of employment, welfare and growth.

Democracy and welfare development

Democracy is defined as a system of government in which leaders periodically renew their mandates through free, fair and competitive elections. In addition, it is a system that acknowledges a set of rights — such as those of expression, organisation and collective action—that allows citizens to exercise political choice and hold leaders accountable. Advances in welfare provision require that the democratic regime is made sufficiently competitive, which will allow citizens acting as voters to change governments that pursue policies that are detrimental to their well-being. It also requires additional mechanisms of interest representation in the policy process if gains are not to be restricted to electoral cycles.

Democracies deliver outcomes that are beneficial to the poor when groups with strong ties to the poor demonstrate capacity for organisation and mobilisation, transcend or reconcile internal divisions, and create structural links for bargaining with actors involved in policy making. This leads, at times, to social pacts. Contestation may block unpopular policies or may lead to the adoption of popular demands in public policy. Electoral competition in which there is a high probability that governments may lose office can also act as an incentive for redistribution and progressive reforms. However, electoral competition without effective group organisation and contestation may produce weak redistributive outcomes. The poor suffer when interest groups and social movements are weak and when the electoral system is not sufficiently competitive.

Implications for Nigeria's democracy

Nigeria has a large and flourishing civil society, including a vibrant and good quality press. Even during the most despotic period of military rule, 1993-98, the state was unable to subdue pro-democracy forces. Indeed, the right to independent organisation and contestation is deeply

94

embedded in the country's political culture even when it is not always respected by political leaders.

The next three sections address three issues arising from the comparative studies of welfare democracies to try to understand the problems of democracy and well-being in Nigeria. These are the failure to conduct credible elections, which are necessary if citizens are to hold leaders to account and force changes in public policies. The second is the seeming inability to embed Nigeria's political parties in broad social movements or coalitions that reflect the interests of the poor. And the third is the failure of developmentalism, which would compel the state to engage constructively with production-based business interests and popular sector groups even if these groups do not have strong ties with state actors.

Democracy without credible elections

The comparative experiences of welfare democracies suggest that competitive elections can act as a mechanism to hold leaders to account and force changes in public policy. Research suggests that pressures for democratisation and welfare provision were driven by similar forces in advanced industrial democracies. For unions, democracy, including the freedoms and rights it provides, was not just an end in itself; it was also an instrument to improve the bargaining power of workers in the distribution of the national product. For the working class and other political groups to accept the democratic rules of the game as a medium of change, the rules had to be credible. The revolutionary posture of sections of the working class movement may not have been successful in overturning existing political arrangements, but they added to the pressure for democratic change with credible elections and the need to incorporate the demands of workers in the political economy.

All successful welfare democracies have been able to conduct free and fair elections, in which there is a strong possibility of incumbents losing office. Fear of losing power through elections can push governments to adopt and sustain social reforms. Indeed, scholars on Indian politics argue that the reason Kerala posts superior social indicators to those of West Bengal, both governed by communist parties, is because elections are more fiercely fought in Kerala than in West Bengal.

Nigeria is one of the few African countries with a vibrant civil society that has failed to organise free and fair elections even though the 2011 elections saw a bold step to correct this problem with the appointment of Attahiru Jega, a former Vice Chancellor with strong ties with the pro-democracy movement, as the chief electoral officer. In West Africa alone, many countries have managed to attain this task. Alternation of parties in government is now a relatively normal practice in Ghana, Benin, Cape Verde, and Mali; and even Sierra Leone with a recent history of war changed its government through the ballot box in 2007. Analysts have bemoaned the fact that the credibility of elections in Nigeria seems to suffer a downward spiral with each election, with the one in 2007 rated as the worst in the country's history. While Nigerians always come out in large numbers to vote, politicians systematically frustrate and devalue voters' choices through rigging and other types of electoral fraud.

Enhancing electoral credibility rests on four factors: an independent, impartial, competent and effective electoral commission; an independent and impartial judiciary; an active citizenry that is capable of monitoring the process and ensuring that the rules are obeyed; and acceptance by the political elite that power can only be effectively managed when all strata or factions of the elite respect the integrity of the electoral process.

Nigeria's electoral commissions have been seriously compromised in past elections. Given his track record as a former president of the Academic Staff Union of Universities and a pro-democracy activist, the appointment of Attahiru Jega as head of the electoral body for the 2011 elections is an interesting and positive development. How much space and authority does he enjoy in the institution and in his relations with the contending political forces? How have popular pressure and his past links with the pro-democracy movement been able to shape the choices he makes? These are issues that are currently hotly debated among Nigeria's pro-democracy forces. While the 2011 elections are generally believed to be more credible than those of 2007, serious questions have been raised about the collation of the results and extremely high voter turn-out in the South-East and South-South regions. The judiciary has historically enjoyed a better track record than the electoral body in upholding the rule of law, although it is also constrained by governmental pressure. It has in recent years delivered a few electoral decisions in favour of gubernatorial candidates that are not from the governing party. What are the political dynamics that allowed the judiciary to deliver those decisions? Can these isolated cases be repeated in really big, national elections?

Many non-governmental organisations have emerged that address issues related to electoral and constitutional reforms. How effective have these been in monitoring and enforcing rules? Why were they unable to change the 2007 election results even when most voters and "even the newly elected president accepted that they were flawed"? These sets of questions lead to the last point: why have the political elite been unable to resolve their differences and organise credible elections? It must be noted that organising free and fair elections is not just a project for "progressives". Successful democratic transitions everywhere involve elite pacts to respect the choices of voters.

Parties without ties to pro-poor social movements

Comparative case studies highlight the importance of strong ties between political parties and social groups that advance the interests of the poor not only for consolidating democracy but also for delivering good social outcomes. It requires that subaltern groups are sufficiently organised to influence the orientation of politicians without reliance on intermediaries. The embedding of political parties in social movements may provide clarity to parties' social agendas, ensure that leaders are held to account by a broad membership base in the choices they make, and the preferences of members acting collectively are reflected in public policy when such parties gain power.

One of the stark anomalies of Nigeria's democratisation is the loosening of links between political parties and broad social movements that defend the interests of the poor. In the past, at least one or two mainstream parties could lay claims to speaking for the poor in terms of membership, ideology and policies pursued while in office. The Action Group of the 1950s and 1960s was based largely in Yorubaland, and is credited with the provision of universal primary education and other basic services in that region. It had effective ties with the cocoa peasantry and other popular strata groups, while it also appealed to the middle classes and sections of traditional authority. The surpluses generated by the cocoa marketing board were central to the construction of effective party-citizen relations. Despite reports of corruption, the regional government used the board to appropriate peasant surpluses and cushion the incomes of farmers against world market fluctuations; as well as provide extension and social services to farmers and the wider public. The Northern Elements Progressive Union (NEPU) also had strong ties with the northern peasantry, or *talakawa*, and gave the ruling party, the Northern People's Congress, a run for its money in northern elections. Its successor party, the People's Redemption Party (PRP), captured two strategic and commercially vibrant states in the north in the 1979 elections. It can be argued that it was the decision to initiate land reform and offer support to small industries in Kaduna state that led to the impeachment in 1981 of the governor, Balarabe Musa, by the National Party of Nigeria, which had strong ties to feudal landlords and commercial interests.

In the current transition, a past leader of the national labour organisation, Adams Oshiomohle, is governor of a state, but the party that took him to office does not have strong ties with the labour movement, even though the governor himself does. And the party floated by the central labour organisation, the Labour Party, won one seat in the National Assembly and the governorship of Ondo state after a judicial challenge. However, the party structure that supports the governor, Olusegun Mimiko, originally of the federal ruling party, is believed to be weak or non-existent, forcing him to work with the more established party in the region, the Action Congress.

What accounts for the seeming decline of radical populism in Nigerian politics? Why are current political parties devoid of strong ties with social movements? A number of studies have highlighted the proliferation of non-governmental organisations in the pro-democracy movement. Is Nigeria witnessing an NGOisation of social movements? Are NGOs crowding out social movements? It is instructive to note that in countries where NGOs have been effective in social transformation, they have often worked with broad social movements that are rooted in popular struggles and political parties with a rights agenda.

Failure of developmentalism

Gains in welfare can be made even if social groups lack ties to parties and state power, as in the cases of South Korea and Taiwan. But this requires high levels of continuous mobilization and a political elite with a development project. Indeed, much of Korea's and Taiwan's poverty was eliminated under authoritarian rule when the ruling authorities embraced an export-led growth strategy of industrialisation. These developmental authoritarian states prioritised strong ties with business through highly effective nodal agencies that provided incentives to selected firms and sanctions when firms failed to deliver on agreements. However, what is often overlooked is that even though the developmental states repressed labour and other groups, repression alone was not sufficient to obtain the compliance of these groups in the development process. Concerns for economic growth and transformation meant that these states had to engage popular strata groups more seriously than simply repressing them. State services—such as infrastructure, subsidised fertilizers, improved seedlings, credit, research support, investment in and regulation of health and education to expand access—and policies of life-long employment and social insurance for workers helped to build state-citizen relations. And after a certain level of transformation had been achieved, top-down strategies of coercion and control proved unsustainable. As economic growth occurred, there was a proliferation of economic and other social interests and an expanding and demanding middle class, as well as an effective and mobilised trade union movement, acting to strengthen civil society and intensify its demands. These factors helped to shape the transition to democracy in the 1980s.

In Nigeria in the 1970s, just after the civil war and surge in petroleum revenue, a case could be made that the power elite had a vision of transforming the country into a modern developmental state. Northern bureaucrats that underpinned the federal authority system facilitated the emergence of a national bureaucratic-technocratic elite. The northern bureaucratic group had close family and aristocratic ties, many of whom were socialised through the Native Authority system/Northern Premier's Office, and attended similar schools and colleges like Katsina/Barewa College before proceeding to the UK for further specialist training. Prominent northern bureaucrats met regularly after the fall of the political class in 1967, as members of the Niima Club, in attempting to forge a cohesive, but informal, northern bloc of elites. Their southern counterparts came from different social backgrounds with less family /aristocratic ties and much less organisational cohesion, but were trained in top British universities and were comfortable with the major currents of intellectual ideas and national policy debates.

The military, supported by the budding technocratic elite, formulated and implemented some of the most important projects of economic development and national integration in the first half of the 1970s. On the economic front, the key policies were the indigenisation of the economy, in which three different types of equity participation in economic enterprises were established aimed at enhancing the power of indigenous entrepreneurs vis-à-vis their transnational and Levantine counterparts; and pursuit of import substitution industrialisation, commercialisation of agriculture, and large-scale infrastructure development. At the level of politics, strong strides were made to create a centralised political system and national identity at the expense of the regional and ethnic cleavages that contributed to the civil war. The major projects included changes in the formula for allocating revenues in favour of the federal centre, the creation of more states and local governments, and the establishment of the National Youth Service Corp and Unity schools. Despite widespread corruption, there was confidence across the political spectrum that the high rate of growth of the 1970s would be strong enough to transform the economy and society. A prominent technocrat, Alyson Ayida, even talked about "The Nigerian Revolution", and there was much discussion among radical political economists, such as Bjorn Beckman, about a "Nigerian bourgeoisie" that was carrying out a capitalist transformation of the state and economy.

The developmental vision motivated the state to engage the expanding industrial working class by imposing labour unity on the workers in 1978. The unions were restructured from over 1000 to 42 and given a new central labour organisation: the Nigerian Labour Congress (NLC). It seemed at the time that the government wanted a single and credible actor it could deal with in promoting industrial change rather than the disparate unions and competing trade union centres that often resulted in wild cat strikes. Although the state's methods of centralisation were authoritarian, the outcome yielded huge benefits to labour. The union was empowered to deduct workers' contributions from their wages to support the new trade unions and a labour bureaucracy similar to those of the civil service was created. Branches of the NLC were established in all states of the federation, giving the organisation much influence in collective bargaining and federal politics. This power was enhanced as radical unionists won the NLC's first elections and imposed their vision on the organisation.

The developmental vision has suffered a blow in the last two-to-three decades as military rule degenerated into kleptocratic and despotic rule, the technocratic elite became less cohesive as ethno-regional competition for power and resources took centre stage, the economy experienced long-running crises, and governments adopted stabilisation policies that were devoid of strategic planning. Eight years of civil rule have seen some growth but the vision of economic transformation has not been restored. More progress has been made in debt repayment and restructuring of the financial sector than in industrial and agricultural transformation. The failure of developmentalism affects the culture of bargaining. If the political elite do not have a development project, they cannot engage the business class and popular forces constructively and citizens cannot hold them to account for their policies. Repression may then become an instrument in the struggle over resources, which does not require compromises and public accountability to ensure the survival of the development project.

The lowering of the development vision and setback in economic transformation have had two effects. The first is on class formation. Perhaps the biggest effect is on the industrial working class, whose numbers have sharply declined across various sectors. For instance, one of the largest unions in the private sector, the garment and textile workers union, has seen its national membership drop by half to some 20,000. The informal economy, which was already large in the 1970s, has grown in leaps and bounds, forcing some unions, especially those in the textile sector, to attempt to extend membership to informal producers and artisans in order to improve their bargaining power. Less than 40 percent of Nigerians---largely smallholders with low productivity -- earn their living in agriculture; but an overwhelming majority of the remaining 60 percent of the labour force is not in industry. Oil still drives much economic activity but is highly capital intensive, with limited prospects for employment. The financial sector has emerged as a growth sector, but it has limited employment capacity. Despite weaknesses in its economic structure, Nigeria exports three big cultural services-- film, music, and Pentecostal churches—which are changing the social landscapes of many African cities today.

A social structure that is dominated by mineral rents; smallholding agriculture; micro-scale informal enterprises; and well remunerated and independent service providers in films, music and religion may not easily facilitate formation of interest group organisations of the type that historically exerted pressure to lift societies out of poverty. However, discussion on welfare democracies in agrarian societies shows that these constraints are not insurmountable. They require political parties with redistributive agendas and strong ties to the poor to effect positive social change.

11
Sierra Leone at 50:
Confronting Old Problems and Preparing for New Challenges[11]

The celebration of a 50 year event in most parts of the world evokes the high sounding phrase "golden jubilee"—with the word golden depicting all that is bright in the history of the person, institution or activity. In this type of celebration, individuals and states share one important thing in common: at 50, a person can no longer blame his or her parents for failures associated with choices during the life cycle; the person may have started life with a weak foundation that can be traced to parental circumstances, but at 50 that person is assumed to be mature and is expected to bear responsibility for at least some of the outcomes in choices made. The same goes for a state. When a state celebrates 50 years of independence, it cannot place all the blame for its failure or backwardness on its former colonial master, even though the colonial encounter may have imposed constraints on the life of the new state. The big question such a state will face, especially from its citizens who did not experience colonial rule, is: what did our leaders do to overcome the constraints of colonialism, improve our lives, and justify our quest for independence?

On the other hand, 50 years is a small step in the life of a nation. Indeed, many countries count their history in millennia. Seen from this perspective, a 50 year old state has many advantages. It can correct mistakes, however terrible they may have been, and get on a different trajectory that will lead to better outcomes. Demographically speaking,

[11] Published in *Review of African Political Economy*. March 2012. Vol. 39, Issue 131, pp.181-192 (www.tandfonline.com); also in S. Ojukutu-Macauley and I. Rashid (eds.), *The Paradoxes of History and Memory in Post-Colonial Sierra Leone*. Lexington Books. 2013; and published as Africa at 50 Discussion Paper Series 6 by the UN African Institute for Economic Development and Planning (IDEP). Keynote speech, Advanced Policy Dialogue on Sierra Leone at 50, Organised by IDEP and the Ministry of Finance and Economic Development, The Government of Sierra Leone. Freetown. 28 October 2011.

Sierra Leone is a youthful nation. The overwhelming majority of its population is under 50. What all this suggests is that if we get our priorities right and resolve to correct our bad ways of conducting the affairs of state, we can catch up very rapidly with countries that have developed. In doing this, we do not have to rediscover the wheel and we have the vibrancy of youth to make things happen.

The history of newly industrialising states suggests that it is possible to transform our economy and society within a generation. Take a country like Malaysia, which was not very different from Sierra Leone or Ghana or Nigeria in 1960 in terms of per capita income, poverty levels and resource endowment. Following the New Economic Policy, initiated in 1970, that set the stage for economic transformation, Malaysia succeeded in attaining middle income status and drastically reduced its poverty rate within a time scale of 30 years. In Malaysia, manufacturing employment expanded rapidly from 7 percent in the 1960s to about 28 percent in 2000. Whereas 55 per cent of Malaysians earned a living from agriculture in the 1960s, this share fell to 16 per cent by 2000. Poverty fell from about 50 per cent in 1970 to less than 6 per cent in 2004. However, overcoming backwardness requires a frank and dispassionate look at how we spent our last 50 years, and a strong commitment to confront old problems and prepare for new challenges. It is to these that I now turn.

Political and economic trajectories

One of the compelling lessons of Sierra Leone's development in its last 50 years is how strongly our political trajectory tracks our economic development. We entered statehood with a boom in the world economy. This was a period development policy analysts have come to describe as a golden age of capitalism. We registered a moderate level of growth during the first 10 to 15 years of independence. We had confidence in the ability of our new leaders to transform our society and make the very limited but fairly well-functioning state deliver the benefits of independence to everyone. We also had a fairly robust multi-party system, which in 1967 set a record in post-colonial Africa as we became the first country on the continent to change a government through the ballot box. Unfortunately, that democratic change was almost immediately thwarted by the military. After the winners were restored in

1968, we then entered within a few years a long period of authoritarian, corrupt and repressive one party rule, which degenerated into further military and thuggish rule as well as a brutal civil war in the 1990s. This series of reversals at the political level correlated with economic decline and institutional decay, from which it has been difficult to recover. We regained democratic life in 1996, and, except for the one year of military usurpation of power in 1997, we have enjoyed in the last decade or so some moderate level of growth. However, as most development policy analysts know, it is easy to restore growth when the fighting stops, but much more difficult to improve the lives of people, restore institutions and make them work for citizens.

The key lesson from our history is that authoritarian rule and economic development are incompatible in our terrain, even if they correlated well in other countries such as those in East Asia. We always make progress, however limited, when our politics are democratic; and regress, sometimes really badly, when we allow a single party, the military, big men or warlords to lord it over us. Indeed, it has been shown for the period 1991-2004 that growth nose-dived into negative territory when there were major rebel attacks (1992, 1995, 1999) or a coup (1997) and rose rapidly when civil democratic rule was restored (post-2000). However, our history also suggests that democracy alone will not generate the kind of growth that will transform our economy for the benefit of all citizens and prevent us from sliding back to dictatorship and conflict. We need to build additional sets of institutions, policies and strategies to direct our growth and sustain our democracy and make both growth and democracy work for everyone.

Old and persistent problems

I would like to focus on three issues that I have characterised as old problems, but which have continued to make it difficult for us to attain our full potential. These are how to harness our abundant natural resources for economic growth and transformation that will improve living standards; how to rebuild and expand our highly degraded human capital; and how to rework our politics to make it serve an agenda of economic and social transformation. I would then use the remaining time to address a few challenges we are likely to confront in the coming decades, which are climate change and global pressures for a green economy. My basic message is that we cannot confront the new challenges if we are unable to deal with the old and persistent problems. So, I will start with the old problems.

Harnessing resource wealth for economic and social transformation

The story of our resource endowment needs no recapitulation. Our resources include diamonds, bauxite, rutile, iron ore, and gold; and there are strong prospects for oil, which, if realised, will produce a sea change in terms of revenues. We are also blessed with rich marine life, lush forests, and arable land. It is difficult to put a value on these resources, but it is clear that if we only harness them well, even the goal now being set by the government of attaining middle income status looks modest. Small mineral-rich countries can jump several stages in the world income classification by simply earning rents from their products. We know that this is what Equatorial Guinea, which is now a high income country, has done. But this corrupt, wasteful and largely dysfunctional country is not what I believe should be our development model. We want a transformation that can be judged not just in terms of economic growth but that also translates into real incomes and supports sectors where the majority of people work. Such a transformation should stimulate and create real value and improve productivity across the economy. In other words, we should be aiming for a world income status that allows for substantially improved yields to the national economy, that cuts capital flight or wealth repatriation by local elites and foreign companies, that transforms our agricultural sector so that we can feed ourselves, that boosts industrial production so we can stop being a nation of imported second hand products, and that transforms our urban informal sector of petty traders into real producers of wealth. In short, such a transformation should connect agriculture, industry and services productively. This kind of transformation will not happen without strategic planning, coordination and discipline.

It is an established fact that mineral resources are often difficult to control and the resource curse tends to define the lives of many mineral-rich poor countries. Even the colonial power, Britain, had problems controlling our mining sector, as it was forced to make deals with chiefs in mining areas who appropriated state transfers and mineral rents for their own benefits. However, even though the colonial mining companies reaped most of the benefits and transferred them overseas, the problem of mass leakage of revenue from the formal state sector was not extensive. The colonial state also had very limited ambitions in developing the country as it administered Sierra Leone and other colonies on the cheap. As a colonial state, we were allowed to spend only what we could generate as revenue: less revenue generation meant less expenditure. Our people therefore did not expect much from the colonial power.

It is, however, a different matter when the state has lofty ambitions or expectations are raised through slogans about independence delivering prosperity for all. The most important change in the way our revenues were harnessed occurred between 1973 and 1985, which also marked our rapid descent into authoritarian rule, large scale corruption and, subsequently, economic decline. It is important to grasp two key issues in this change as they came to define the path that transformed us into a failed state in the 1990s.

The first was the failure to develop a healthy and productive relationship between the state and the budding business elite for economic growth and transformation. Concerned primarily about political domination and illicit accumulation of rents from our natural wealth, the political elite distrusted indigenous African entrepreneurs and refused to cultivate them as partners in the lucrative mining sector that would have provided a foundation for investment in other sectors of the economy. Instead, Lebanese businessmen, who were perceived as apolitical and therefore non-threatening to the political elite, became the state's partners in the production and sale of our natural resources. The American political scientist, William Reno, provides data on licensed diamond dealers, which show that whereas in 1968 African dealers accounted for 85 percent of the licenses and Lebanese dealers only 15 percent, by 1973, the Lebanese had become the dominant players, accounting for 78 percent of the licenses and Africans only 22 percent Now, the unfortunate thing about this development is that the same state that favoured Lebanese enterprise in the mining sector had (and indeed still has) a racist citizenship law that discriminated against this key business group. The Lebanese were thus given free rein to exploit our resources and make money, but the citizenship law was such that this group did not have the incentive to invest that money locally in productive sectors; and nor did the state, which was now run by a kleptocratic elite, compel members of the group to do so despite the enormous patronage given to them. Compare this experience with Malaysia, which is also a multi-ethnic state. Even though the Malay were considered indigenous, the citizenship status of the Chinese, who dominated business, was never questioned; and the Chinese joined the Malay (even if as unequal partners) in forming the political coalition, Barisan Nasional, which governed the country and advanced the project of economic transformation.

The second development that formed the basis for economic decline and state collapse was the informalisation of our economy and public sector. The institutions established during colonial rule and the first decade of independence to manage our resources were systematically dismantled after 1973. The transnational mining company, the Sierra Leone Selection Trust, was rendered ineffective; and the state-dominated company, the National Diamond Mining Company (NDMC), was stripped of its monopoly in carrying out mining operations on its rich diamond deposits and export activities. Individuals with strong patronage links with the state took control of the mining sector. The end result was a concentration of the national wealth in the hands of a few powerful individuals (the most well-known being Jamil Mohamed and Tony Yazbeck) but without state incentives and sanctions to channel such wealth into the productive sectors. By 1980, Reno reports that the official mining company, the NDMC, accounted for only 29 percent of legally produced diamonds, compared to 94 percent in 1973. The informalisation of the mining sector was extended to other sectors, such as the produce marketing board and a host of parastatals, such as the ports and the trading, hotel, transport, communication, banking and utility sectors. Government revenue dried up very quickly, debts mounted, especially after the organisation of the extravagant Organisation of African Unity Summit in 1980 that was estimated to have cost USD200 million, and the state became highly dependent on foreign aid. All of this occurred in an international environment that was now highly unfavourable, as terms of trade for primary commodities deteriorated. Informalisation of the economy and the public sector meant that the state even lacked the discipline to implement IMF reforms in the 1980s, leading to a triple pain for the nation: austerity that further reduced living standards, more debt and no growth.

What does all this mean for nation building and economic transformation today? We have surely made important strides since the war in rolling back informalisation, as can be seen in the increase in domestic revenue and value of exports that pass through official channels, as well as efforts to revive the agricultural sector and improve our infrastructure and energy supply. However, we are still a long way from combating the problem. The indictment of a large number of public figures by the Anti-Corruption Commission and emergence of new cases underscore the point that the private interest continues to trump the public good when individuals are entrusted with public office. Indeed, the challenge of effective resource management and dangers of informalisation, corruption and capital flight are even more acute today because of the exponential growth of our resource base and rise in global prices of mineral resources. And the danger of a few players monopolising our resource wealth and colluding with political and administrative elites for ridiculously high tax concessions, low royalties, and to transfer wealth illicitly overseas is still real. The recent decision to renegotiate mining contracts, in response to pressures from donors and civil society advocacy groups, and attempts to rush through new mining legislation in parliament without proper debate, send conflicting signals. They buttress the point that there are still huge governance problems on matters relating to resource management.

Controlling the resource curse and informality is not rocket science, as there are successful models around the world to learn from. Even if we ignore the experience of high income Norway (and I would recommend that we seriously study that experience and engage their researchers and policy makers), there are a number of positive examples of resource management in developing countries that we can learn from. Mineral-rich Botswana adopted policies that discouraged exchange rate overvaluation, as well as fiscal strategies that set targets on government spending, and created special funds that stabilised mineral revenues. Through such measures, the government has consistently maintained a stable macro economy that has avoided the resource curse. However, its success in governing its economy has not translated into broad-based and diversified growth. The share of agriculture in GDP has fallen drastically since 1960, but per worker output in agriculture has not increased. The diversification of the economy into manufacturing has not been seriously pursued since the share of manufacturing in GDP has declined as well. Levels of unemployment, inequality and poverty remain high.

However, the story is different in mineral-rich Malaysia and Indonesia. These two countries, which are among the top 10 developing-country exporters of manufactured products, have fared much better in transforming their economies from minerals to manufacturing. In these countries, the resource sector was not treated as an enclave, but was firmly anchored in, and supported, the primary goal of industrial transformation. Although informality and corruption existed in the two countries, they adopted variants of East Asian industrial strategies, by building strong and effective states, which were able to influence investment decisions of foreign and domestic entrepreneurs, forcing them to adopt labour-absorbing and export-oriented manufacturing strategies.

Sierra Leone cannot become another Malaysia or Indonesia or Korea. It will have to chart its own development path. But building strategic and enforcement capacity will be vital in the search for that path and in supporting state-business relations that will deliver agricultural and industrial transformation.

Rebuilding and expanding human capital

No country can develop without strong and sustained investment in human capital. The value of human capital—principally education and health—in promoting growth, improving well-being and reducing inequality is now widely acknowledged in development circles. An educated and healthy workforce contributes to economic growth by improving skills and labour productivity, which in turn leads to improved incomes and life chances. To talk meaningfully about a transformative agenda in the context of Sierra Leone is to take human capital formation and its expansion seriously.

Educationists, historians and social sector analysts have over the years documented the major trends and challenges in our educational and health sectors. My reading of what they say can be summarised into a few basic points. We entered statehood with severely limited health and educational services that touched the lives of just a fraction of the population. The literacy rate was just 9 percent and we had only 52 doctors and a little over 1,000 hospital beds for a population of 2 million.

Most services were concentrated in Freetown, rural towns performed better than villages, and women had less access to these services than men. The new state had a big ambition to provide education and health for all, but could not match its policy rhetoric with concerted action.

Spending on education and health as a proportion of the national budget increased but was insufficient to meet the very real and high levels of need. Economic crisis in the 1980s and implementation of market reforms in a highly disorganised and corrupt political environment plunged the education and health sectors into protracted crisis. The funding share of education and health in the national budget remained largely stable even when the economy experienced crisis. But this stability disguised the uselessness of the allocations in real terms as the value of the Leone depreciated dramatically and inflation skyrocketed. Salaries lost their value and could not even be paid on time; primary and secondary school teachers and nurses moved out of the middle class as they struggled to make ends meet; books, drugs and other supplies could not be bought; school and hospital infrastructure experienced decay; class sizes expanded; and standards of instruction and delivery of health services collapsed. This happened well before the civil war in the 1990s, which plunged the sector into further decay, from which it is slowly recovering.

One important point stands out in this story of human capital degradation. The first one to two decades of independence could be characterized as a period in which a limited and uneven social sector had centres of excellence, not only in Freetown, but also in the provinces. I am referring to the good primary and secondary schools that produced students who could compete anywhere and were the envy of our African neighbours. Indeed, these schools and the university –the oldest in the region--trained many public servants and academics in Nigeria, Ghana, Gambia and other African countries. Significantly, at independence, the state assumed an active role in sustaining these schools. Indeed, during my time, only those considered as under-achievers or who could not compete in what was then called "common/selective entrance examination" for admission into these schools attended private schools. Today, even though more schools have been built and more children are enrolled in school, we seem to have lost these centres of excellence that offered opportunities to children from poor backgrounds with good grades to rise to the ranks of the modern middle class. Instead, a very pernicious two track system has developed in which the really rich parents send their children to private schools, which now clearly out-perform these former great schools, and children from poor backgrounds are condemned to very poor schools or none at all.

Rebuilding and expanding our human capital requires a focus on several fronts, many of which have been articulated by our educationists and those concerned with human capital development in poor countries. A major report on educational reform dubbed "The Professor Gbamanga Report" was also recently submitted to the government. There is clearly a need to build new schools and rehabilitate existing ones in order to ensure that all children who are supposed to be in school are actually in school at both primary and secondary levels. Indeed, progress has been made in the building of new schools and enrolment levels have risen sharply. But building schools or tackling infrastructural deficits and raising enrolment levels is only one part of the solution. The other is the software part. What is put in the schools in terms of books, modern teaching aids or equipment, keeping the schools clean with properly functioning toilets, and class sizes manageable; motivating teachers through training and retraining, decent salaries and housing; providing feeding programmes to keep children healthy and mentally alert; and quality control constitute the other vital part of reversing the human capital degradation and moving the country up on the skills ladder. It is the quality of the software that will keep children and teachers in school and motivate them to achieve good grades.

An often neglected part of human capital development is extra-curricular reading and the value of public bookshops and libraries. There is need to balance the explosive interest in popular music by our youth with a reading culture that is not tied to textbooks. In the 1960s to 1980s, many young people had easy access to, and read, popular magazines, books and comics, such as *Reader's Digest, Drum, Spearman, West Africa,* and most of the African Series novels, such as *Things Fall Apart, No Longer At Ease, A Man of the People, Weep Not Child, The Beautyful Ones Are Not Yet Born, Mine Boy* and *Passport of Mallam Ilia* even before proceeding to university. We memorised interesting passages to impress each other about our knowledge of these books, and adopted the names of key characters as guy names, such as Okonkwo, Lans Spearman, Rabon Zolo, and Mallam Ilia. Compare this to the preference for more war-like names today among our youth, such as Bomb Blast, Leather Boot and

555. There is a strong need to restore and deepen the culture of extra-curricular reading through production of interesting reading materials and incentives for their absorption by youth.

Rebuilding our human capital obviously requires substantial funds. World Bank estimates suggest that households are the main contributors (44 percent) to the funding of education, followed by the government (35 percent) and donors (22 percent); and that households' contribution is half of total expenditure at the primary school level and 60 percent at the secondary school level. Given the low incomes of most households, it is clear that the burden of financing human capital formation for transformative change cannot rest on them. Education at the primary and secondary levels has a high social return and should be collectively funded through the state. A strong case can be made to tie some of the revenue collected from the goods and services tax to education and health, as Ghana has done; and to also pursue the possibility of including a social tax in mining contracts that will support these two sectors. Part of the tax proceeds can also be used to finance our tertiary institutions, which also require massive investment in infrastructure and facilities and decent remuneration for those who work in them.

Politics of transformation

Let me now turn my attention to the problem of how to rework our politics for economic and social transformation. Perhaps, our biggest problem is how to engineer our politics to achieve the high goal of transformation we have set ourselves since the war. Kwame Nkrumah once famously said that Africans should first seek the political kingdom, by which he meant political independence, and "everything else will be added on to it". We now know that the struggle for progress is more complicated than this. Africans can mess up their independence through bad politics, which can retard economic development. We have only really enjoyed 21 years of relatively stable competitive politics in our 50-year life—and those 21 years were interspersed with a long period of one party and military dictatorship, and a brutal civil war. Part of the reason for our failure to consolidate democratic rule is our inability to manage our ethnic divisions in ways that are inclusive, transparent and respectful of difference. We have also been unable to embed our political parties in broad movements or organisations concerned with welfare or redistributive issues. And we have taken delight in infusing thuggery into our politics. Indeed, thuggery, which involves recruiting sections of the poor and marginalised into the security wings of parties, compensates for our failure to make our parties meaningful to the aspirations of the poor.

Before I address these issues, let me state that there is one area of public life that we have done extraordinarily well as a nation—that is in the sphere of religious tolerance. I recently watched the wedding video of one of my nieces and I was pleasantly surprised that even though it was a Muslim wedding, during the opening part of the ceremony when the leader of the bridegroom's group was doing the rituals of greeting and paying tribute to the bride's relations and friends, which is often done with gifts in envelopes, he had an envelope for an anonymous Christian representative. Small gestures like these reinforce my belief that ordinary people can handle social divisions if they are not manipulated by power-seekers. And I want to add that even though our politics seems to be polarised along ethno-regional lines, there is a lot of inter-marriage across ethnicities and regions and people get along socially when the politicians and elites who are greedy for power, resources and positions keep out of their lives.

But we should take our ethno-regional division seriously. In the two elections when power was transferred from one political party to another (in 1967 and 2007), the margin of victory was very small, and voting tended to mirror, though not absolutely, ethno-regional lines. Such sharp divisions may cause winners to monopolise state power and exclude individuals from regions that belong to opposition parties from government jobs. Individuals from opposition regions in turn may withdraw support from the government even if it is doing well in the development front. This may lead to multiple and competing publics. When this happens, political parties may only be credible to one segment of the public at best. And if some parties want to be credible across the ethnic divide, voters may be less flexible, rewarding primarily parties that are perceived to be led by kinsmen and women. The vote may thus lose its significance as a sanctioning device against bad performance. Politicians may perceive the ethnic vote as a vote bank that cannot be claimed by rival politicians or parties from other groups, making electoral politics unlikely to work for development and the poor. A government that functions on the basis of an ethnically-bifurcated public is also deprived of all available talent to implement a transformative agenda. Indeed, it may become captive to less talented or less capable ethnic bigots who may perceive inclusiveness as a threat to their access or control of posts, power and resources. The state then performs below optimum and fails to deliver on its promise of transformative change. It may also run the risk of militant opposition from excluded groups and regions.

No democracy can embark on transformative change if it fails to pursue a policy of inclusiveness. Indeed, many of the laudable programmes, such as tapping the savings and talents of the diaspora through the Diaspora Office, and developing a long-term plan of economic development that transcends the electoral cycle, are unlikely to work without elite consensus across ethnic groups and regions. Developing a depoliticised and professional army and police force is also difficult without consensus that cuts across ethnicities and regions. We also need to think seriously about a programme of national service that is targeted to the youth. But this will not work without political consensus that allows individuals from all regions and ethnicities to feel included in the national project.

The solutions have been recounted many times and in many places. They can be summarised in two parts. The first is to ensure that cabinet and other top level government appointments, including the bureaucracy, reflect the ethno-regional make-up of the country. In Nigeria today, no government can be formed that does not include at least one minister from each of the 36 states. And the rule of power rotation adopted by the governing party ensures that no region can now dominate politics indefinitely if the rules are followed. The composition of the federal executive thus tends to reflect the ethnic make-up of the federation. Where I live, Switzerland, which has three major groups-- German (74 percent), French (21 percent) and Italian (4 percent) --the executive council is composed of seven members (at least two are often French and sometimes there is one Italian); the presidency rotates every year among the seven members, so that someone of French origin can also become president within a seven year cycle; and the federal bureaucracy is amazingly balanced in terms of the representation of the three groups.

The second policy is to transform our political parties into multi-ethnic parties. The real test of our success will come when the average person in Bo and Makeni can walk into a polling booth and is not held hostage to the perceived ethno-regional identities of the candidates' parties. There are a number of rules that can help to bring this about. Today, the leading political party in Nigeria, the People's Democratic Party, is highly multi-ethnic. The series of electoral reforms introduced in the last 30 or more years has led to a situation in which Nigerian politics has been transformed from ethnic competition "between parties" to ethnic competition "within parties". There are a number of rules that can be adopted if we want our parties to become truly multi-ethnic. These include primaries of the US type, threshold rules of vote shares across regions for declaring winners of presidential elections, and the alternative vote that ranks candidates, all of which may force candidates to appeal to voters outside of their ethno-regional strongholds in order to win elections; and power alternation among the key ethno-regional clusters.

However, ethno-regional elite pacts are not sufficient to drive economic and social transformation. The masses need to be brought into the bargain. Pacts that address the interests of popular sector groups are needed in order to filter out non-developmental, predatory elites in the political system. If the political elites are to be made to take development seriously, elite bargains need to be complemented with development bargains between governments and citizens involving the participation of groups in agriculture, the informal sector and industry. This will help to set the country on a trajectory of growth that will deliver jobs and equity. One positive point to note here is that in Sierra Leone, many economic activity-based groups are non-ethnic. Even in cases where they are ethnic, encouraging groups to scale up for effective bargaining may ultimately weaken the ethnic dimension for collective action.

Unfortunately, rather than meaningfully incorporating the poor into the political and economic system, sections of the poor have instead been allocated the task of doing the dirty work of political parties. They guard politicians and party offices; and are fed, drugged and given money to intimidate opponents or unleash violence during election rallies or when parties are dissatisfied with election outcomes. During the 2007 elections, both parties used ex-combatants with a history of marginality as security insurance. With a huge youth bulge and high levels of underemployment, this kind of popular sector incorporation into parties can be very destabilising. One danger in incorporating individuals with a propensity for violence into the security wings of mainstream parties is that even if parties do not want to provoke violence, the self-interest of those who serve as security guards will be to provoke violence in order to remain relevant and keep their jobs. Political parties and the government must find better ways of keeping these young people productively engaged if they are serious about a transformative agenda.

New challenges

I have spent considerable time on our old problems because I believe that our success in meeting new challenges depends on how well we are able to tackle the old problems. In the limited time that remains let me quickly address two big challenges we are likely to face in the coming decades. These are climate change and global pressures for a green economy--that is, pressures to make our economies less dependent on resources, technologies and production systems that are carbon-intensive. Sierra Leone, like other poor countries, faces a triple injustice, as one speaker described the problem in a recent conference on the subject organised by UNRISD. Because of our underdevelopment, we are less responsible for carbon emissions, but because of our location, we are likely to pay a higher price than the countries responsible for the pollution if the planet warms up; and our underdevelopment makes us less resilient to cope with the catastrophe when or if it happens. Most of the emissions were, and are still, caused by the industrialised countries, with fast-growing, energy guzzling China now the biggest polluter in the world. In this crime against nature, Sierra Leone's contribution is really insignificant. In one estimate, Sierra Leone ranks 192 out of 214 countries in terms of carbon dioxide emissions per capita—spewing only 0.2 metric tons of carbon per capita between 1990 and 2006. However, much of our coast, from Kambia to Pujehun, hardly rises above sea level. If global temperatures rise, the sea level will also rise, and large parts of our coastal towns and villages will be submerged and become part of the Atlantic Ocean. The world is already witnessing the gradual disappearance of small islands in the Pacific. We lack the infrastructure, resources and organisation to cope with a disaster of such magnitude.

Two issues inform the global debate on climate change: mitigation and adaptation. It is clear from my analysis of our old problems that we can only be successful in adapting to climate change if we manage our resources and economy well, improve our human capital and system of social organisation, and develop an inclusive political system. Mitigation on the other hand refers to measures that can slow down or reverse climate change, and it involves targets on, and strategies for, reducing global emissions generated from various aspects of human activities. The details are complex and should not detain us here. But one issue I would like to address and which is likely to profoundly affect us is pressure to adopt green technologies, production systems and habits. Again, this is a very complex subject that is likely to dominate debate at the Rio plus 20 Summit next year. One thing seems clear: despite strong opposition from business sectors that benefit from carbon-intensive industries and fossil fuels, many industrial countries, including China, are already investing heavily in alternative, low carbon energy and technologies. The world may not get rid of old industrial and consumption practices in the next 50 years, but it is quite possible that much progress could be made in this area, rendering old energy sources, methods of production and habits illegitimate. I should add here that part of the reason Sierra Leone's and many poor countries' economies are not in recession, as they often tend to be when Western economies stagnate, is largely because of high growth in China and other emerging economies. Such growth is fuelled by rising consumption of raw materials from poor countries. It is doubtful that this demand can be sustained when these countries complete their industrial transformation and join the ranks of rich countries.

These developments have serious implications for a resource-rich country like Sierra Leone. It underscores the need to move up the value chain in industrial and agricultural development. I think it was the famous Guyanese historian, Walter Rodney, who said that the African farmer entered colonialism with a hoe and left colonialism with the same hoe. A similar point can be made about our natural resources. Since we started mining diamonds and iron ore and exporting them in their raw form during colonialism, we have not moved from this very basic level of specialisation that devalues our effort and offers higher value to foreign companies and lands. There is a strong case for a bold and systematic strategy, coordinated with our neighbours –Guinea and Liberia who are also rich in minerals—for better bargains to be struck that can allow for processing of our minerals and adding real value to our domestic economies. We should not wait to manage the negative consequences of other countries' transitions to the green economy. We should actively strategise to shape the transition to our benefit.

The drive for green energy in industrialised countries is also having one big effect on us—land grabbing. There is a big rush by Western and Asian companies to control African land. This land is needed to grow crops, such as sugar cane, sweet potatoes, cassava, and corn, which can be processed as ethanol fuel for use in automobiles. High global food prices are also pushing some emerging economies with less arable land, such as those in the Middle East, to buy African land and grow crops to feed their population. And there is the speculative side to this new development. As the financial crisis deepens and interest rates become unattractive in Western economies, investors shift to African lands, which can be acquired very cheaply. Such land is often not put to productive use, but held in reserve for speculative purposes. As the value of land transactions is often very low, investors believe that land prices can only go up in future, thus providing huge gains if they want to sell back the land. The net effect of these developments is likely to be higher food prices. Africa is the site for land grabs because it is believed that it is the only continent with surplus, or underutilised, land, which is priced very cheaply. Given the system of shifting cultivation practiced in many countries, in which land is left to fallow for many years before reuse, it is doubtful whether much of the land being grabbed, including in Sierra Leone, is actually free.

The danger of future land scarcity, pressure on rural livelihoods and missing the goal of food security should be taken seriously. External investments in agriculture can stimulate growth and bring benefits to rural producers, but such investments need effective scrutiny and regulation to ensure that the benefits are real and that the investments do not end up crowding out our poor farmers from their land. They should also not be in conflict with the primary goal of food security.

12
Resource Wealth and Development[12]

One of the big challenges I often face when trying to understand Sierra Leone's contemporary history is how little there is of scholarly work that connects past and present efforts in generating economic, social and political development.

There is a lot of historical and contemporary work on various aspects of development. However, much of this work is fragmented. We lack a grand, systematically structured narrative that draws on the work of early writers, who focused on the 1960s, to tell the story of multiple shocks on, and revival of, the present economy, society and politics.

This lacuna has led to the unfortunate situation where popular understanding of critical developments, especially in our politics, is not informed by expert opinion or archival knowledge. There is much amnesia and revisionism, including rehabilitation and even glorification of actors who may have laid the foundations for our underdevelopment.

Efforts to rehabilitate or glorify discredited leaders owe much to the fact that most of today's youths cannot easily connect what they currently experience to events in the first two decades of independence; and there are very few, if any, authoritative and easily accessible books they can read to make these connections.

My contribution to the book, *Paradoxes of History and Memory in Post-Colonial Sierra Leone*, which is the basis for this panel, is based on a keynote speech that I gave at a policy dialogue organised by the UN African Institute for Economic Development and Planning based in Dakar and Sierra Leone's Ministry of Finance as part of the celebrations to mark Sierra Leone's fiftieth independence anniversary.

I was concerned with three issues that still confront us in our efforts at nation-building:

---

[12] Published in *Sierra Express Media* (Freetown), 20 June 2014; and *Patriotic Vanguard* (Vancouver), June 18, 2014. A Note for a panel discussion on launch of *Paradoxes of History and Memory in Contemporary Sierra Leone*; edited by Sylvia Ojukutu-Macauley and Ismail Rashid; Lexington Books, 2013.

- how to harness our abundant natural resources for economic growth and transformation that will improve national well-being;
- how to rebuild and expand our highly degraded human capital; and
- how to rework our politics to make it serve an agenda of economic and social transformation.

Because of time constraints, I will limit my comments to the resource wealth dimension of the problem of nation-building. Indeed, I would like to suggest that our failure to properly manage our natural resources contributed substantially to the degradation of our human capital and the series of crises that ultimately led to our war and collapse of institutions.

Three issues stand out in discussions on resource management:

- ability to capture a large part of the resource rent;
- ensuring that the agricultural and manufacturing sectors of the economy are not disadvantaged when formulating macroeconomic policies—in other words avoiding overvalued exchange rates and large budget deficits; and
- spreading the benefits of the resource rent, including savings for future generations, and preventing environmental degradation.

Historical developments

Sierra Leone, like most resource-rich countries in the 1960s, tried to use its resource rents to support industrialisation and development. Places where such strategies have been successful have involved a strong state project that either nurtures a national entrepreneurial class to lead the industrialisation process, or attracted foreign direct investors and linked local capital to such investors. Whatever the strategy chosen, no successful industrialisation has taken place without strong state support for local capital.

In Sierra Leone, diamond extraction and exportation was the dominant form of wealth generation in the early period of independence. There were two types of diamond extraction.

The first was small and medium scale mining, in which the granting of diamond licenses to domestic dealers played a key role. Many of the commercial and service activities in the big towns and capital city were fuelled by the proceeds from diamonds. A strategy that seeks to encourage local business groups to upgrade from commercial to manufacturing activities requires, therefore, effective management of the process of granting licenses to small and medium scale dealers.

The second type of diamond extraction was industrial large scale mining, involving the participation of foreign capital. State capture of rents from this sector is important in supporting human capital formation, infrastructural development, import-substitution industrialisation and diversification of the economy.

Unfortunately, the state failed to capture much of the resource rent or cultivate indigenous African entrepreneurs as partners in the lucrative mining sector that would have formed a foundation for investment in other sectors of the economy. Instead, a pernicious process of informalisation was encouraged that created massive leakage of the diamond revenue from the state sector; and Lebanese businessmen, who were perceived as apolitical, became the state's partners in the production and sale of our natural resources.

Consider these numbers. In the 1960s, African dealers accounted for 85 percent of diamond licenses, compared to 15 percent for Lebanese business dealers; but by 1973, the Lebanese had become the dominant players, accounting for 78 percent of the licenses and Africans only 22 percent.

In addition, the institutions established during colonial rule and the first decade of independence to manage large scale mining in the resource sector were systematically dismantled after 1973.

- the Sierra Leone Selection Trust, the transnational mining company, was rendered ineffective;
- the National Diamond Mining Company (NDMC), the state-dominated company, was stripped of its monopoly in carrying out mining operations on its rich diamond deposits and export activities; and
- individuals with strong patronage links with the state (the top players were of Lebanese descent) took control of the mining sector.

By 1980, the NDMC accounted for only 29 percent of legally produced diamonds, compared to 94 percent in 1973. This leakage, when

122

combined with worsening terms of trade for Sierra Leone's export commodities and hosting of the extravagant OAU conference in 1980, contributed to the state's fiscal crisis, the inability to fund the limited import-substitution industrialisation that had started in the 1960s, the dramatic decline in educational and health provisioning, and the fall in household incomes in the 1980s. All of this happened well before the war of the 1990s.

One may argue that there is nothing wrong with Lebanese dominance of the mining sector if the mineral rents can be used in activities that will lead to a diversification of the economy. To borrow the late Chinese leader Deng Xiaoping's famous statement when carrying out market reforms in China after the death of Communist leader Mao, "what does it matter whether the cat is black or white as long as it catches the mice?"

Unfortunately, in our case, the pampered "cat" did not catch any mouse. This was largely because the same state that favoured Lebanese enterprise in the mining sector had a racist citizenship law that discriminated against this key business group. We ended up with the worst possible outcome where the Lebanese were allowed to exploit our resources and make money, but the citizenship laws acted as a disincentive for them to invest the resource rent in local productive sectors on a large scale.

In Malaysia, which is also a multi-ethnic state, even though the Malay were considered indigenous, the citizenship status of the Chinese, who dominated business, was never questioned; and the Chinese collaborated with the Malay (even if as unequal partners) in forming the political coalition that governed the country and advanced the project of economic transformation.

Current developments

Where do we stand today? Some progress has been made since the war to improve natural resource management. The rampant informalisation of the 1970s-1990s has been checked. However, huge challenges remain.

Studies suggest that the state is still very far from capturing a large share of the resource rent. This applies to most African countries. Part of this is tied to the very generous concessions, in the form of royalties, corporate taxes, value added taxes and import duties, given to mining companies. Despite the renegotiation of mining contracts by the Sierra Leone state, the danger of a few companies monopolising the resource wealth and providing kickbacks to political and administrative elites for ridiculously high concessions is still real.

ActionAid estimates that the Sierra Leone state lost about $224 million in 2012 largely because of generous tax concessions given to the five largest mining companies and a cement factory; the value of the concessions given to these companies was much higher than the goods and services tax revenue (GST) collected by the National Revenue Authority in 2012; despite a statutory corporate income tax rate of 30%, the big companies succeeded in negotiating customized deals, resulting in one company paying 0 percent rate and another 6 percent; none of the four largest companies pays the statutory 30 percent rate.

In Guinea, under Lansana Conte (the country's previous president), an Israeli company, which bought the mining rights of the Northern part of the rich iron ore deposits at Simandou for $160 million, sold those rights to a Brazilian company for $2.5 billion. In Zambia, an Indian businessman was caught on video mocking the Zambian state that although he paid only $25 million for a copper mine, he makes $500 million every year from the mine.

Expert opinion on the extractive sector, as highlighted in the *Africa Progress Report* of 2013, affirms that the current boom in the prices of mineral resources may turn out to be a super cycle boom comparable to the commodity boom associated with American industrialisation in the late 19th century and the boom of the 1940s and 1950s that was linked with the recovery of Europe and Japan. The current boom is driven by China's rapid pace of industrialisation. Estimates suggest that China's share of global import of base metals rose from 12 percent in 2000 to 42 percent in 2011. While China's economic growth may fluctuate and importation of metals such as iron ore may falter, as happened early this year, most projections highlight an overall upward trend, with the country continuing to rely on resources on a massive scale.

A consensus is emerging among scholars of extractives that large scale concessions are not necessary to attract mining companies. Studies suggest that it is the quality of infrastructure, the cost of conducting business, a stable macroeconomy and political order that attract foreign investors.

Furthermore, most of the new ore discoveries are located in Africa, with the continent accounting for seven of the ten biggest mining deals in 2012. This gives considerable leverage to African states to strike favourable deals since there are very few alternatives elsewhere that are attractive to mining companies. It may explain why Rio Tinto decided to stick with Guinea, promising new investments of about $20 billion in the Simandou iron ore mines, despite the state's new resolve to increase its share of mineral revenues by renegotiating all mining contracts signed by Lansana Conte. The Simandou iron ore deposits are reckoned to be the largest in the world, prompting speculation that any company that gains control of them may ultimately dominate the global supply of iron ore.

Mining concessions, of the scale that we have seen in Africa, transfer huge amounts of money to foreign firms, especially in contexts where countries do not have capital gains taxes to recapture some of the gains that arise when prices of commodities rise.

Let me conclude. Political scientists use history to understand development paths or trajectories, critical junctures, and institutional change. When one studies the dynamics of resource management in Sierra Leone from a historical perspective, we have clearly not been successful in charting a new development path that will usher in a politics of economic and social transformation even when new slogans are coined, such as *Agenda for Change* and *Agenda for Prosperity*.

13
Street Traders and State Power[13]

There have been sporadic confrontations between state authorities and street traders over the use of public spaces in Freetown. These confrontations on the streets and pavements of the city now seem to occur every year with no sign of meaningful resolution. Streets are, by law, meant to facilitate the movement of vehicles, and pavements help pedestrians to move around cities without fear of accidents. In the current confrontation, state authorities want to uphold the law and reclaim ownership of the streets, while traders complain about the lack of alternative spaces to sell their wares and survive in an economy that has failed to generate productive jobs for the mass of underemployed or unemployed youth.

Many people will agree that Freetown is one of the most congested, filthy, unplanned and under-resourced cities in the world where the law hardly operates in terms of how public spaces are used. The basic infrastructure of roads, electricity, water and housing that served about 130,000 people in 1965 now serves more than one and half million people. Public spaces are regarded as open spaces that are devoid of ownership, and can be appropriated by anyone to the exclusion or discomfort of others.

A "stroll" through the central business district, starting from the intersection of Percival Street and Lightfoot Boston Street (now called Belgium) to Up Gun at the end of Kissy Road can be a real nightmare, especially to a first visitor. Howe Street, Wilberforce Street, Ecowas Street, Garrison Street, Upper East Street, Short Street, Back Street, Lumley Street, Sackville Street, Regent Road, Regent Street, Abacha Street and Fourah Bay Road have been comprehensively transformed into a single seamless market that is virtually out of the reach of the law. Some of these streets were abandoned to the traders and became full markets when Operation WID was launched in 2013 and traders were forced to leave Siaka Stevens Street, the thoroughfare at the centre of

---

[13] Published in *Sierra Express Media* (Freetown), 3 February, 2014; *Patriotic Vanguard* (Vancouver), 3 February 2014; *Daily Trust* (Kaduna), 4 February 2014; *Global Times* (Freetown), 5 February 2015; and *Sierra Leone Signposts* (Freetown), 11 February 2014.

town. That operation simply produced a balloon effect and police or state power was overstretched and ultimately rendered ineffective.

Can the state succeed in its current drive to rid the streets of traders? Why have traders succeeded in defying the law under all governments since the 1980s? What needs to be done to restore the rules that governed the use of public spaces in the 1960s and 1970s when most citizens, including traders, obeyed the rules?

One popular explanation for state failure in evicting the traders from the streets is that the traders are a key constituency of the ruling party, which will lose votes if it resolutely executes the law. I want to suggest that the problem of state failure to reclaim the streets goes well beyond partisan politics. Over the years, the state has experienced two kinds of failure that may explain its lack of success in dealing with the traders: development failure and failure of state provisioning of mega markets that will serve the majority of traders.

Institutional analysis offers insights on why the state is unlikely to succeed in its current track of decongesting the streets. The cost of enforcing rules is high when a large number of people do not believe in them. The pathology of mass street trading can be traced to two shocks: the economic crisis of the 1980s when state provision of basic services and living standards plummeted, and the war of 1991-2002, which fuelled an unprecedented mass migration of people to the city.

The crisis and the war strained the capacity of state officials to enforce rules of any kind. An institutional vacuum emerged. The urban dispossessed or underclass and new migrants with few employment opportunities moved into public spaces, encountering little or no resistance from public authorities. Over time, the old rules lost their significance, and new rules were created by the new occupants. These new rules emphasise effective and continuous occupation of a spot on a public space as a right of ownership or right to trade. Networks of group support and self-policing were constructed to sustain livelihoods. These new informal or illegal rules have been in force for more than three decades; they now regulate in significant ways how public spaces are used by a large number of people.

Reverting to the old formal rules through appeals to the traders or the use of force is unlikely to be effective if attention is not given to the institutional change that has occurred, including the unregulated and unprotected livelihood strategies that have spawned the change. The key issue is how to get the majority of street traders to become law abiding citizens. Relying only on law enforcement to revert to the status quo ante of more than 30 years ago has very high policing costs and may generate strongly negative social outcomes.

Getting the traders off the streets requires one or two big initiatives, which have so far not been forthcoming from the state. The first is how to tackle the development failure. By this I mean generating development that will provide jobs to the youths who now rule the streets. Surely, employment-generating growth is recognised in the government's Agenda for Prosperity, and economic growth has been spectacular in the last few years, thanks to the mining sector. However, mineral resource-led growth has done little to absorb the surplus labour on the streets; and the various small-scale public works, training and micro-finance programmes and state-created youth agencies and activities have had limited impact. Indeed, the micro finance programmes may have the unintended effect of further keeping the traders who receive loans on the streets.

Agri-business and strategic partnerships between the state and local entrepreneurs, including the top cadre of financially-rich "Belgium Traders", to diversify into productive industrial activities may hold promise, but will require effective industrial policy, which a weak state, such as Sierra Leone's, may not be able to pursue or sustain.

The second initiative is the construction of mega markets that will absorb the majority of street traders. Sierra Leone cannot boast of a single market that is comparable to markets in Guinea, Nigeria, Ghana, Cote d'Ivoire or Senegal, for instance. Markets in Freetown have not been improved beyond what they were in the 1960s and 1970s when street trading was minimal. The most spectacular illustration of state failure in market provision is the so-called market that has been constructed at Sewa Grounds (Park), which is meant to accommodate the Abacha Street traders. The market consists of a small building, which looks like a school, and a few rows of tin shacks (*pan bodi*) that can hardly accommodate 20 percent of the traders at Abacha Street. Most of the traders at Abacha Street do not have tables on the pavements, but are actually on the street itself hawking a few items. It will be difficult to lure such traders to the *"pan bodi"* structures at Sewa Grounds. A mega market with four floors and underground parking facilities can be built at the park to release a lot of the pressure on the surrounding streets.

A standard refrain of city council officials is that most of the markets are empty, so traders should not complain about lack of market provision. However, on this issue, traders seem more rational than council officials. If a market cannot accommodate more than 50 percent of traders in an area, no trader will want to occupy it, since the majority will be trading on the streets and will enjoy an advantage in reaching buyers who may not enter the market if they can get what they want on the streets. This may explain why only three markets are fully occupied by traders in Freetown: Big Market, Up Gun Market and Congo Town Market. In these three markets, there are hardly any street traders.

In conclusion, I submit that development failure and failure of mega market provision should be taken seriously by state officials. They impose serious constraints on the capacity of the state to enforce its rules on street trading. The failures in development and provisioning may explain the choice of sporadic intervention by the state to reclaim the streets. To demonstrate its legitimacy, the state wants to be seen by the broad public to be restoring sanity on the streets, but it has been consistently shown that it cannot sustain its interventions. Sporadic intervention itself is a reflection of state weakness. The state cannot implement its rules routinely. In this sense, it is not a law and order state; so, it engages in sporadic threats and punitive actions.

It is only in this context that we can understand the additional problem of partisan politics in constraining state actions. The traders know that the state cannot sustain its punitive actions; they may withdraw for a few days or even weeks and return on the streets and pavements with a vengeance.

14
Spectre of Ebola Protectionism[14]

A new kind of protectionism is haunting the world: the spectre of ebola protectionism. As the ebola virus disease ravages the Mano River Union (MRU) states of Guinea, Liberia and Sierra Leone, there are increasing calls to prevent people from MRU states from interacting with the rest of the world. The protectionist measures range from exit and entry controls, such as temperature checks and mandatory monitoring and quarantining of travellers from MRU states, to flight bans and denial of visas to holders of MRU passports.

The virus poses less of a threat to rich countries with sound public health systems than poor West African countries that have extensive links with the MRU states. Exit and non-intrusive entry controls, not flight bans and visa restrictions that Australia and Canada have imposed, may be enough to manage the few cases that are likely to pop up in rich countries.

It is amazing that Australia, which is more than 15,000 kilometres away from West Africa, and which has no confirmed case of ebola, is the first Western state to adopt mean-spirited protectionist policies. North Korea, a reclusive country in the far corner of Asia, is also fuelling the global panic by announcing that all foreign visitors regardless of travel history will be quarantined for 21 days.

As health experts have repeatedly affirmed, the ebola virus is not easily transmitted if a carrier is not symptomatic. Besides, it is health workers, home caregivers, and those engaged in customary practices of washing dead bodies that are mostly at risk. Indeed, more than half of the cases of infection have been linked to unsafe burial practices. It is hard to imagine a major ebola outbreak in Western societies where such practices do not exist and communal ways of living are rare.

---

[14] Published in *CODESRIA Bulletin* (Council for the Development of Social Science Research in Africa). Nos. 3-4, 2014; *Premium Times* (Abuja), 5 November 2014; *Sierra Express Media* (Freetown), 6 November 2014; *Patriotic Vanguard* (Vancouver), 6 November 2014; *Daily Trust* (Abuja), 7 November 2014; *People's Daily* (Abuja), 7 November 2014; *Think Media* (Nassau, Bahamas), 12 November 2014; and *The New Citizen* (Freetown), 13 November 2014.

If the voices of ebola protectionism become dominant in global public policy, the effect on the MRU states, diaspora citizens of such states, and Africa in general, will be catastrophic. It will gravely undermine the fight to tackle the disease at its source, make a mockery of the multilateral system of cooperation, and ultimately transform the ebola epidemic into a pandemic.

When living beings encounter external threats, they tend instinctively to withdraw into a mode of self-preservation. Our house cat, Maki, always relies on her own judgement, not ours, to protect herself from unknown visitors and disturbances. However, humans do not always act on instincts alone. They can build institutions to constrain the impulse for self-preservation that may make everybody worse off in the long-run.

Economic protectionism in the 1930s had a devastating effect on world trade and output. It disadvantaged all countries, rich as well as poor. A multilateral system was later crafted through the Bretton Woods Institutions of the IMF and World Bank and the United Nations network of organizations, in which countries would cooperate to solve common economic, social and security problems. When the spectre of protectionism threatened again to engulf the world in 2008, following the US financial crisis, a new kind of multilateralism, which included the active participation of emerging economies through the G-20, saved the day.

Ebola protectionism is likely to be more pernicious than protectionism that is driven by economic dynamics. In addition to fuelling capital flight and undermining trade, investments, tourism and government revenues in the MRU states, ebola protectionism affects human bodily contact, social trust, and free movement of people, and may reawaken or feed xenophobic and racist attitudes and practices.

Already in some Western countries, there are cases of children or students who are ebola-free being denied schooling or university education because they have lived in MRU states or their parents may have originated from, or travelled to, such states; Africans from ebola and non-ebola infected countries are being disinvited from external professional events; landlords are refusing to rent apartments to people from MRU states; and diaspora Africans, especially from the MRU states, are being harassed by neighbours in some countries. *Time* magazine reported on 28 October that two children from Senegal, which has had only one ebola confirmed case and has been declared free of the disease by the WHO, were beaten up in New York City by classmates yelling "Ebola".

Two points in President Obama's defence of a vigorous multilateral response to the ebola crisis need emphasising: protectionism will severely compromise the movement of essential health volunteers, medicines and facilities to the affected region and make it harder to defeat the virus at its source; and there can be no full protection in any country against the disease if it becomes a pandemic.

Advocates of ebola protectionism may believe that the rest of the world will not bat an eyelid if it loses the MRU states' 21 million people with a GDP of only USD12 billion, which is less than 2 percent of the West African region's GDP, 80 percent of which is accounted for by Nigeria. However, if the virus is not eradicated in the MRU states, it is likely to spread to neighbouring countries with bigger populations and large non-African developing countries that cannot easily be isolated. It may then ultimately find its way in the rich world in much larger numbers than the few cases that are currently causing panic.

By the standards of low-income countries, the MRU states were doing relatively well in growing their economies and rebuilding chronically-neglected roads and electrical power systems. Progress was being made in domestic revenue generation, even if the optimisation of revenues, especially from natural resources, remained a huge challenge. Unfortunately, the MRU states woefully failed to pay sufficient attention to the software of development---building institutions that can ensure citizens' trust in government policies. Governments are hardly present in the lives of most people for the most fundamental things, such as jobs, social services, and social security. People invariably fend for themselves and have learned to not depend on, or trust, the word of government. Even though most people are aware of the danger of ebola, they continue to ignore government instructions about how to handle the sick and the dead, especially when the instructions are not fully backed by provision of adequate health facilities and resources. In a sense, the ebola crisis underscores the point that rampant informal coping strategies are an index of underdevelopment that disconnects citizens from states.

State failure in the MRU countries was compounded by health policy failure at the multilateral level during the early period of the crisis when the virus could have been snuffed out at its epicentre in the forest region where the three countries meet--Gueckedou in Guinea, Lofa in Liberia and Kailahun in Sierra Leone. Now that the virus has spread massively to large towns and cities, combating it through contact-tracing is like looking for the proverbial needle in a haystack.

What accounts for the tardy multilateral response? According to *The New York Times*, budget cuts at the WHO resulted in the dissolution of the organisation's epidemic and pandemic response department, and large scale retrenchment at its Africa office of staff that were skilled in containing viral epidemics. Surely, the leaders of the MRU states initially showed incredible sluggishness and poor vision in responding to the crisis. However, their multilateral partners also failed to provide sound technical advice on how to combat the disease. The significance of the crisis was downplayed even when the non-governmental emergency response agency, Médicins Sans Frontières, was warning of a health catastrophe as early as June. The surge in international assistance in recent weeks, especially from such countries as the US, Britain, China, Cuba and France may hopefully help to stem the tide.

To conclude, if ebola protectionism takes root in the public policies of rich countries and millions of lives are lost to the disease, as some experts predict, the MRU states may be condemned to a wasteland of poverty and instability. It may confirm Robert Kaplan's prophecy in the 1990s of *The Coming Anarchy*, and render untenable international development assistance, which is already facing strong criticism from sections of the policy and research community for its alleged failure to deliver results. Research suggests that aid is only effective when it is combined with efforts at domestic revenue mobilisation and recipients improve their competitiveness in global trade and investments. Ebola protectionism will undermine such efforts and make it harder to optimise key components of development policy.

15

Sierra Leone's Traditional Bondo Female Society under Siege: A Case for Reform[15]

The issue of whether or not the traditional Bondo female society should be banned because it harms and disempowers women has asserted itself in the debate on gender equality. I have a few ideas I would like to share on the subject. I know that this subject is taboo for bona fide Bondo graduates (*an'shayma*), but as it is an issue that is likely to be with us for a long time, I feel it has to be discussed. It would be good, therefore, if our sisters with first-hand experience could join this discussion. This is not an invitation to tell it all. It is simply an invitation to shed light on key aspects of the institution that the public ought to know before hasty conclusions are made.

Currently, there is much hysteria in Europe and North America about the value of female circumcision societies in Africa. The dominant view is that they cause unnecessary physical injury to children (genital mutilation) and painful deaths, and undermine female sexual rights, or the rights of women to have unrestrained sexual pleasure. This view is important but ignores what I believe to be other vital aspects of the institution, viz. the formation of traditional conceptions of womanhood, at least in the Sierra Leone context, and the power which women acquire in the process to relate to men in male-dominated households, which may explain why a ban may be resisted by many women despite the harmful effects of circumcision. It is important, therefore, that a discussion on the institution should focus on three things: what I will call the surgical or circumcision aspects of the ceremony; the formation of traditional conceptions of womanhood; and the power which the institution traditionally confers on women in society.

---

[15] A version of this article was discussed extensively on Leonenet (an on-line forum for discussion of Sierra Leone issues) in March and April 1996. Non-English words in italics are in Temne.

On the circumcision aspect of the ceremony

To most people, including members of the Bondo society, circumcision is indeed the institution's raison d'être: the institution will not survive without the ritual of circumcision. My view is that alternative ways of initiation should be developed that do not require circumcision; a debate on alternatives should be promoted and government must establish a time frame to effect this change; children should not be initiated into the society; adults who do not wish to be initiated should be given legal protection; and in the transition to alternative initiation rites, the state should ensure that circumcision is safe for adult women who willingly choose it.

There is general agreement that circumcision can go wrong, children can be dangerously ill, and lives can be lost. Under such circumstances, there is a compelling argument to impose a ban on the practice as it will deter custodians of the society who may not want to get into trouble with the law. However, a ban may be difficult to enforce because of the institution's strong cultural underpinnings. Widespread disapproval of a ban may drive initiation ceremonies underground and simply enrich the pockets of law enforcement agents. A ban, in other words, may ultimately fail to protect a large number of *an'bonka* (freshly initiated) against the health hazards associated with circumcision at the *yarrma* (place for initiation). It will absolve the state of its responsibility to engage constructively with the institution and make it safe for adults who wish to participate in it.

While searching for alternative initiation methods, there is a strong case for upgrading the conditions in which surgical operations are conducted. Well trained doctors and nurses (who should also be *an'shayma* or graduates of the institution) could be inducted into the institution's technical stream so that they could become *e'digba* (highest rank of traditional professionals who carry out the operations), after going through the stages of *ta'wothoh* (recruits who spend between three months and one year in the bush learning all the tricks of the profession) and *an'sampa* (in charge of dancing, but knowledgeable enough about surgical operations to be able to conduct operations in the absence of *e'digba*). In the alternative (a much more realistic option), the traditional *digba* and *sampa* should be given simple training in modern methods of hygiene and sterilisation, similar to what many governments now provide

135

in rural areas to traditional birth attendants (TBAs). Health professionals, with background experience in the institution, should be sent to inspect the tools and place of initiation (*ro'yarrma*) before each ceremony. We should note that all *digba* have very rich knowledge of the healing properties of herbs, especially those relating to the curing of wounds.

Does circumcision make Bondo initiates less sexual than their non-society (*an'gborrka*) female counterparts? This is a difficult question to answer. It is quite possible that those who first decided that the road to womanhood should pass through this operation might actually have believed that the operation might serve to reduce the sexual appetite of women. Given the central role which the excised part of the female organ plays in arousing sexual feeling, it is also possible that the goal of circumcision is to restrain the sexual drive of women. However, the extent to which it does this is an open question. It is also debatable whether non-Bondo women are more sexually active than Bondo women. I am not aware of any empirical study on the sex lives of Bondo and non-Bondo women to make me speak authoritatively on the subject.

Is this an infringement on women's sexual rights? Again, it is a difficult question to answer. It is quite possible that the original idea to treat women this way may have originated from men (there are other practices in the Middle East which involve use of locks and other devices to prevent "unofficial" sexual activities; and where even men perform the surgical Bondo operations on women). What one can say is that in most societies in Africa where Bondo is practised, women are in full control of the institution. Men are not supposed to go near the *yarrma* or discuss Bondo secrets with wives or female relations. I vividly recall how terrified I was when my sisters were inducted into the society during one of our holiday trips to our village. Even though I was a little boy, I was only allowed to see them after the main ceremonies had been conducted. Before the initiation we were warned to keep off the *yarrma* if we did not want to be captured and punished by the women participating in the ceremonies. Indeed, there is a certain mystic about the Bondo society that completely confounds men. It is the most autonomous and all-embracing female institution in Sierra Leone.

As is the case with all our traditional institutions, the problem with Bondo is that modern elites and state authorities have not engaged it in ways that will lead to its modernisation: making it safe and clean, upgrading the curricula in the *yarrma*, enforcing standards, and

136

introducing alternative initiation ceremonies that will not require circumcision.

The question of womanhood

In many ways, the Bondo society is an integral part of the formation of traditional womanhood. It provides training and education that help women to handle their complex lives in traditional social settings -- which still rule the lives of most women in Sierra Leone. In these settings, and even among certain strata of people in urban areas, a woman is considered worthless or inferior if she has not been inducted into the Bondo society. The word *o'gborrka* (the uninitiated) carries very powerful connotations in female-female relations. Someone who is referred to as *o'gborrka* is regarded as dirty, third-rate and incapable of assuming responsibilities. Such a person is an outcast in society. Therefore, women who go through the Bondo ceremonies feel that such ceremonies are the foundation of their womanhood. Try to question this aspect of the institution and they will go mad at you or become emotional. It is central to their identity as women. Modernising the institution and protecting women who do not want to be members may require changes in the way womanhood is conceptualised in traditional settings.

In rural areas and in more traditional times, ceremonies can last between three and four months -- during which time women learn many things about society; how to take care of their households when they get married; how to relate to their husbands and in-laws; how to conduct relations with co-wives in the same households, etc. The institution is also a powerful tool of social control. In rural areas, for instance, initiates are usually those who have passed the stage of puberty and are considered by families and communities to be suitable for marriage. Suitors are encouraged to start proceedings for marriage during initiation ceremonies or just after the graduates (*an'shayma*) are out of the *yarrma*. This way, the communities or families do not have to face problems of "unwanted" pregnancies and other social vices. In addition, the Bondo society, where it is strictly practised, helps to prevent pre-marital sex. Fresh initiates (*an'bonka*) go through rigorous virginity tests. The imminence of such tests in the *yarrma* imposes obligations on parents to conduct regular tests of their own on their daughters before the Bondo

137

ceremony and marriage. Girls who are found to have been dis-virgined before their induction into Bondo society bring shame to their families.

In urban areas, many of these strict practices no longer hold. Even toddlers can now be initiated into the society and virginity tests seem to have lost their significance. The educational value of the institution is being eroded by city practices. The main reason why children are now inducted into the society at a very early age is to reduce costs, which have gone up astronomically over the years. Also, ceremonies are much shorter in the cities than in rural areas because of the need to conform to urban school calendars. And there is a trend to even allow the *bonka* to recuperate at their homes after the brief surgical operation. The feeling of solidarity in womanhood, which the *yarrma* creates, is thus being lost or undermined.

The educational value of the society can be criticised as nothing more than a scheme to perpetuate female submissiveness to men. If this is the case, feminists could intervene at the level of the *yarrma* to introduce more gender-balanced subjects in the socialisation and training of women. Indeed, because of the very large number of women who are members of this institution, the *yarrma* provides a perfect site for feminists to promote gender-sensitive values and claims-making that will reverse centuries of female subordination to men. There is no other institution in Sierra Leone that can rival Bondo in terms of mass membership.

Bondo society as female power?

What is often ignored in discussions on Bondo society is the sense of power which graduation in the society provides women. At the core of this power is the skilful use of secrets. There are certain issues which women are forbidden to discuss with men or their husbands whatever the level of their subordination to men. The secrets of how to take care of households, how to deal with problems in marriage, how to relate with co-wives, etc. are very often honoured. Men are always at a loss about the strategies of their wives. They can only guess what the overall strategies are likely to be, but can never be in full control of their wives or know the full dimensions of their strategies. Indeed, it is well known that as co-graduates in the Bondo society, co-wives can hide many joint secrets from their husbands. Such secrets often outlast even very serious conflicts between wives.

We should note that traditional African families are fundamentally different from Western families. Western families are generally small and closely-knit (wife, husband and children). In Western societies also, property tends to be jointly shared within family units and couples and children (at least during this century) often socialise as single units. On the other hand, traditional African families are large and open-ended. Complete loyalty does not always go to the head of the household, who is usually the man. Especially in cases where a household has more than one wife, wives are likely to cultivate the support of their brothers who are expected to intervene on their behalf when things go wrong in their households. Husbands always have tremendous respect for (or fear of) the brothers of their wives. Those brothers may hold secrets about a husband's household which the latter may not know about. Property is also not always jointly shared. Women, of course, collaborate with men in productive activities, but the former are also expected to fend for themselves independently of their husbands' economic activities. They can farm; raise chicken, sheep and goats; and trade independently of men. They also have the right to dispose of their incomes as they deem fit without seeking the advice of husbands.

Unlike the pattern of close and intense social relations that one finds in Western family systems, men and women do not always socialise as single units in traditional African family set ups. In the African case, each member is encouraged to cultivate an independent network of friends. I suspect that traditional African families are better able to handle the stresses of social life than Western family systems, which can get easily over-heated in the relatively small spaces that couples have to negotiate and resolve differences. Does this account for the exceptionally high divorce rates in the West? One obverse of this difference is that traditional African families tend to have less emotional bonds than European ones. Children can even be raised by extended family members without any sense of emotional loss to the children. Indeed, one of the biggest problems Africans face in Europe and North America is that of making the transition to Western models of family life, where husband, wife and children are expected always to be together. It has been a source of considerable strain in many family households. Back home, even in highly urbanised settings, open household relations are, in the main, largely practised by most elites.

Because of the open family structures that one finds in much of Africa, and the power that is invested in men, it is always important that women should have independent resources and skills to control their lives and manage the problems that are likely to emerge in their households. It seems to me that the Bondo society is (or can be) a powerful tool for this purpose. Men are overawed by the institution of Bondo, and find it difficult to predict the behaviour of their wives. It helps to enforce a sense of solidarity among wives in polygamous households, and among women in our male-dominated society.

To conclude, problems of gender inequality should not be located in the Bondo society even though it may reproduce or reinforce such inequality. The quest for gender equality should point elsewhere: in laws or customs relating to inheritance and property ownership; attitudes relating to the education of children of both sexes; gender discriminatory practices in labour markets; appointment of individuals to positions of authority; and access to information, incomes and resources that often influence life chances of individuals.

16

Reforming the Traditional Bondo Female Society: A Reply to Critics[16]

There have been several responses to the posting on the traditional Bondo female society. Instead of responding to each posting separately, I will instead address specific themes and refer to individual authors where appropriate.

When I set out to write the article on Bondo, I was aware of the risk involved in discussing this subject in public. I grew up in an environment where this issue was never discussed. Men or boys had some knowledge of what Bondo is about, but not the full story, and were forbidden from asking questions. Like Joe Afrique, I did not want to use Western terms like "clitorectomy", "female circumcision", or "female genital mutilation", which do not bring out the cultural aspects of the institution. Nor did I feel that a document that describes in graphic detail what goes on at the *yarrma* (place for initiation), or that names the parts of the female organ that are affected by the operation would serve much purpose. In any case, there are so many versions and experiences that I felt I would leave such details to those with first-hand experience on the subject to decide on how best to proceed on such issues. I decided that one way to conduct a discussion like this is to address the general issues of the institution, hoping that most people, including initiates, may feel able to join in the debate.

Like Lemuel Johnson, since my adult days, I have agonised over the blanket silence that prevails over discussions about many of our secret societies, even though they seem to command so much space in the lives of the vast majority of our people, with implications for public policy and social standards. Like Kelfala Kallon, I knew or suspected that our sisters may not want to discuss this highly sensitive issue. Indeed, my wife warned me not to expect much input from Bondo women because of their vows and the emotions which the subject is likely to throw up. However, as someone who is concerned with public policy issues I felt

---

[16] This article was discussed extensively on Leonenet (an online forum for discussion of Sierra Leone issues) in March and April 1996. Non-English words in italics are in Temne.

that the issue is important enough to provoke a discussion. Perhaps, the Net is not the best place to do this, but I thought we could start here in a modest way before we reach the right medium where key decisions are likely to be made.

There are two reasons why I feel a discussion on Bondo, and indeed other traditional institutions, is crucial. First, like Ibrahim Abdullah, Hassan Sisay, Ben Weller, Lemuel Johnson, Ahovi Kponou (and Mariama Barrie), I believe that there are many things that are wrong with the institution. Many practices need to be changed to help people like Ben Weller resolve the dilemmas which he eloquently expressed in his mail. Ben, you are not the only one who has faced this dilemma. I was first confronted with it in 1984 when one of my junior sisters, who my wife and I raised, turned 13 and my mother and other relations felt it was time to initiate her into the society. All along I had taken her as my daughter and felt that I had full control over decisions relating to her well-being. I did not realise how powerless I was to speak on her behalf on Bondo issues, which traditionally are considered the sole prerogative of women, until my mother broached the subject. Of course, my reaction was a flat No. I was very careful to show respect for the institution but was emphatic about the health hazards and physical pain that I knew were associated with the ceremony. My view then, which I continue to push in discussions with women, was that I would be willing to allow my sister to take part in the ceremony (as I valued some of the cultural aspects of the institution) only if there was no surgical operation.

My mother was visibly startled that I could hold an opinion on the subject, let alone express it. She and my other relations told me in very clear terms that my views were not important. They were only informing me about their plans out of courtesy. The only thing that I think saved the situation was the respect that my mother and I have for each other -- she did not want to upset me on the issue -- and the fact that our holiday was only for three weeks. A very close friend who was normally resident in the country was not so lucky. He had expressed similar misgivings about the ceremony to his wife and relations. Unfortunately for him, he was only informed by his wife about what had happened to his children and sisters after the ceremony had been performed at the *yarrma*. It caused a lot of strain in their relationship. Ben Weller, I do not think that there are any laws that protect those who do not wish their children or wards to take part in the ceremony. Unlike you, I do not have strong family links with the guardians of the institution, so I can understand your double dilemma. It is precisely for reasons like this that I think that a public discourse on the issue is important. Should fathers not have a say on matters relating to the physical status of their daughters?

What are the public policy issues that arise out of this discussion? I hold the view that the Bondo society is so strongly embedded in the values of the great majority of our women that it should not be treated as a purely private institution or dismissed out of hand as worthless. Ibrahim Abdullah, I am really intrigued by some of the points you raise in relation to the status of the institution and what looks like an attempt to treat your "informants" as a representative sample of the Bondo population. I have great respect for women who do not want to be associated with the institution on the grounds that you cite. But surely, they are currently a very tiny minority. I respect the fact that they are Ph.D. and Master's degree holders but that does not make their views more important than the countless women, including educated women, who hold very different views on the subject. It would be useful if you could widen your network of informants to get a full picture of what is really happening in the institution. After reading your social history papers and recent postings on ethnicity on the Net, you left me with the impression that you tackle social and cultural problems from the bottom up. Why do you not want to do the same for the Bondo society? Let me emphasise that women are in "full control of the institution". The only visible role men play in the ceremony is the construction of the *yarrma*, a task seen as inappropriate for women. The construction work is usually done by *an'soko* (members of a male secret society). If Ben Weller was in Moyamba he could play that role.

In the traditional contexts in which the Bondo society operates, it will not be too far-fetched to argue that the institution has a semi-public character (all women are potential members), even though its activities are done in secret, and it is not accountable to one half of the population (men). Because of the central role of the institution in the lives of the majority of women, some form of public regulation is needed to maintain minimum standards of clinical and social practices. Some might say that the institution is capable of regulating the behaviour of its members and should be left alone to do this. However, like all corporate entities, self-regulation is not always enough, especially when what goes on in the institution has implications for the rest of society and for dissidents like Mariama Barrie and Ibrahim Abdullah's informants. What are the key issues in regulation? These range from a total ban (Hassan Sisay and Ibrahim Abdullah) to measures that emphasise reforms.

Those who advocate a ban are, of course, entitled to their positions if they feel that the institution serves no useful purpose. I am sure that there will be women who will hold this position, but I would like to believe that if a survey is carried out they are likely to be in the minority. Ibrahim Abdullah, how will we know that the majority of women who believe in the institution do not want it? This sounds very much like Marx's problematic views on "false consciousness". Like you, I feel that the institution may have been a product of the historical process in the formation of male domination over women. But this is a very blind spot in our history. I do not think we will ever be able to know the truth. Whatever the history, the truth is that in present day Sierra Leone, men have no serious input in the institution. I hold nothing "sacred" in my life, but I respect the rights of those who want to hold certain things sacred provided they do not hurt others. The view that men made the institution sacred can only be a guess. And I do not understand why Sierra Leone or any other country for that matter should have only one view or tradition of Islam; or why in fact Muslims in Sierra Leone should copy hook, line and sinker what is written in the Koran. The fact that Islam has not been able to conquer this African institution is something many people will be proud of. By the way, Egypt and Sudan -- Islamic countries -- continue to practice female circumcision.

The very painful memories that Mariama Barrie recalls in her article in *Essence* are real and need to be taken seriously, as Ibrahim Abdullah and Hassan Sisay have pointed out. They also worry me a lot. But how far will a ban go in the real world of women in Sierra Leone? What use is a ban if it cannot be enforced? And why should public policy be restricted only to one aspect of a problem if there are other components of the institution that may be worth preserving or reforming? If a ban cannot be enforced, what can the state do to protect women from the health problems associated with circumcision? Should the state refuse to protect the health of these women because they may be doing something illegal? It is on the basis of this that I come down strongly on the side of reform. This is why I also find David Keili's comments on Mariama Barrie very apt. Although I strongly empathise

144

with Barrie's experience in the Bondo society, I feel that she may have decided to play the role of an outside critic, which is very fine. External critics are always useful in the process of social change.

However, the point I think David Keili makes in relation to her exposé has a lot in common with positions adopted by Communists and Social Democrats in Western Europe on how to change society. Communists were adept at criticising capitalism and its decadent socio-economic order, and in urging workers to overthrow it. Social Democrats also disliked much of what capitalism did to workers but felt they could bring enormous changes to the lives of workers by criticising the system from within. Result? The real reforms that left a mark on the lives of workers (such as the welfare system) were carried out by Social Democrats. Today, all communist parties are dying to be labelled social democratic parties. Condemning a social act because it offends one's social values does not always help the mass majority of victims, especially if such victims have a very different world view and the person who condemns has not made much effort to link his/her own personal experience with those of the putative victims, and understand why they wish to stick to their old ways.

If a ban is not likely to be effective, how can we help our sisters and children who are likely to be taken to the *yarrma*? In my previous posting I suggested several ways this could be done: basic health training to *e'digba* (highest rank of traditional professionals who carry out the operations) and *an'sampa* (in charge of dancing, but able to conduct operations in the absence of *e'digba*); induction of doctors and nurses (who are *an'shayma* or Bondo graduates) into the technical stream of the institution so that they could perform the surgical operations; providing basic health services at the *yarrma*; making it mandatory for health professionals with experience in the institution to inspect working tools and the *yarrma* before each ceremony; giving legal and social protection to those who do not wish to be inducted into the society; starting a debate on, and establishing a time frame for introducing, alternatives to circumcision. A debate has to develop among the Bondo women themselves.

Hassan Sisay and Ibrahim Abdullah, I do not understand how you can describe an institution that has the support of most women in our society and has a powerful living reality as "outdated". Whose "date" are we using here? Are we to assume that the women who engage in the

145

practice are also outdated? What should we do with them? All institutions change with time. History teaches, however, that not all aspects of an institution easily disappear because of the passage of time or the acquisition of higher education. Relying on history as the final arbiter on the status of Bondo may, therefore, be premature, and may not help the search for appropriate policies to guide the evolution of the institution. Bondo is very much alive, and cherished, by the great majority of women even in urban areas. A very high proportion of these women are educated. Many have completed secondary school education. Those among the educated Bondo women who no longer initiate their daughters into the ceremony are mainly a small group of high-brow professionals. However, a good number of these professionals participate in the entertainment aspects of the ceremony. They provide financial support and act as advisers to practicing families during initiation ceremonies.

It is, of course, the case that most urban women are not likely to be degree holders or to hold professional posts. Non-professional women who take part in the ceremony may be aware of some of the health risks and pain, but their socialisation in urban society involves a high dose of traditional practices, adapted to suit their changed urban life styles. Among these groups of women, Bondo ceremonies are solidly built into their yearly entertainment activities. The culture of showing off the best "ashobi" (uniform dresses worn in ceremonies), the composition and singing of new songs or time-worn classics (the popular hit single "Somebody" in the album "Lek Yu Culture" by Ahmed Jankay Nabay is derived from a Bondo classic), open feasts, and the showering of gifts to initiated children or relations are deeply embedded in their social practices. I suspect that for a large number of these women, the entertainment value of these ceremonies may now be more important than other aspects of the institution that still hold sway in the rural areas. What should the majority of these women do in the interim while they wait for the progressive wheel of history to roll?

The second reason why a debate on Bondo is important relates to a general problem I have with the way African traditional institutions and values have been treated since colonial rule. These institutions and values, including our secret societies, health care provisioning cultures, military defence systems, religious practices, the art of telling stories, parables and proverbs, music, as well as our languages have been

146

confined to the non-formal, traditional sector. Even though the great majority of our people are still exposed to these values and institutions, they are no longer accorded the status they enjoyed before the Western conquest. The result has been what the Nigerian sociologist, Peter Eke, has described as "the two publics". How can these institutions grow and adapt when they have not been effectively engaged in defining the values of the dominant post-colonial public space?

Africa is one of the few places in the world where the process of modernisation is taking place outside of the institutions that the vast majority of people can identify with. Is this not one of the reasons why our formal institutions are so unstable, so unrepresentative, so unaccountable, and so undynamic? Some of the traditional institutions, such as the secret societies, including Bondo, clearly have harmful practices, and need to be changed. However, change is only possible if states and elites engage these institutions constructively rather than confining them to the second or informal public where they can continue to cause harm to citizens and make it difficult for individuals in traditional settings to participate effectively in the development project.

Part II: Democratic Politics

17

Economic Policy Making and Democratic Accountability[17]

The Issue

Many new democracies have emerged since the late 1980s following worldwide demands for respect of human rights, accountability and transparency in policy making. Aid donors have promoted the view that democratisation improves the quality of public policies and services. However, democratisation is occurring at a time when the power of investors and financial institutions is changing both the parameters and styles of governance. Financial globalisation, high levels of indebtedness and neoliberal prescriptions narrow economic policy options to a limited set of objectives that emphasise fiscal restraint, privatisation and liberalisation.

In order to meet these objectives, policy making is increasingly restricted to "technocrats", or those with highly technical knowledge or expertise whose decisions are unconstrained by political processes. Technocrats tend to work in those executive institutions of government that are the most insulated from public pressure and therefore the least democratically accountable—such as central banks, and finance and trade ministries.

Technocratic styles of policy making pose problems for democracies. They distort structures of accountability, as governments become more answerable to multilateral agencies and investors than to representative institutions and the public at large. Such styles of policy making also affect responses to employment and social protection, poverty reduction and conflict management. Even those these issues are important in consolidating new democracies, they may be sidelined by policy objectives that emphasise macroeconomic stability. Furthermore, citizens may lose confidence in the democratic process if they believe their votes are irrelevant in decisions that affect their lives.

Yet if governments are to be responsive to citizens' demands, policies—including economic policies—must be decided democratically.

---

[17] UNRISD, *Research and Policy Brief.* No. 3. August 2004. Geneva: UNRISD.

The role of legislative institutions in holding the executive accountable is crucial in this regard. In democracies, legislative institutions—parliament or congress--are expected to articulate citizens' choices, scrutinise policy proposals and provide legitimacy for policy outcomes. But economic policies affect social groups and institutions differently, and democratic processes and accountability suffer when important decisions about trade-offs are entrusted exclusively to technocrats. Central bank chiefs and ministers of finance, for instance, may be beholden to special interest groups in the financial world, which may privilege strategies for inflation reduction, or financial and trade liberalisation, over those of employment generation or more inclusive social protection.

Research findings

Between 2000 and 2002, UNRISD carried out research on economic policy making and parliamentary accountability in eight developing and transition countries: Argentina, Benin, Chile, the Czech Republic, Hungary, India, Malawi and the Republic of Korea. The case studies sought to understand the inter-connections of economic and social policies, the salience of these policies in government strategies, the influence of societal interests on the making of such policies, and the trade-offs or complementarities between policies in parliamentary bargaining. Insights into these issues were gained by focusing on the budget, which is a major policy instrument for government spending and taxation.

The research shows that countries have managed the tensions between technocracy and democratic accountability differently. Exposure to different types of financial pressure, the nature of the economic situation before democratic transition, elite consensus, party behaviour, party representation in the legislative branch, technical skills and knowledge of legislators, and activism of civic groups may determine the extent to which policy making may reflect democratic choices.

The imbalance in expertise and power between the executive branch of government and legislative branches grows as economies become globalised. Countries that are dependent on the multilateral institutions for finance and advice show high levels of policy capture by these institutions. However, the rise of technocratic behaviour in the executive branch can serve as an incentive for legislators to become more technically competent. This may check the growth of technocracy if it is accompanied by improved levels of accountability to citizens, and if the latter also become more aware of the technical issues involved in policy making. Citizens often do not have enough information or expertise to make informed judgements on public policies, hold governments accountable, or effectively scrutinise and influence the work of their legislators. This affects all democracies—old as well as new.

Politics, not systems of government, determine technocratic or democratic outcomes

According to many observers, parliamentary systems are more effective than presidential systems in checking technocratic behaviour. Under a presidential system, the president is elected for a fixed term and tends to be insulated from the dynamics of parliamentary politics. The office-holder need not necessarily seek to build consensus in exercising power. In a parliamentary system, on the other hand, the prime minister is largely dependent on the strength and representation of political parties in parliament, and can be removed from office after losing a vote of confidence. This means that prime ministers may spend more time than presidents cultivating parliamentary support for their policy proposals.

However, the UNRISD research suggests that the linkages that produce either technocratic or collaborative behaviour are complex. The studies on Argentina, Chile and the Republic of Korea indicate that despite their strong presidential systems of government, governments may indeed seek parliamentary legitimacy for their policies. This may happen when opposition and governing parties have narrowed down their differences on economic policies, and when legislators have developed expertise that enable them to bargain with the executive based on the technical merits of proposals.

A parliamentary system of government is not a guarantee against technocratic behaviour if the political party of the prime minister enjoys an overwhelming majority in parliament. However, coalition or minority governments may enhance the policy making power of the legislative branch. The reforms that liberalised the Indian economy in 1991, for example, were implemented gradually, in part because of the need to cultivate support within the loose governing coalition. The bill allowing foreign investment in the insurance sector was only passed after the executive conceded four amendments to it. Similarly, amendments to bring India's Patents Bill into conformity with World Trade Organization commitments were passed only after the executive agreed to parliament's demand to grant licences for patented drugs in the event of a health emergency. Although in both cases the delays were costly, the final legislation was perceived as an improvement on the initial proposals.

Constructive relations between the executive branch and political parties, as well as improvements in expertise improve parliamentary oversight

Parliamentary accountability can be enhanced when ruling parties engage in critical—not rubber-stamp--support of government policies, and when opposition parties develop expertise to bargain with the executive and dispense with strategies of non-cooperation. A technocratically-inclined executive cannot be held accountable if the legislative branch itself lacks comparable levels of expertise. And if parties fail to strengthen their members' technical capacity, then parliaments will remain equally uninterested in enhancing technical capacity.

Until the early 1990s, the Argentine Congress was seriously disadvantaged in dealing with the executive. Very few efforts were made by the president to consult parliament, and a record number of decrees were used to push through tough economic reforms. The rise of technocracy in the executive coincided with a decline in the operational budget, staff size and competence of the parliament. Unable to scrutinise the technical merits of policy, opposition parties in parliament adopted strategies of non-cooperation. However, the technical knowledge and expertise of the legislative branch improved between 1995 and 1997, as it emulated the executive by incorporating more economist-legislators; economics-related committees experienced greater diversification and specialisation; and there was more willingness by members of the opposition and governing parties to question the executive, introduce legislation and modify government-proposed bills. Requests for reports increased after 1997, an indication that legislators were showing greater interest in the technical details of the executive's policy proposals.

In Chile the number of economist-legislators has grown dramatically since 1990, and they now dominate the finance committees of both houses of parliament. These economists have played an important role in moderating executive dominance in economic policy, particularly by asserting their professional jurisdiction over parliamentary economic committees and in informal negotiations with the executive's economic experts. However, legislators still feel disempowered in the budgetary process despite improvements in the quality of the information sent by the executive to parliament. Attempts to institute mechanisms for independent policy analysis in the legislature, in the form of an independent budget office, have failed and parliament still lacks sufficient expertise, information and resources to scrutinise all economic policies.

Low technical capacity hinders effective scrutiny of policies

The lopsidedness in executive-legislative relations in the economic policy field in low-income countries is often compounded by the lack of technical expertise of most legislators. More than 60 percent of Malawi's first democratically elected parliament had qualifications below a college diploma and only about 15 percent had a first degree or more. While donor interventions have strengthened the technical knowledge and expertise of the executive, those of the legislative branch remain severely underdeveloped.

However, the issue of technical capacity is not restricted to formal education alone. The India study suggests that despite the high level of education of Indian legislators (about 90 per cent hold a college degree), their familiarity with budget issues is limited and most lack sufficient knowledge of economics. As a result, they focus on "visible" policies-- such as subsidies--that affect their constituencies, and ignore the much larger effects of less visible policies—those on exchange rates, interest rates and tariffs, for example. In 1999, 2001 and 2002, the Indian parliament passed the federal budget with virtually no scrutiny or debate.

An additional constraint on the development of capacity is the proliferation of small parties, which find it difficult to meet the cost of investing in expertise. In such situations, parliamentary parties may resort to threats of obstruction or the strategic formation of coalitions in order to achieve their objectives, with such behaviour replacing bargaining based on technical knowledge. In 2000, Benin had 118 registered political parties, and 35 party lists representing 62 parties were present in parliament. Most parties revolved around their leaders, who largely financed the parties and used them to further their own agendas. The interests of civic groups were not well integrated into the work of political parties.

Elite consensus and democratic transitions may favour the executive

If a democratic transition is preceded by an authoritarian regime with a good economic record, as in Chile, the new government may be forced to accept the former regime's policy-making parameters. Elite consensus on economic policies may also emerge if past approaches to policy making are discredited, and parties and citizens yearn for a new beginning. In the Czech Republic and Hungary there was strong consensus among the political elite on economic policy reform, and the governments enjoyed a honeymoon period among voters, during the initial period of the transition. Widespread distrust of central planning, and strong faith in the market and EU membership as vehicles for reversing the economic decline and improving living standards served to bring elites together across the political spectrum. During this period, parliamentary oversight of the executive branch mainly entailed acquiring information about the executive's activities and acting in ex post facto ways--establishing committees to examine cases bordering on corruption, for example.

In Hungary, executive-legislative consensus broke down in 1995 as a result of economic crisis. A hard-hitting stabilisation programme led to party splits and intense parliamentary debates on the budget, especially on taxes. In the Czech Republic, the crisis of 1996-98 led to government criticism of the monetary policy pursued by the independent central bank. When the government later collapsed, it was replaced by a caretaker administration headed by the central bank governor. Parliamentary oversight on the executive improved when a new parliament was constituted in which no party had a majority; the executive's scope of action was limited following signature of a pact between the government and opposition parties relating to the budget and the staffing of economic and other strategic committees.

Aid dependence and indebtedness strengthen technocratic tendencies

Technocratic approaches to policy making tend to have deep roots in aid dependent countries that are highly indebted to the multilateral financial institutions. In Malawi and Benin, these institutions have played important roles in identifying, supporting and, sometimes, recruiting technocrats for vital economic ministries. In Malawi, there is tension between government proclamations on poverty alleviation and the technocratic requirements of economic reform. Aid dependence and the strong influence of the multilateral financial institutions have imposed limits on the extent to which the government can pursue its social programme. UNRISD research found that technocrats in the economic ministries had rejected a welfare-focused approach to policy making. The poverty alleviation programme launched in 1995 was never implemented because of the subsequent introduction of cash budgeting, the need to control expenditures, and the transfer of many of the technical staff entrusted with the implementation of the poverty alleviation programme of the National Economic Council to the Ministry of Finance and Economic Planning.

As a member of the CFA franc zone, Benin has long surrendered monetary sovereignty to a regional central bank. Economic reform is largely concerned about fiscal stabilisation, privatisation and liberalisation. The government's budget is submitted to the multilateral financial institutions to ensure that spending plans meet agreed targets. These institutions have also intervened at critical conjunctures to influence budget debates in parliament. Two major crises have underscored the tense relations between the executive and parliament on economic policy making. The first was in 1994 when the CFA franc was devalued and Benin's parliament, acting in alliance with labour groups, called for an increase in salaries and social spending. The second was in 1996 when the national oil company was privatised, and opposition parties, which dominated parliament, joined the national public sector workers' union in resisting privatisation because of its assumed effects on employment. In both cases, parliament refused to approve the proposed budget, forcing the president to use emergency powers to govern.

Policy implications

The democratisation of economic policy making is essential if social and other issues of public concern are to be integrated in ways that contribute to cohesion and the well-being of citizens. This view currently enjoys some support in the poverty reduction strategies of the multilateral financial institutions. Strategies for poverty reduction are to be brought into adjustment policies, and civic groups are to participate in the formulation of such policies. But participation has so far been limited to consultation, and parliaments are yet to be fully engaged in the process.

The growth of expertise in both the executive and legislative institutions of government is essential for development in a complex world. Democracy is threatened when decisions are not subjected to public scrutiny and the dynamics of bargaining that are at the heart of politics.

The UNRISD research suggests that technocratic policy making can be moderated when:

- political parties invest in expertise and are willing to engage the executive on the technical merits of policy;
- parliaments establish effective mechanisms—such as specialised committees with technically qualified members--for information gathering and independently analysing policies;
- the technical knowledge of legislators, especially on economic issues, is enhanced;
- there is high probability that the government will lose a vote of confidence if it tries to circumvent proper parliamentary scrutiny of economic policies;
- aid dependence and indebtedness are reduced, and countries reclaim their autonomy in the economic policy field; and
- citizens and civic groups are well informed about the choices governments make on their behalf and are willing to hold policy makers to account.

18

Reflections on Recent Patterns of Political Development in Africa[18]

Introduction

African countries approach the end of the twentieth century with much disquiet about the kinds of institutions that would guide the social, economic and political lives of their citizens. It is difficult to predict what these institutions will be, given the incredibly rapid pace of change that most societies have had to endure during the last 15 years. Except perhaps for Eastern Europe, which has had to shed an entire social system that was based on central planning in favour of one that is largely driven by market incentives, no other region can compare with sub-Saharan Africa in terms of the multiple shocks its institutions and peoples have suffered in recent years.

My purpose in this discussion is to attempt to explore some general socio-economic and political trends that will enable me to discuss some key options that I believe will need to be confronted in efforts to build institutions that are likely to be much more sustainable than what is available at present.

Pitching the discussion at this level already raises a lot of problems since we are not dealing with a homogenous continent. Even when countries face common problems of economic decline or civil strife they may differ in terms of the specific constraints they will have to overcome because of their history, social structures and power relations. What is more, African countries have not been exposed to the same level or intensity of socio-economic and political vulnerability; some have, in fact, done pretty well on the basis of available resources and levels of development. However, despite these caveats, I do not intend to treat each country separately. Instead, I will try as much as possible to classify countries when key arguments are made in order to highlight differences.

---

[18] Published in *Southern African Political and Economic Monthly* (Harare), September 1995. Speech delivered at the Graduate Institute of International Studies on "International Security". Geneva. 20 July 1995.

Let me state the broad processes of change that I believe are likely to affect whatever African leaders and people do in their search for stable economic and political institutions. I would like to highlight three of such processes, viz. those relating to the informalisation of economic life; those which deal with the challenges of political liberalisation; and those which fall under the domain of ethnic conflicts and civil wars. The three issues are very much inter-related. As we proceed, it should be clear that one set of problems provides a context for the development, and thus an understanding, of the others.

Economic restructuring and informalisation

I will not spend much time on this first issue since my talk is supposed to focus on political trends. I discuss restructuring and informalisation, however, in order to prepare the background for an understanding of the political trends themselves. I address three issues here. The first is the decline of most economies in much of the 1980s and 1990s. Except for Botswana, Mauritius and Swaziland, annual GDP growth rates of most countries were either negative or hardly sufficient to account for their annual rates of population growth. Employment levels, inflation rates, balance of payments deficits, debt ratios and the overall fiscal situation worsened for most countries. Indeed, Africa's competitiveness in the world economy has suffered very sharp declines. For instance, Africa's share of world exports dropped from 4.7 percent in 1980 to 1.9 percent in 1991. What is more, its share of total exports from developing countries declined from 16 percent to 8 percent over the same period; and its share of LDC manufactured exports fell from 9.3 percent in 1960 to 0.4 percent in 1985.

I do not intend to delve into the causes of this decline, which most scholars have linked to worsening agricultural prices, poor volume performance in the export sector, weak incentives, inadequate physical and social infrastructure, capital flight and corruption. However, the profile of decline is important as a backdrop to understand the second issue, which is the loss of control by African leaders in the management of their economies. Through policy-based lending programmes, or structural adjustment as they came to be called, the international financial institutions have, over the last decade and half, massively intervened in reshaping these economies by recommending deflationary policies of tight money, balanced budgets, flexible exchange rates and liberal markets. About 241 IMF/World Bank structural adjustment programmes were initiated by African governments between 1980 and 1989.

Again, the record of recovery has been largely poor or, in a few cases, barely satisfactory. Countries that have done relatively well, in terms of checking the decline, have also been large recipients of foreign finance. Independent researchers who have studied the outcomes do not find much difference in growth rates between countries that have rigorously implemented the reforms and those which have stalled in their commitments. It has been much easier to liberalise exchange rates and prices than to carry out institutional reforms, such as in privatisation, financial markets and public sector management; inequalities and the incidence of poverty have increased; and the flow of private investment funds or direct investment has been pathetically dismal. In fact, there has been a secular process of dis-investment from Africa in recent years.

If one adds the interventionist programmes of other multilateral agencies in the social and humanitarian fields, Africa must rank as the most heavily penetrated continent by the United Nations system and its specialised agencies. Yet, there is an inverse relationship between such high levels of multilateral penetration and actual economic and social development. The really dynamic forces of economic transformation, transnational corporations (TNCs) and private capital markets, have largely avoided Africa, except in the mining sector. One issue that beckons for serious thought is the question of how to break out of the recurring syndrome of UN/Bretton Woods/bilateral donor/NGO dependency and work towards rebuilding these countries as properly functioning and dynamic economies. This requires long-range strategic thinking.

Economic decline and programmes of stabilisation or restructuring have combined to produce rapid and high levels of informalisation of the public sector and economic activities in general. This has taken several dimensions. First, the public sector and modern private businesses have considerably contracted as a result of retrenchment, company bankruptcies and cuts in social service provisioning. Those who have been directly affected by this contraction have had no option but to relocate to the informal sector. Second, devaluation and inflation have introduced steep cuts in real incomes, forcing individuals and household members to take on multiple jobs, again largely in the informal sector. Third, employers have come to increasingly rely on non-formal, sometimes non-legal, ways of making profits, such as casualisation of the workforce; sub-contracting of lines of economic activities where this has been possible; and the concealment of business practices in order to avoid taxes. Thus, informalisation has greatly contributed to the fiscal crisis of most states as companies and individuals work out various schemes to evade public authorities. Even enterprises that have been empowered and enriched as a result of liberalisation and globalisation have become very difficult to reach. In other words, crisis and adjustment have weakened the regulatory regimes of most African countries and deepened the fragmentation of their economies. It is one of the ironies of social change that programmes that were meant to improve efficiency and regulation have largely produced the opposite effects.

The challenge of political liberalisation

Alongside the restructuring of African economies and the rise in informal practices, there has been a major upsurge in political liberalisation or competition. In the face of other major ills, such as civil wars, it is all too easily assumed by media commentators that not much constructive political activity goes on in the continent. The single most important political development of the 1990s is obviously the breakdown of the post- independence structures of monolithic politics and the emergence of a plurality of actors, centres of authority and viewpoints. African countries have handled this development in very different ways, some much more creatively and competently than others, with implications for national stability, social cohesion and regional security. Before 1990, there were only five countries (Senegal, Botswana, Gambia, Mauritius and Zimbabwe) which had anything resembling multi-party political systems; and except in Mauritius, in none of the remaining countries had the parties which led the struggles for independence been defeated in elections. All other countries on the continent were run by military or one party dictatorships.

The situation is now completely different. However, my purpose in this discussion is not to celebrate political liberalisation. I would like to believe that the exciting moments of the early 1990s are somehow behind us. What is interesting at this stage is to take a sober look at the patterns of political liberalisation and raise questions about how they help us to understand the challenges facing African people at the end of the twentieth century.

Liberalisation has produced uneven results across Africa. Three clear trends are discernible. The first concerns a set of countries where military rulers and one-party civilian governments have been unseated by new political parties through the medium of elections. These countries include Benin, Mali, Niger, Cape Verde, Zambia, Malawi, Lesotho, South Africa and Madagascar. In these countries, political competition is now fairly well tolerated; the number of non-government owned newspapers has increased dramatically; and there are some attempts to separate political parties from governmental institutions and the military.

However, one should resist the temptation to call these countries democracies as many commentators, including some respectable political scientists, tend to do. I do not think that democracies can be built in a year or two or even in five or ten years. This is a process that takes a long time to mature. Democratic practice needs to become an inseparable part of a country's social and political culture for it to be sustainable. Underpinning the formal attributes of a democratic polity are three very important values: the need for political actors to recognise the limits of power, including the readiness to surrender that power to democratically elected opponents without fear of the consequences; acceptance of the principles of moderation and compromise as fundamental aspects of the process of political bargaining; and a commitment to live with, and support, plurality in social and political life. These values are still very much at a low level of development in these countries and it is quite possible that many of the gains in the past five years could be reversed. A major question which needs to be asked is whether stable political liberalisation can be sustained under conditions of economic decline and loss of opportunities for the vast majority of people who were led to believe that democratisation would bring tangible benefits to their lives.

A second pattern of liberalisation refers to cases where ruling regimes, whether derived from the military or a single party, are still very much in control of government even though many of the attributes of formal democracy, such as multi-party elections, non-homogenous legislatures, growth in the organisations of civil society and independent media, are in place. Examples include Cote d'Ivoire, Guinea, Togo, Cameroon, Ghana, Burkina Faso and Kenya. In this set of countries the principle of free and fair elections is still highly contested; opposition political parties and organisations in civil society have not been able to wrest power from the governing groups through elections; and the activities of ruling parties are still very much inseparable from governmental practices. This means that governments enjoy considerable power to limit the scope of political participation, representation, organisation and expression. Extra-judicial forms of protest by opposition political parties and civic organisations, which sometimes threaten the social order, are also more prevalent in this set of countries than in the first type. Those of you who follow developments in these countries should be aware of the constant attempts of governments to detain political opponents, obstruct the activities of opposition groups and close down newspapers. You should also readily recognise the tendency for opponents to resort to riots or violent forms of demonstration, often as a result of governmental intolerance. Much needs to be done in this set of countries to break the deadlock in electoral competition, which seems to frustrate attempts to focus on other pressing issues of institutional reform.

A third pattern refers to cases where military rule continues to be a dominant feature of the political process. Unlike in the second set of countries where military rulers have transformed themselves into civilians in order to hold on to power, in this latter case the military continues to rule primarily through the institutions of the military itself. Examples in this category are Nigeria, Gambia, Sierra Leone, Sudan and, in some ways, Burundi. In this set of countries, national legislatures are non-existent, talk less of whether their membership is homogenous or diverse. Also, open party competition is not tolerated even though there may be a high level of political activity in civil society. As is the norm in political liberalisation, however, an independent media has grown even though it works under extremely hazardous conditions. Newspaper closures and harassment of journalists, politicians and social activists are routine, but new ones tend to emerge to fill the void. The persistence of military rule in an era of liberalisation underscores the fragile nature of the process of political change. While I was preparing this talk I did a rough count of the current sub-Saharan African leaders who have a military background. It might interest you to know that about 57 per cent (28 out 49) of them do. The process of disengagement from the military is still a long way off. Obviously, there is not much to choose between military dictatorship and one party rule, but the historical record at least disadvantages military dictatorship in one vital domain: apart from the wars in Southern Africa that were associated with decolonisation, almost all other wars in the continent have occurred under military rule.

The resurgence of ethnic conflicts and civil wars

I would now like to examine the third and final trend, viz. the resurgence of ethnic conflicts and civil wars. From 1980 to the present, one could count up to thirteen major wars that have occurred in Africa - viz. in Angola, Mozambique, Zimbabwe, Uganda, Ethiopia, Sudan, Rwanda, Burundi, Sierra Leone, Liberia, Chad, Somalia and Namibia. Although these countries represent only about 15 % of the total sub-Saharan African population, the incidence of war, especially in the last five years, constitutes a serious problem. One should, of course, distinguish among different types of wars. Those of Angola, Mozambique, Zimbabwe and Namibia, for instance, were linked to decolonisation even though ethnic differences were intensely exploited in all four cases. The presence of a racist regime in South Africa and super-power rivalry in the sub-region made the outcomes much bloodier than perhaps would have been the case. In most of the other countries, ethnicity, elite rivalry, the gradual weakening of state capacity and, in some ways, the spill-over effects of conflicts in neighbouring countries combined to produce very destructive and vicious wars. The demise of secular ideology in the 1990s helped to fully expose the ethnic dimensions of most of these wars. The main point is that irrespective of their origins, conflicts tend to take on alarmingly negative ethnic dimensions when they turn into wars.

Ethnicity is, of course, not a new phenomenon in our continent. Africa is home to more than one thousand language groups, to take just one of ethnicity's defining characteristics. It is obviously the most ethnically diverse region in the world. Apart from a few empires which incorporated several ethnic groups, most pre-colonial societies were relatively integrated self-governing polities. Ethnic groups were at varying stages of development and used a complex of institutions to maintain social order and political stability. They also had mechanisms for promoting inter-ethnic relations and integration, as well as for accommodating immigrants or "ethnic strangers" in local communities.

Colonialism radically restructured these varied polities in the process of integrating them into the world market. Previously autonomous language groups were forcibly brought together under one polity, ignoring - or distorting- the patterns of social, economic and political relations that were evolving in many regions. Much of this experience is already well documented in history books so I will not repeat it here. My interest is on the social and political consequences of the dual society project: viz. the incompleteness of the colonial/western impact and the crisis which this project faced in the 1980s and 1990s.

At independence, African rulers inherited states which did not set out to consciously promote social integration or improve the governance capacities of the various groups that were incorporated in the new territorially-defined societies. The colonial authorities were more concerned about promoting the values of modernisation or westernisation - viz. a single language, an impersonal bureaucracy, scientific rationality and secularism - in the new public sphere. These so-called modern values were largely confined to the state sector. This sector was efficient but its reach was extremely limited in scope, as its primary purpose was to facilitate international trade and mining activities, as well as maintain law and order. One need not belabour the point that only a small number of Africans had access to this sector. The lives of most people continued to be regulated by traditional African values and institutions. Partly because of the strategy of discouraging a united opposition to colonial rule and partly also as a result of the sheer dynamism of ordinary Africans themselves, traditional institutions remained resilient at local and regional levels. But these institutions were not only ineffective in shaping the development of the new states, they had also lost their capacity for innovation and autonomy in decision making and governance.

In the run-up to independence in the 1950s and early 1960s, Africans were faced with the choice of whether to return power to the pre-colonial self-governing polities or to consolidate the new states and build cohesive nations out of them. They emphatically chose nation-building. Indeed, the question of redrawing state boundaries to reflect pre-colonial experiences was laid to rest in the Charter of the Organisation of African Unity, which called on governments to respect the inviolability of existing frontiers. While this decision looked sensible at the time, it failed to address the question of how to reconstruct the new states on the foundations of local culture and institutions in order for these states to be inclusive and sustainable. The colonial state's dual society model of development was, instead, deepened. The various states were to become "nation states" as opposed to multi-ethnic or multi-national states. In other words, concerted efforts were made to give the nation-states single identities. But the source of values for the construction of those identities remained Western. The foundations of African social life, viz. traditional institutions of property rights, social security, military defence, health provisioning, educational training, and governance were downgraded or simply ignored. Also, with very few exceptions, official languages remained Western; very limited efforts were made to develop the indigenous languages despite the rapid evolution of several of them as national or regional lingua franca. Many governments even went as far as to ban or discourage reference to individuals' ethnic or language group origins in public discourse.

These nation-building efforts had one big salutary effect. Despite the existence of ethnic differences and attempts to manipulate them for political ends, most elites resolutely believed in the one nation ideology: the commonly expressed view that "we are all Zambians, Senegalese, Kenyans, Tanzanians, Nigerians, Ivorians, Zaireans or Ghanaians", for instance, was really deep-seated. Perhaps because of the long process of separation of elites from traditional systems of authority and the material incentives which the one-nation ideology provided through jobs, social services, credit, subsidies, etc., even when elites used ethnicity to pursue their goals, their strategies were often devoid of demands for self-determination. Indeed, it is instructive to note that throughout the 1960s and 1970s, there were only three cases of ethnic conflicts based on separatist demands: Eritrea, which was forcibly incorporated into Ethiopia; Biafra in Nigeria; and Katanga (now Shaba) in Congo.

However, the downside of this development was that rulers were led to believe that the political corollary of the one nation ideology was a single political party or military rule. Since single party regimes and the military were themselves not democratically organised or administered, it was easy for one ethnic group or region to exercise hegemony in national political processes and for excluded groups to label public institutions as ethnically-biased. If we are to learn anything from our history, it is that monolithic or centralised institutions of governance are terribly inappropriate for the long-term stability of plural societies.

Unfortunately, Africa has had three such monolithic institutions: colonial rule, one party government, and military dictatorship.

The rapid expansion of the state sector in the 1960s and first half of the 1970s, including the fairly impressive economic growth rates that underpinned such expansion, helped to moderate the political demands of elites on the new "nation states". However, economic crisis and restructuring as well as political liberalisation have undermined the national consensus and made ethnicity visible and potent. Recession and economic restructuring have reduced the resources available to the state sector, and thus the incentives for disadvantaged groups or individuals to remain loyal to previous social and political arrangements offered by the state. In addition, ethnic affiliations and forms of mobilisation have become important as the scope for plural forms of organisation has widened. It is impossible to liberalise ethnically plural societies under conditions of economic decline without ethnicity becoming a major feature of political organisation. The demand for forms of politics that are devoid of ethnicity under current conditions is a pipe dream.

There are two principal ways ethnically-driven politics could have been moderated: if the Western project of "one nation" had succeeded in eliminating the multiple language groups and their corresponding social institutions as is the case in parts of the Caribbean and Latin America, for instance; or if sufficient autonomy had been given to local societies so that the institutions that inform the values of those societies would have formed the basis for the construction of national states with plural identities. The latter option would have required also a democratic system that would allow for institutionalised forms of power-sharing or political accommodation at local, sub-regional and national levels; and the protection of various types of minorities that multi-national polities can readily throw up. I consider this option the more viable of the two in the African context; and it would seem to me to be the most challenging act of institutional engineering that most African countries will have to confront today.

The good news is that there has been a time-lag between the rapid rise of ethnic claims and the demands for separate states based on exclusive ethnicity. Predictions of a thousand or so republics of mini-states, or an upsurge of mass conflicts to establish, or deny the emergence of, such states have been premature. Commitments to the territorial integrity of the current states are still fairly strong among most

Africans even when they disagree on how such states should function in practice. But this is no cause for celebration. Work needs to focus on how to set in motion processes of institutional reform that will change the way Africa's states are currently structured and managed.

19
Elections and the Transfer of Power: Lessons from Ghana[19]

Elections have become an important mechanism in current attempts to reorder Africa's faltering political systems. As most states come under the combined pressures of domestic and foreign forces to institute multi-party systems of governance, the concept of democracy tends to lose much of its substance and gets reduced to questions of conducting free and fair elections.

The first election invariably becomes a test case and an end in itself. It is either completely free and fair, in which case the country is proclaimed to have joined the ranks of democratic nations, or, if the election is flawed, the entire democratisation process is perceived to have suffered a serious setback.

As most current elections in Africa turn out not to be free and fair, there is bound to be some disillusionment with the very ideal of democracy, which might give credence to the view that the African soil is not conducive to the growth of democratic institutions and values; and that, perhaps, the old ways of authoritarian rule, which ensured some measure of security and peace, would be preferable to the protracted instability that characterises many of the transitions underway.

Questions of realpolitik would then continue to define ways in which the major powers relate to the unfolding changes on the continent. Current difficulties in conducting free and fair elections demand a fresh look at the underlying structures of power in African societies, in order to be able to evaluate the role of elections in the politics of change.

Any such effort must attempt to understand some of the unique and complex features of authoritarian rule in various country settings, and must be placed within the context of the on-going economic crisis and the doctrinaire application of neoliberal adjustment policies in poor

---

[19] Published in *CODESRIA Bulletin* (Council for the Development of Social Science Research in Africa, Dakar), No. 1, 1993; *South Letter* (South Centre, Geneva), No. 16, Winter, 1992-93; and *Africa Demos* (Carter Center, Atlanta), Vol. III, No. 1, February, 1993.

and fragmented societies. Basic systems of livelihood and national power structures have been challenged in ways that have imposed considerable strain on political institutions and the legitimacy of governmental authority.

The ensuing stalemate in many on-going transitions has opened up ethnic, regional and other types of social grievances that were rooted in the unequal distribution of power. This has allowed discredited rulers, and weak aspiring opposition groups, to cultivate deep ethnic roots in their respective local communities, and has tended to frustrate the emergence of social forces with a national base and vision for democratic change.

Theoretical and policy issues

Current interest in democratisation centres around three inter-related themes. The first concerns the issue of effective governance, i.e. the ability of governments to initiate and implement rational public policies. It is not always the case that democratically elected governments are better placed than authoritarian ones to achieve this primary attribute of state power, but the protracted African crisis convinced donor agencies, Western governments and local pressure groups of the need to link improvements in governance and well-being to the conduct of free and fair elections.

The second theme concerns the democratic and peaceful transfer of power from one set of rulers to another. It is assumed that the absence of competitive elections limits the choice of competent individuals and policies, promotes institutional decay, and entrenches the logic of violence in the political system.

Those that have special access to the instruments of violence, or to the single party machine, enjoy undue advantage over other competitors in the way political values are allocated. Such an advantage easily gets translated into economic rents, which can lead to non-rational policies and misallocation of national resources.

The third theme concerns the social relevance of the democratisation process and its differential effect on various groups in society. This deals with the issue of whether the evolving democratic institutions provide a wider sense of participation, accountability, liberty and well-being to those affected.

It is possible for societies to achieve a high degree of effective governance and peaceful transfer of power, based on elections, without addressing the fundamental questions of social relevance and popular participation.

The regulation of deep social divisions in liberal democratic societies, through the welfare state, succeeded in blunting the primary role of social struggles in the consolidation of democracy. Elections in such societies have become largely a technical and routine exercise, and do not threaten basic socioeconomic interests and arrangements.

However, the failure to achieve both effective governance and peaceful transfer of power in Africa underscores the need to probe deeper into the underlying relations of power and coalitions of interests, in order to understand why elections produce different outcomes from those in liberal democracies.

Elections and power

The recent presidential elections in Ghana (November 1992) provide a useful context for addressing some of these issues. We are concerned less with the elections results, which have been adequately discussed in several observer mission reports, newspapers and magazines, than with the problems posed by the electoral process in understanding the configuration of interests and the dynamics of power.

The elections highlighted three main problems. The first relates to the impartiality of the electoral system and deals with the roles of elections officers, party polling agents and the judiciary, as well as the availability of a reliable electoral register and voter identification system.

The second concerns the question of how to minimise the incumbency factor in order to give opponents a fair chance of winning. This calls for the regulation of the use of state resources and personnel, control of acts of bribery and intimidation of public functionaries and traditional rulers, and establishment of rules that will ensure equal access to the media.

The third problem deals with questions relating to parastatal forces whose activities are not regulated by the conventional structures for the management of public force, such as "the committees for the defence of the revolution", the "mobisquads" and the "people's defence committees".

Most African countries have experienced problems of incumbency and impartiality in their transitions, but countries that have had populist-oriented governments have faced additional problems of how to regulate parastatal forces. Problems of incumbency and impartiality arise from conflicts embedded in the structure of power and cannot be reduced to mere technical and logistical difficulties.

Indeed, technical and logistical problems are often allowed to fester because of the political calculations of office holders and seekers. Authoritarian rule provided wide-ranging opportunities to local and foreign interests in areas such as natural resource exploitation, investment capital, markets in guns and manufactured goods, global security, and the consolidation of Western culture.

Political leaders, concerned with the protection of a combination of such interests, relied on traditional relations of authority and the global structure of power to hold down dissent and to resist early post-independence pressures to preserve or create plural forms of politics.

The current transitions are occurring at a time when many of the existing regimes and rebel groups have been invested with considerable military and financial resources to be able, at least in the short run, to ignore the advice of their foreign patrons, who now seek to develop new arrangements in the global security and economic system.

Part of the strategy of the local regimes and groups seems to be based on the expectation that protracted post-elections instability would force foreign patrons to revise the principles of free and fair elections and render support to their tenuous hold, or claims, on power.

We may ponder the view that the most difficult transitions have occurred in countries where foreign patronage had been central to the operations and effectiveness of incumbent regimes and opposition groups, such as Angola, Cameroon, Cote d'Ivoire, Ethiopia, Kenya, Liberia, Malawi, Somalia, Togo and Zaire.

The least complicated transitions have occurred in countries where foreign influence had been limited, and where the major powers and financial institutions had a vested interest in the defeat of the incumbent regimes: Benin and Zambia.

Adjustment and social polarisation in Ghana

The PNDC (Provisional National Defence Council) regime in Ghana received a very high degree of patronage from the international financial institutions and donor governments in establishing some reasonable degree of effective governance and reversing the serious economic decline of previous decades. The high level of foreign financial resources it has enjoyed since 1983 is unprecedented for crisis economies in Africa, and tends to make the Ghana case special.

This had two implications. Firstly, the reform programme produced a deeply divided society. On the one hand, the reforms struck a positive cord among most middle class self-employed groups in urban areas and the bulk of the rural folk, who benefited from improvements in infrastructure and changes in relative prices.

On the other hand, many other social groups, such as industrial workers, public sector employees, urban unemployed/underemployed youth, and former business and political elites, felt deeply aggrieved by the new economic and political order. In the cocoa-growing region of Ashanti, where farmers were perceived to have been among the leading beneficiaries of the programme (even though on the basis of the results, it was the only region that voted overwhelmingly for the opposition), grievances against the government seemed to be linked to traditional ethnic issues.

This complicated the electoral outcomes in ethnically-mixed Brong Ahafo, and Eastern and Accra regions, where it was widely believed supporters of the regime played the anti-Ashanti card against the main opposition party that had a strong base in the Ashanti region.

The second factor relates to the concern of the donor agencies and governments for an outcome that would ensure the continuity of the reform programme. Doubts were raised about the capacity of the opposition parties to restrain the inevitable demands that would follow from their supporters for a relaxation of budgetary discipline, if any of such parties were to be voted into power.

This gave the regime an extra sense of security and confidence. Given its track record of proper economic management, the regime might have been led to believe that it could not be subjected to the kind of political conditionality that was recently imposed on such countries as Kenya and Malawi to force their leaders to hold multi-party elections.

Under such conditions, the regime could not be persuaded to treat the opposition parties seriously and discuss with their leaders some of the important queries relating to the conduct of the elections. Governmental intransigence was buttressed by calls from leading sections of the opposition to try key members of the regime for what were alleged to be crimes committed during their tenure of office.

The government and the opposition could not agree on a pact that would have provided the conditions for hitch-free elections. In the event, the elections were perceived as an act of war, in which losers were expected to suffer the full weight of governmental repression from winners. In such situations, the losers were bound to reject the results, whatever their validity.

Parastatal forces, populism and intolerance

Problems of parastatal forces relate to the populist traditions of the regime. The PNDC government had approached the question of social relevance from a perspective that sought to change the basic institutions of governance. It had created a few parastatal forces at various levels of society that, in many ways, usurped several of the functions and powers of the bureaucracy and traditional centres of authority.

When it overthrew the corrupt and inefficient administration of the elected Third Republic in 1981, the PNDC's rallying cry was to dispense with party politics, which, it believed, had allowed corrupt politicians to get into power and swindle the resources of the country. Attempts in the 1980s to develop the institutions of district councils and the national assembly, along essentially corporatist non-party lines, should be seen from this perspective of distrust of civil opposition.

Populism created a culture of messianism and intolerance on the part of the government and influenced the attitudes and strategies of the opposition, as the latter, in turn, refused to recognise even some of the more obvious achievements of the government. Each party believed it alone had the correct answers to the country's problems. Against the background of the failure of previous civil administrations to halt the economic decline, coupled with the loss of faith in government by most sections of the populace, the regime capitalised on its widely acclaimed record of economic success to frustrate genuine pressures for democratisation.

173

The parastatal forces, which were resentful of losing their privileged status in the new political dispensation, were central to the strategy of frustrating fundamental change. Most uncommitted voters still harboured deep-seated fear of previous excesses of party politics. It is possible for any regime under such conditions to rationalise its victory at the polls, even if the results were to have been invalidated.

Conclusion

Elections will continue to be a problematic medium of democratic change unless effective strategies are developed to confront local and transnational interests that have shaped the structures of power and social divisions in Africa. There is a pressing need to initiate open, democratic and consistent policies, unencumbered by considerations of global realpolitik, and economic development programmes that will take into account the basic livelihood concerns of the majority of the populace.

This means paying a lot more attention to questions of participation, accountability and liberty, relevant to wider groups in society. For in the final analysis, it is enlightened, economically secure and active citizens that would compel governments and opposition groups to act responsibly and conduct elections that would be seen as free and fair.

20

The International Monitoring of Elections in Africa[20]

Introduction

This essay reviews the Swedish Ministry of Foreign Affairs' Independent Electoral Institute Commission's proposal of 1992 for the establishment of an international institute for the monitoring of elections in countries experiencing democratic change. The Commission's document raises a number of interesting points on current attempts to provide international electoral support to on-going political transitions in developing countries. Much too often, decisions to hold elections are not based on careful preparation, and the outcomes leave the countries concerned much worse off than they were before the elections. Most of these countries have not had competitive multi-party elections since authoritarian rule became the dominant form of third world politics in the 1960s. Some have not even had any national competitive elections in their post-independence history. The problems that are emerging in many on-going transitions call for careful study and planning if elections are to occupy a vital component in the process of democratisation and have lasting meaning to the aspirations of wider groups in society.

One major shortcoming of the Commission's document relates to the way it defines the problem posed by rapid transitions in various continents: as an issue of supply constraints in the field of electoral support; a problem of mandates and roles of foreign observers; and a question of providing long term support covering pre and post-elections phases.

This approach to the problem would make sense if a decision has already been taken to establish an institute for elections monitoring, and all that remains is to examine the mandate, scope and tasks of such an institute. It would seem inadequate if the purpose is to address wider

---

[20] Published as "Some Reactions to the Independent Electoral Institute Commission's document of 2 November, 1992" in *CODESRIA Bulletin* (Council for the Development of Social Science Research in Africa), No. 2, 1993. The Commission's document was also published in the same edition of the *CODESRIA Bulletin*.

questions of why elections have been problematic in many developing countries, and to examine what effective strategies are to be adopted, locally and internationally, to ensure that the transitions are sustainable.

Implicit in the definition of the problem is the assumption that the elections are largely a technical issue. The document ignores the complex ways relations of power and interest articulation affect the conduct of elections. It also does not discuss the key problems created by the post-war global security and economic system in the emergence and consolidation of authoritarian systems in low-income countries; as well as the devastating impact of economic crisis and neoliberal adjustment policies on the social fabric of many of the countries that are expected to embrace democratic practices. There is also no mention of ways in which local groups concerned with issues of human rights and democracy can be encouraged to play active roles in the monitoring of national elections, including strategies for building and strengthening the autonomy of national electoral offices.

The politics of elections

Let me emphasise that elections monitoring is important and ought to be encouraged where this is deemed to be necessary. My experience as a foreign observer in the recent presidential elections in Ghana (November 1992) shows that the presence of observers does affect the local situation in a number of ways: opposition groups feel relatively more assured in several instances where they have good reason to doubt the intentions of incumbents; voters feel a bit less intimidated and may be ready to point out problems to observers; elections officers may be encouraged to defend the integrity of their office and may seek to overtly distance themselves from government; and victorious incumbents may use the approval ratings of observers to legitimise their rule.

There are obviously technical and logistical problems to tackle even if all parties are committed to the conduct of free and fair elections. Some of these technical issues relate to the availability of a reliable register and voter identification system; ensuring that elections officers, party polling agents and security officers are properly trained to handle elections issues and laws; providing the right quantity of elections materials, such as ballot boxes, indelible ink, authoritative registers, seals, vehicles and secure polling sites; and ensuring that voters have a good knowledge of where and how to vote. These are real technical problems, the resolution of which may be beyond the competence of many countries that are just being exposed to the rigours of competitive elections. The international community may have a role to play in helping to solve some of these problems.

However, in many situations where political relations are highly polarised, many of these seemingly technical problems provide ample opportunities for incumbents and opposition groups to fraudulently influence the choices of the electorate. Political calculations and strategies often allow many technical problems to fester. In many recent elections, such as in Ghana and Kenya, the strategies of incumbents to control the electoral process and return a verdict favourable to their parties, led to the holding of elections at extremely short notice. This did not allow for the establishment of the institutional infrastructure and relations of goodwill necessary for the conduct of fair elections. In such situations, it is not clear how the technical problems can be solved without tackling the political ones. It raises the question of whether resources, time and money should be spent in providing support to such kinds of elections, which are bound to be disputed by losers and plunge the country into chaos, or whether such resources should be used in projects that would minimise some of the social and political problems that make it difficult for governments and opposition groups to agree on a minimum working arrangement for the conduct of competitive politics.

International dimensions

Strategies aimed at influencing political change in developing countries in a democratic way should also take into account the wider international dimensions of the problem. The Commission's document highlights the need to provide professional backup to interested parties at the international level in the context of a long term strategy of engagement, covering pre and post-elections phases. The argument that the crucial test of democratic success is usually the second and third elections, and not necessarily the first, holds mainly in cases where the first election passed off peacefully and without much controversy. In many other situations, the test of success does not really depend on how many elections a country holds, or the number of observer missions sent to cover such elections. Putting the electoral system on an acceptable growth path could be a rather difficult and long term process involving a combination of strategies and pressures. Recent positive pronouncements by the major Western powers on what are generally believed to be highly questionable elections results in Kenya strengthens the view that considerations of self-interest and realpolitik are likely to remain central factors influencing how elections in poor countries are interpreted by such powers. This tends to weaken the efforts of more independent organisations that attempt to stick to the basic principle of fairness in assessing elections results. In such situations, a precondition for upholding the principle of electoral fairness is to regulate the self-interests of the major powers.

A related issue is the need to recognise the fact that some of the political problems many countries currently face can be traced to the way they were integrated into the international security and economic system. This led to a massive transfer of arms to extremely fragile societies that were grappling with the onerous tasks of nation-building and economic development: Angola, Mozambique, Somalia, Ethiopia, Afghanistan, Cambodia, El Salvador and Nicaragua. The end of the cold war coincided with the current attempts to change the political systems of developing countries. The old system has left many local leaders and client groups with a lot of financial and military resources. This has given them some leverage, at least in the short run, in defying some of the pressures from the international community. Despite the laudable attempts to promote the values of human rights and democracy in the world system, the major principles guiding the international behaviour of the dominant powers are still based on self-interest and power politics. Such countries decide on when and how to intervene in the world trouble spots, which elections results to underwrite and which to condemn.

Since the end of the cold war, the international system has tended to become more authoritarian in the way basic decisions that affect a number of developing countries are taken. It is doubtful whether democracy in developing countries can be encouraged to grow in an authoritarian international environment, as local despots can always bank on the self-interests of the major powers that dominate the global agenda to frustrate demands from their populace for genuine democratic change.

Some of the problems highlighted above can only be handled within the context of a general restructuring of the United Nations. The points raised in the Commission's document about the inherent difficulties of mandating the UN to extend its functions to cover the field of elections monitoring are sound, and need to be raised in order to provoke further discussion. The UN itself has not given sufficient thought to the numerous problems it has had to cope with in recent years. It has tended to opt for the "fire brigade" approach, which puts the spotlight on countries of the South, leaving untouched many of the underlying factors that give rise to most of the problems it seeks to tackle. Its effectiveness and moral authority has also been eroded in recent years by the political manipulations of a few powers, and it risks becoming an arm of the foreign policies of such powers. It is not clear, however, how an independent institute outside of the UN could fare better, especially as some monitoring situations would require the presence of a large force, which an independent private institute cannot provide.

Adjustment and democracy

Another important area that the document has not addressed is the link between economic crisis, adjustment policies and democracy. Only a few countries that have adopted market-driven adjustment policies have received sufficient resources from the donor community for adjustment to make a significant impact on their macroeconomic situation. Where such resources have not been forthcoming, countries have had to face the dual problem of macroeconomic decline and massive disruptions in livelihood. This can only complicate the political situation and encourage elites to opt for easy authoritarian solutions.

The doctrinaire way adjustment programmes have been implemented in developing countries makes the international financial institutions and donor governments to be less than neutral in some elections of countries where there has been a heavy commitment of foreign resources. This was obviously the case in Ghana, where the donor agencies and governments were worried about the advent to power of opposition parties that they suspected would revise some of the stringent policies of the PNDC regime on the budget, as it was believed such parties would be forced to respond to the varying interests of their supporters for various kinds of expenditure schemes. This attitude may have strengthened the hands of the incumbent regime and contributed to its refusal to allow for more open and democratic contestation. The way the adjustment programme was executed, with many groups having virtually lost out in the process, exacerbated the divisions in the country and made it difficult for the elections to be conducted fairly. There was very little foreign monitors could do in such situations to avert the inevitable instability that was to follow.

Local monitors and national elections offices

One final point that has not featured in the Commission's document is the role of local monitors and strategies to strengthen the autonomy of national electoral offices. The latter may have been implicitly recognised in the section on "capacity building...", but not articulated in ways that would demonstrate its significance. It must be stressed that the primary responsibility for the proper conduct of elections should rest with the nationals of the country where such elections are to be held. The polarised nature of politics in many countries in transition no doubt calls for some level of international intervention. But such intervention should make the question of developing effective local monitoring groups a central strategy of the operation. Otherwise we are likely to see a dependency syndrome in which major decisions that affect the political lives of poor countries are taken by outsiders who are not accountable to local people.

There are already a number of human rights and pro-democracy groups in a number of countries that are not affiliated to any of the major political parties. These should be encouraged to play active roles in the monitoring of elections. During our observer mission in Ghana, the Carter Center attempted to train a number of local monitors to complement the work of the foreign observers who were only 18 and could not cover the 18,000 polling stations in the country. In any case, Ghanaians ought to be involved in the monitoring of their elections. It should be pointed out that sections of the press were suspicious of the link between the Carter Center and the local monitoring groups; and the elections monitoring office, INEC (Independent National Electoral Commission), refused to grant independent accreditation to the local monitors, insisting that the Carter Center should be responsible for their activities. What is stake, however, is the principle of encouraging local groups to become an important part of the monitoring system. Where local monitors have become part of the political culture of a country, they could play a major role in getting elections officers to be independent of the parties in power.

Conclusion

Should an independent institute be created for electoral support in developing countries? There is obviously the need for some form of electoral support and monitoring in many developing countries trying to introduce multi-party systems of government. But it would seem to me that the kind of coordination and technical support the Commission identifies as the basic rationale for an independent institute can be organised within the auspices of a restructured and strengthened UN. I would want to believe that no institute, however independent, can avoid the problems other monitoring institutes and organisations currently face in the field, and it is highly unlikely that such an institute would have the last say on matters of elections and democracy in developing countries.

It would seem to me that countries that are interested in advancing the frontiers of democratic space in developing countries, and that have played a more neutral and progressive role in world affairs, have a responsibility to widen the search for strategies that would lead to the establishment of more open, consistent and democratic policies at the international level, in order to create a healthy environment for democratic ideals to sink deep roots in developing countries. The spotlight ought to be turned on both local and transnational forces that have made the business of conducting elections in developing countries so problematic.

At the local level, it is not always the case that electoral support should be given the major priority in assisting the process of peaceful democratic change. One can identify three possible strategies based on recent experiences in Africa. The first concerns countries that have made a good start in conducting elections, the results of which have not been seriously contested, such as Zambia, Benin, Cape Verde and Mali. These countries need a lot of support and encouragement to enable them overcome some of the technical problems relating to the conduct of free and fair elections, and ensure that institutional and structural constraints are constantly addressed in order to avoid a relapse into authoritarian

181

practices. Some viable strategies would include working with national electoral bodies in order to give them sufficient autonomy, encouraging local NGOs to take an active interest in elections monitoring, and getting government and opposition parties and organisations to hold regular meetings on ways in which the electoral system could be further depoliticised. Some of these meetings have been attempted in Zambia, even though there are still some problems in getting the former governing party, UNIP (United National Independence Party), to participate in such meetings. The second and third elections the Commission's document identifies as vital to the consolidation of democracy are important for these cases. The success of these cases could even influence developments in other countries.

The second strategy concerns countries that have experienced a prolonged period of internal strife, where prospects for viable elections are slim: Somalia, Ethiopia, Liberia, Mozambique, Angola, Sudan, Chad and Rwanda. The holding of premature elections in these countries is likely to compound the problems of such countries, if the structures for the functioning of their national political systems and the conduct of peaceful relations and trust have not been put in place. What is needed in such situations is mediation, institution building, reconstruction of the basic infrastructure, organisation of political parties, and a revival and strengthening of civic institutions that are likely to provide the foundations for peaceful elections at an agreeable time frame. The interim period could allow for all major parties to be represented in government, and for the granting of a wide range of political freedoms and civil liberties. Uganda has attempted to follow this path, although it has experienced difficulties in implementation because of resource constraints, difficulties in controlling some of the activists of the resistance committees and the military, as well as problems generated by the implementation of an IMF adjustment programme on a war-torn society.

The third arrangement concerns countries whose leaders have been reluctant to hold elections (Zaire, Togo, Malawi) or where elections have been conceded grudgingly and the results have been seriously disputed (Cameroon, Kenya, Cote d'Ivoire) leading to protracted crisis and instability. The prospects of organising free and fair elections in such societies are bleak, and the stability of such societies could be further endangered by holding early elections without the institutional structures in place. A lot more work needs to be done in such cases to break the political deadlock and get the various parties to be committed to democratic change, including getting the major patrons of some of the regimes to be consistent in their commitment to the principles of democracy. Sufficient pressures for national conferences, which would review the basic constraints on the political system, and establishing institutions and rules for organising competitive politics and elections would be appropriate.

In countries where elections have already been held and the results disputed, there is no guarantee that subsequent elections would be free and fair, even with foreign monitoring, especially as incumbents have been able to rule on the basis of questionable results which have received the backing of the major powers. The idea of "national conferences" which have been established in a number of "Francophone" African countries is sound, although these conferences have been held without the other ingredients in place, such as political pacts among the major contenders for power, and a favourable external environment that will make the national conferences respectable institutions. The absence of these ingredients has tended to allow incumbents to sit tight, play on ethnic differences and hope that instability would force foreign patrons to revise the policy of free and fair elections.

21
The 1996 Elections and Peace in Sierra Leone[21]

Since the removal of Captain Valentine Strasser as head of Sierra Leone's military government on 16 January, 1996, debate on the political future of the country has sharply divided into two seemingly irreconcilable camps: those who think that the elections promised for 26 February should go ahead, and those who believe that the elections should be postponed to allow for greater concentration of efforts in the procurement of peace. We are told that a meeting is scheduled to be held in Freetown on Monday, 12 February, to decide what steps the new government should take on the matter. Both sides have excellent arguments, but the problems seem to be larger than what we have been offered in the debate. In these brief comments, I will try to review the key arguments on both sides and offer some suggestions about where I think we should be headed in our difficult search for stable government, national reconciliation and peace.

The case for the elections

Central to the argument of those who insist on holding the elections at the promised date is the commonly accepted and valid view that the military -- any military -- has no business in government. As an institution, the military is too close to the instruments of violence and cannot be trusted to seek civic and flexible forms of conflict resolution, which are often required to run societies with sharp social cleavages. Societies need to be governed by people who do not derive their authority and legitimacy from guns, but from the wishes of the populace, as expressed through periodically organised free and fair elections. Such elections provide a medium for checking the excesses of government and for throwing out bad leaders. During periods of civil wars, in which military governments command the reins of government, it is difficult to differentiate between the moral claims of soldiers and those of rebels,

---

[21] Abridged version published as "The Way Forward" (Co-authored with A. Fowler and B. D. Komba-Kono) in *West Africa* (London). 26 February-3 March, 1996.

since the strength of both types of fighters largely depends upon the amount of fire power they control rather than the support they claim to derive from the populace, which both sides will always dispute. Only when one side annihilates the other can the conflict be brought to an end. Even in relatively normal times, changing governments under military rule always involves the threat or use of force, which can cause instability or chaos to the national body politic.

These general views about the shortcomings of military rule seem to fit recent experiences in Sierra Leone. The RUF (Revolutionary United Front) rebels obviously command no significant support in any part of the country, and therefore cannot lay claims to any form of legitimacy. They rely instead on terror to impose their presence in society. The NPRC military government is the de facto government of Sierra Leone. It enjoyed large scale support when it got rid of the pathetically incompetent and visionless government of General Joseph Saidu Momoh. However, public opinion has always insisted that welcome though the April 1992 coup was, military rule is a political aberration, and that power should eventually be transferred to a properly elected government. Indeed, the NPRC seems to recognize this fact by its decision to call itself a *provisional* ruling council. In any case, the early support for the military dipped tremendously when the war got out of control and life became miserable for the majority of people. Indeed, it is a measure of the general indifference of most people to the military government that Strasser, the darling of the youth in 1992, could be overthrown without any political tremor in any part of the country.

It is now widely recognized that the war has virtually engulfed most parts of the country since the military seized power in 1992. The military itself, we are told, has expanded from 3,000 to 10,000 in strength. Part of this expansion is related to the hawkish stand which the government took against the rebels, believing it could end the war by military means alone. Also, a number of news reports have shown that atrocities have been committed by both soldiers and rebels -- in some places where the fighting is most intense people find it difficult to tell the difference between the rebels and what is now being referred to as "sobels" (soldiers-turned-rebels). The rebels do not accept the legitimacy of the soldiers -- indeed, RUF advocates state that it is the soldiers that are rebels! They believe that the only barrier to their road to power is the superior armoury of the soldiers, and not the widespread social support the soldiers claim to enjoy. In this kind of struggle, which is defined by military logic and prowess, the views of the people do not seem to matter. Both sides believe that any group which controls more guns or holds the military balance will govern. Finally, if we are to believe media reports about the physical assault which Strasser is said to have received from some members of the new government during the transition to Brigadier Julius Maada Bio, we should thank our stars that the scuffle did not spill over into the barracks and onto the streets of the capital. It only confirms the view that military rule is inherently unstable and strengthens the case of those calling for elections on the 26th of February.

The case against the elections

What are the arguments of those who call for a postponement of the elections? Here the arguments revolve around five sets of positions: one general and theoretical and the others specific and practical. The general position relates to the glaring shortcomings of civil rule across Africa, even under "democratic" dispensations. In Africa, politicians are more powerful than public institutions. Thus, political institutions have been unable to hold national leaders accountable for their behaviour. The electorate is largely illiterate, and votes according to sentiments and ethnic or other forms of primordial loyalties. Electoral outcomes may not, therefore, reflect the national or public interest. Leaders get easily re-elected even when their public record turns out to be an unqualified disaster. In the context of Sierra Leone, the All People's Congress (APC) transformed a multiparty system of government into a single party regime, and kept fielding political incompetents largely because of the party's control over the electoral process and the local-level patronage networks individual politicians had developed to stay in power. People rightly believe that there is no guarantee that this will not happen again. Indeed, many of the old politicians are back in the political game (just listen to the record "*Big Berin*" by Musical Flames, composed and sung by a group of blind youth).

Those who advance these arguments do not always reject electoral politics. Indeed, in the current climate of global democratisation and the poor record of military rule in Africa and elsewhere, it is very rare to find die-hard authoritarians who believe that the military is an alternative to multiparty politics. So, my interpretation of this otherwise valid criticism of civil rule in Africa is that one needs to work hard on the institutional fabric of politics before one can be confident about electoral politics producing desirable outcomes. On this score, the case against elections does not translate into a valid case for the prolongation of military rule. The question that needs to be asked, though, is whether such an institutional fabric can be nurtured under military rule? Does this argument not give the military and their supporters an excuse to cling to power indefinitely since institution-building is always a long-term project? Think about the disaster that is now stalking Nigeria as military rulers continue to manipulate the good sense of the populace under the pretext of searching for viable institutions even after eleven years.

The practical arguments for postponing the elections are formidable. First, it simply does not make sense to hold the elections when anything between one third and two fifths of the population has been displaced. If the elections go ahead, they will largely be restricted to the towns -- Freetown, Bo, Kenema, Makeni, Port Loko, Kambia and Koidu. Areas which have been hardest hit, such as in Kailahun, Pujehun, Moyamba, Kono and Tonkolili, will be disenfranchised. Second and closely related to the first argument is that even those who have been registered to vote will not be able to do so because the logistics for organising the elections are not yet fully in place: INEC's (Interim National Electoral Commission) sums for the elections do not add up as donors have not warmed up to INEC chairman James Jonah's pleas for adequate funds; the electoral register is incomplete or chaotic; and travelling between towns or villages to cast votes or defend ballot boxes will be extremely hazardous in the absence of equipment or infrastructure to protect willing voters and elections officers.

Third, if the elections are an instrument for peace, then the main actors who have mounted the insurrection, the RUF, should participate in them. Otherwise, the RUF would not only sabotage the elections but would continue to wage war even after the installation of a civilian government. One indication of the RUF's plans to incapacitate people or prevent them from voting is the set of horrible pictures of maimed hands that are now all too familiar to readers of newspapers and television viewers. This third argument is impeccable only if we restrict the elections to questions of peace and give equal status to the military and the rebels in the power equation. If the elections are meant to provide a representative, accountable and legitimate government to Sierra

Leoneans, then the case for suspending them simply because an armed faction has not been included is rather weak. Should Sierra Leoneans continue to wallow under the weight of military rule if there is no peace? Is the RUF really interested in peace? Are Sierra Leoneans not entitled to show the RUF that they can rebuild their country through constitutional means and make hollow the rebels' claims to legitimate social support?

The fourth practical argument emerged after the recent coup that brought Bio to power. More than ever before, the military government seems interested in ending the war. Bio has called for talks without any preconditions and has shown a single-minded determination to pursue the peace objective. The RUF rebels have declared an interest in Bio's peace overtures; a temporary cease fire is in place; and Bio has for the first time talked by radio with Corporal Foday Sankoh, the RUF leader. If these moves are to yield dividends then they should take precedence over the elections -- the government needs to concentrate on one big issue at a time; and the RUF might, indeed, be interested in the elections. If this is the case, why not postpone the elections so that Sierra Leoneans can have both peace and legitimate government?

What can be done?

How does one square up these contending positions, most of which seem valid? What can Sierra Leoneans do under current circumstances to restore peace, constitutional legitimacy and political order in our country? In this third part of the discussion I focus on the need to introduce constraints that will support whatever position or plan Monday's meeting in Freetown is likely to yield. I divide the analysis into two parts. The first is short-term and looks at the question of what to do with the February 26 plan; and the second takes a much longer-term view of political development.

One thing seems clear in the debate. Nobody is calling for the cancellation of the elections, only their postponement. In other words, there is a minimum agreement that the military should not continue to rule Sierra Leone and that whether on February 26 or later, Sierra Leoneans should put in place political structures that will ensure the exit of the military from power. This makes the job relatively easy. There is already a moral disapproval of military rule -- a powerful constraint, which any military ruler aspiring for a long-term tenancy of the presidency will have to contend with. But this basic constraint is not enough if the Monday meeting or the military government decides to postpone the elections and pursue the peace process.

What additional constraints would be needed to ensure that the military does not go off on a limb, perpetuate itself in power, or encourage one of its members to do a Lansana Conte or Jerry Rawlings on Sierra Leone -- in other words, become a "civilian", contest the elections and "win"? The history of Africa is littered with too many leaders who show early promise only to renege on their promises and lead their countries to destruction or failure. We should, therefore, always strive to bank on institutions and not on leaders.

If the elections are postponed, Sierra Leoneans should insist on three things. First, we should make sure that the postponement is not open-ended, but that a firm date is put in place, which is reasonable in order to upgrade the conditions for orderly, free and fair elections. Second, since postponement is linked to peace, the current government should be judged on whether it has been able to deliver peace within a clearly established timetable. Failure should result in a change of government in order to consider new options. Third, the only way the second constraint can be effective is if Sierra Leoneans insist upon the establishment of a Consultative Assembly along the lines of what was already emerging when the February 26 date was fixed. The composition of the Assembly should reflect a cross-section of the country, which should give it much moral authority to defend the public interest. The Assembly should be an autonomous institution, with powers to censure the military government and elect a new leader if the current one does not deliver peace. The new leader should then be mandated to prepare the country for nation-wide elections. Such a leader should not contest the elections.

Institutional reform

However, even if things go well under the short-term plan, the fears expressed about the limitations of elections in Africa will not go away simply because the war has ended or all parties are agreed about the virtues of an election. How do we make sure that public institutions are stronger than politicians; that people are able to recall bad leaders from office; that politicians are held accountable for their policies whilst in

189

office; and that people feel that their interests are fairly represented in government and other public institutions? How do we ensure that the errors of politicians do not plunge the country into another round of civil war and incompetent government? In other words, if those who want the elections to go ahead on February 26 win the argument, or if the short-term plan for eventual elections comes into play at some point, what needs to be done to give the country a more stable and viable political system?

The issues here are complex and many and would take up a full article. They also require much more thought than I have been able to devote to them at this point. I highlight only the main threads of the argument. Sierra Leone is an extreme case of a capital city state. All elites of consequence are located in Freetown. This has obviously helped to check some of the more rabid forms of ethnicity that one sees in other countries. Elites in Sierra Leone are likely to share common experiences in education, jobs and urban associational life. Despite this high level of integration, ethnicity has not gone away. Elites manipulate it intensely and a sense of insecurity pervades their lives during elections or when new governments are being formed: "are we going to be in it or not?" Because of the centralisation of power and facilities in the city, we have the abnormal situation where a member of the elite who lives most of his/her life in the capital lays claims to representing folks in his/her "home town" by virtue of having relations who reside there or having, perhaps, been born there. What are the results? Rural folks are visited with violence every four or five years by strangers from the city, whose only interest is to win power and settle in the city. Since they do not live in the areas where they contest elections such elites do not have to worry about the social and economic costs of their electoral forays in the villages or rural towns. They do not also have to worry about development in those areas.

Several issues beg for attention. First, there is need to decentralise political power in the country. The primary areas of political life, local government and district councils, need to be taken seriously. They need to be given a certain level of autonomy, sufficient funding and allowed to generate resources for local development; local institutions of government need, therefore, to be upgraded; and a structure of incentives and constraints introduced to get elected representatives to reside in local constituencies or district councils and contribute to local and regional development. In other words, local and district assemblies, with elevated powers and responsibilities, should be allowed to become functional again.

Second, fears of ethnic domination are real and need to be taken seriously. Fortunately, whether under civil or military rule, all governments have been ethnic coalition governments since the time of independence. But the decision on how ethnic groups are to be reflected in government has always rested in the hands of the president and his group of advisers. Not surprisingly, this essential pluralist principle for managing ethnically divided societies has tended to be widely abused. Governments set up one set of community leaders against another, pursue a witch-hunt against vocal dissidents of other ethnic groups in the national arena, and in some cases encourage the use of violence against ethnic opponents to ensure complete compliance. This practice was very common under Siaka Stevens and Joseph Mommoh. Chiefs would be deposed; opposing elites would be prevented from living in a contested village or town; thugs would be hired to beat up families and supporters; and national "representatives" of ethnic groups would be given enhanced status over those who are critical of government. The case of the so-called "*Ndorbryosoi*" revolt in Pujehun, which some people have tried to connect to the current civil war, is a vivid example.

One way to prevent such strong-arm tactics and fears of alienation is to develop a scheme that would allow political parties with some measure of popular support to be represented at all levels of government -- local, district or national. This should not compromise the relative autonomy of opposition parties that participate in such governments. An alternative will be to establish rules that will make political parties highly multi-ethnic so that individuals from different ethnic groups or regions can serve in government even when a governing party draws its core support from a specific region or regions. A winner-takes-all approach to governance in the context of war will make it difficult to confront the Revolutionary United Front as a united country.

Third, our civic institutions should be upgraded and extended to district and local areas: NGOs, the press, political parties, trades unions, students unions and other professional organisations. They help to uphold and defend values of liberty, transparency, accountability and cross-ethnic solidarity. Also, the courts and INEC should be made autonomous of government. Indeed, the record of impartiality which

INEC has developed under James Jonah in this short period should be defended. INEC should not be allowed to degenerate into a lame duck institution or used as a corrupt instrument as was the case with the APC's National Elections Office.

If the correct steps are taken to develop institutions that will be all-inclusive, transparent and accountable, a case could be made to the outside world for some support for the political transition. This support would involve funds for the transformation of the military and re-integration of the rebels into society as citizens with viable means of livelihood and responsibilities.

22
Dark Clouds on the Horizon?
Reflections on the SLPP Convention of 2011[22]

The election of ex-junta leader Julius Maada Bio as flag bearer of the Sierra Leone People's Party (SLPP) for the 2012 presidential elections has sent shock waves around the country and in the Diaspora. Although Bio was one of the front-runners among a motley crowd of 19 aspirants, people with less partisan attachments had hoped that the delegates would settle for a less controversial figure with no history of violence and elect an executive that is inclusive. Unfortunately, it seems that the party has decided to narrow its political appeal to its core support base, which is the South and East of the country, and adopt a candidate with a troubling background.

Before addressing the political implications of this choice, it is worth noting that the SLPP has always distinguished itself from the ruling All People's Congress (APC) on the basis of its aversion to violence, respect for the law and regional inclusiveness under its catchy and all-embracing slogan "One Country, One People". The APC was indisputably a by-word for violence when it ruled the country from 1968 to 1992.

There are also more Northern elites in the SLPP than there are Southern elites in the APC. Part of the reason for this lopsidedness was Ahmad Tejan Kabbah's (the first post war president) policy of inclusiveness, the political fragmentation of the North into multiple parties after the collapse of the APC in 1992, and the calculations by Northern elites that association with the ruling party would yield real material benefits. It is, indeed, a great credit to the SLPP that about half of the contestants for its presidential ticket claim to have Northern roots.

The current APC started off badly by creating a highly skewed Northern-dominated cabinet. The SLPP chairman John Benjamin's characterisation of the first APC cabinet as Wusum Stars was spot on.

---

[22] Published in *Sewa News* (London), 4 August 2011; *Patriotic Vanguard* (Vancouver) 5 August 2011; and *Cocorioko* (New York), 5 August 2011.

Benjamin promised the nation that the SLPP will not create its Southern equivalent, Kambui Eagles. Sadly, this has happened with the new SLPP executive. Public pressure and protests have nudged the APC government towards a trajectory of inclusiveness, even though more needs to be done. It has also tried to remake its image of a violent party by having as leader a charismatic personality with roots in the business sector and who was not part of the political class of the 1970s and 1980s that wrecked the country.

We thus have the unbelievably strange irony that just when the APC is trying to be inclusive, the SLPP has decided to waste its political asset of inclusivity by having a Southern-dominated executive and leader; and just when the APC has a leader with no history of violence and who enjoys considerable respect at home and abroad, the SLPP has decided to impose upon itself a leader with a lot to account for in the field of violence.

Why did the SLPP decide to field a militarist or warrior from its own base? I offer three insights, all of which bode ill for the country. The first is that the choice is a gut reaction from a hard core of party chauvinists who believe that since the APC government has alienated Southern elites, Northerners have no business occupying top posts in the SLPP. This may have the unfortunate effect of locking the country into a tight bipolar ethnic polity with dire consequences for those who want to straddle and dilute the ethno-regional divide.

The second explanation is that the party may have calculated that it does not stand a chance of winning the 2012 elections given the development record of the current government and the power of incumbency. Its preference therefore is to unify its base, which was seriously fractured when Charles Margai failed to get the party ticket for the 2007 elections and decided to form a rival party, the People's Movement for Democratic Change, and urged his supporters to vote for Ernest Koroma, the APC leader, in the runoff of the presidential election. The reported speech of one of the party elders, Sama Banya, to the delegates urging them to listen to the voices of the "people" massed outside of the voting centre is instructive in this regard. At the party's Makeni convention in 2005, delegates ignored the voices of the "people" clamouring for Margai and paid a heavy price in the 2007 elections. A generous reading of the 2011 delegates' view is that the real election for a presidential change of guard is 2017, when the APC will not enjoy the power of incumbency and its members are likely to fight over Koroma's crown. The SLPP will then behave rationally and field a more electable candidate.

The third explanation is that the SLPP intends to play ugly by injecting uncontrollable violence in the electoral process, forcing a stalemate that would lead to a government of national unity. Some would argue that the ground work for this scenario has been crafted by the party's refusal to recognise the authority of the head of the National Electoral Commission, Christiana Thorpe, who was first appointed to the job by the SLPP government of Tejan Kabbah. There are many in the party who believe that Solomon Berewa, the SLPP's presidential candidate, should not have conceded defeat in 2007; and that the international community would have had no choice but to urge both parties to form a government of national unity as they did in Kenya. Indeed, the reason Tejan-Kabbah is unpopular today in the party is because of the pressure he exerted on Berewa to accept defeat. It is important to point out that after the Kenyan experience, and as events in Cote d'Ivoire have shown, the international community has become weary of governments of national unity.

However, the danger of increased electoral violence should not be minimized. During the 2007 elections, both parties used ex-combatants as security insurance, and individuals with previous links to military and rebel outfits, such as the National Provisional Ruling Council, the Armed Forces Revolutionary Council, and the Revolutionary United Front, are members of both parties. The implications of having a presidential candidate that was part of a group that used violence to sack two governments and engaged in extra-judicial killing of 26 or 29 citizens should not be taken lightly.

What can be done? Here I offer three suggestions, two short-term and the other long-term. The first is the need for vigilance by the public, the international community and the political parties themselves. The SLPP as a party and Maada Bio as leader now have an enormous burden to prove their critics wrong. This assumes that the relations of the citizens murdered without trial will not make life difficult for Bio by pursuing him in the courts to account for the murders, especially if he travels overseas. So the SLPP has inflicted on Sierra Leone a political leader who is likely to encounter problems overseas and make it difficult to redeem the country's image that has been associated with violence and horrendous crimes against humanity.

In his acceptance speech, Bio has already started the process of cleaning up his image as a violent man. A public apology for the crimes of the NPRC is also in order. But speeches are not enough. He needs to be seen to be controlling his supporters and eschewing violence in all its forms. There have been widespread and persistent reports about the unruly behaviour of his core supporters during the process leading to his victory at the conference. Even Sama Banya reported in his column in the *Global Times* on 26 July 2011 that "A gang of unruly young people two of who wore Maada Bio T-shirts were openly defiant outside the Party headquarters last Wednesday where they rained invectives at National Chairman Benjamin and the National Women's Leader Isata Kabbah. The scene was absolutely disgusting".

The SLPP has a large number of decent people who now have the herculean and patriotic task of holding their leader to account and disciplining him if the party is to regain its image as a party of decency and win support across the ethno-regional divide. The use of ex-combatants in the electoral process should also be discouraged, even outlawed. This applies to both the SLPP and the APC. And public debate on the need to end political violence needs to be sustained. It ought to be stressed that in a mineral rich economy, such as ours, elite conflicts to control rents and other spinoffs are likely to be rife and destabilising. Our recent history suggests that it is very easy to sustain warfare and the livelihoods of combatants from mineral resources.

The second suggestion is for both parties to reassert their commitment towards inclusive parties and government. The immediate task of the SLPP in this regard is to ensure that it does not experience Northern flight as happened in 1964 when our first prime minister, Sir Milton Margai, died and power was transferred to his brother, Sir Albert Margai, instead of to John Karefa-Smart, a Northerner, who was more senior in the government. The public interest requires that the SLPP remains multi-ethnic and improves on the representation of Northerners and Westerners in the party hierarchy. The government of Ernest Koroma also needs to accelerate the recruitment of Southerners into the APC and the government. Part of the reason the SLPP has turned inwards and to its base is because of the perceived lopsidedness of government appointments. Northern hegemonists who want to grab all public posts need to be checked.

The third suggestion is long-term, which involves changes in rules governing election of political representatives. It seems from the SLPP flag bearer election results that only 39.5 percent of the delegates wanted Bio to lead them. It is not clear what would have happened if last-placed candidates were eliminated and their votes shared among the top candidates. Again, if 60.5 percent of delegates did not really want Bio, the outcome is a commentary on the SLPP's propensity to produce electoral rules that act against its interests.

The other time the party inflicted this problem upon itself was when it changed the voting rules from the list system of proportional representation to single-member, first-past-the-post constituency rules. If voting is ethnic, as it tends to be in Sierra Leone's elections, it is difficult for the SLPP to win seats in the Western area even though it has about 30 perent of the votes in that region. This means that unless ethnicity is transcended, the SLPP will always be deprived of a majority in parliament even if it wins the presidency. The combined seats of the North and Western Area are much more than those of the South and East.

In terms of long term strategies, there are a number of rules that can be adopted, including primaries of the US type and the alternative vote that ranks candidates, both of which are likely to force candidates out of their ethnic cocoons in order to win elections; power alternation among the key ethno-regional clusters; and flexible rules on proportionality in the staffing of government jobs. Linking political parties to the aspirations of popular classes can also be a strong antidote to ethnicity-based politics, especially when underpinned by other rules, such as those above. When parties become rooted in popular aspirations, development and public service delivery are bound to take centre stage and the power of ethnic entrepreneurs across regions weakened. A public debate is needed on these issues. Sierra Leone needs to grow out of the prism of ethnicity-based parties and political violence.

23
Further Comments on the SLPP Convention of 2011[23]

The feedback I have received on the opinion piece "Dark Clouds on the Horizon? The SLPP Convention of 2011" has been highly positive. However, a few issues have emerged in three critical responses that I would like to address. I do not intend to turn this into a debate with partisans as this can easily degenerate into name-calling and point-scoring, which may produce more heat than light.

The first issue I would like to address is the ethno-regional composition of the SLPP executive. Patrick Kagbeni Muana claims that the appropriate comparison between the APC and SLPP is their respective executives rather than the comparison I made between the APC cabinet and the SLPP executive. He then proceeded to argue that the SLPP's executive is more national in scope than the APC's. I have three points to make on this issue.

My piece was not about which of the two party executives has a better national spread. Information that highlights the highly Northern-dominated character of the APC executive is not news to me. My focus was on the SLPP, which, as I argued, has an unquestioned advantage over the APC in terms of elite membership. I was disappointed that the SLPP failed to utilise this advantage and instead turned to its core South-Eastern base in its choice of flag bearer and executive. I honestly thought that with so many non-Southern/Eastern candidates vying for leadership of the party (the first time this has happened in its recent history), the SLPP would have set the bar high for the APC by transforming the ethno-regional trajectory of our politics into one of inclusiveness. It is, sadly, a missed opportunity, which the party may come to regret. This point is completely lost on Kelfala Kallon who insists that since the SLPP executive is less than 80% South-Eastern, the party has already done well for the North and Western Area, which enjoy about one third

[23] Published in *Patriotic Vanguard* (Vancouver) 18 August 2011; and *Cocorioko* (New York) 18 August 2011.

of the delegates even though they only supply a fraction of votes to the party at national elections.

When a party is in government, the party executive tends to take a back seat. The public face of the party becomes that of cabinet ministers and the president. For an opposition party, the interesting organ is its executive, which speaks on public issues. In fact, if the opposition party's parliamentarians are well-resourced and policy-focused, the party's executive may not even play a substantial role in public discourse. In the United States, for instance, one hardly hears the voices of Republican Party executive members. It is the party leaders in the House of Representatives and Senate who call the shots. It is a sad commentary on the calibre of our parliamentarians on the opposition benches that the voice of the party is only seriously heard at the party's headquarters. Let me hasten to add here that this is a problem for most African political parties. Once they lose power, and by implication access to the state bureaucracy for policy guidance, they become bereft of ideas on the core areas of government.

The SLPP executive list of 31 members that shows a relatively equal distribution of members across the four regions is deceptive. The 31 members are the same "green" oranges alright, as Muana would like readers to believe. However, only some have enough juice to be called oranges. The core offices of most party executives are the flag bearer, the chairman, the secretary general, the organising secretary, the publicity secretary, and the financial secretary (these are two posts in the SLPP executive). All these positions, except for the secretary general (Sulaiman Banja Tejan-Sie almost lost to a Southerner) went to the South and East. Deputies are mere shadows; they hardly do anything. Similarly, the positions of Northern, Eastern, Southern and Western Area Chairmen do not carry much weight especially in countries with unitary polities and party systems. The relative insignificance of these offices is the same as the superfluous positions of resident ministers for the South, North and East in a context where there is a substantive minister of the interior. In addition, creating party wings for women and youth does not cut it in the real dynamics of power. The best way to improve gender and youth representation in party systems is by electing women and youth to the top seven or eight posts. Women and youth leaders who head party wings are likely to stay on the wings and not at the centre of policy

199

making. And other posts, such as Chief Imam and Chaplain, are, surely, purely decorative.

The second issue I would like to address is the dynamics that led to Maada Bio's election. I am really surprised that Kelfala Kallon leans on Mancur Olson's *Logic of Collective Action* to explain Bio's victory. Olson's theory applies to situations in which a small group of people that are highly organised and feel strongly about their interests can impose their choices on society if they are the only organised game in town. It assumes a very large electorate in which other citizens do not hold strong views on the issue the organised group is interested in. However, in the SLPP election, the electorate (the 602 delegates) is very small, highly partisan, strongly mobilised, and willing to act out its choices on the only issue at stake, which is the election of a flag bearer. It is spurious to assume that only Bio's mob had strong preferences without considering the external supporters of the other candidates who surely must also have strong preferences. Recall that Bio only scored 39.5 percent of the vote. More than 60 percent of delegates still rejected his group's pressure.

The best explanation for Bio's victory in plain political science analysis is the voting system and fielding of too many candidates for the same post. Immediately I saw the results for the chairmanship position in which Abbas Bundu, the reported candidate of the Bio camp, obtained 35 percent of the votes, I concluded that Bio stood a very strong chance of winning the election if those who voted for Bundu decided to vote for him and the remaining 65 percent of the votes were spread equally among the other 18 candidates. Under the first-past-the-post rules the party adopted, and with 19 candidates, it is quite possible for a winner to have emerged with even less than 6 percent of the votes. A candidate that appeals to the party's ethno-regional base could have been defeated if a majoritarian system, such as the alternative vote, had been used that ranks candidates and progressively distributes the second and other preference votes of last-placed candidates to top candidates until a winner emerges with more than 50 percent of the votes.

Kallon also states that he spoke to delegates at the convention who told him that the reason they voted for Bio was because he brought democracy to Sierra Leone that lifted the SLPP out of the political wilderness. Marx once famously remarked in his critique of empiricism that 'things do not always appear as they are; a stick dipped in water may appear broken when in actual fact it is not'. It is poor scholarship to accept what people say at face value. The job of an analyst is to get behind ideological justification of choices and reveal what people really want and do. Recall that Foday Sankoh and the RUF also told the public that their war was to liberate Sierra Leone from poverty, underdevelopment and corruption. Their actual practice revealed otherwise. I am not a party member but would like to believe that I am a good listener and do not respect political boundaries in my social interactions. The three hypotheses I posited on the choice of Bio are not mere inventions but reflect strongly held views among party supporters. There are many in the party who are not only chauvinistic but who believe that only a militarist like Bio stands a chance of winning power back from the APC since he has done it before. Urbane professionals with no history of political violence, such as Andrew Keili and the other Southern candidates, do not fit this bill and, therefore, lost out.

The third issue deals with Bio's past record as a military leader. Here the best submission of the three is by my good friend, Lans Gberie, who recognises the gravity of the issue of extra-judicial killings and calls on Bio to apologise to the public on behalf of the NPRC. I would like to remind Gberie that collective responsibility does not mean that no one is responsible even if they are not named individually; indeed, it means that all members of the NPRC government were responsible for the crime, which is very serious. To use a Krio proverb, *"noh wais yu fayn pauda pan kondo"* (when something is bad, no amount of facelift will make it look good). Let me also state that Bio's problem is not the overthrow of the APC—an act that was highly popular at the time. The NPRC coup, unlike that of the Armed Forces Revolutionary Council (AFRC) in 1997, enjoyed international recognition. The argument by APC partisans that Joseph Saidu Momoh's government was democratically elected and that he would have handed over power to a democratically elected government is hollow. Momoh's government was illegitimate, authoritarian and rotten to the core by the time the NPRC boys struck.

Equally nonsensical is the view that Bio is the father of Sierra Leone's democracy. Bio was literally forced down the path of democratisation by civil society, James Jonah (the elections chief), the international community and paramount chiefs who were fed up with the atrocities of both the RUF and sobels (soldiers turned rebels—a phenomenon that emerged during NPRC rule and reckless recruitment of marginalised youth on drugs into the army, as eloquently recorded in the Truth and Reconciliation Commission report). Indeed, it was under the NPRC that Sierra Leone achieved the notoriety of an archetypal state of "the coming anarchy" in the world system (See Robert Kaplan, *Atlantic Monthly*, February 1994).

Bio's problem is the extra-judicial killing of 26 or 29 citizens and, as has been alleged, the sale of state assets, such as our passports, for personal gain. There are laws of war even in the battlefield. For instance, it is criminal and morally repugnant to kill without trial opponents who have been arrested, and torture is abhorrent even if prisoners had also engaged in similar acts during the course of war. In Bio's case we are dealing with people who were unarmed, some already in prison, and all of whom were far removed from the theatre of war. Bio is on record in the Truth and Reconciliation Commission (TRC) report that he witnessed the torture of the victims. The questions posed by Citizen's Advocate in *Awareness Times* are poignant: As a citizen and a senior member of the government, what did he do to prevent the torture and killing of these people? As Secretary of State for Information (!), why did he not challenge the government's press release that the victims were tried by a military tribunal and found guilty of treason? The TRC report was very damning in its verdict: "The Commission is dumfounded to think that the Government of Captain Strasser, first killed people and then put them on trial"; and "The Commission holds all the leaders of the NPRC responsible for the murder of these men". The torture and subsequent extermination of these people reportedly at Lumley beach are a crime against humanity. As I intimated in my piece, the SLPP cannot bluff its way out of the mess it has inflicted upon itself. Contrary to what Kallon, Muana, Gberie and others may want to believe, the party and their flag bearer may have to contend with legal challenges, especially from family members of the victims, human rights groups, and governments that prohibit individuals with links to human rights violations from entering their countries.

Let me conclude by saying that it is the responsibility of intellectuals to provide a mirror to society for self-reflection, ask difficult questions, uphold ethical and human rights standards, and suggest options in terms of how to move forward. The most unfortunate thing that can happen to an intellectual is to be trapped in narrow, ideological and exclusionary partisan politics. It is a double tragedy when the partisan politics is bereft of developmental ideas and driven instead by ethno-regional sentiments.

24
Thoughts on Sierra Leone's 2012 Presidential Elections[24]

In less than three weeks, Sierra Leoneans will go the polls to elect a president, parliamentarians and local government officials. The contest that is most keenly watched and has raised the most heat is that of the presidency, which, because of its winner-takes-all character, will give the victor enormous powers to chart the country's development path in the next five years.

Each of the two main parties, the All People's Congress (APC) and the Sierra Leone People's Party (SLPP), is convinced that it has the numbers to clinch the top job, with APC partisans confident of victory on the first ballot.

It is difficult to predict election outcomes in countries where there is no tradition of scientific polls. Crowd turnout at rallies may provide insights, but can be misleading as Solomon Berewa (the SLPP's previous flag bearer) found out in 2007.

The situation is more complicated when the electorate is divided into two relatively equal ethno-regional blocs. In Sierra Leone's three previous elections, two (1996 and 2007) went into a run-off, and in the third (2002, which was a post-war election), the incumbent won handsomely in the first round with 70 percent of the votes.

Are we in a 2002 moment when the rhetoric of peace consolidation resonated widely with voters and gave the incumbent an overwhelming advantage over his challengers? Does the current government's rhetoric or narrative of development enjoy the same cross-country appeal as that of peace consolidation in 2002? Do ethno-regional sentiments still weigh heavily in the choices of voters? And do recent shifts in electoral demographics render the ethno-regional calculations of parties obsolete?

In this piece, I interrogate the contradictory claims of the two main parties using information from past voting behaviour and insights from current dynamics. The aim is to inject some "realism" into

---

[24] Published in *Patriotic Vanguard* (Vancouver), 29 October 2012; and *Sewa News* (London), 4 November 2012.

expectations by highlighting a variety of plausible paths and challenges that parties face in achieving desired outcomes.

Let us start with the SLPP. The source for the SLPP's electoral optimism can be traced to two issues that party chieftains believe are unlikely to be repeated in 2012: the schism that led to a third party, the People's Movement for Democratic Change (PMDC), in the South-East, and cancellation of votes from more than 400 polling stations in the party's stronghold of Kailahun. The PMDC took 41 percent of the votes in the South and 15 percent in the East in the 2007 election. Since the PMDC has lost its potency, SLPP partisans are convinced that the PMDC's voters will return home and give the SLPP the critical edge to win on the first or second ballot in 2012.

It is true that if Charles Margai's PMDC votes were added to Solomon Berewa's, the latter would have won the 2007 election with 52 percent of the votes. However, this view fails to take into account the profound change that has occurred in the electoral demographics with the introduction of the biometric voter registration system. Under the biometric system, Sierra Leone is being transformed into a lopsided bipolar polity. In 2007, the ratio of registered voters in the North and Western Area to the South and East was 55:45; in 2012, according to the National Electoral Commission's biometric registration figures for the three phases of the registration exercise, the North/Western Area—South/East difference has risen to more than 18 points, producing a ratio of 59.35:40.65.

All the three districts in the East (Kailahun, Kenema and Kono) lost voters in the biometric system of 2012; Bo and Moyamba made slight gains in the South, but Bonthe and Pujehun registered losses. The East lost a staggering 72,355 voters, with Kailahun losing 21 percent or 39,528 of its 2007 registered voters. In contrast, all districts in the North and Western Area gained voters, with Western Rural gaining 45 percent or 51,179 new voters. If Kono, which seems to have strongly tilted towards the APC after the 2008 local council elections, is removed from the South-East voting bloc, we are dealing with a ratio of 65.46:34.54.

Over-voting was observed in Kailahun, Pujehun and Bonthe in previous elections. In 1996, the elections office simply eliminated the excess votes, giving these districts a 100 perent voter turnout, which was far higher than the national average. In 2007, only Kailahun experienced over-voting, and the elections office cancelled the results from the polling stations where this occurred. The key question is: have some districts in the East and South been guilty of both over-registration and over-voting?

If the 2012 biometric voter registration list is used (voter turnout has tended to be relatively equal across regions, except for a few districts that have experienced over-voting), adding Margai's (PMDC) share of the South and East votes to Berewa's votes would have given the latter only 47 percent of the total votes; if Margai's Western Area votes are included (PMDC had a diverse following that transcended Southeasterners in Freetown), Berewa's total would have been 48.6 percent.

This suggests that simply maximising votes in the South and East will not be enough for Julius Maada Bio to win the presidency. He can force a run-off, but will not win without improving upon Berewa's performance in the North and Western Area. A 50 percent plus one majority in favour of Bio will require a 40 percent share of the Western Area vote (Berewa received 31 percent) and at least 18 percent of the Northern vote (Berewa received 15 percent). If the goal is to win on the first ballot, then Bio's share of the Northern vote will have to be more than 30 percent.

The possibility of Bio achieving these results cannot be ruled out in the absence of credible polls. However, such a spectacular feat in the Western Area and North will require that he also wins back the mass of Kono voters in the East who switched to the APC in the 2008 local elections, as well as check the inroads that the APC is reported to be making in Kailahun, Kenema and Pujehun as an incumbent party with resources to undertake visible vote-catching projects and activities. My impression, after three months in the country, is that Bio is less popular than his party; he has a difficult path to cause an upset.

What about the APC? There is high expectation among the party faithful of a landslide victory that is comparable to what Ahmad Tejan Kabbah of the SLPP achieved in 2002. How realistic is this expectation? The 2002 landslide can be explained by two factors. The first was the trauma of the war and voters' desire for peace (largely assured by the United Nations and British military presence) and the association of peace with the policies of the incumbent government. The second was the collapse of the two main parties in the North, the United National People's Party and the People's Democratic Party, and the absorption of a large number of their leaders into the SLPP. The APC in 2002 was still in the process of reinventing itself and did not offer the kind of virulent opposition it has received from the SLPP between 2007 and 2012.

The APC in 2012 faces an energised SLPP that has accused the government of undermining the assumed national cohesion of 2002-7 by removing Southeasterners from top public sector jobs and running a Northern-dominated government. This discourse is very strong among core supporters of the party in Freetown, who are generally dismissive of even the positive developments the country is experiencing under the current government. The discourse of this group resonates with a large part of the 31 percent of voters in the Western Area who supported Berewa during the first and second rounds of the 2007 elections. This should not be surprising as it is in Freetown that competition for jobs and resources is fiercest.

The APC has countered this discourse by pointing to the government's development record, which, it argues, is ethnicity and region-blind. Road construction, the free health care for special groups, and agricultural support schemes are visible in most parts of the country. The implication of this argument is that 'inclusive and transformative development' compensates for the shortcomings in 'inclusive government'.

Has the electorate across the country bought the rhetoric of transformative and inclusive development? This is not the place to evaluate the impact of the government's development programme. In the larger scheme of things, using any socio-economic yardstick, Sierra Leone is without doubt very far from being a transformed economy, society or polity.

However, what I have found in my three months in the country is that people compare what was there before 2007 and what is there now. In Freetown, most people I spoke to complained about the high cost of living, but were also quick to point to the now fairly regular electricity supply (thanks, perhaps, to the rainy season; I went to bed without light only once in three months!), the number of roads under construction, and the free health care for special groups, which were not there when the SLPP was in power. My sense is that Koroma is hugely popular in the city—he seems to be much more popular than his party. In a country with a low literacy rate and countless broken promises from politicians, voters attach less importance to manifestos or promises than to what parties actually do in office. On this score, I feel that the government is winning the argument in Freetown in a big way.

Does the government's argument enjoy support in the South and East? The kind of landslide expected by party activists is only possible if Koroma makes substantial inroads in the South and East. Maximising votes in the North and Western Area will not be enough to achieve this feat.

Let us look at some numbers and possible paths or outcomes. If Ernest Bai Koroma repeats his first round performance of 2007 in 2012, he is likely to get about 47 percent of the votes, which suggests a run-off. If he repeats his second round performance of 2007 when many of the votes of the PMDC and other parties were transferred to him, he will get about 56 percent of the vote, avoiding a run-off. A third path will be if he repeats his second round performance in 2007 in the North (85 percent) and Western Area (69 percent), maximises the Kono vote (to say 70 percent) and repeats his first round 2007 performances in the South, Kailahun and Kenema. This will yield about 54 percent of the vote, which is still short of the magic 55 percent to avoid a run-off. If he raises his votes in the Western Area to 75 percent and to 90 percent in the North (Northern parties obtained 91 percent of the votes in the first round of the 1996 presidential election) and assumptions for Kono and other districts in the East and South remain the same as in the previous scenario, he is likely to get 57 percent of the votes and win on the first ballot.

This suggests that the landslide that the party expects can only happen if Koroma exceeds his second round performance of 2007. With the rupture of the alliance with the PMDC, this will amount to the East and South voting for the government's avowed development record in large numbers.

I offer three scenarios by way of conclusion. First, there could be a run-off; however, it might be a different kind of run-off in which the front-runner scores more than 50 percent of the votes and does not require new votes to win in the second round. The absence of a strong third party in 2012 makes it possible for a winner to score more than 50 percent of the votes on the first ballot. Second, it is also very possible for Koroma to win on the first ballot, but this may not be a landslide. Third, a landslide will occur only if the reported inroads the party claims to have made in the East and South translate into real votes. *Over to you voters.*

25

Lopsided Bipolarity: Lessons from the 2012 Elections[25]

The results of the 2012 elections confirm a point in my previous piece ("Thoughts on Sierra Leone's 2012 Presidential Elections") that Sierra Leone is being transformed into a lopsided bipolar polity. Bipolarity in this context refers to a situation in which two ethnic groups or ethno-regional blocs dominate politics and influence voting behaviour. It does not mean that every person in each of the contending blocs votes the same way, but the majority often do. The two groups or blocs can be relatively equal, as in Fiji, Guyana and Trinidad, or unequal, as in Rwanda, Burundi, Belgium and Latvia.

In a 15-country study I coordinated at the UN Research Institute for Social Development (Y. Bangura (ed.), *Ethnic Inequalities and Public Sector Governance*, Palgrave Macmillan 2006), we showed that for countries with highly fragmented ethnic structures, such as Tanzania, in which no group has the numerical strength to dominate politics or construct a regional coalition for governance, successful parties are likely to be substantially multi-ethnic, producing a highly representative public sector. The difficult cases are countries with bipolar or tripolar (Nigeria, Malaysia) ethnic cleavages, which tend to generate a politics of exclusion and militant or zero-sum types of contestation. We argued that achieving stability and cohesion in these types of countries will require ethnicity-sensitive institutions and policies.

Prior to the 2012 elections, most informed analysts would agree with the characterisation of Sierra Leone as a relatively equal bipolar polity. This old model of bipolarity can be summarised as follows: the two main ethnic groups, the Mende and Temne, are roughly equal in size, accounting for about 60 per cent of the population; the two groups are also geographically separated, with the Mende located in the South and East, and the Temne in the North and Western Area. The fact that the two largest groups vastly outnumber other groups in their respective regions may explain why most groups in the South and East coalesce

---

[25] Published in *Patriotic Vanguard* (Vancouver), 3 December 2012; and *Cocorioko* (New York), 3 December 2012.

around the Mende, whereas those in the North revolve around the Temne. The voter registration list of 2007, which showed a ratio of 55:45 for the registered voters in the North and Western Area vis-à-vis the South and East, seemed to support this model of equi-bipolarity.

However, the 2012 biometric voter registration system, which makes it difficult, if not impossible, to over-register voters, has produced a ratio of 59.35:40.65 for the two ethno-regional blocs, suggesting a lopsided bipolarity in favour of the North-Western Area. The East lost more than 72,000 voters, with Kailahun (where the ballots in 477 polling stations were voided in 2007 because of over-voting) losing 21 percent of its 2007 registered voters. SLPP partisans have always maintained that the cancellation of those Kailahun ballots cost them "hundreds of thousands of votes", which would have tilted the outcome of the election in their favour.

However, any close look at the 2007 registration and voting data for Kailahun will show that this is a spurious claim. If we assume that "hundreds of thousands" is at least 200,000, it means that the SLPP had 325,414 votes in Kailahun (it received 125,414 votes in the second round), when the total number of registered voters in that district was 185,583.

The key question is whether the lopsidedness in voting power between the two ethno-regional blocs is a recent phenomenon, or it has been there for some time but suppressed since 1996 by over-registration of voters in the South and East. It is difficult to believe that this lopsidedness will be corrected in a future registration exercise, as some have argued, when voters in the South-East will register in large numbers. Interestingly, the ethno-regional imbalance has also been revealed in data on middle school enrolment. Figures released for the Basic Education Certificate Examination (BECE) for 2012 show that the North and Western Area accounted for 63.5 per cent and the South and East 36.48 per cent of the 82,907 students who took the examination. The North accounted for 30.5 per cent and the Western Area 33 per cent, compared to 21.4 per cent for the East and 15 per cent for the South. Such figures should caution those who believe that the sharp reduction of registered voters in the South and East was because people in those two regions failed to register for the 2012 elections.

The elections of 1967, 1996, 2007 and 2012 showed a strong pattern of ethno-regional voting. It was only in 2002 that a single party won a landslide, or 70 percent of the votes. Therefore, analysis of the 2012 elections results will have to start from the lopsidedness in the electoral demographics, which the biometric system has revealed.

In an equi-bipolar electorate, it is difficult for a winner to get more than 55 percent of the votes on the first ballot. However, Ernest Koroma has been able to avoid a run-off because of the lopsidedness in the regional distribution of voters in favour of his traditional strongholds (the North and Western Area), his achievement of a comfortable majority in Kono in the East, and penetration of his opponent's strongholds in Kailahun (22.7 percent in 2012 versus 5 percent during the first round in 2007), Kenema (18.7 percent in 2012 versus 12 percent in 2007), Pujehun (15.5 percent in 2012 versus 2.8 percent in 2007) and Moyamba (26 percent in 2012 versus 18 percent in 2007). He also raised his share of the votes in Bo (16.7 percent versus 10.9 percent in 2007) and Bonthe (11.7 percent versus 3 percent in 2007). Indeed, Koroma improved upon his 2007 performance in all the 14 electoral districts.

One major lesson of the results is that even though the regional distribution of voters favoured Koroma, he was only able to avoid a run-off when his votes in the South and Eastern districts of Kailahun and Kenema were added to the votes he received in the North, Western Area and Kono. In 2007, he could not have won the second round ballot without Charles Margai's PMDC votes in the South and East. However, Koroma did not need the PMDC alliance in 2012. Amazingly, he scored more votes combined in Kailahun, Kenema and the four Southern districts in 2012 than when he had Margai's help in the second round of 2007. The big loser in the breakup of the alliance is the PMDC, which lost all its parliamentary seats to the SLPP and can boast of only one local council member in Pujehun.

In 2012, if Koroma had relied only on the North and Western Area, he would have scored only 48.6 per cent of the vote; adding Kono would have raised his share of the vote to 51.6 per cent; his votes in Kailahun and Kenema get him to 54.5 per cent. It is only when the Southern votes are added that he crosses the magic 55 per cent that guarantees him victory on the first ballot. This suggests that maximising votes in the North, Western Area and Kono will only deliver a second ballot victory.

I commend the framers of the 1991 constitution, which requires a winning candidate to score more than 55 per cent of the vote to avoid a run-off. In a bipolar polity, this rule forces candidates to construct winning coalitions beyond their traditional strongholds. To the best of my knowledge, Sierra Leone is the only country that has this 55 per cent rule on diversity management in electing leaders. In Nigeria, the winner in a presidential election must obtain at least 25 per cent of the votes in two thirds of the states.

The results show that there is a strong SLPP presence in Kono, which even Koroma's Kono running mate, Sam Sumana, was unable to comprehensively dislodge. Kono seems to be the only "battleground district" in the country, if such a characterisation is applicable in a presidential system that is based on the popular vote that forces candidates to maximise votes everywhere. I suspect that the ethnic Kono vote was split almost equally between Koroma and Bio. Northern parties have always performed well in Kono because of the large number of Northerners in this diamond-rich district. These Northern voters may have tilted the balance in favour of Koroma to give him a comfortable win of 58 percent in the district. In 1996, the United National People's Party and the People's Democratic Party (both Northern parties) received more than a quarter of the Kono vote. In the first round election of 2007, when Sam Sumana's influence in the district was minimal (he lost the parliamentary contest in his own area), Koroma received 35 percent of the Kono vote.

What accounts for Koroma's respectable numbers in Kailahun, Kenema, Moyamba and Pujehun? One interesting highlight is that Koroma is the first president in our history to ask voters to judge him on his development record. This is a boon for our young democracy as voters may in future be encouraged to transcend ethnic loyalties and assess leaders on public policy issues.

The Old APC of Siaka Stevens and Joseph Momoh could not deliver on development and relied on repression and single party elections to stay in power. The key message of Kabbah's SLPP in 2002 was peace, reconciliation, resettlement and humanitarian assistance--not development. In contrast, Koroma was very confident that his record on road construction, electricity, free health care for special vulnerable groups, and agricultural support schemes in the 149 chiefdoms would trump ethnic loyalties and deliver a large part of the South and East to the party. Any objective evaluation of these programmes will surely find shortcomings, some of which are very serious. However, voters tend to compare what was there before 2007 and what is there now.

The results suggest that the expectations of a landslide (he received a comfortable 58.7 percent of the vote) were largely misplaced, but solid inroads were made in the South-East. We do not have exit polls like those in the United States that gauge voter preferences on a range of issues on polling day. However, it is quite possible that visible infrastructural and social programmes on the ground, however imperfect or incomplete, as well as the large number of defections of prominent SLPP activists to the APC before the elections may have convinced many people to vote for Koroma and his party. However, perceptions by South-Eastern elites that Koroma was running a Northern-dominated government may have also blunted the appeal of the development discourse among the majority of South-Eastern voters. This suggests that the APC can only get a landslide victory if it runs a more-inclusive government. It certainly needs the support of South-Eastern voters to avoid a run-off.

Why did the SLPP perform so poorly---scoring only 37.4 percent of the votes in the presidential election? What lessons can the party draw from the new reality of lopsided bipolarity? Bio's 37.4 percent share of the vote is the worst performance by an SLPP flag bearer in any competitive election. Solomon Berewa, who lost the 2007 election, received 38.3 percent of the vote on the first ballot and 45.4 percent in the second round. The appropriate comparison should actually be Bio's first round performance (there was no strong third party in 2012) and Berewa's second round performance when the third party had been eliminated from the race.

The results suggest that the party gambled very badly on its flag bearer. In an equi-bipolar electorate, a party can rely largely on its stronghold and hope for a few decisive votes from its opponent's stronghold to clinch victory. Both the APC and SLPP have historically used this strategy to win elections, which explains why the two parties are still largely ethno-regional institutions. However, in a lopsided bipolar electorate that favours the North-West, this strategy is no longer feasible for the SLPP. The party needs to get out of its ethno-regional cocoon and effectively engage voters in the North and Western Area if it wants to bounce back to power. This requires a flag bearer with cross-regional appeal, which Julius Maada Bio was unable to provide.

The results in the North and Western Area reveal the following: Bio is less popular than the SLPP, which is less popular than the APC, which is less popular than Koroma. Bio performed worse than the SLPP parliamentarians in the North and Western Area, whereas Koroma outperformed his party's parliamentarians in the two regions. Many parliamentarians and councilors, especially the councilors in Freetown, may have benefited from Koroma's popularity to win seats. The magic slogan was 4For4---a call on voters to cast all four ballots for the president, MPs, mayors and councilors for the APC candidates (the Freetown city council of 2008-12 behaved like the Old APC—its record of service delivery was a real disaster; therefore, 4For4 was a boon for the councilors).

Bio performed worse than Berewa in the North-West. Berewa got 31 percent of the votes in the Western Area, whereas Bio could only manage 26 percent; and Berewa received 15 percent of the Northern vote, while Bio scored a miserable 6 percent in that region. Koroma, on the other hand, increased his performance in the two regions: 72 percent in 2012 as opposed to 69 percent in 2007 in the Western Area; and 87.5 percent in 2012 as opposed to 85 percent in 2007 in the North. The SLPP lost its three parliamentary seats in the North, failed to win a single seat in Freetown for the second time in two consecutive elections, and has been reduced to a regional party. I wonder what the founding fathers would be saying about a party that was founded on the slogan "one country, one people".

The SLPP faced two problems in 2012: a self-inflicted unpopular flag bearer; and a very popular opponent in the North and Western Area. The party was unable to ward off the very serious allegations against Bio on matters such as the extra-judicial killing of 29 citizens when he served the regime of the National Provisional Ruling Council in 1992-96; and the sale of passports and award of contracts for helicopter parts for self-enrichment. The interesting point is that it was the former SLPP president, Ahmad Tejan Kabbah, and Solomon Berewa, the party's flag bearer in 2007, who first made the corruption allegations against Bio when the party was in power. It did not dawn on the party members that their persistent allegations of corruption against Koroma's government could only be credible if they had a clean flag bearer. When the APC lost the confidence of the electorate after its disastrous rule in the 1970s and

1980s, it reinvented itself by electing a leader who was not implicated in the corruption and human rights violations of the party.

The SLPP was not able to explain why Bio got stuck in Canada and could not travel to the United States to honour a series of widely publicised party events. It reinforced the belief among many people that he was denied a visa to the US because of his past human rights record. The party refused to change gear, but its stubbornness only resonated with its core supporters in the South-East and parts of the Western Area. One of the low points in the campaign was when the party tried to rewrite its own history of active participation in the forces that fought against the attempted prolongation of NPRC rule in 1996 by supporting Bio's ridiculous claim that he is the "father of democracy".

The results reveal that the SLPP enjoys about a quarter of the votes in the Western Area. It has about 120,000 votes in Freetown, which is the third district after Bo and Kenema that gave Bio the most votes. His Freetown votes are enough to mobilise large crowds during election rallies and give the impression of competitiveness in the capital. Half of these voters can fill the national stadium (30,000; plus 10-15,000 for the football and track areas) without importing supporters from elsewhere as alleged by APC partisans and commentators. But the SLPP is outnumbered by about three to one by the APC, making this region an APC stronghold.

The APC has consistently relied on a Northern-Krio coalition to win the Western Area, starting from the 1967 elections when the party won all the seats. This coalition accounts for perhaps about seventy or seventy five percent of the Western Area electorate. The only time the SLPP made inroads in the Western Area was in 1996 when the North fragmented into multiple parties, and in 2002 when voters wanted the incumbent to continue with the policy of peace consolidation, which boiled down to the security provided by the United Nations and British military forces. The APC has been adept at managing the Northern-Krio coalition, such as the informal rule that grants the party's mayoral ticket to Krio politicians, even though the Krio are outnumbered by Northerners in Freetown. There is no sign of a similar coalition being constructed by the SLPP.

Managing bipolarity

How can bipolarity be tamed or managed? First, it is crucial to note that bipolarity of whatever type may encourage opportunistic behavior by politicians, which may undermine national cohesion and stability. The situation may even be more dangerous in a lopsided bipolar polity, which may condemn losers to permanent or long-term opposition. Sierra Leone needs to re-engineer its politics in ways that can allow politicians and voters to transcend bipolarity.

There are two diametrically opposed options: power sharing, involving the participation of the SLPP in government; and transforming the main parties into truly multiethnic institutions and setting rules that will facilitate formation of inclusive governments. The first option will be bad for development, since the government will lack the scrutiny and bite of an effective opposition to get things done. There will be no incentive to perform since a share of power will be guaranteed to all key parties. I suspect that the commitment that Koroma has shown in implementing his development agenda can partly be traced to the uncertainty of electoral outcomes and his fear of losing the presidency to the opposition. Power sharing, or a government of national unity, makes sense only when a country is at war or facing a generalised and protracted crisis.

The second option is a winner-takes-all settlement with a difference. It aims to transform the key parties into truly multi-ethnic entities and ensure fair distribution of government posts to reflect the ethno-regional character of the country. Transforming the political parties is a medium-to-long term project that will require constitutional reforms. In the short term, Koroma could start by ensuring that each of our 14 electoral districts has a full cabinet minister. In a cabinet of 24 members, the remaining 10 posts can be filled in such a way that the final distribution gives the South-East at least 40 percent of the total cabinet posts. It should be the prerogative of the President to appoint the ministers, who will serve in his pleasure.

There is no valid reason why some districts can boast of three or four ministers when others have only one or none. With the inroads that the party has made in the East and South, it should not be difficult to find suitable people from those regions. I will even add that the party will go a long way in shedding its image as a Northern institution if it chooses a Southerner as its flag bearer in 2017. Koroma received 149,021 votes in the 6 Mende-dominated South-East districts, compared to his 67,238 votes in Kono. The myth that the SLPP is in the DNA of all Mende, who will never vote for any other party, let alone the APC, has been deflated in two consecutive elections. The ethnic Kono vote is important, especially at the parliamentary level, but readers may be surprised to know that more Mende than Kono voted for Koroma. It is instructive to note that in Nigeria, each of the 36 states is entitled to a cabinet minister, and the ruling party has a policy in which its flag bearer alternates between the North and South.

A bigger challenge faces the SLPP. Its refusal to accept the elections results, even though all the international and domestic observer groups have given the elections a fairly clean bill of health, and instructions to its MPs and councilors to boycott parliament and local government institutions, puts it on a slippery slope with unpredictable outcomes. I suspect that there will be a backlash from MPs and councilors who will be eager to take up their new jobs as the stalemate continues and the fear of losing their seats becomes imminent. Interestingly, the flag bearer and top members of the party executive are not prospective holders of national elective offices; therefore, their threshold level for risk taking that can cause instability can be very low.

Quite frankly, the party's reaction to the results borders on the infantile. It is comical to expect "the international community" to investigate the party's claims of rigged elections. What about our courts? Why are they being ignored? Which organ of the "international community" should carry out the investigation—the UN, which has already praised the elections and called on all parties to accept the results? ECOWAS? The African Union? The European Union? The Commonwealth? The US? Britain? Since all these entities believe that the elections were largely free and transparent, accepting the SLPP's demands will mean that these organisations and states will have to negate their own judgement.

Conflict analysis teaches that when a party side-steps formal institutions and legal processes, it may open itself up to capture by more extreme elements that may eventually call the shots, using even violent means to achieve their aims. The Kenya option of violence, paralysis and ultimately power sharing that has been advocated by some party activists may be difficult to replicate because the balance of power and opinion at the domestic and international levels does not favour the SLPP. However, by boycotting our legislative institutions and ignoring our courts, the party may well believe that it can still delegitimise the government, discredit public institutions, paralyse the political process, and ultimately get a share of power without firing a bullet or inciting violence. The party should avoid boxing itself into a corner like the RUF and AFRC in the 1990s, whose leaders foolishly believed that they could impose their will on the majority of Sierra Leoneans and the rest of the world.

It is obvious that the SLPP needs a New Direction that will prepare it for governance through the ballot box. Insisting on the current path of non-cooperation will delay the need for critical reflection and blue sky thinking unfettered by old myths and calculations. The party needs to absorb the implications of the new reality of lopsided bipolarity and strategise on how to overcome it. It needs to fully transcend the South-East, which now provides it with all its MPs and local councilors. It cannot afford to be perceived as a protest party that is not ready for governance.

Even though the APC is currently dominant in our politics, it is not immune from defeat. Firstly, a broad coalition is often difficult to manage. Success often contains the seeds of failure. Now that the party has become much more national, there are likely to be tensions within it as individuals from different parts of the coalition struggle for dominance. These struggles are likely to intensify as we approach 2017 and the party begins the process of electing a new flag bearer. A re-fragmentation of the North into multiple parties or defection of some non-Northern parts of the coalition should not be ruled out. Intra-party squabbles that encourage splits and cross-overs often occur in political settings where the parties are less driven by ideology or core values and politicians are often in the game largely to enhance their self-interests. On this score, there really is no difference between the APC and SLPP.

Second, it is true that the electoral demographics when combined with an effective implementation of the government's Agenda for Prosperity that may be fueled by billions of dollars of new investments in the mining sector may be a nightmare for the SLPP in 2017. However, if the government fails to deliver jobs, food security and housing for the poor and lower middle income earners, a party that is anchored in popular aspirations with a non-ethnic agenda could cause an upset and exploit the divisions that are likely to emerge within the APC. The more the party's discourse focuses on development, the more voters will be less likely to be beholden to ethnic loyalty and to demand instead their own share of the development dividend. The problem with the SLPP is that it is not good at connecting with popular or subaltern groups in Freetown. Will a new leadership or party emerge with a new vision for the masses?

I will end with a note on the National Electoral Commission (NEC). There is no doubt that NEC deserves the praise it has received from all the observer groups that monitored the elections. Organising multiple elections with a new voter registration system is not an easy task. However, it should be obvious that NEC still has some house cleaning to do. According to the NEC Chair, Christiana Thorpe, over-voting took place in only five polling stations in the Western Area. I would like to believe that there should be zero tolerance for over-voting in even one polling station.

Over-voting is not supposed to happen under the new biometric system without the complicity of NEC officials in the affected polling stations. It means that there are still bad apples in NEC who are not afraid to flout the rules and regulations. Over-voting can only occur if people who are not on the register of a polling station are allowed to vote. Other lapses, such as missing registers in some stations, use of mobile phones to provide light in some stations, and failure to post the results on the walls of some polling stations need to be fixed. These are basic flaws that should not be allowed to reoccur.

26
Unelected Party Leaders and the Supremacy of Parliament[26]

The press release reportedly issued by three leaders of Sierra Leone's opposition parties, the Sierra Leone People's Party (SLPP), the People's Movement for Democratic Change (PMDC) and the National Democratic Alliance (NDA), instructing members of parliament of their respective parties to boycott parliament is a challenge to the supremacy of parliament and independence of parliamentarians. The action may undermine one of the key arms of government and shift parliamentary power to individuals and institutions that lack popular mandates.

In well-established democracies, parliamentarians represent the will of the people; they make the laws and scrutinise the policies of the executive, which cannot spend or raise money without parliamentary approval. Parliamentarians' right to perform these tasks rests on the fact that they are the direct representatives of the people. In early times of direct democracy, when people had the time, ability or resources to represent their interests directly, and when the affairs of state were less complex and organised in small city states or village republics, there was no need for intermediaries or representatives. Today, no democracy can function without representatives. But these representatives have to earn their power of representation through elections. It is the only way they can legitimately claim to be the bearers of the interests of the people.

In modern democracies, political parties attempt to aggregate the interests of the people, since it is impossible for every individual interest to be heard in the public arena. And in any case, many of the core interests that people hold dearly tend to cluster, making it easier for parties to aggregate choices and for individuals to choose among parties that are best suited to represent their interests. This gives party leaders considerable powers in shaping the direction of public policy. However, it should always be clear that party leaders are not popularly elected unless when they also win elections for parliament or the presidency.

Under a parliamentary system of government, the party leader is also a member of parliament and acts within the confines of the

---

[26] Published in *Cocorioko* (New York), 21 October 2011.

parliamentary system when he/she mobilises other party members for collective action. MPs can be influenced by extra-parliamentary politics, and, indeed, should listen to the voices of voters who put them in parliament. But even electors cannot dictate to their MPs. If they are dissatisfied with the performance of their MPs, they have to wait until the next election when they can exercise their right of recall and elect someone else to represent their interests. Even party leaders in parliamentary democracies do not enjoy automatic loyalty from parliamentary members of their party. This is why party leaders appoint whips whose job is to ensure maximum support for the party leaders' positions in parliament. The fact that it does not always work underscores the point that MPs are, in principle, autonomous actors who are expected to use their individual judgement to defend the will of their electors.

In presidential systems of government, party leaders may find themselves out of parliament, especially if their party is in the opposition. However, when this happens, it is the party leader in parliament (referred to as Minority Leader, if the party does not have the majority of the seats) who decides how the party should conduct itself in parliament. This ensures the independence of MPs and supremacy of the legislature over parties. It is only in communist systems that MPs are less powerful than party leaders and politburo members. For instance, it will be unthinkable for the party chairman of the Republican Party to instruct Republicans on how to act in the US Senate or House of Representatives. The best that the party leader can do is to influence the positions of party members in the legislature through informal party channels. Indeed, because of the supremacy of parliament in democracies, when party leaders are not in parliament, their job of directing party affairs becomes largely administrative.

In Sierra Leone, it seems that our parliamentarians do not really cherish the job of being parliamentarians. The job seems to be second choice, thus attracting the least powerful, influential or talented among party members. It is clearly an affront to parliamentary leaders of the SLPP and PMDC and a betrayal of the people's trust for them to take instructions from individuals who are not members of parliament. What this suggests is that the powerful members of our political parties are not in parliament. This applies to both the SLPP and All People's Congress (APC). In the case of the SLPP, the strong members of the party did not contest the parliamentary elections of 2007 because of confidence that the party's presidential candidate would win and they would get back their ministerial posts. We need only to compare the calibre of the 19 aspirants for the post of flag bearer of the party for the 2012 presidential elections and that of their current MPs to see where the best or strongest members want to be. Similarly, some of the strong members of the APC contested the parliamentary elections of 2007 because of uncertainty about the outcome of the presidential election. However, as soon as the party won the presidency, some of the MPs exerted pressure on the president to be made ministers. The Majority Leader of the party even preferred a diplomatic posting to the job of Majority Leader. Imagine John Boehner of the US Republican Party giving up his powerful job when he was Majority Leader of the House of Representatives from 2006-2007 for an ambassadorial post.

What is also troubling about recent developments is that the SLPP now seems to have two leaders: John Benjamin, who doubles as party leader and chairman, and Julius Maada Bio, the flag bearer. There are persistent reports even from newspapers sympathetic to the SLPP that the two do not get along very well. We should be wary of remote control of leaders in our democratic institutions. Nigeria suffered such a fate during its First Republic when the most powerful figure of the land, the leader of the Northern People's Congress (NPC), the Sardauna of Sokoto, refused to lead the NPC in the federal executive and decided instead to opt for the regional post of Northern Premier. He allowed Abubakar Tafewa Balewa to become the Prime Minister and leader of the country, but real power rested with the Sardauna, who pulled the strings from Kaduna, the capital of the Northern region. The federal polity was unsustainable under such arrangements, and it fell in 1966.

In a young democracy such as ours, it is dysfunctional for party leaders who do not want to be mere administrators of party affairs to operate outside of parliament. Since they are not in parliament where negotiations and compromises define the dynamics of parliamentary activities, the threshold level of party leaders for risk-taking that can lead to instability can be very low. If party leaders want to be powerful leaders of their parties, then their parties should endeavour to make them parliamentarians, as happened when Ernest Koroma and John Karefa Smart were in parliament as leaders of the APC and the United National People's Party respectively. If party leaders do not want to be in parliament then they should refrain from controlling the activities of parliamentarians.

I will end by stating that this note is not about the series of complaints made in the press release of the opposition parties. It is about the dangers of extra-parliamentary forces usurping the powers of parliament and parliamentarians. I consider one of the complaints –the delay in publishing and acting on the Shears-Moses Report—valid. If we are to succeed in fighting political violence, then all violence should be treated with an even hand. Having said this, I believe that the appropriate step the opposition parties should have taken is to have their parliamentarians raise the issue in parliament before resorting to boycotts, especially when it has been reported that a white paper is being prepared on the issue.

27
The Electoral College and Representation: Right Direction, Wrong Track[27]

Sierra Leone's two main political parties, the All People's Congress (APC) and the Sierra Leone People's Party (SLPP), have introduced new rules for choosing candidates for the forthcoming parliamentary and local council elections. The rules seek to give more say to voters at the constituency level than was the case in previous elections when party big wigs called the shots. Both parties are aware that the award of party symbols by the party hierarchy had in the past been fraught with problems, as defeated candidates transferred their loyalties to other parties or became less enthusiastic in campaigning for winning candidates or working for their parties in general elections.

Under the new rules, the APC has adopted what it calls an electoral college: influential voters in the constituencies who putatively represent key groups, such as traders, drivers, okada bike riders, hunting and Bondo societies, teachers, religious bodies and other community-based organisations are identified by a committee of the party to act as an electoral college.

The SLPP, on the other hand, has appointed committees to assess the popularity of contestants by speaking to groups and individuals in the various constituencies. The party strives for a consensus candidate after such consultations, and holds elections that are similar to those of an electoral college if divisions are irreconcilable.

The new rules for selecting the flag bearers of the two parties are clearly a step in the right direction. First, they are likely to ensure that those selected will enjoy broad support within their party in the constituency they seek to represent rather than rely on the patronage of powerful individuals in the party hierarchy.

Second, the rules may have the added advantage of making incumbents work hard in defending the interests of their constituents. This may introduce a double process of holding office holders to

[27] Published in *Sierra Express Media* (Freetown) 20 September 2012 ; *This is Sierra Leone,* September 2012 ; *Patriotic Vanguard* (Vancouver), 19 September 2012;

account: within the parties at the primaries, and between the parties during general elections.

This double process of accountability is especially important in constituencies where one party is overwhelmingly dominant and voters are reluctant to switch allegiances even when their traditional party has performed poorly in office. In such situations, the electoral college may offer a party the opportunity to renew itself by replacing incumbents who are perceived to have underperformed. Already, the primaries for local councils have produced many surprises, with many incumbents, including mayors and chairpersons, losing elections. We should expect future incumbents to work harder in improving the lives of their constituents if they are to be assured of re-election.

However, the actual operation of the electoral college has thrown up a number of problems that are likely to discredit the system and undermine the goal of popular democracy at the grassroots level. Three such problems stand out. First, the primaries for local councils have shown that party leaders and executive members in local constituencies, who are also members of the electoral college, wield undue influence over the selection of individuals from various community groups in constituting the electoral college. There have been a large number of complaints that those entrusted to organise the elections at the local level skew the selection process in favour of candidates of their choice. One women's leader at Aberdeen complained that her name was removed from the list of delegates because she was suspected of supporting a candidate that did not enjoy the confidence of the committee. This problem will not be eliminated even if, as is being suggested by some party officials, the selection committee is made up of "neutral" individuals who do not have voting rights in the constituency.

Second, because of the small size of the electoral college (it varies from 100–200 members), it is easy for rich candidates to bribe voters at the primaries. One incumbent parliamentarian from a constituency in Kambia has complained that two of his challengers from the Diaspora with strong financial resources have been distributing money and goods to members of the electoral college in his constituency.

Third, the preferences of group representatives (such as those for okada riders, traders, market women, teachers, etc.) who constitute the electoral college do not always reflect the wishes of the individuals they claim to represent. This is especially the case when elections are not held by the groups to determine the individuals who should represent them and express their voting preferences in the electoral college.

These three problems can be overcome by giving the vote to party members at the constituency level, as happens in mature democracies. Empowering local party members with one vote each to choose their representatives will check the biases of party leaders, ensure a level playing field for all candidates, and make it more costly to bribe voters. It will deepen the democratic process; force incumbents to deliver on promises; as well as improve local party organisation, recruitment of party members, and systematic updating of membership lists. It will also encourage active citizenship and party activism at the local level.

28

The Will of the People Transcends the Will of Parties in Presidential Democracies[28]

Sierra Leone has been plunged into a major constitutional crisis following the President's decision to sack the Vice President.

The President based his decision on three grounds: having been expelled from the ruling All People's Congress (APC), the Vice President is no longer a member of a political party, which the President claims is a "continuous requirement" for the post of VP; Section 40 (1) of the 1991 constitution gives the President "supreme executive authority" to relieve the VP of his post without going through parliament as stipulated in Sections 50 and 51 of the constitution; and by seeking asylum from a foreign embassy, the VP abandoned his job, demonstrating an unwillingness to serve the people of Sierra Leone.

Eminent legal scholars and practitioners, including the erudite jurist and chief architect of the 1991 constitution, Justice Abdulai Conteh, have challenged the legality of the President's action; and the Vice President has petitioned the Supreme Court to deliver a verdict on the issue.

The two questions posed by the VP's legal team to the Supreme Court are simple, clear and to the point: whether the President can sack the Vice President without using the parliamentary procedures in Sections 50 and 51 of the constitution; and whether the President's "supreme executive authority" mentioned in Section 40 (1) of the constitution includes the power to sack the Vice President without using the procedures of Sections 50 and 51 of the constitution.

My contribution in this piece is on the danger of the idea of "continuous requirement" of membership of a political party for the posts of President and Vice President.

Political parties aggregate voter choices by selecting individuals to contest public office and advancing policies that represent the

---

[28] Published in *Awoko* (Freetown), 31 March 2015; *APC Times* (All Peoples Communication, On-line Sierra Leone News) 27 March 2015; *The Sewa Chronicle* (London), 27 March 2015; *Daily Trust* (Kaduna), 31 March 2015; *This is Sierra Leone*, March 2015.

preferences of voters. Although sovereignty belongs to the people, direct democracy, in which every citizen can directly represent his or her interests in the public domain, is hardly feasible outside of micro-level village settings. Modern democracies require elected representatives who, for the most part, are processed through political parties. This is why political scientists refer to modern democracies as "representative democracies".

Despite the central role of political parties in the functioning of modern democracies, they do not usurp the will of voters in constituting public institutions. Especially in established presidential democracies, even the entry requirement of membership of a political party for the election of President and Vice President enshrined in Sierra Leone's 1991 constitution may be frowned upon because it undermines the sovereignty of voters as individuals in contesting public office.

Political parties can discipline erring representatives when they seek re-election by denying them the party's symbol; they can also expel such representatives, making it impossible to seek re-election under the same party. However, expulsion may not affect the status of an elected official whose tenure has not expired and who refuses to resign his or her post. The reason is simple: parties nominate, and voters elect. Party members are just a fraction of the totality of voters who are the primary bearers of sovereignty and democracy.

In Sierra Leone, it is understood that a nine-member committee of the ruling party's 49-member National Advisory Council investigated allegations against the VP and recommended his expulsion from the party, which the NAC upheld. Compare this 49-member group to the more than two million voters who participated in the 2012 elections that propelled the President and VP into office. If membership of a political party is a continuous requirement for the posts of President and Vice President, then a small bunch of unelected party officials may arrogate to themselves the power to decide whether a VP or President with a popular mandate can continue in office. In authoritarian communist states that fuse the powers of party, state and government, parties enjoy such dominance over voters' choices.

The situation is different in democracies. Presidential democracies and constituency-based, first-past-the-post parliamentary democracies share similar characteristics in recognising the sovereignty of voters over parties in determining the status of elected representatives.

This is why even when MPs switch sides or are expelled from their parties, they are often not required to quit office. Some new democracies, such as Kenya, Zambia and Sierra Leone that use constituency-based rules to elect MPs, stipulate that such MPs should lose their seats, but fresh elections in which the affected MPs are free to contest should be held, thus ensuring that voters, not parties, still have the final say on who represents them.

The sovereignty of voters may be compromised in parliamentary democracies that are based on the closed list-system of proportional representation where voters elect parties rather than individuals. In such a system, if an MP ceases to be a member of a party, the next person on the party list automatically replaces the affected MP without going through elections. Many West European parliamentary democracies with PR systems have thus opted for open-list systems where voters have the freedom to select individual candidates on party lists, making it difficult for party bosses to scuttle the verdict of voters. The Organization for Security and Cooperation in Europe affirms that it is individual MPs who own the mandates of parliamentary seats, which, in the absence of elections, can only be revoked through a judicial process.

In presidential democracies, a Vice President enjoys the same popular mandate as a President. In this sense, a VP's status is fundamentally different from that of ministers who are presidential appointees. It is virtually impossible for a President to fire an elected Vice President even when relations become irreconcilable. The two offices are like Siamese twins. This is why the procedures that govern the removal of a president are usually the same as those for the removal of a Vice President.

For instance, after 1986, the impeachment of a Vice President in the United States also requires (as is stipulated for the impeachment of a President) the Chief Justice to preside over the Senate chamber that will vote on the impeachment. No US Vice President has ever been impeached; but Spiro Agnew, Richard Nixon's Vice President, was forced to resign in 1973 because of charges related to financial fraud. Instructively, Nixon would not have been able to replace Agnew with Gerald Ford without Agnew's resignation or impeachment by Congress.

Two recent cases in Africa of political differences between presidents and vice presidents are also instructive. In Nigeria, Vice President Abubakar Atiku fell out with President Olusegun Obasanjo over the latter's bid for a third term in office. Atiku was suspended from the ruling party on charges of corruption and anti-party activities, and when he joined the opposition Action Congress as the party's presidential candidate, Obasanjo relieved him of the post of VP. However, the court ruled that Obasanjo did not have the constitutional authority to sack him. When the national elections office tried to prevent Atiku from contesting the presidency under the AC on the basis of his conviction on corruption charges, the court ruled that it did not have the power to disqualify him. Similarly, President Bingo wa Mutharika of Malawi was unable to sack his Vice President, Joyce Banda, even when the latter was expelled from the ruling party. Banda formed her own party and remained Vice President, succeeding Mutharika as President when the latter died before the end of their joint mandate.

In the African context, the brinkmanship displayed by presidents may reflect the "strong man" syndrome or refusal to respect and grow institutions, which President Obama warned against in his speech to the Ghana Parliament in 2009. At least in Nigeria and Malawi, the constitution and courts imposed limits on presidential power and the vice presidents remained in office.

If in democracies there are limits to presidential power in hiring and firing vice presidents, presidents have no alternative but to manage such power professionally. There is no reason why a professional working relationship cannot be crafted to allow for co-habitation between a president and his vice even when personal relations deteriorate. Democracies are full of cases where leaders and their deputies do not have amicable relations, but have worked professionally as a team to serve the public interest.

It is difficult to understand why the All People's Congress and the President decided to plunge the country into a constitutional crisis in the middle of our worst health crisis in living memory. It was an open secret that relations between the President and Vice President had become frosty even before the 2012 elections, and many observers felt the President would dump the VP by selecting a new running mate, especially as the VP had become mired in too many scandals (although he strenuously denied the allegations).

Electoral calculations, not concern for the public interest, may have influenced the decision to retain the VP as a running mate, even though, as it turned out, the votes that the VP may have mobilised in

Kono, his home district, were not decisive in clinching the election for the President. If one adjusts for at least Northern voters in Kono, who constitute at least a third of the electorate in that district, and who tend to vote for Northern parties, the ethnic Kono vote may have been equally split between the Koroma-Sam Sumana and Bio-Sesay tickets in the 2012 election. Indeed, more voters from the Southern region and the two Eastern districts of Kenema and Kailahun supplied more votes to the Koroma-Sam Sumana ticket than the Kono voters (67,238 votes from Kono versus 149,021 votes from the 6 Mende-dominated Southeast districts). Future historians and public policy analysts may well interpret the current crisis as poor management or abuse of executive power.

29
People Power Shames Qaddafi's Appeasers[29]

The events in Libya signal once again that dictatorship of whatever brand, strength or age is unsustainable and that the people ultimately have the final say on who governs. Western and African leaders believed that Qaddafi's hold on power after forty two years was impregnable and that his regime, which was built on a camouflage, the Jamahiriya or "People's Republic", enjoyed broad support.

They assumed that his support for international terrorism and authoritarian rule could be tamed and his obnoxious regime given international respectability if a bargain could be struck. In this bargain, Qaddafi would share his oil loot through reparation and gifts, offer business contracts to Western companies and give up his weapons of mass destruction. It has taken the extraordinary courage of the Libyan people through mass action to expose the hollowness of these beliefs.

Qaddafi's rule has always been based on a small clique of loyal supporters drawn largely from his Qaddadfa "tribe"; placing family members in strategic positions in his highly centralised state system; manipulating tribal, clan and regional differences; using oil wealth to bribe or reward followers; and decisiveness in applying terror on opponents.

Realising that his so called Green Book ideas of the "Third International Theory" did not resonate with youths and fellow leaders in the Middle East, he turned to Africa south of the Sahara where he financed, trained and armed some of the most despicable rebel groups in the continent's history.

He was a key driver in getting African leaders to transform the Organization of African Unity into the African Union, even though nothing substantially changed after the change of name. He lobbied to be made the leader of all Africa in the new AU.

His diplomatic forays included courting African traditional leaders with gifts and extracting from them the title of King of Kings. He almost embarrassed the Ghana government in 2009 when he organised

---

[29] Published in *Daily Trust* (Kaduna), 1 March, 2011; *Patriotic Vanguard* (Vancouver), 1 March, 2011; *The Nation* (Nairobi), 4 March, 2011.

an international conference of West African traditional leaders in Accra where he was hoping to be crowned their overall king. This coronation was to have happened a week after the historic visit of Obama to Ghana.

Qaddafi's appeasement in Britain and Sierra Leone where he committed some of his vilest crimes is dishonourable. After slaughtering 270 innocent passengers over the skies of Lockerbie in Scotland in 1988, the British government under Tony Blair and Gordon Brown sought to pacify him and clean up his image in return for US$2.7 billion as compensation for his crime, lucrative business contracts, and dismantling of his weapons programme.

The only person convicted of the Lockerbie murder, al-Meghrai, was flown back to Libya from his Scottish jail. The British establishment opened its doors to Qaddafi's son, Saif al-Islam, who gave £1.5 million to the Centre for the Study of Global Governance at the London School of Economics and Political Science.

To add insult to injury, Saif al-Islam, who only received his doctorate in 2007 and had no distinguished record of public service, gave the Ralph Miliband Lecture in May 2010. Miliband, we should note, was a great Marxist intellectual whose two sons, David and Ed (currently the Labour Party's leader), occupied top ministerial posts in the last Labour government. The co-director of the Centre for the Study of Global Governance, David Held, described Saif, who has vowed to resist the popular will to the last bullet, as "someone who looks to democracy, civil society and deep liberal values for the core of his inspiration". It is a sad period to be an alumnus of the LSE.

Qaddafi's appeasement in Sierra Leone was equally offensive even though the payoff was scandalously flimsy. Sierra Leonean academics and journalists had in the 1990s done a great job of documenting Qaddafi's role in training, financing and arming Foday Sankoh's Revolutionary United Front. It is ironic that residents in Tajura where Sankoh and Charles Taylor received their training and agreed to help each other in making war in Sierra Leone and Liberia are today being brutalised by Qaddafi's special forces.

Sierra Leone's Truth and Reconciliation Commission implicated Qaddafi in the war that led to more than 30,000 deaths, numerous amputees, and hundreds of thousands of displaced people, and called on the government to obtain reparations from him. And David Crane, former prosecutor at the Sierra Leone Special Court, recently informed the world that he "named and shamed" Qaddafi "in the actual indictment", but could not indict him because of pressure from Western powers.

The government of Ahmad Tejan Kabbah failed to follow through on the recommendations of the Truth and Reconciliation Commission, preferring instead to strike deals that turned out to be puny: Qaddafi gave the government a few buses, garbage collection trucks and some bags of rice. And in 2009 the current parliament through cross-party support conferred on Qaddafi the status of an honorary member of parliament. The irony of this award was lost on both the benefactors and the recipient. QGaddafi's Green Book berates parliamentary democracy as fake democracy. To him, the only true democracy is one based on people's committees and congresses, which he obviously controls.

Why did our parliamentarians devalue their own institution by making a tyrant who has Sierra Leonean blood on his hands an MP? And why did Qaddafi want to become a member of a "fake" democratic institution? Students of international politics and diplomatic history have their work cut out in unravelling the intricacies of these deals.

Qaddafi's fall opens up opportunities to revisit the reparations issue. His victims in Sierra Leone, Liberia, Chad and Libya deserve justice and full compensation.

30
The Arab Spring, Democracy and Well-Being[30]

The popular revolts in the Arab world underscore the importance of grounding governments in foundations of democracy, well-being and equity. When Mohamed Bouazizi, a street vendor in Tunisia, set himself ablaze after losing his livelihood to the police, no one predicted that the event would signal the beginning of a mass movement that would challenge long-standing dictatorships in the region.

Occurring in the midst of a food crisis that has brought hardship to millions, the Bouazizi tragedy caught the public imagination because it summed up deep-seated vulnerabilities that define the lives of many people: high rates of unemployment, precarious livelihoods, limited social protection, and lack of redress when governments ignore citizen demands.

The Arab region has of course made progress on a number of social indicators, such as literacy, life expectancy and access to basic services. One UNDP study by Rodriguez and Samman ("The North African Miracle", *Let's Talk Human Development*) even toasts North Africa as an unsung "miracle" because education and health components of its human development index grew faster over a 40-year period than the world average. However, the uprisings have exposed the limitations of such indexes, which ignore asset and income inequalities as well as basic freedoms in measuring well-being.

The outcome of the revolts is far from clear. Basic freedoms and credible elections may take root in some countries, but incumbents may use repression and oil wealth to stifle opposition in others. Armed external intervention may be necessary in situations where leaders vow to unleash mass terror on populations. However, such interventions may distort the democratisation process, especially when civic activism takes a back seat and authoritarian governments seeking to maintain their own rule join the interventions. Furthermore, as experiences elsewhere suggest, even credible elections may not translate into improved well-

---

[30] Published in *UNRISD e-Bulletin* No. 4. March, 2011.

being for all if governments' agendas are not developmental and redistributive.

Three issues need to be addressed if the Arab Spring is to have a lasting and positive impact for the poor. These are equity-based growth strategies, social protection for all, and inclusive politics.

In many countries, dependence on oil rents has fuelled corruption, conspicuous consumption and overvalued exchange rates. This has affected sectors of the economy where the majority earns its living. However, with the right policies, institutions and practices, this resource-endowed region with a population of more than 300 million can become an industrial powerhouse, provide decent jobs (especially for its rapidly growing youth population) and feed everyone. There are resource-dependent countries, such as Malaysia, that avoided the resource curse and climbed up the global industrial ladder within a generation.

Social policies are also needed that protect all citizens from basic risks of unemployment, underemployment and ill health and assist with the care of children and the elderly. Such policies should depart from the region's fragmented and patronage-based systems of social protection, as well as the practice of distributing money to citizens when leaders are under siege. Instead, governments should treat social policies as acquired rights. Arguments of affordability are untenable in a region where six countries are classified as high income, three as upper middle income and eight as lower middle income.

Inclusive politics is also important. Governments are unlikely to pursue redistributive policies if political parties are disconnected from people's aspirations. Thus the quality of emerging parties in the region will have to be nurtured and gendered in terms of membership, participation and policies. Gendering the democratic process is particularly important because of the region's historically sharp gender disparities and exclusions, and considering women's active participation in the protests.

Finally, even though the region has one overwhelmingly dominant language and religion, it is far from homogeneous. The transition is likely to be more complicated in countries such as Bahrain, Libya and Yemen that are fractionalised along dimensions of "tribe", clan and religious denomination. If such cleavages polarise into a few clusters, organising elections without building institutions that can moderate these cleavages could produce outcomes in which incumbents with flawed mandates cling to power, reopening a new round of instability, as has happened in Côte d'Ivoire.

The Arab spring holds promise, but it has to be democratically anchored in the right institutions and made to serve the interests of the broad mass of the people.

Part III: Cohesion and Security

31
Managing Ethnic Diversity and Inequality in a Development Context[31]

The title of my talk is "managing ethnic diversity and inequality in a development context". I want to explore the links between diversity and inequality, and why a developmental approach to social cohesion is likely to improve the plight of the poor and make societies more cohesive and stable.

The problem of ethnic diversity and inequality, including their potential to generate conflict, has received much attention in academic and policy circles. When inequalities reflect group differences, ethnicity may become important in shaping choices and mobilising individuals for divisive collective action. High levels of ethnic inequalities may also make it harder for countries to sustain growth and lift people out of poverty. If ethnic groups are geographically clustered, development may bypass groups that are not located in dynamic zones, intensifying poverty in the neglected areas. Such outcomes may fuel ethnic animosity and weaken the bonds of citizenship. Exclusion, in turn, may make it harder to achieve growth, by constraining the productivity of the poor and thus their potential contribution to growth.

Managing difference and inequality in ethnically diverse societies has, therefore, become a central objective of development policy. However, how diversity and inequality are managed will vary depend on whether governments adopt a development focus in their strategies. Policies that focus only on cohesion often privilege elite bargains, or social integration at the top, which may not address the problems of the poor or development more broadly. Citizens may find it difficult to hold

---

[31] Keynote speech, "Conference on Reflections 2010: Managing Diversity, Reconciliation and Development", Organised by GTZ-Sri Lanka, the Sri Lankan Ministry of National Languages and Social Integration, and the European Union Office in Sri Lanka. Colombo, Sri Lanka. 31 October-3 November 2010. Based on Y. Bangura (ed.), *Ethnic Inequalities and Public Sector Governance*. Basingstoke: Palgrave Macmillan and UNRISD, 2006; and UNRISD, "Tackling Ethnic and Regional Inequalities", in UNRISD, *Combating Poverty and Inequality: Structural Change, Social Policy and Politics.* Geneva: UNRISD.

privileged elites to account or get them to deliver developmentally uplifting outcomes.

Many post-war reconstruction programmes that emphasise sequencing of policies tend to adopt this approach—i.e. countries are advised first to get warring parties to work together through inclusive government, deliver humanitarian assistance, and then they do development. By the time the development phase is reached, patterns of behaviour that are non-developmental may have set in, and confidence in peace improving the well-being of most people may have waned, making the political settlement ultimately unsustainable.

An alternative approach is one that places development at the centre of reconciliation and social integration. It focuses not only on providing incentives for the emergence of moderate leaders, but also for leaders to be developmental in formulating and implementing public policies. It is concerned not only with elite pacts, but also with development pacts that reflect the interests of the poor. Such an approach has implications for the construction of party systems, the kinds of bargains struck at different levels of society, the development strategies pursued, and the social policies embraced by governments.

The developmental approach to social cohesion is different from approaches that downplay the salience of ethnicity in development. Some analysts and policy makers believe that if a country is put on a strong growth path that improves livelihoods, ethnic divisions will become a thing of the past. They draw their inspiration from a finding in econometric studies that the risk of violent conflict tends to be higher in poor countries than in rich ones. However, the fact that rich countries also experience violent conflicts suggests that development strategies that are ethnicity-blind may not be a guarantee for long-term social cohesion and stability. There is, therefore, a strong case for strategies that actively promote cohesion, equality and development. This requires taking both development and ethnicity seriously.

I will first provide an overview of the links between diversity and inequality and then address issues related to their management in different contexts.

Ethnic diversity and inequality

Ethnic diversity per se does not necessarily produce inequalities or conflicts. Unfortunately, there is a large body of literature that associates ethnic diversity with pathological outcomes, such as conflict, dictatorship, underfunding of public services, and poor growth.

A major pitfall of the pathological view of ethnic diversity is its tendency to treat all multi-ethnic societies as undifferentiated. Analysts see ethnicity as a problem irrespective of the way it is configured in countries' social structures. Efforts to develop an index of ethnic fragmentation have surely not helped matters. By ranking countries according to the extent of their ethnic fragmentation, the index of fragmentation helps researchers to make generalisations about countries, but it is a poor guide for understanding the conditions under which fragmentation aids instability.

Fragmentation aids equality

The effects of ethnic diversity on behaviour and inequality are complex. In a 15-country UNRISD study on ethnic inequalities and the public sector, we found that a high level of fragmentation—meaning that no group is large enough to dominate the public sphere—leads to less inequality and encourages good inter-group cooperation.

Indeed, ethnic structures assume various forms. They vary from cases in which one ethnicity is overwhelmingly dominant and coexists with numerous small groups (as in Botswana and Lithuania), to cases where two or three groups predominate in a multi-ethnic setting (as in Belgium, Bosnia and Herzegovina, Fiji, Latvia, Malaysia, Nigeria, Switzerland and Trinidad). A third possibility includes cases in which the ethnic structure is very diverse. This includes cases of high levels of fragmentation (as in Tanzania and Papua New Guinea), and cases where fragmentation is interspersed with a few large and relatively equal groups, which may encourage polarisation (as in India and Kenya).

The findings suggest that in cases where one ethnic group is overwhelmingly dominant, ethnicity is less likely to be important in constituting the public sector. Electoral competitiveness may open up conflicts within the dominant ethnicity, allowing individuals from minority groups to play important roles in parties led by individuals from dominant groups. In Botswana, even though most Tswana vote for the ruling party, a sizeable percentage also support opposition parties; and minorities have not formed separate parties from those led by Tswana. Candidates from the three dominant Tswana subgroups and the second largest group, the Kalanga, have occupied more than two-thirds of the cumulative parliamentary seats of the main political parties since 1965. Although the Tswana constitute 70 per cent of the population, they accounted for only 58 per cent of cabinet posts in 2000, 50 per cent of top civil service posts in 2003, and 61 per cent of parliamentary seats in 2000, suggesting strong representation of minorities in the public sector. Voting patterns have assumed an urban-rural divide, with the opposition winning most urban votes and the government winning rural ones.

In highly fragmented settings with relatively small ethnic groups, as in Tanzania with 120 groups, ethnicity is less likely to be important in the governance of the public sector, since it is difficult for a single group to be dominant under free, fair and competitive conditions. Since political parties may have to appeal to a cross-section of groups to be electorally viable, they are bound to be multi-ethnic. No single ethnic group dominates Tanzania's public sector in terms of their share of posts. The largest ethnic group (which makes up only 13 per cent of the population) and the second largest group (4 per cent of the population) were not represented at all at the top layer of the civil service in 2000. This is not surprising, since it is rare for an ethnic group to have more than one member at the top cadre of the civil service and cabinet. In the 1990 cabinet, for instance, the largest group had only 7 per cent of the posts, the second largest had none, and the third largest (4 per cent of the population) had 4 per cent. A similar distribution was found in the 1995 and 2000 cabinets.

The more difficult cases are countries with bipolar and tripolar ethnic structures or cases where ethnic fragmentation is interspersed with a few large and relatively equal groups that may form selective ethnic coalitions. Countries with these types of ethnic structures that are relatively stable and cohesive have introduced institutions and policies that are sensitive to ethnicity in order to influence the composition of the public sector.

Structural shocks and inequality

However, even in countries where the ethnic structure can be a risk factor, it is important to stress that inequality and conflict are not automatic outcomes. Inequalities are often historically constructed or arise as a result of what Graham Brown and Arnim Langer have called foundational or structural shocks.

Three well know shocks are slavery, colonialism, and transitions from communal to feudal land tenure systems in which the ethnicity of landlords is different from those of peasants. For instance, the racial inequalities in the United States can be traced to 300 years of discrimination based on race, with slavery as the foundational shock. The persistence of South Africa's racial inequalities is also tied to the foundational shock of Apartheid. In Malaysia, the Malay's economic disadvantage is linked to the ethnic division of labour that developed during British colonial rule. While Europeans, Chinese and Indians were mostly employed in high-value modern sectors as entrepreneurs, managers and workers, the Malay mostly worked in low-value peasant agriculture.

Similarly, inequalities in Africa's agrarian economies, such as Ghana and Cote d'Ivoire, can be traced to the differential effects of colonial rule on communities. Under British and French colonialism, investment was largely concentrated in regions with raw materials and facilities for export, which was in the south of both countries. There was very little development of infrastructure or human capital in the north. However, local ethnic groups in resource-endowed regions may be disadvantaged if more influential outside groups use state power to appropriate the resources, as in the Niger delta of Nigeria; or if outside groups that have settled in the endowed regions dominate the production or marketing of the resources, as in the case of minority regions in Indonesia with Javanese migrants.

Patterns of diversity and inequality vary across countries. They include situations where a minority group may dominate both the economy and governance institutions (apartheid South Africa, Burundi before the current transition) to situations where a majority group is dominant in both spheres (the marginalisation of indigenous groups in Latin America). Other patterns include minority dominance of the economy and majority dominance of governance structures (post-apartheid South Africa, Malaysia), and situations where a minority dominates public institutions, but not the economy (African countries in which minority dominance of the military expands the reach of the group to other arms of the public sector usually under military rule or one party dictatorships).

In some situations, different groups may specialise in different economic enterprises that are not hierarchical: the nomadic, cattle-raising activities of the Tutsi versus the settled agriculture of the Hutu in pre-colonial Burundi and Rwanda. However, inequalities and conflicts may occur when individuals with one tradition of enterprise gain control of the state and establish a hierarchical social structure that privileges their line of activity. A related type may be the ethnically bifurcated labour markets in Fiji and parts of the Caribbean, such as in Trinidad and Guyana: Indians in these two countries dominate rural agriculture and small business enterprises and Africans are prevalent in urban employment and the professions. Bifurcated markets confer veto or hostage powers to both groups and can be used to devastating effects during conflicts.

Drawing on a number of sources on ethnic diversity and inequality, the UNRISD report *Combating Poverty and Inequality* argues that ethnic inequalities that arise out of structural shocks tend to persist because of several reasons: i) deprivation or wealth at one point in time make it harder or easier to accumulate assets in the future; ii) some groups may make gains in one area (say education), but may lack other endowments (say employment and finance) to forge ahead; iii) individuals from poorer ethnic groups may lack the social ties or capital to make progress, since poor people have more contacts with each other than with rich ones; iv) group members may also face discrimination or favouritism by non-group members in accessing jobs, credit and services by virtue of their group characteristics; v) and group inequalities may include political inequalities, which may reinforce social and economic inequalities.

The dynamics of these factors can produce vicious and virtuous cycles: groups with a privileged head-start accumulate more and are able to sustain their privilege, while those who started from a position of disadvantage find it difficult break out of backwardness. Transforming these cycles is important if poverty and inequality are to be effectively tackled and national cohesion promoted.

Managing diversity and inequality

Let me now address the management of diversity and inequality. Managing diversity and inequality requires trust among ethnic groups as well as in the way the state relates to its citizens. Trust can be achieved by tackling inequalities in the cultural, governmental and socioeconomic domains.

Cultural recognition

Overcoming cultural inequality deals with issues of recognition. It is about making the public domain reflect, or not discriminate against, the cultural identities of groups. How issues of language rights, religious practices, and traditions that do not violate human rights are treated is important in building trust and reconciliation. Some states, such as the nation states of Europe, are based on the assumed values of one ethnicity, in which those who share common blood ties, history and culture enjoy primary claims on the state. Others are based on civic republican values, such as in France, which appeal to notions of a community with shared political territory, institutions and history – but not culture— and stress the principle of equality before the law regardless of group membership. However, civic republicanism can be assimilationist, with the dominant culture enjoying supremacy over other cultures.

A third type is the nation-building project of multi-ethnic societies, especially those in early independent Africa, in which ethnicity was discouraged as an organising principle of statecraft. Use of foreign languages and secular values implanted by colonial authorities underpinned the identities of the state. A good example is Tanzania, which discouraged references to ethnicity in public discourses and developed a national language, Swahili, in addition to English, to support its egalitarian policies. The multi-ethnic state is the fourth type. Under this model the state does not only recognize the multi-ethnic character of its society; it also develops rules to create a multi-ethnic public. It seeks to create ethnic balance in the way the state is culturally defined and constituted. Examples are Switzerland, Belgium, Bosnia-Herzegovina and, to some extent, Nigeria and India.

245

It is important to stress that if groups do not feel attached to the identity of a state, even progress in reducing inequalities in governmental and socioeconomic domains may not compensate for feelings of alienation and may render the polity unstable. Therefore, the first rule for creating national cohesion and accommodation in multi-ethnic societies is to get the cultural issues right. My focus, however, is on the other two dimensions of inequality—representation in governance and access to socioeconomic resources—in underscoring the developmental imperative in building cohesive societies.

Elite bargains

Two competing frameworks have been advocated for managing diversity and ensuring political inclusivity in government institutions: (i) reforms that seek to promote large majorities by encouraging vote pooling, ethnic integration and moderation, while also supporting adversarial politics; and (ii) consociational or power-sharing arrangements that accommodate ethnic divisions.

The first type of reform (majoritarian) promotes plurality within party systems by encouraging political actors to seek votes outside of their ethnic strongholds if they are to gain the second, third or subsequent preferences of voters in the preference or alternative vote system that underpins this framework. Voters are asked to rank candidates on the ballots. If no candidate receives more than 50 percent of the votes on the first count, the last candidate is eliminated and his/her second preference votes are transferred to the remaining candidates. The process is repeated if no candidate scores more than 50 percent in subsequent rounds of counting, until a winner emerges. Under this arrangement, parties may become multi-ethnic rather than ethnic. It forces candidates to adopt centrist positions since their chances of winning elections depend on their ability to appeal to a wide range of concerns. The maximisation of votes encourages parties to work with individuals from other ethnic groups. As all electable parties are likely to be multi-ethnic, governments will be plural and may not discriminate against particular ethnic groups.

The second type of reform—consociation or power-sharing— accepts ethnic parties as given and seeks to promote plurality, not within the contending parties, but at the governmental level itself. It is grounded in the list-proportional representational (PR) vote system, which does not require parties to have a majority of the votes to be represented in the legislature. Because of PR, even smaller groups which feel alienated from the political process may form their own parties and then bargain at the top to gain representation in government. The consociational model is inclusive rather than adversarial. Some notable consociations are Switzerland, Belgium, Malaysia, Lebanon, and Bosnia.

Both systems can be characterized as elite bargains since they provide incentives for inter-elite cooperation. However, the capacity of voters to influence the behaviour of politicians is rather weak in the consociation model. Indeed, the list-PR electoral rule that underpins this model may weaken the accountability of parliamentarians to their electorate and strengthen party control over parliamentarians, since it is parties that draw up lists and decide where to place candidates on the lists. Voters will not be able to vote out underperforming parliamentarians. Power sharing among elites from different ethnic parties may also blunt the effectiveness of voters to hold leaders to account and change them if their performance is unsatisfactory. In inter-ethnic elite bargains, parties or politicians may only be credible to one segment of the voting public at best. The vote may lose its significance as a sanctioning device against bad performance. Making these kinds of elite bargains work for development and the poor can be difficult. Developmental democracies require adversarial politics and uncertainties in electoral outcomes to get elites to deliver on promises.

The majoritarian vote pooling system is adversarial and voter empowering, and can encourage politicians to pursue moderate policies. However, this can only happen if the constituencies are mixed and not homogenous, or if the entire country is taken as a single constituency. In homogenous settings, or where ethnic groups are geographically clustered, voters will elect candidates from the same ethnic group even if they belong to different parties. Furthermore, by producing majoritarian outcomes, the majoritarian vote pooling system may exclude from government key politicians of other groups, who may decide to not play by the rules since they may have no opportunity to be in government. In addition, even though it may allow governing parties to get votes from regions or groups other than their core areas of support, cases where transferred votes are decisive in choosing winners may be limited. A large number of voters from other regions may in fact not vote for the governing party. In Australia, which uses a majoritarian alternative vote system, in the 1993 elections, 46% of voters did not support the winner.

UNRISD research suggests that some form of power sharing is unavoidable in societies where only two or three groups exist, or where two or three dominant groups coexist with smaller groups in a multi-ethnic setting, as well as in settings with strong ethnic or regional clusters. However, even in these cases of ethnic polarisation, if elites are to be held accountable by voters across ethnic divides, parties must be made multi-ethnic, as in Switzerland, rather than ethnic, as in Belgium.

Two mechanisms can be used to facilitate this outcome. The first is to insist on primaries in the election of party leaders. If delegates are fairly distributed across regions and ethnicities, leaders will be forced to win the trust of voters that are not in traditional ethnic strongholds. This may work best in situations where the two or three dominant groups are roughly equal in size, producing a roughly equal distribution of delegates across regions and ethnicities. The effect is that parties' lists of candidates will be drawn from multiple ethnicities and candidates who aspire to lead political parties will have to appeal to a cross section of the country to be elected. This approach can be backed by a rule that compels parties to alternate their leaders between the key ethnic divides. The two mechanisms can transform ethnic parties into national parties and liberate the electorate from the burden of having to endure the poor performance of parties on grounds of ethnic loyalty.

Equitable growth

Elite bargains are important but not sufficient to transform societies along developmental lines. The specific interests of non-elites also need to be addressed. These groups benefit when employment levels and incomes that accrue to the poor are high. Most poor multi-ethnic countries have not been able to generate and sustain strong growth that can transform their economies and deliver decently paid jobs. They tend to be stuck with low productivity agriculture and services or mineral extraction with few employment opportunities. Often there is widespread poverty across the ethnic divides. This takes the form of large scale underemployment and low incomes in informal and agricultural activities; or persistent and large-scale unemployment in situations where the informal economy is restricted.

Elite bargains need to be complemented with development pacts between governments and citizens involving the participation of groups in agriculture, the informal sector and industry to set countries on trajectories of employment-centred and equitable growth. Development pacts should grant recognition to representatives of farmers, workers, informal petty producers and employers to address issues related to wages, incomes and price support, working conditions, services, welfare and employment; ensure that group representatives can enforce members' compliance when decisions are reached; and facilitate ways that the state can be held accountable in delivering agreements. It is instructive to note that in many multi-ethnic countries, economic activity-based groups are often non-ethnic. Even in cases where they are ethnic, encouraging groups to scale up for effective bargaining may ultimately weaken the ethnic dimension for collective action.

Development pacts create consensus. They can empower governments to mobilise domestic revenue through progressive taxation and incentives for high savings; pursue policies that will support the agricultural sector and connect it more effectively to industry and other sectors; stimulate the economy in ways that will expand domestic production and demand for domestic goods and services that will generate strong demand for labour; invest in infrastructure as well as education to improve skills across sectors, groups and communities; and manage the process of structural change fairly.

Conclusion

Let me conclude. Managing ethnic diversity and inequality is a major challenge for multi-ethnic societies. However, diversity itself does not necessarily create inequality or conflict. It is certain types of diversity, such as situations in which two or three groups are pitched against each other, which may constitute a risk factor. However, even in these cases, ethnic structure per se does not generate inequality and conflict. Inequalities are often a product of structural or foundational shocks that propel countries along a development path that disadvantages some groups. The persistence of ethnic inequalities may be due to the concentration of growth in certain lines of activities and regions, weak social ties between the poor and those who have forged ahead, deficiencies in one or several types of capital, subtle and overt forms of discrimination, and differential access to governance institutions.

Managing diversity and inequality, therefore, requires trust. Trust can be achieved by tackling inequalities in the cultural, governmental and socioeconomic domains. However, strategies for the promotion of social cohesion that improve the livelihoods of the poor require a development focus. They demand not only elite bargains, but also development pacts that involve the participation of the poor. Such an approach calls for different ways of constructing party systems, making bargains at different levels of society, formulating employment-centred development strategies, and pursuing social policies that are both developmental and redistributive across ethnicities and classes.

32
Racism, Citizenship and Social Justice[32]

The third World Conference against Racism, Racial Discrimination, Xenophobia and Related Intolerance will be held in Durban, South Africa from 31 August to 7 September 2001. World leaders will examine progress made in the fight against racism since the adoption of the Universal Declaration of Human Rights and related conventions and resolutions; discuss ways of improving the application of existing standards and instruments to combat racism; review the social, economic, political, cultural and historical factors that drive racism and racial discrimination; and recommend effective measures at the national, regional and international level for combating racism, xenophobia and intolerance. While the preparatory meetings for the world conference have exposed sharp differences among countries and groups on some of the core agenda items, they have simultaneously underscored the need to understand racial cleavages and discrimination in formulating development policies. Drawing on some of the papers that have been prepared for a parallel UNRISD conference on Racism and Public Policy scheduled for 3 –5 September, I address two main issues in this article: how the construction of race and racism affects social solidarity and citizenship; and the promotion of social justice in societies with deep racial divisions.

The social construction of race and citizenship

Racism, racial discrimination, xenophobia and intolerance are worldwide problems. They affect social relations, influence structures of opportunity and life chances of individuals. They provoke violence and wars. Slavery, colonialism, genocide, the Holocaust and apartheid represent the most extreme forms of racism; but other overt and subtle forms of racism persist to this day. The legacy of institutionalised racism

---

[32] Published in *Social Development Review*. London: International Council on Social Welfare. Vol.5, No. 3. September 2001. Based on papers commissioned for the UNRISD conference on Racism and Public Policy; a public event at the World Conference Against Racism, Xenophobia and Related Intolerance. Durban, South Africa. 31 August-7 September 2001.

continues to weigh heavily on the development prospects of entire groups and countries, influence prospects for social integration and accommodation, and affect the efficacy of public policies for promoting equality, justice and social development.

Race is socially constructed, not biologically determined. The practice of classifying humans according to distinct races has been discredited by genetic research. On average, 99.9 percent of the genetic features of humans are the same; and of the remaining percentage that accounts for variation, differences within groups are larger than between groups. However, physical differences structure perceptions and constitute a significant source of prejudice in social relations. Racial ideas may influence discourses on integration, encourage insular or xenophobic practices, and distort perceptions about rights and citizenship.

In the United States, as George Fredrickson and Manning Marable remind us, commitment towards universal human rights coexisted with a strong historical tendency to exclude non-white groups from citizenship. Despite the proscription of racial discrimination by the Civil Rights Acts of 1964 and 1965, structural inequality associated with race persists. A substantially higher proportion of blacks than whites are likely to be unemployed, imprisoned, in poverty or destitute. More than 1.2 million African-Americans (more than half of the prison population) reside in US prisons. Of the 4.3 million Americans who have lost the right to vote 1.7 million are black. Although African Americans constitute only 14 percent of all illegal drug users, they account for 35 percent of all drug-related arrests, 55 percent of convictions, and 75 percent of all Americans imprisoned or jailed for drug crimes. In addition, Sheldon Danziger and his colleagues point out that although the official poverty rate declined during the boom years of the 1990s from 15.1 percent in 1993 to 11.8 percent in 1999, its effects were unevenly felt by racial groups: in 1999, this rate was 23.6 percent for African-Americans and 22.8 percent for Hispanics, but only 7.7 percent for non-Hispanic whites.

South Africa is comparable to the United States in terms of its historical commitment to institutionalised racism. Bernard Magubane points out that racism in South Africa is associated with the colonial quest for raw materials and the settlement of Europe's social outcasts. Before apartheid, the subjugation of the African population took two forms: slavery and peonage. Laws devised for indentured white immigrants, free "coloured" workers and emancipated African slaves provided the backdrop for South Africa's notorious master and servant laws, which from 1910 were transformed into segregatory laws, and from 1948 into apartheid, effectively denying the African population citizenship rights. The 1994 constitution and the new Government of National Unity proscribed apartheid, upheld universal citizenship for all South Africans, and committed itself to both racial and gender equality. However, as Renosi Mokate points out, sixty-five percent of Africans still live below the poverty line. The average annual income of African-headed households is R23, 000, compared to R32, 000 for coloured-headed households, R71, 000 for Indian-headed households and R103, 000 for white-headed households. Black rural women are particularly disadvantaged.

In South East Asia, a recurring theme as Lily Rahim, Khoo Bhoo Teik and Jomo K. Sundaram report, is the problematic relationship between the Chinese population and "indigenous" groups. However, since the economic crisis of the late 1990s, ethno-racial conflicts have also emerged among different categories of indigenous groups seeking rights, autonomy or self-determination. More orthodox Muslims, raising the spectre of religious intolerance and conflict, have rejected Indonesia's *pancasila* ideology. Malaysia's *bumiputera* or "son of the soil" policy has narrowed the socio-economic gaps between Chinese and Malayas, and in the process helped the country to avoid Indonesia's type of ethno-racial implosion. The *bumiputera* policy is, however, challenged by non-Malays as discriminatory.

Racial discrimination has not always thrived only in societies with laws, policies and practices that classify individuals according to biological differences. In Peru and other parts of Latin America, as Marisol de la Cadena contends, nation-builders rejected biological determinism and produced a notion of race based on morality and reason to defend social hierarchies. In this framework, education was vested with the power to dissolve differences based on physical appearances. It gave rise to what has been referred to as *silent racism*, since the bulk of the non-white indigenous population remained excluded from the transformatory benefits of education.

In South Asia, as Vijay Prashad informs us, caste, which is also not based on physical appearance, is derived from ancient practices associated with occupations, marriage bonds, dietary habits and religious customs. It constitutes a significant source of discrimination, which by many accounts is comparable to social practices under apartheid South Africa and racial segregation in the southern United States. The Dalits, or Untouchables, could "touch" most things owned by the dominant *jati* or ruling groups if their labour was required, but when they worked for themselves their touch was regarded by the *jatis* as social pollution. Caste discrimination has been outlawed in India and, as in the United States and South Africa, affirmative action policies exist to help Dalits bridge the socio-economic gap. However, the enforcement of laws is lax and discrimination, intolerance and caste-related violence persist.

Another issue of relevance to discussions of race and citizenship is migration. Globalisation is associated with mass migration of people from different regions to countries perceived to offer opportunities for self-advancement. Immigrants may arrive with differences in physical appearance, culture, religion and language, which native populations may perceive as threatening to their values and notions of what a society should be. Jeroen Doomernik reports that there have been three broad types of European responses to immigration. The first stresses the importance of equality before the law for both legal long-term residents and traditional citizens and grants the former easy access to citizenship. It also acknowledges the ethnic origins of residents and, if they do not conflict with the principle of equality, supports the public display of such differences. This is the multicultural approach. The second is the republican ideal, which also stresses the principle of equality before the law for residents and citizens, but discourages the display of cultural practices that are different from the dominant native culture. The third type is the most exclusionary. It is founded on the old notion of nation state homogeneity in which only co-ethnics are entitled to citizenship.

In Western Europe, a new form of exclusionary populism, exemplified by right-wing political parties and movements, poses a threat to that region's democratic and liberal order. Hans-Georg Betz argues that these parties rely on charismatic leadership, political marketing with a pronounced customer or voter orientation, and mobilisation of popular anxieties, prejudices and resentments. They advocate a comprehensive programme of social change, which includes strong hostility towards foreigners and multiculturalism, as well as other issues relating to national identity, which tend to vary according to country experiences. The electoral base of these parties encompasses several groups, although young male voters with low to medium education tend to predominate. Far-right parties have been included in governing coalitions in Austria and Italy.

A related issue is the fate of migrant workers in oil-rich countries of the Middle East. The Middle East, as Ray Jureidini reports, has experienced massive waves of immigrants engaged in short-term work – from household helps to highly qualified professionals. The migration of cheap Asian and African workers has produced a racialised secondary labour market in that region. These workers are associated with the dirty, dangerous and difficult jobs, which nationals refuse to do despite widespread poverty and unemployment. A central feature of the contract that underpins labour recruitment for these jobs is its bondage character: workers are not free to access local labour markets without state approval, and are attached to a sponsor for the duration of the contract. Conditions of slavery pertain to many female live-in domestic workers: threats of violence, restriction of movement, exploitative working conditions and widespread abuse.

Racial discrimination and social justice

A number of policies exist for tackling racism, racial prejudice, discrimination, xenophobia and inequalities. Public policies range from legal instruments and socio-economic programmes, to educational policies that seek to change behaviour and promote inclusiveness. They may involve sensitivity to racial cleavages in devising economic and social policies and reforming governance institutions. Targeted programmes may be adopted to correct historical injustices or to assist excluded groups to get out of poverty and exploit opportunities. Public policies may be implemented in macro- and micro-level settings where groups compete for resources and public offices. They have differential impacts, including among targeted beneficiaries. They are also often contested by different groups. This makes it difficult to predict their overall effects on social change or draw universal lessons that may be applicable to all situations.

Correcting racism and racial discrimination may involve reform of governance institutions. It is often not enough to introduce legal instruments or educational policies to transform the public sector into a non-racial institution. The question of who makes and administers the laws and public policies is equally important. All groups in society ought to feel a sense of belonging, representation and shared interest in the institutions that govern their lives if the public sector is to function effectively. As Ralph Premdas points out, at the core of these reforms is 'recognition': the need to accord juridical and social equality to all communities, including promotion of their languages in relevant educational institutions and public places. Linguistic rights, Neville Alexander affirms, are inalienable human rights.

The elimination of racial discrimination and injustice requires competent, neutral, responsive and accountable law enforcement agencies. However, police departments in multi-racial societies may constitute part of the problem of racism; in many countries, their preferential treatment of individuals has been queried. Benjamin Bowling and his colleagues discuss these abuses, which include excessive use of force, torture and racist language against people they perceive as different. Measures to eliminate abuse of power from police work may include creation of a police force that reflects the racial diversity of the communities served; promotion of equality of opportunity and equality of service; establishment of structures that will aid legal, political and community accountability; introduction of civilian oversight and transparent and effective methods for handling complaints; development of ethnic minority staff networks; and innovative educational and training schemes.

Public policies that promote social justice are a fundamental requirement for achieving the goals of the World Conference. These include affirmative action policies and anti-poverty programmes and policies that seek to eliminate disparities in health status and environmental racism. Affirmative action policies are associated with efforts to correct socio-economic disabilities, which certain groups may have suffered as a result of past discriminatory public policies. They focus on issues of employment, admission into educational institutions, government contracts, and broad areas of social policy. Their content and application may vary according to whether the targeted population constitutes the majority group and has strong access to policy-making institutions, or whether beneficiaries are a minority whose influence on lawmakers, the executive branch of government and administrators is limited. Policies are thus likely to vary in countries as different as the United States, South Africa, Malaysia and Brazil.

Affirmative action policies have come under considerable attack in the United States in recent years: sections of the white population see them as open-ended commitments, reverse forms of discrimination and a violation of individual rights. As Glenn Loury reports, the dominant ideology that drives opposition to affirmative action is liberal individualism, which espouses a policy of colour-blindness: the practice of not using race when carrying out a policy. Colour blindness should be distinguished from race-indifference: the practice of not considering how a chosen rule might impact various racial groups. Both can ameliorate or exacerbate the social disadvantage of blacks and other minorities. However, given the history of institutionalised racism in the US, Loury argues that the effects of race-blind or race-indifferent policies should be evaluated asymmetrically: those that harm blacks or minorities should be repudiated; those that assist blacks and minorities should be seen as necessary to the achievement of just social development. It may require a reordering of moral concerns: racial justice before race-blindness or race-indifference. It may also require rejection of the idea that racial equality has already been achieved. Racial discrimination and injustice, which spanned a period of about four hundred years, cannot be overcome in a few decades of implementing affirmative action policies.

Disparities in health status between ethno-racial groups are endemic. As Varnellia Randall points out, they are linked to differences in education, employment, housing options and incomes, exposure of racially disadvantaged groups to high health-risk occupations, past discriminatory public policies and, in some cases, racial prejudice by health care providers. Racial prejudice may influence the choices of scientists and industrialists in selecting sites, individuals or groups, for experiments and clinical trials. There have been a number of well-reported cases in recent years of scientists abusing their professional codes of conduct and causing harm to populations that look different from the scientists. While data on ethno-racial disparities in health status are routinely collected in the US, the health statistics of most countries are not disaggregated according to race or ethnicity. It makes it difficult to fully comprehend the enormity of the problem and fashion effective policy responses. Effective regulation of discrimination in health care will require proactive policies against institutional racism as well as routine and systematic collection of health status and health care statistics disaggregated according to race, gender and socio-economic status.

There is the additional problem of what has been called environmental racism, which provides benefits to corporations that pollute the environment and shift costs to people of colour. As Robert Bullard points out, environmental racism influences local land use, encourages lax enforcement of environmental regulations, and legitimises human exposure to harmful chemicals and risky technologies. In the United States, environmentalists and local residents have described the Lower Mississippi River Industrial Corridor, whose inhabitants are overwhelmingly African American, as Cancer Valley. More than 125 companies enjoying a variety of tax breaks manufacture a range of items including fertilizers, gasoline, paints and plastics. Native Indian lands have also been exposed to radioactive waste. And the health of poor communities in poor countries has been threatened by the obnoxious North-South trade in industrial waste products. Combating environmental racism in the twenty first century will require acceptance of environmental protection as a basic human right; enforcement of existing environmental, health, housing, and civil rights laws in non-discriminatory ways; closing of corporate tax loopholes that encourage corporations to pollute the environments of the poor and disadvantaged; and the development of effective international regulations and agreements.

33

Ten Theses on Ethnicity and National Unity in Sierra Leone[33]

Ethnic Identities

I

The world is populated by innumerable ethnic groups, which are often identified by language, religion, territory, history and culture. Africa alone is home to more than two thousand language groups. And Sierra Leone, a country of just five million people, has within its borders about 16 ethno-linguistic groups. Today, no country in the world can be said to be homogenous. Ethnic groups or affiliations are, however, not pre-ordained but are socially constructed and evolve over time. In other words, there is no group existing in the world today that has always been the way it was from time immemorial. The "pan-ethnic" or "nation-state" idea which proclaims that people who speak the same language and share similar cultures or traditions should constitute a single ethno-political entity is of recent origin. The rise of nationalism in 18th and 19th century Europe has a lot to do with the world-wide spread of this doctrine. In other places and in pre-nationalist Europe, people tended to identify with smaller village/clan/municipal-level configurations or multi-ethnic empires where they were free to criss-cross ethnic and, at times, religious divides. In the context of Sierra Leone, surely before the colonial intrusion none of the 16 or so ethnic groups in the country could be said to have been united under a single polity. A study of each group will reveal that there are social and even linguistic differences among individuals who currently identify themselves as belonging to any one of the 16 ethnic groups.

II

Migration and inter-marriage have been the lot of humankind, in Africa and the world at large. This makes it difficult to speak about a pure culture, tradition and language. Societies borrow, give and adapt social values and ideas when they interact with others through communication, trade, migration and conquest. It would be difficult to identify groups of

---

[33] This article was discussed extensively on Leonenet (an on-line forum for the discussion of Sierra Leone issues) in March 1996.

Sierra Leoneans whose genealogy would be restricted to only one ethnic group. If we trace the genealogy of individuals to two or more generations, there is likely to be at least one off-shoot of the genealogy reaching out to one or several other ethnic groups. For instance, many present-day Temne people have ties with the Soso, Loko, Fula, Madingo, Koranko, Yalonka, Limba, Krio, Frobay/Fulaton people (Muslim Krio). The Mende also have strong ties with the Vai, Krim, Sherbro, Kono, Madingo, Fula, and Krio. The Krio are the great melting pot of Africans of various backgrounds and traditions -- some indigenous to the area, others from other parts of Africa. The Madingo, Kono and Koranko spring from the same ethnic base. They share a lot in common, including language vocabulary. The Yalonka and Soso are two sides of the same ethnic group, and together with the Madingo, Kono, Koranko and Mende, form part of the larger West African Mande linguistic group.

At the boundaries of society where two or more ethnic groups meet, inter-marriage and resettlement are more likely to be the norm. For instance, people located between Southern Tonkolili and Northern Moyamba are likely to produce individuals with a fusion of Temne and Mende backgrounds or Temne and Sherbro backgrounds. Those in the Kabala region of Koinadugu district may produce any combination of hybrids of Koranko, Madingo, Yalonka, and Fula. The Fula of Gbinti have been almost completely assimilated into Temne culture because of the dominance of the Temne in the area. Some parts of Bombali may produce a fusion of Limba and Temne off-springs. The same is true of parts of Kambia and Port Loko districts which have experienced a long tradition of inter-marriage between the Temne and Soso. Parts of Kailahun, Kenema and Pujehun have seen a massive fusion of Mende and Kissi and Mende and Vai. In Southern Kono district and Northwestern Kailahun, Kisi and Kono are also linked by marriage and other forms of integration. The Sherbro and Mende are known to be strongly linked through inter-marriage; and like the Vai, Kissi and Krim, may easily be absorbed into Mende culture because of the presence of both groups in Bonthe and Moyamba, two adjacent districts that share many social practices. As they occupy the South-Western part of the area leading to Freetown, the Sherbro are also known to have converted on a massive scale to Krio. Because the Loko share common locations with the Temne and Krio in the Western area and in the Northern province, many have converted into Temne and Krio. Historically, it was easy for individuals with no previous knowledge of the cultures and traditions of host communities to migrate to such communities and become completely assimilated -- even to the point where their off-springs could ascend to leadership roles or occupy chieftaincy positions.

III

As a result of this very fluid situation of social integration, most of Sierra Leone's ethnic groups share a lot of values and cultural practices. Surnames such as Kamara, Turay, Koroma, Sillah, Bangura, Sesay, Mansaray (Masallay), Kemokai, Sankoh (Saccoh), Sheriff (also a first name for some groups), Fadika, Williams, etc. cut across several ethnic groups. Even surnames like Wurie, Timbo and Jalloh are no longer confined to one ethnic group -- not to talk of first names like Kemoh, Bangali (which could also be a surname), Bockarie, Foday, Kelfala, Musa, Almamy, Lansana, Momoh, John, Patrick, Hawa, Aminata, Susan etc. Customs relating to ways of honouring the dead, welcoming a new born baby, initiations leading to manhood and womanhood, secret societies, and respect for elders are very similar among most groups. Because of the dominance of Mende in the Southeast and Temne in the North, people in those areas who do not speak Mende or Temne respectively as first languages are likely to be multi-lingual. However, as our historian, Cecil Magbaily Fyle, notes the process of "Mendenisation" in the Southeast is much deeper than the "Temnenisation" of the North. Krio serves as the lingua franca in the city. Indeed, as a result of the widespread use of Krio, the English language, in its more standard form, has very shallow roots in Sierra Leone when compared to countries like Ghana or Nigeria where English is also the official language. When two Sierra Leoneans meet outside of Sierra Leone the use of Krio as a medium of communication comes naturally.

IV

Apart from cultural differences among individuals in each of the 16 groups, there have also been other types of social divisions, which make it difficult to see ethnic groups in homogenous terms. Firstly, in the context of the traditional social division of labour, some families or individuals, for instance, are likely to be musicians (*yeliba*), historians (griot), herbalists/doctors (*an'men*), fortune-tellers (*an'thupus*), hunters (*an'kapr*), craftsmen (*an'camd'err*), etc., while others may be farmers,

261

soldiers (*an'kurgbah*), midwives (*an'comsr*), and judges (*an'dikali*). Although these groups may obviously share many values with people who may be associated with their specific ethnic group, they also often share aspirations and values with individuals of the same professional specialisation located in other ethnic groups. The question of secrecy, for instance, is commonly valued among all herbalists, doctors, hunters, those who perform special ceremonies, and highly specialised craftsmen. It is amazing that several rituals and ceremonies performed by these special groups in the different societies tend to be very similar. This could only have come about through exchange of information and collaboration.

Modernisation introduced an additional layer of division of labour and sharpened social and economic differences between people within similar ethnic groups. New identities have emerged, which are unevenly distributed among individuals depending upon their location in the economy and society. Such identities relate to issues such as the status of being an industrial worker, a professional, an urban petty trader or artisan, a business person, a social activist, or a modern artist and musician. These identities complicate the picture of ethnicity. The drive for modernisation facilitates the coming together of people of different ethnic backgrounds to experience common social and work experiences. This has led to mass social movements like trades unions and student movements, whose strengths and successes often depend upon their ability to transcend ethnicity and mobilise members for a common corporate or social goal.

V

Thus multiple identities are the natural order in human evolution. At any given point an individual, for instance, can be a teacher, a Muslim or Christian, a trader, a woman, a member of an association or union, an actor with international NGO or professional links, and a person with family ties that reach out to one or several ethnic groups. Multiple identities should be applauded, not denigrated. Our lives are shaped by a constant process of negotiating our various identities as we move from one social setting to another. Multiple identities demonstrate the complexity of human relations, and help to hold in check propensities for forms of politics or social relations that seek to affirm ethnic exclusiveness. In other words, identities become a problem only when ethnic entrepreneurs enter the ring and totalise only one aspect of individuals' social affiliations for political mobilisation or for attack. In this regard, Siaka Stevens' constant reference to his multi-layered ethnic background -- his links with the Limba, Mende, Kissi, Vai and Krio -- should be seen as progressive, and not retrogressive. Each time he made those claims he was affirming the social reality of most Sierra Leoneans and helping to bridge ethnic differences. His problem was located elsewhere: he was greedy, ruthless and anti-developmental.

Ethnic politics

VI

The current patterns of ethnic identities started to take shape during the colonial impact when two different types of administrative systems were imposed on the country (Freetown and the Protectorate), and when the central state system itself failed to provide a political framework that would facilitate an equitable distribution of power among the key political actors who came from different ethno-linguistic formations and regions. The colonial state expected Sierra Leoneans to shed their African values and traditions and embrace only Western or British values. African traditions and values were devalued in such diverse fields as language, education, health provisioning, community defence, social security, music, storytelling and religion. Even though the power of traditional authority was recognised in the colonially-constructed native authority system, this was now subordinated to British power in Freetown. And the elites who should have played a vital role in modernising African traditions became much more interested in learning about British social ways and living their lives accordingly -- most often in hybrid fashion. Sierra Leone, like most African countries that experienced Western conquest, became a bifurcated society: a small Westernised sector pitched against the mass majority of people, who continued to practice their traditions but without the autonomy and resources to transform them into modern institutions.

It was this small elite that was to transform the process of ethnic identity formation in the country and made it much more difficult for people to criss-cross ethnic divides as they had done in the past. Even though this elite was drawn from all ethnic groups and shared more things in common -- such as their Western outlook and location in the city -- than they did with commoners in their assumed ethnic groups, they would quarrel over the resources and posts that had been created by the British to run the country. This quarrel was to take on virulent ethnic dimensions as the date of independence from Britain approached, and as Africans finally assumed the seat of power itself.

The first fault-line was the Freetown-Protectorate divide, with the bulk of the Krio elite (the most Westernised stratum of the elite) on one side supporting the United People's Party, and the Protectorate elite uniting under the Sierra Leone People's Party (SLPP). Of course, the SLPP also had several Krio elites, but not the other way around. One fall-out of this split was that the process of conversion into Krio by people from the protectorate slowed down or was reversed. Prior to this, the main route to Westernisation, which all elites cherished, passed through Krio or Frobay society. We now have a situation where a so-called provincial person in Freetown who has lost all links with his or her original language and a significant part of its corresponding culture will still refuse to regard himself or herself as a Krio or a Frobay--something that would have been a natural outcome in the past.

The second fault-line occurred within the ranks of the Protectorate elites themselves. The Protectorate was divided into three provinces: North, South and East. The Temne were dominant in the North, and the Mende in the South and East. The SLPP assumed power under the leadership of Milton Margai, a Mende. Upon his demise in 1964, the party decided to make his brother, Albert Margai, the party leader and Prime Minister, even though the latter had left the party at one stage to form his own People's National Party (PNP), and even though there were other senior members in the party like John Karefa Smart, M. S. Mustapha and Kandeh Bureh. Most members of the Northern elite saw this move to give the premiership to Albert Margai as ethnically-biased and nepotistic, and left the party to join the All People's Congress (APC). The APC then was still comprised largely of disgruntled ex-SLPP/UPP/PNP politicians in the city, and had no firm roots in the North. The split in the SLPP along ethno-regional lines strengthened the APC's hold on politics in the North. The Krio also joined the party in large numbers. As the group which supplied the bulk of the administrative cadre at the early period of independence, it's members felt threatened by what they saw as Albert Margai's attempts to

264

redistribute civil service posts among the various ethnic groups. The dominant view in Freetown was that the redistribution was skewed in favour of the Mende. Thus by 1965, elites had succeeded in transforming Sierra Leone's relatively fluid ethnic structure into a cluster of competing ethno-political centres.

VII

Ethnic politics took on a different pattern under the long reign of the All People's Congress. Siaka Stevens, the first president, was widely seen as a Limba because of his paternal links, even though those close to him felt he did not fully understand the language. His mother was Mende -- some said he was more fluent in Mende than in Limba -- and he spent a large part of his life in various mining towns and in Freetown as national secretary of the mine workers union and as a policeman. Perhaps, because of this mixed heritage, he was a very adaptable politician, who knew one or two things about the cultures of each group, and could mix very well. However, since the post-Milton Margai politics had split the country into a struggle between North-West and South-East elites, Stevens and his party colleagues decided to make the North-West the base of the APC, while at the same time undermining the hold of the SLPP in the South-East through intimidation, thuggery, violence, the cajoling of more pliable South-Easterners with political posts, and the transformation of the political system into a one party regime. Politicians in the South and East could only be tolerated in national politics if they joined the APC. Any form of Northern dissent was also repressed. The fate of the United Democratic Party, floated by Hamid and Ibrahim Taqi, Mohamed Fornah, Karefa-Smart and others is illustrative of the hegemonic grip of the APC on all of society.

Within the North-Western core constituency of the APC, Temne elites were dominant for a while, but the intellectual wing -- represented by Ibrahim Taqi and Mohamed Fornah -- lost the battle for control of the party to the mass activists – largely Siaka Stevens, "Agba Satani" S. I. Koroma, and C. A. Camara-Taylor. S. I. Koroma's ascendancy to the post of Vice President strengthened the grip of an aspiring group of Temne elites on the party. During this period, because of his relatively weak links in the North, Stevens had very little choice but to concede much power -- including the power to form cabinets -- to S. I. Koroma, who very quickly emerged as the dominant figure in the North by

265

shifting his electoral base from the Central One constituency of Freetown to an adopted constituency in Port Loko. A newly reconstituted Temne elite was ready to exchange the loss associated with the execution of Fornah and Taqi for senior posts and power in the party under the protection of S. I. Koroma. Within Northern elite circles, a small Limba elite that was in formation at the time was seen as a junior partner in the relationship, especially as most spoke Temne. However, with time, Stevens regained the initiative, and was skilful enough to not allow the Northern or Temne group to have complete control over the party. Elites from the Western area, Kono and co-opted/willing members of the South and East were equally rewarded with government and party posts.

The situation changed radically when Stevens and his cohorts decided to hand over the reins of the party and government to Joseph Saidu Momoh, who had not shown any interest in politics (as a nominated member of Parliament for 10 good years he never made a single speech). Stevens' flare for presenting himself as a man of all or most ethnic groups could not be matched by Momoh, who allowed a small cabal of Limba elites operating under the organisation "*Ekutay*" to take control of State House and become the clearing house for access to the presidency. The tragedy of this group was not only that its vision was marred by inward-looking ethnicity; the members were also driven by insatiable greed, playfulness and indiscipline; and they demonstrated gross incompetence and a pathetic inability or refusal to comprehend the depths of the social and economic malaise that had become all too visible to almost everybody else.

VIII

Even though the APC had a clear North-Western slant and South-Easterners were not treated as equals in the party, it would be wrong to conclude that the vast majority of people in the North benefited more from APC rule than those from the South or East, or that the thuggery and violence of the party was directed only at the people of the South-East. The violence of the APC knew no ethnic boundaries. All groups suffered from it in the party's drive to exercise hegemony over society. Individual elites from all ethnic groups also participated in the violence. The best known cases are the Sanda and Pujehun massacres. In the case of Sanda, a minister, Thaimu Bangura, locked horns with Timbo and

Ajibou Jalloh -- all three long-standing residents of Freetown. Even though the latter two individuals had been socialised into Temne culture and had therefore become less-Fulah, the ethnic card of Temne origin was played in the struggle for power in the constituency. Families that had lived peacefully together for generations were divided, and hundreds of people lost their lives, houses, cattle and other valuables in the carnage that followed. Murder charges that were initiated against the politicians involved in the massacre were quietly allowed to lapse in the interest of "party unity".

A similar situation occurred in Pujehun when the APC, under the influence of Francis Minah, who hailed from the area but spent most of his time in Freetown, tried to impose a candidate of his choice on the people during the parliamentary elections of 1982. The refusal of the people to yield to this pressure led to the recruitment of local thugs to beat up and harass the opposing candidate and his supporters. A very respectable school teacher and activist in the area was even captured by the government and imprisoned in Freetown. Again, families were unnecessarily split into antagonistic camps. There followed a period of large-scale violence and mass rebellion, dubbed *"Ndorgbryosoi"* (i.e. invisible spirit in Mende), which was only contained when the army was sent in. This, of course, further complicated the situation. Many observers believe that the RUF was able to take control of Pujehun during the early period of the war because of this history of local resentment of central government rule.

National Unity

IX

Multi-ethnic societies can only be governed peacefully if political systems are sensitive to ethnic cleavages, and if serious efforts are made to create civic publics that transcend ethnicity and allow every group or individual to feel at ease with those who govern, or aspire to govern. Forms of electoral politics that are based on the principles of "first-past-the-post" or "winner-takes-all" are clearly inadequate for the tasks of building multi-ethnic and civic polities. If they are not backed by institutional reforms for inclusive politics, they may activate latent ethnic fears, encourage winners to monopolise power and manipulate differences within losers' communities, and force losers to impose ethnic boundaries

267

on communities. The results can be devastating. A discourse of "us" versus "them" may emerge where none existed before, individuals who wish to straddle ethnic divides may find it difficult to do so, and those who wish to assert multiple identities may encounter resistance from ethnic bigots.

The elections of February 26 and 27, 1996 provided a window of opportunity for Sierra Leone to rebuild its battered politics away from the winner-takes-all formula of the APC, SLPP, and colonial eras. In both the presidential and parliamentary elections, no single party scored up to 50 percent of the votes. About five or six parties scored at least 5 percent of the votes to have some representation in parliament and for a cabinet based on a coalition of parties to be constructed. All regions had more than one party and voting did not strictly follow ethnic or regional lines. However, the second round of voting for the presidency transformed this fragmented outcome into a bipolar ethno-regional contest.

X

Multi-ethnic societies also suffer from socio-economic inequalities – such as in education, access to health facilities, electricity, transport and road networks, food security, employment, and housing. Ironically, despite the salience of ethnicity in our politics, most Sierra Leoneans of all ethnic groups today are immersed in poverty and suffer equally from the consequences of failed leadership, rundown infrastructure, a poorly functioning public service, and near national economic collapse. The few who benefit are also drawn from all ethnic groups.

Despite the hegemony of Northern elites under the APC, living conditions in the North are just as bad as in the East and South. And even though *Ekutay* enjoyed unquestioned hegemony in Momoh's government, the plight of the average Limba is not better -- it may, in fact, have deteriorated -- than it was before the ethnic concentration of power in the executive branch. In Brookfields and Kongo Market areas of West II constituency in Freetown, where many Limba in the city reside, the only monument of APC rule is a small dilapidated market, which has recently been given a face-lift by the NPRC government. For the vast majority of Limba in those areas, housing, education, water supply and incomes deteriorated very seriously from their already very pathetic state before the advent of the APC; and all were united with the rest of the city population in the daily struggle for light as Freetown was thrown into a state of complete darkness during much of Momoh's rule.

The lesson from this experience is that in the game of ethnic politics commoners are always used by their so-called ethnic elites as cannon fodder. A progressive government with a vision of national unity should be sensitive not just to elite differences in the struggle for the national cake; it should also be sensitive to inequalities within ethnic groups and between elites of all ethnic groups and the masses of all groups. Post-war reconstruction programmes should have this mass appeal, without ignoring ethnic cleavages.

34
Building a United and Cohesive Society[34]

I would first like to thank the organisers, the National Commission for Democracy (NCD), for inviting me to chair the opening session of this important conference.

Institutions like the NCD are essential in the consolidation and expansion of democracy. Such institutions can be effective and credible when they enjoy relative autonomy and are run by competent professionals with a commitment to the public good.

I commend the Chairman and staff of the NCD for raising the profile of the organisation, especially in the run-up to the 2012 general elections.

This conference, which will focus on ways of building a peaceful, tolerant and cohesive nation, could not have been organised at a better time.

Sierra Leone has just conducted national elections, which, like previous elections, especially those of 1967, 1996 and 2007, revealed a deeply divided electorate and lack of trust between the main political parties.

However, I should emphasise that despite our enormous problems, we have made important strides in consolidating our young democracy.

- the guns are silent and have, to a large extent, been destroyed;
- the press enjoys remarkable freedom despite its abrasiveness and serious shortcomings in the quality of reporting;
- there are no political prisoners; and
- some of the core institutions of governance are beginning to enjoy the trust of the people despite the challenges.

---

[34] Published in *CODESRIA Bulletin* (Council for the Development of Social Science Research in Africa), Nos. 1& 2, 4 June 2013; *Sierra Express Media* (Freetown), 23 March 2013; and *Patriotic Vanguard* (Vancouver), 24 March 2013, Opening Remarks at Consultative Conference on Building a Cohesive Nation; Organised by the National Commission for Democracy. Freetown. 20-22 March 2012.

It is important that the search for institutions and policies that can make us a tolerant and inclusive nation is taking place within a democratic setting. Democracy offers opportunities to identify, debate and rectify problems without resorting to violence. The best period to solve problems that require constitutional change is usually after a general election when passions have cooled and the issues that cause division, intolerance and exclusion are still fresh in the minds of voters.

I believe that this conference is part of a wider conversation that has been inspired by the President's post-elections speech to parliament in which he called for a review of the constitution to make Sierra Leone a more inclusive and tolerant polity.

Sources of intolerance

Intolerance thrives in divided or non-cohesive societies. It has many sources and dimensions, and can express itself at various levels of society.

It may be attributed to relations of domination, which may have a long historical trajectory, in the spheres of race, ethnicity, gender and class.

These may breed feelings of superiority among dominant groups as in apartheid South Africa; the effects of slavery on White-Black relations in the USA; male superiority over women spanning centuries or millennia; and peasant and working class subordination by property owners in feudal and industrial societies.

Intolerance can also occur even when relations of domination are not clearly defined or established. This may happen because of unregulated competition over scarce resources and positions in government and the private sector.

Individuals and groups may develop a sense of entitlement or exclusion, depending on their relations with the power structure, and may perceive politics as a zero-sum game in which losers are excluded from key resources and offices and winners take everything. Again, such intolerance may assume racial, ethnic, gender or class dimensions.

From the programme, it is clear that the organisers are mainly interested in the ethnic dimensions of the problem. We should however not lose sight of these other dimensions as they may be inseparable from ethnicity. In some contexts, progress in building united and cohesive

271

societies and overcoming intolerance in the ethnic domain may require equal attention to these other cleavages.

The ethnic problem

The first task for the policy analyst in devising mechanisms for inclusion and tolerance is to identify the key cleavage or cleavages that policy should address.

If the focus is on the ethnic cleavage, then some understanding of the distribution of ethnic groups and their inter-connections is important:

- is one group overwhelmingly dominant numerically?
- is the society made up of only two or three ethnic groups?
- do two or three groups dominate in a multiethnic setting?
- is the ethnic structure fragmented in such a way that it is difficult for any group to dominate politics or form regional coalitions?

Research suggests that countries with fragmented cleavages are much easier to manage than those that are polarised. Unfortunately, Sierra Leone's ethnic structure tends to be polarised:

- two dominant groups, which are roughly equal in size, account for about 60 percent of the population;
- the two groups are also geographically separated, making it possible for smaller groups in regions where each group is dominant to coalesce around the dominant group; and
- the two main political parties and voting patterns tend to reflect this ethno-regional bipolarity.

One of the dangers of bipolarity is that voters may be less flexible in relating to parties that are perceived to derive their core support from other regions.

This may lead to a bifurcated public. Groups that lie outside of a ruling party's stronghold may dismiss government initiatives even if the public good is served by such initiatives.

Similarly, a ruling party's voters may discredit everything that opposition parties from other regions do. Bifurcated publics may encourage non-cooperation between parties, and may plunge societies into conflict.

Despite Sierra Leone's bipolar ethnic structure, we do score very well in many other dimensions that measure tolerance:

- there is a high level of inter-ethnic marriage;
- we rank highly on religious tolerance, perhaps unsurpassed by no other country;
- there are no large-scale ethnic settlements or ghettoes in the capital city;
- a lingua franca, Krio, helps to depoliticise language, which is an important marker of identity and a source of conflict in other countries;
- our schools are not ethnically segregated;
- food, dress and music preferences tend to be uniform across ethnicities; and
- our professional organisations are highly multi-ethnic.

It is at the political level that intolerance tends to manifest itself. However, if political intolerance is not well managed, it can easily affect other facets of society and poison relations between people in their everyday lives.

Solutions

How can united, tolerant and cohesive societies be built? There are a variety of policy and institutional mechanisms that address issues of intolerance and exclusion. They focus on two issues: inequality reduction and recognition of cultural differences.

Recognition deals with issues of language rights, religion and cultural traditions. Fortunately, we have a lingua franca, and groups do not fight over language rights as in other countries, such as Sri Lanka, Latvia and Belgium. And the holidays of our two major religions are equally observed.

The major challenge is in inequality reduction, which deals with incomes; employment; asset ownership, such as land; and access to services; as well as the way cabinets, the civil service and law enforcement agencies, such as the military and police, are constituted.

How representative are these institutions? Do groups feel excluded? Are the institutions inclusive enough?

Institutions and policies

There are a number of rules that can promote inclusion in public institutions. These include:

- electoral rules, such as proportional representation; the alternative vote; the two round system; primaries; threshold rules, such as our 55% rule in determining whether there should be a run-off in presidential elections, and requiring winners in presidential elections to score a certain percentage of votes in all states or districts as in Nigeria and Kenya;
- affirmative action or positive discrimination can also be used for disadvantaged groups if inequalities are durable; if the inequalities are not sharp and deep-seated, the principle of proportionality can be used in constituting public bodies; and
- constitutional provisions can also be devised to ensure that political parties are substantially multi-ethnic.

We will have the opportunity to address these issues in the substantive sessions of this conference.

Having said this, I would like to emphasise that all policies and institutions that seek to promote tolerance and inclusion should pass an accountability and development test. Not all policies that promote inclusion are effective in promoting accountability and development.

Let me give two examples.

The first is the argument over power sharing and winner-takes-all systems. Donors have been in the habit of recommending power sharing systems to countries at war or that have experienced protracted conflict. This often involves distributing cabinet posts to the contending or warring parties, with the belief that a share of power will kill the appetite for war or conflict.

However, while power sharing has helped to minimise conflicts or end wars, it has not been a good instrument for promoting accountability and development.

- those who are given power may take it as a right and not something that should be exercised on behalf of the people;
- there is often no incentive to perform, since a share of power will be guaranteed to all parties even if they lose elections;
- voters may find it difficult to punish poor performers; and
- the country may be denied the advantages of an effective opposition that can hold the government to account.

I believe that a winner-takes-all system with constitutional guarantees for the representation of major groups or districts in the cabinet is preferable to power sharing systems in young democracies that are grappling with the problems of development. In Nigeria, which practices a winner-takes-all system, the constitution stipulates that each of the 36 states should have a cabinet minister.

The second example is the choice between the closed list-system of proportional representation, such as the one used for the 1996 elections, and constituency-based electoral systems. There is no doubt that the proportional representation system promotes more diversity than the first-past-the post system, as it makes it possible for smaller parties to organise and gain representation in the power structure.

However, the closed list-PR system scores poorly on accountability.

- it gives enormous powers to party leaders, who may decide how individuals are placed on party lists;
- besides, voters may find it difficult to throw out non-performing MPs. They can withdraw their support from the party, but not from individual MPs. Thus, non-performing MPs that enjoy the support of the party hierarchy will be shielded from the wrath of voters; and
- the system can also be abused by party leaders. This happened in 1996-7 in our parliament when the leader of the United National People's Party expelled more than 80 percent of the party's MPs

275

and attempted to replace them with other party members on the list. It is important to note that by-elections are not held in list-based proportional representation systems.

I will end my opening remarks by emphasising two points.

First, institution-building is a long-term project. It involves compromises and experimentation, and can be messy. There are no magic bullets.

Second, people make institutions work. The best institutions will fail if people do not believe in them or are ready to subvert them without fear of the consequences. Leaders' commitment to the rules of the game matters a lot.

35

Ethno-regional Divide and National Cohesion: Five Proposals for Constitutional Reform[35]

The national conversation on the review of the 1991 constitution is about to start in earnest. Already, a wide range of ideas and proposals are being canvassed in the media by advocacy groups, party officials and informed citizens. The process promises to be engaging and educative. It will enable citizens to understand the basic law of the land that defines rights and obligations, the powers and functions of the various arms of government, and how political leaders and other public officials are chosen and held to account by the populace.

This is the first of a series of interventions I intend to make as the review process unfolds. In this piece, I focus mainly on how to overcome the seemingly chronic ethno-regional divide that has structured our politics, and suggest ways of achieving national cohesion.

The 2012 elections, like most of our previous competitive elections, revealed a deeply divided electorate. Even though the All People's Congress (APC) made inroads into the Southern and Eastern regions, about 80 percent of the votes it received for the presidency came from the North and Western Area. Similarly, the Sierra Leone People's Party's (SLPP) presidential candidate obtained about 76 percent of his votes from the Southern and Eastern regions. The composition, leadership and electoral base of the two parties are unequivocally ethno-regional.

This bifurcation in the party system and voting behaviour has led to two relatively antagonistic publics that have the potential to disturb the peace and make it harder to sustain any development agenda. Party activists and sympathisers have developed a sense of entitlement or exclusion, depending on their location in the ethno-regional divide, and perceive politics as a zero-sum game in which losers believe they are excluded from key resources and offices and winners take everything.

---

[35] Published in *Sierra Express Media* (Freetown), 25 July 2013; *This is Sierra Leone*, July 2013; *Patriotic Vanguard* (Vancouver), 24 July 2013; *The Salone Monitor*, 24 July 2013.

Losers and their supporters, in turn, tend to discredit most development efforts by the government even when they serve the public good. Under such conditions, the two main parties are not held to account by their respective supporters who are ready to believe anything they hear from their party leaders. One only needs to listen to the numerous phone-in radio programmes on current affairs to understand the depth of the division in our body politic.

Constitutional reforms are clearly required to make Sierra Leone a more cohesive country. Even though the 1991 constitution is fairly good in many areas of governance, it does not offer sufficient provisions that can help politicians and voters to transcend the ethno-regional divide and embrace the values of national cohesion. Chapter III, article 27 of the constitution prohibits discrimination on the basis of "race, tribe, sex, place of origin, political opinions, colour or creed"; and Chapter IV, article 35 affirms that a political party should not be restricted to only one ethnic group; the "name, symbol, colour or motto" of a party should not have exclusive significance to any ethnic or religious group; a party should not "advance the interest and welfare" of only one ethnic group, community, geographical area or religious faith; and a party should have a "registered office in each of the Provincial Headquarter towns and the Western Area". It is clear that these provisions have been insufficient to tame the scourge of ethnic division and antagonism in our politics.

I offer five proposals for consideration. These are in the areas of cabinet formation, internal democratic practices of parties and election of flag bearers, time limits for determining electoral disputes, and fixed dates for holding general elections.

The principle of representation, which is the bedrock of modern democracies, assumes that those who govern, do so on behalf of the people. Individual interests are often aggregated into larger group interests, such as those of industrial workers, entrepreneurs, farmers, landlords, traders, artisans, professionals, women, and ethnic and religious minorities.

In advanced industrial democracies, interest groups and political parties tended in the early period of democratisation to cluster according to the basic capital-labour cleavage associated with industrialisation. Indeed, the ideologies of most political parties reflected the aspirations of the key interest groups they sought to promote. Interests based on horizontal cleavages, such as those of women and ethnic groups, were ignored. However, most industrial democracies were relatively homogenous nation-states, and even though women's representation in public institutions was limited, women as voters could be found in all major political parties. It was, therefore, relatively easy to incorporate women's demands in public policy when women's voices grew louder for greater representation and empowerment.

However, in most developing countries today, political parties do not cluster according to economic class interests. Most parties lack clearly defined ideologies that are based on economic aspirations or what people do for a living. Most developing countries are also multi-ethnic, making it possible for class interests to be downplayed by individuals in their choice of parties, and for parties that seek to draw support from specific economic interest groups to be restricted to only one ethnic segment of such groups. Even though the APC likes to claim that it is a "common man's party", this message, even if true, resonates only among commoners in the North and Western Area. The danger of having a public sector that is highly skewed in favour of one ethno-regional group is very high in situations where the public sphere is strongly bifurcated.

How have multiethnic democracies tackled this problem? Two methods can be highlighted: coalition governments or power sharing and constitutional provisions for multi-ethnic representation in cabinet.

Coalition governments work in parliamentary systems that use either proportional representation rules (which may encourage a fragmentation of large ethnic groups into multiple parties), as in Belgium; or first past the post constituency rules where a dominant ethnic group (which may also fragment) enters into an alliance with smaller parties that draw their support from minority ethnic groups, as in Malaysia. The current Belgian cabinet is composed of six political parties, three each from the two dominant ethnic groups of Walloons (French) and Flemish (Dutch). Because of the fragmentation of the two ethnic groups into multiple parties, no single party has the numerical strength to form a government alone. Malaysia's cabinet is composed of a Malay party, the United Malays National Organization, and parties representing Chinese and Indian communities, with UMNO as the dominant party. Because of the fragmentation of the Malay vote into multiple parties, UMNO increasingly relies on the Chinese and Indian parties to win elections. In Switzerland, all the four main political parties, which are multi-ethnic in character, share the seven ministries that constitute the cabinet based on their performance in the popular vote.

The second method -- that of constitutional provisions for multi-ethnic representation in cabinet-- has been tried in several countries, including Nigeria, Belgium and Switzerland. In Nigeria, which has a presidential system of government with first past the post electoral rules, the constitution compels the president to appoint at least one cabinet minister from each of the 36 states. In Belgium, the constitution limits the number of cabinet ministers to 15 and stipulates that these should be equally distributed between the two ethnic groups: French and Dutch. In Switzerland, there is an informal rule, now institutionalised, which requires that at least two of the seven members of the federal executive council should be French in order to prevent German speakers from using their numerical strength to grab all seven cabinet posts.

What can be done in Sierra Leone? Sierra Leone practices a presidential system of government with first past the post electoral rules. I have argued elsewhere that the proportional representation system tends to empower party leaders at the expense of voters, and is weak on accountability. At the same time, a parliamentary system in a context where the political culture does not promote compromise or moderation may lead to grid-lock and frequent elections and change of government. Besides, even if Sierra Leone had a parliamentary system today, the APC would not need a coalition to govern since it has more than 60 percent of the contested parliamentary seats. Combining a parliamentary system with proportional representation might produce a coalition government, but the voting behaviour of the two dominant ethnic groups will have to fragment into multiple parties for viable small parties to emerge and the cabinet to be substantially multiethnic. It is also worth pointing out that coalition governments do not work well in presidential systems of government, unless if the president's party does not enjoy an absolute majority in parliament. The coalition between the SLPP government of Ahmad Tejan Kabbah and Thaimu Bangura's People's Democratic Party ended in failure, as did that of Ernest Koroma's APC government and Charles Margia's People's Movement for Democratic Change. The lesson here is that a president who has already won an election can dispense with the support of the junior party in the coalition without fear of losing power.

My proposal is to retain the presidential system of government and first-past-the-post constituency rule and introduce constitutional provisions for the formation of multiethnic cabinets.

So, my **first proposal** is:

> *The President shall appoint at least one cabinet minister from each of the fourteen electoral districts; and no two regions shall account for more than 60 percent of cabinet appointments.*

The last part of the proposal is derived from the fact that no two regions combined—North-West, South-East, North-East, North-South, South-West, East-West--- account for more than 60 percent of registered voters or the country's population.

The second and third proposals focus on ways of de-ethnicising our political parties. Part of the problem here is the lack of internal democracy in the two main parties, and association of party identities with the ethnicities of those who lead them. Both parties have not succeeded in embedding open democratic practices in the way they choose their representatives. Powerful individuals and groups often manipulate internal electoral processes in order to produce outcomes that favour their preferences. Lack of internal democracy empowers those who thrive on the ethno-regional identities of the parties and makes it difficult for modernisers with a national outlook to emerge and take root in party structures.

In the run-up to the 2012 elections, the two parties took important steps to democratise their methods of choosing representatives by introducing electoral college rules. However, the implementation of the rules for conducting the primaries was fraught with difficulties. In a number of cases, those entrusted with the responsibility to organise the primary elections skewed the selection process in favour of candidates of their choice.

One recent development is the return of the culture of "zero competition" (unopposed candidates) in the ruling APC. This was vividly demonstrated in the party's last national convention when all the candidates for the key party posts went unopposed. The public now refers to this practice as "politics of compensation"---i.e. giving jobs or resources to those who withdraw from contests. This is not only bad for democracy, it is also a cost on our treasury. Some members of the SLPP, on the other hand, have resorted to threats or use of force in their own primaries to impose their will on the party (the so-called "pa-o-pa syndrome") because the party lacks the resources to buy off those who seek to challenge candidates of influential personalities.

My **second proposal** is:

> *A political party shall conduct primary elections in choosing its candidates for presidential, parliamentary and local council elections; each registered party member at the local, constituency, district or national level shall participate in such elections and shall be entitled to one vote.*

Transforming our main political parties into substantially multiethnic institutions also requires changes in the way flag bearers are chosen in presidential elections. Individuals from all regions and ethnicities must have equal opportunities to contest and win the top jobs in the main parties. In Nigeria, the ruling party, the People's Democratic Party, has a policy of rotating the post of flag bearer between the Northern and Southern regions, which are divided into six geo-political zones. In Switzerland, the presidency rotates every year among the seven members of the federal executive council, which means that a French person will have the chance to become a president twice within a seven year cycle. In Bosnia, the presidency rotates very eight months among members of the executive council that is made up of the three main ethnic groups of Serbs, Bosniaks and Croats.

My **third proposal** is:

> *A political party shall not choose its flag bearer from the same region or ethnic group in more than two consecutive elections; however, a flag bearer who has served for only one term as President can be chosen as a flag bearer for a second and final term of office.*

My fourth and fifth proposals are about fairness in the electoral process. The constitution needs to be amended to compel the courts to decide election petitions within a defined period. Petitions emanating from the

2007 elections dragged on for several years, and it took about six months for the Supreme Court to decide on the petition relating to the 2012 presidential election. Right now the courts are yet to determine petitions on two parliamentary constituencies. This means that voters in those two constituencies have not been represented in parliament since November 2012. This is a messy and unacceptable state of affairs. Confidence in the judiciary can only be enhanced if losers believe that their grievances can be heard and resolved not only fairly but also speedily. We should take a leaf from the new Kenyan constitution, which stipulates that all electoral disputes on presidential elections should be decided within two weeks, and that winners should not be sworn in or inaugurated before electoral disputes have been resolved by the courts.

I quote the relevant sections of the Kenyan constitution as my **fourth proposal** to guide our discussion.

> *"Within fourteen days after the filing of an election petition (against the President-elect), the Supreme Court shall hear and determine the petition and its decision shall be final.*
> *If the Supreme Court determines the election of the President-elect to be invalid, a fresh election shall be held within sixty days after the determination.*
> *The President-elect shall be sworn in on the first Tuesday following--*
> *a) the fourteenth day after the date of the declaration of the results of the presidential election, if no petition has been filed; or*
> *b) the seventh day following the date on which the court renders a decision   declaring the election to be valid, if any petition has been filed".*

We may wish to select a different day for the swearing in of the President-elect--say the first Saturday following the fourteenth day after the declaration of the results if there is no petition, or the seventh day after fresh elections have been held after a successful petition.

My final proposal is to establish a fixed date for holding presidential and parliamentary elections. The present arrangements in the 1991 constitution are rather clumsy. The date shifts after every election. Chapter V, article 46 (1) states that "No person shall hold office as President for more than two terms of five years each whether or not the terms are consecutive". And yet, article 43 allows for an interval of up to three months after the expiration of the five year term of the president for elections to be held. This means that a president can enjoy an extra three months in office after his or her term has expired. If that president serves two terms, he or she would have served ten and half years instead of ten. Currently, there is speculation that the next election might not be held in 2017 but in 2018. This culture of "bonya" (extras) should be terminated. We do not run a parliamentary system of government where it is impossible to fix a specific date for a general election. Incidentally, one advantage of having a fixed date is that we can avoid organising an election in the rainy season when movement of people and vehicles within the country is difficult.

My **fifth proposal**, again drawing on the Kenyan constitution, is:

> *An election of the President shall be held on the same day as a general election of Members of Parliament on the second Saturday in November in every fifth year.*

I will conclude this piece by stressing the point that the constitutional review process offers us a fresh opportunity to fix our chronic ethno-regional problem and create a level playing field in the electoral process. We were lucky that our brutal war was not fought on ethno-regional lines. However, we should not wait for a Kenyan type of ethnic crisis before we try to solve the problem, which everybody knows exists. It is more costly to rebuild a broken house than to carry out timely and incremental or moderate repairs. The five proposals that I have offered may even encourage the emergence of new parties with a social justice agenda that is not constrained by the ethno-regional divide.

36
Why a Government of National Unity will not be good for Zimbabwe[36]

The suggestion by some Commonwealth leaders that Robert Mugabe and Morgan Tsvangirai should form a government of national unity to heal the divisions in Zimbabwe is mistaken and should be rejected by both parties. The constitutional referendum of 2000, the parliamentary elections of 2001, and the just-concluded presidential elections, however flawed they are, point to a significant development in African politics and democratisation. The elections signal a decentring of ethnicity and assertion of policy issues over sentiments in public debate.

Zimbabwe is a multi-ethnic society in which the Shona account for well over 60 percent of the population. The second largest group, the Ndebele, are slightly less than 15 percent of the population, and the third largest group is about 2 percent. There are about 15 ethnic groups in the country. There has been a tendency in academic and policy circles to view ethnicity as pathological. Two development economists, William Easterly and Ross Levine, have even identified ethnic fragmentation as a major cause of "Africa's growth tragedy".

A recently launched project entitled *Ethnic Structure, Inequality and Governance of the Public Sector* at the UN Research Institute for Social Development questions this reading of politics in multi-ethnic societies. It develops a typology that distinguishes countries according to levels of polarisation or dispersion of ethnic segments. One of its hypotheses is that if the largest group accounts for an overwhelming majority of the population, it is likely to fragment, allowing individuals from smaller groups to play active roles in the parties formed by the dominant group. Ethnicity may constitute less of a problem in such societies than in those with only two or three ethnic groups, or in multi-ethnic settings in which groups have coalesced into regional formations that may limit the scope for bargaining.

As in all post-liberation countries in which nationalism was an organising principle of politics, Zimbabwe's first elections were a

---

[36] Published in *The Herald* (Harare). April 2002.

referendum on white settler rule and colonialism. The tendency for dominated groups to act as a single entity in the first years of independence is usually very strong. The ruling party, Zimbabwe African National Union-Patriotic Front (Zanu-PF), embodied the aspirations of all sections of society disadvantaged under white rule. Despite problems of funding, the party held out the prospect of land reform in order to keep its rural constituency happy. At the same time, its inheritance of a healthy budget and economy meant it could pursue progressive social policies in the educational and health fields for all Zimbabweans, as well as provide job opportunities and good incomes to the urban middle class and workers. At 87.2 percent, Zimbabwe's literacy rate is the highest in Africa and higher than that of most middle income countries in the world.

The major political divide among Africans in the early years of independence was ethnic: Shona versus Ndebele. Joshua Nkomo, who was Ndebele, and his Zimbabwe African People's Union (ZAPU), were worried about marginalisation for good reason. Nationalism, use of state resources for political ends, and majoritarian electoral rules would prevent the fragmentation of the Shona vote, thus ensuring that Zanu-PF would govern without reference to ZAPU, which had its base among the Ndebele. The decision to form a government of national unity, following the violent conflicts between the two parties in the early 1980s, was a rational and welcome development. It brought the Ndebele into the social contract that underpinned nation-building. Indeed, ZAPU's policies, unlike those of Abel Muzorewa's party that was sponsored by the white regime to obstruct socio-economic transformation, did not differ from ZANU-PF's on the core issue of national development.

The situation today is different. Nationalism is in decline and the state is no longer able to meet much of its obligation under the social contract that helped it hold together two different constituencies: the rural and the urban. It can only appease the peasantry by speeding up land reform, which seems less interesting to urban dwellers.

Significantly, the Shona vote has fragmented, allowing elites from the Ndebele and other minorities to play central roles in both parties. In the 2000 referendum, which the government lost, most urban dwellers voted against the government whilst the rural people supported it. In the 2001 parliamentary elections, the opposition Movement for Democratic Change (MDC) won 57 seats and ZANU-PF 62. All 15 seats in

Matabeleland, the heartland of the Ndebele, and most urban seats were won by the MDC. ZANU-PF won most rural seats. The two largest cities, Harare (with a majority Shona population) and Bulawayo (majority Ndebele) voted overwhelmingly for the MDC. The pattern in the 2002 presidential elections is similar to previous ones except that the Ndebele vote fragmented for the first time. The cities in Matabeleland still went to the MDC but Mugabe was able to make substantial inroads into that region's rural areas, winning about 33 percent of the regional vote. The MDC won the majority of the council seats in cities for which elections were held.

These trends suggest that ethnicity is becoming less important in Zimbabwe's politics. The major dividing line is now rural-urban, and the two main parties reflect this. ZANU-PF has failed to connect with the urban workers and middle class, whereas the MDC, which is heavily supported by the West and local whites, offers no credible message to the land-hungry peasantry. Indeed, the MDC is seen as an instrument to reverse the gains of independence and block land reform. ZANU-PF supports state intervention in the management of the economy whereas the MDC, like many new opposition parties that depend on the West for support, champion neoliberal economic policies. As an opposition party, the MDC is strong on the rule of law, whereas Zanu-PF still has to shed its authoritarian baggage.

A national unity government will not work in Zimbabwe under these conditions. This is one of the few cases in African democratisation in which policies rather than ethnicity and other types of primordial sentiments are driving the political contest. Let the policies contend as in Western democracies where ethnicity is an insignificant predictor of political behaviour. A unity government will fudge, not resolve, the issues. Unity governments work best when countries are in a state of war or emergency, or when they are polarised by ethnic conflicts with no clear policy differences between contenders. The control of city councils by the opposition gives them a stake in governance and may force both parties to dialogue and tone down the unsavoury aspects of their discourse and behaviour. The international community should help Zimbabwe resolve once and for all its land problem, which makes it difficult to organise free and fair elections. A mobilised peasantry and nationalist party with a liberation history will not accept a situation in which 4,500 white farmers control 42 percent of the agricultural land and 1.2 million black families subsist on 41 percent of the land.

37
Rebuilding Cote d'Ivoire: Lessons from Sierra Leone[37]

The demise of Laurent Gbagbo's regime offers fresh opportunities to tackle Cote d'Ivoire's intractable problems. Hundreds of people have lost their lives, about a million have been displaced from their homes, infrastructure and properties have been destroyed, and economic life remains precarious. Gbagbo's continued hold on power would have emboldened leaders who lose elections to stay in office, dealing a blow to the region's fragile democracies.

However, Gbagbo's exit does not solve the problems of Cote d'Ivoire, which remains a divided country. Although Alassane Ouattara won the elections, almost half of the population voted for his opponent. The country's 20 million people of 70 ethnicities form five regional clusters: the Akan in the eastern and central parts of the country; the Krou and allied groups in the southwest; the Southern Mandé in the west; and the Voltaic and Northern Mandé in the north. The southern groups tend to be Christian, and those in the north Muslim. The influx of migrants from predominantly Muslim Burkina Faso, Mali and Guinea in search of work during the boom of the 1960s and 1970s changed the ethnic distribution in favour of Muslims.

As demands for competitive elections grew and the political elite that succeeded the founding president, Houphouet Boigny, sought to consolidate its rule, a xenophobic discourse of *Ivoirité* or indigeneity emerged that elevated the Muslim-Christian/North-South divide over other cleavages. Bold and creative efforts are required to drain the poison of *Ivoirité* from the body politic, manage the North-South schism, and develop a culture of shared citizenship.

Sierra Leone's post-conflict experience offers lessons on security, inclusive government and development.

Sierra Leone's conflict was of course more destructive and less ethnic than Cote d'Ivoire's. Still, Cote d'Ivoire will have to rebuild its divided army, disarm militias, and provide security to its traumatised

---

[37] Published in *Open Democracy* (London). 3 May 2011; *Daily Trust* (Kaduna), 6 May 2011; *UNRISD eBulletin.* Issue 5. 5 May 2011.

citizens. In highly polarised settings, security sector reform should not be left to winners alone. In Sierra Leone, the government worked with the United Nations peacekeeping mission (UNAMSIL) and Britain in providing security for a number of years before full responsibility was transferred to national authorities. Fortunately, soldiers in UN peacekeeping missions in Africa today are largely drawn from the continent and other developing countries, avoiding the stigma of neo-colonialism. In Sierra Leone, the bulk of the force was Nigerian. Britain's military back-up to UNAMSIL mainly served as deterrence.

The UN may have to expand its mission in Cote d'Ivoire. Can France play a similar role in Cote d'Ivoire as Britain did in Sierra Leone? The French have been more forceful in carrying out regime change in Cote d'Ivoire than the British were in Sierra Leone. Surely, without French power, the stalemate would have continued and more lives lost.

However, there are constraints on the use of the French military as deterrence because of distrust of French motives among sections of the Ivorian elite. Differences between British and French engagement with their ex-colonies may account for this. The British establishment has fewer social ties with African elites whereas France has nurtured strong bonds with elites in its ex-colonies. Jean-Christophe Mitterrand, son of former French president François Mitterrand, and Martin Bouygues, head of the French industrial group, Bouygues, attended Ouatarra's wedding in 1991. France retained military bases in most of Francophone West Africa and has often been accused of defending friendly authoritarian leaders. Today, partly because of weak post-colonial ties, most Sierra Leoneans consider Britain's military presence in Sierra Leone as benign. The same cannot be said about elite attitudes towards France in Cote d'Ivoire.

The winner, Ouattara, also needs to form a government that is perceived as inclusive by those who did not vote for him. Again Sierra Leone provides useful lessons. The immediate post-war leader, Ahmad Tejan Kabbah, reached out to sections of the country (the North and West) that disliked his party. He even incurred the wrath of party stalwarts in the South for insisting on a balanced cabinet. In the 2002 elections held just after the war, he recorded 70 percent of the vote as president, and his party won 18 of the 40 parliamentary seats in the North. Today there are a large number of Northern elites in his party; and at least 8 of the 19 candidates for the party's 2012 presidential ticket claim to have Northern roots. The current Northern-dominated government has recently borrowed a leaf from that experience of inclusive government after some faltering steps that alienated Southern elites.

Finally, governments should avoid an incremental approach to reconstruction that privileges reconciliation and humanitarian assistance over development. This is because by the time the development phase is reached, confidence in peace improving the well-being of most people may have waned, forcing voters to turn against incumbents. If Kabbah's government did well on reconciliation, it scored poorly on development, preferring to focus on small projects, such as rehabilitating schools, clinics, traditional courts, markets, and police stations that are essential in resettling populations but inadequate in moving economies forward. Issues of infrastructure development, energy provision, agricultural transformation and employment are only now being seriously addressed. Voters rejected the party in the 2007 elections.

The lessons for Cote d'Ivoire are clear: security sector reform, reconciliation, resettlement and development must work in tandem; and governments must ensure that the people, especially the youth, see improvements in their lives.

38
The Case for a Nigerian-Led ECOMOG Force in Sierra Leone[38]

Events in the past two weeks in which a group of non-commissioned soldiers and low-ranking officers of the Sierra Leone army joined forces with the rebel Revolutionary United Front to overthrow the year-old democratically elected government of Ahmad Tejan Kabbah, indicate that the situation in the country is slowly disintegrating into anarchy. The Armed Forces Revolutionary Council/Revolutionary United Front (AFRC/RUF) have been unable to restore order, guarantee the safety of citizens, and hold in check the loose underclass elements of the army and rebel movement that made the coup. The vast majority of city and rural dwellers are opposed to the coup, and have resolved to not cooperate with the coup leaders and their rebel collaborators. Offices remain closed, and a rally which was called on Sunday, 8 June to support the actions of the AFRC/RUF attracted only 5,000 people in a 50,000-capacity stadium in Freetown. Most parts of the provinces remain outside of the control of the AFRC/RUF, have vowed to resist military/rebel rule, and have mobilised armed militia forces to challenge the coup. Without an international force to help stabilise the situation and disarm the AFRC/RUF, and ultimately the militias, the country seems destined to be trapped in its present state of anarchy for a considerable time. ECOMOG, the West African peace keeping force that has helped to bring order to Liberia, is in Sierra Leone to arrest this spiral descent into anarchy and restore constitutional order.

The legitimacy of the ECOMOG force has been questioned in certain quarters on three grounds. The first, put forward by Bolaji Akinyemi (former Foreign Minister of Nigeria under the military ruler, Ibrahim Babangida) in the UK Guardian of 5 June and the International Herald Tribune of 10 June, and by an editorial in the New York Times of 6 June, claims that since Nigeria is a military regime that has subverted the democratic wishes of its own people, it has no moral right to lead a multinational force that is aimed at restoring democracy in another country; and that all that the military operation is likely to achieve is to

---

[38] Published in *West Africa* (London). 30 June-6 July 1997.

rehabilitate General Sani Abacha's regime in the eyes of the world community. The second argument, coming from Abbas Bundu (former Foreign Minister of the military NPRC regime in Sierra Leone), in an open letter he addressed to the Secretary General of the UN on 4 June, states that the Nigerian action violates Sierra Leone's sovereignty; and that the ECOMOG operation flouts the Economic Community of West African States' (ECOWAS) protocols on military engagement in the sub-region. The third argument, put forward by individuals of various political persuasions, questions the intervention on the basis of the likely destruction it may bring to the city. There may be useful lessons to learn from these three objections, but they ignore or downplay the basic realities of, and offer no viable solutions to, the crisis.

Nigeria has regional responsibilities, whose defence can be justified independently of whoever happens to be in power in that country. It accounts for 55 per cent of West Africans, the biggest economy in the sub-region, and the largest number of professionals in Africa outside of South Africa. In a world of regional economic blocs, the country's industrialisation and well-being ultimately depend upon its ability to nurture a stable regional economy in West Africa. It has, over the years, developed a proactive Africa policy, especially after the advent to power in 1974 of the radical military ruler, Murtala Mohammed, and played a leading role in the formation of ECOWAS itself. It has been actively involved in both Sierra Leone and Liberia since 1990 when these two countries were threatened with instability. Surrounded by four potentially volatile states -- Chad, Cameroon, Niger and Benin -- Nigeria is bound to be worried about the spread of instability in the region. The country's strategic interests in the region surely transcend the interests of the current policy makers, even if they may seek to derive dividends from their current operations in pursuing their own agendas.

Besides, the world is going through such disturbingly rapid change that regional anchor states (or blocs) are likely to become the guarantors of global security. This is the case in Europe, the Americas, East and South Asia, and Southern Africa. Africans are slowly learning to accept the current reality that the UN or Western powers cannot, will not, and should not, police African problems. African people and their leaders will have to work out their own regional security arrangements if they are to live in stable and prosperous nations. In West Africa, whether we like it or not, it is Nigeria that can, and will, provide the leadership for regional security. And support for Nigeria's progressive role in Sierra Leone should not mean that Nigerian military leaders' assault on the democratic process in Nigeria should be condoned. Indeed, if the restoration of democratic constitutional rule in Sierra Leone succeeds through Nigeria's efforts, the case for democratic governance is likely to be enhanced in Nigeria itself.

From March 1996 to May 1997, Sierra Leoneans enjoyed a constitutional order that was predicated on a democratically elected government and parliament. Despite its shortcomings, it provided a foundation for the development of a civic culture, as well as respect for human life, the rule of law, and public/private property. People felt safer under that constitutional order than what the gun-toting gangs who are marauding the streets of Freetown are now promising. There is even the danger that the military coup will undermine the unity of the country by accentuating the ethnic fault lines that Sierra Leoneans have been trying to manage through constitutional means in the last year. Sierra Leone needs an international force to stop the looting, killings and assault on people's property, as well as to check the further disintegration of the country.

The legal arguments against Nigerian intervention look shallow on closer inspection. There is a military treaty between the government of Sierra Leone and Nigeria, the Status of Forces Agreement (SOFA), in which the Nigerian government undertakes to "make available military and security assistance" (Nigerian Forces Assistance Group) to Sierra Leone (Article 2.1). President Ahmad Tejan Kabbah is on record as having invited the Nigerian-led intervention force to put down the rebellion and prevent the disintegration of the state.

On the question of the legal status of the military action under the ECOWAS protocols, these protocols were never used to justify the ECOMOG operation in Liberia. As Executive Secretary of ECOWAS at the time, Abbas Bundu and the West African leaders who took the decision relied on humanitarian arguments in setting up ECOMOG. The same humanitarian conditions that justified the deployment of ECOMOG forces in Liberia apply in Sierra Leone today -- indeed, in much greater force. The city of Freetown has been exposed to unprecedented large scale insecurity in the hands of highly undisciplined armed gangs who are now trying to administer the state; and large parts of the provinces are up in arms against the AFRC/RUF. It is the moral responsibility of ECOMOG to restore order in the country.

The international community should support it in what it is trying to do. Only the presence of an ECOMOG force under Nigerian leadership can guarantee that the peaceful solution to the crisis, which everybody wants, will be realised. ECOMOG is needed in Sierra Leone for disarmament and medium-term national security, as well as for rehabilitation and resettlement of all armed combatants.

39
The Tragedy of the Lomé Accord and the Way Forward [39]

Recent events in our troubled country, in which the Revolutionary United Front is reported to have seized about 500 UN peacekeepers, have laid bare the folly of decision-makers who believe that individuals with a record of horrific crimes against humanity can be appeased with a general amnesty, government posts, and a neutral peacekeeping force. Sierra Leoneans are once again left to ponder the awful consequences of the failure of their government to establish a security system that will bring lasting peace to their country. The spectre of the RUF's acts of barbaric executions, grotesquely cruel mutilations and mindless arson haunts the homes of most citizens. The people of Sierra Leone and their supporters need to take hard decisions if the perennial lapses in security are to be corrected.

A deeply flawed accord

One does not need to be a Clausewitz, Kissinger or Cabral to know that the Lomé accord is a profoundly flawed strategic document. The accord has four major shortcomings. First, the granting of amnesty and ministerial posts to the rebels makes a mockery of the basic principles of human rights and democracy. The accord is not only a terrible injustice to victims. It also reinforces a deeply held view by the rebels that gross atrocities can yield handsome political dividends. It is a dubious instrument for conflict management. It represents the first time that armed gangs have been rewarded with power by the international community without the benefit of a democratic mandate. In Cambodia, Bosnia and Northern Ireland, for instance, power sharing with rebels was at least based on popular choices. For all the horrors of Charles Taylor, it was not the Abuja accord that gave him power, but the people of Liberia

---

[39] Written on 14 May 2000 after the RUF reneged on the Lomé Accord and seized about 500 UN peacekeepers in Sierra Leone. Circulated at a conference in London on Sierra Leone's civil war. May 2000.

in elections. It will be difficult to reclaim by democratic means the power the Lomé accord has granted the RUF rebels.

Second, the Lomé accord utterly fails to grasp the conditions under which violence-prone rebel movements can be made to reclaim their humanity and observe peace agreements. This is the third time that the RUF rebels have reneged on an agreement. The Abidjan accord of 1996 stalled when Foday Sankoh refused to send representatives to the key disarmament committee that would have helped the United Nations to disarm the RUF. The Conakry accord of October 1997 collapsed when the AFRC and RUF leaders refused to allow ECOMOG to disarm their warriors. Central to this pattern of failures is a fundamental logic and reality about conflicts that the Lomé peacemakers fail to understand: the interconnections of territory, resources and civilisation.

Events in Africa and elsewhere suggest that peace accords with rebels in resource-rich countries can only succeed when rebels use territory and resources to cleanse their record of atrocities. Territory helps to restore civility and offers power to defend gains in power sharing agreements. Resources facilitate a scaling down of terror, less extraction of the personal assets of the population, and prospects for winning the people's confidence. Complete disarmament, the expected dividend of the Lomé appeasement, is, thus, an incredibly naïve objective. It defeats the basic rebel project of reclaiming their humanity and cultivating political legitimacy.

In this regard, the weapons buy-back policy that is at the heart of the disarmament programme is unlikely to be effective. This policy worked in a place like Mozambique because that country is resource-poor. The US$300 that the disarmament agency has pegged to an RUF gun -- the reward for handing in a weapon -- is far less than the gun's real market value in the diamond areas. Interestingly, disarmament has been relatively more successful with the AFRC soldiers in non-diamond areas than with the RUF rebels in the diamond fields.

Third, the assumption in the accord that participation in the government will persuade the rebels to adopt the democratic road to power is terribly misplaced. Sierra Leone, unlike Liberia, is a multi-ethnic bipolar polity: the dominance of two relatively equal ethnic groups in a multi-ethnic setting. Sierra Leone's politics since the 1960s have starkly reflected this bipolarity: the North and South, where the two main ethnic groups are substantially located, provide the primary axis for political affiliation. Sankoh is highly unlikely to repeat the feat of his mentor, Charles Taylor, who opted for the democratic route and recorded a stunning 75 percent of the votes in elections to become president of a much less polarised multi-ethnic Liberian polity. The SLPP is deeply entrenched in the South and parts of the East of Sierra Leone. Sankoh also has to contend with northern politicians who are unlikely to yield the northern region to him in an open democratic contest. Force, not elections, is, therefore, always likely to be the ultimate option of Sankoh's RUF in its quest for full executive power.

Fourth, by reversing ECOMOG's strategy of peace enforcement and opting instead for peacekeeping, the Lomé accord offers the rebels much more leverage than they hitherto enjoyed. It is irresponsible to have deployed a peacekeeping force "on a shoe string", with a limited mandate, to disarm a rebel group with a track record of horrific violence and duplicity without a regional or international power that can provide backbone to that force. For all its shortcomings, ECOMOG was able to contain the rebels because of the political commitment of the regional power, Nigeria, in enforcing the peace. The rebels went into power sharing with light weapons and have come out of the agreement with at least 12 armoured personnel carriers and plenty of weapons seized from peacekeepers. The rebels also believe, for the first time, that they can overrun the capital and keep it.

What must be done?

Three things need to be done. First, Sierra Leoneans and policy makers at home and abroad should reject the view that the Lomé accord can be rescued. Jesse Jackson, one of the godfathers of the accord, has been reported as saying that the signing of the accord represents only the first step to peace; the difficult task is to implement the peace plan and overcome the obstacles: "after a long night, joy cometh in the morning". Nonsense. Even if the accord is put back on track, it will only be a matter of time before it unravels again. Lomé will not deliver meaningful disarmament, nor will it encourage the rebels to hand over the territories they control.

The lifeline of the rebels, diamonds, can only be disconnected by a change in the balance of power, not diplomacy. The recalcitrance of Savimbi's UNITA movement in Angola is there for all to see. Rebel movements will resist attempts to deny them access to their resource base even when they are part of a power sharing government. Indeed, it is instructive that the peacekeepers were seized when they tried to get into the diamond fields. Dialogue can only be effective when the balance of power, measured in terms of territorial and resource holdings, has shifted decisively against the rebels.

Second, the most important priority now is to prevent the rebels from over-running the capital and taking over the government. The four military outfits that are ranged against the RUF are the British paratroops, the UNAMSIL force, the Kamajoi militia and the rump of the ex-Armed Forces Revolution Council or Sierra Leone Army. After three wasted years of dependence on outsiders for security provision, Sierra Leone does not have the capacity right now to protect itself comprehensively against the RUF's terror. Besides, the limited disarmament that has been carried out has affected pro-government forces more than the rebels.

There is, thus, a strong case for outside support. The British paratroops have secured the airport ostensible to evacuate their nationals and other Europeans. However, it would be grossly irresponsible if they abandon the airport and refuse to provide support to the other forces pitched against the RUF. After all, Britain is a key driver of the Lomé accord. In the summer of 1999 when its leaders, Tony Blair and Robin Cook, were raving over Kosovo and targeting Milesovic for war crimes, the Brtish government was urging the Kabbah government to embrace the rebels who are a much more vicious breed of terrorists than Milesovic. There is a lot that Britain can do if it wants to help in containing the situation. However, the Labour government has recently experienced setbacks in local elections and there is discontent in its traditional heartlands. With national elections barely a year away, the British government is wary of "mission creep" and is unlikely to expose its troops to prolonged warfare.

On the other hand, UNAMSIL cannot take on the rebels without the backing of a major power. The US and the UN should fund the return and operations of Nigerian troops under a Nigerian high command. Adding more troops to UNAMSIL from countries with no political commitment to the conflict and without the participation of a regional or international power will complicate, not solve, the problem. Whatever the external support, international intervention forces should not substitute for a national defence initiative. As the January 6 1999 invasion shows, foreign armies are unlikely to absorb the full costs of rebel attacks and remain committed in the long run to the defence of the country.

Third, the last three years have shown that Sierra Leone cannot afford to delegate security provision and other aspects of its development to foreign governments or organizations. Sierra Leone is the only war-torn country in the world where the primary responsibility for security rests with outside governments and bureaucrats, and not its elected government. It has been painful to hear a cabinet minister describe the current conflict as one in which the government has no responsibility since the UN is in charge of security. Over-dependence on outsiders blocks creativity, initiative and capacity building. International interventions have a way of constraining the policy choices of local decision makers and blocking credible alternatives that may be offered by their citizens. The sad thing is that only the nationals of a country will suffer the consequences of policy failure, as there are no mechanisms for holding international actors accountable for their errors.

Sierra Leoneans have been clamouring for a truly national and effective civil defence force as the only antidote to the rebel menace. This will involve a massive programme of mobilisation, security education, methods of arms use, ways of guarding homes, securing food and medical supplies, and local or neighbourhood capacities for collective and self-defence. The primary strategy of the rebels has been to terrorise defenceless citizens, not to engage armed opponents. The only areas in the country where civil defence forces are fully operational - Bo, Moyamba, Bonthe and Pujehun districts -- have been free of rebels. With the decision of Johnny Paul Koroma's AFRC to join forces with the Kamajoi militia, it has become highly imperative to formalise the civil defence force as the primary unit of national defence. If this is not done in an organised and transparent way, there is a strong possibility that the conflict between the army and the kamajoi that provoked the coup of 1997 will recur.

The choices outlined above require dynamic political leadership. Unfortunately, the Kabbah leadership in the last three years has poorly served us. Many external actors who have been involved in our conflict share this view. Without a leadership that is ready to take initiatives and gets penalised for its policy errors, or has the honour to bow out when it has failed the nation, Sierra Leoneans will continue to be abused and tormented by a few thousand war-drugged individuals. We will also forever remain captives of the policy choices of international actors. These options require restructuring of the governance regime to ensure that our political institutions operate in tandem with our security needs.

Yusuf Bangura

40
An Outline of a Policy Framework for Military Security in Sierra Leone[40]

Introduction

As Sierra Leone celebrates the routing of the Armed Forces Revolutionary Council (AFRC)/Revolutionary United Front (RUF), and the return of constitutional government, it is important to focus on the theme of military security as one of the crucial elements in the provision of lasting peace and stability. National security always has social, economic, political and military dimensions. A secure nation is one which is able to provide gainful employment and basic social welfare protection to its citizens; whose governance system is transparent, as well as accountable to, and representative of, the different strata of its population; and which consistently upholds the rule of law. Where the economic, social and political fundamentals of national security are in place, the military dimensions of security are either redundant or exist mainly as insurance against external threats. As a war-and-coup-torn country, however, Sierra Leone's reconstruction of its national security system will have to address not just the socioeconomic and political factors but the military dimensions as well.

The events of May 25, 1997 and after have been very traumatic for the vast majority of our citizens. We almost lost our country to warlords, thugs and a tiny group of disaffected elites whose trade mark has always been the pursuit of power by authoritarian and corrupt means, and the plundering of the state's revenue and resources. Without the help of Nigeria and the countries that supplied troops to the ECOMOG force, Sierra Leone could have become another Somalia, Burundi, or Afghanistan. As President Kabbah put it so eloquently in his maiden speech at the restoration ceremony on March 10, "we have

[40] Prepared for conference on "Sierra Leone Towards the New Millennium: Post-Crisis Reconstruction and Democratic Rule", Organised by the National Organisation of Sierra Leoneans in North America (NOSLINA). Washington DC. USA. March 28, 1998.

undergone our baptism of fire, and we have survived". The government and the public should resolve that our survival does not turn out to be a short respite, but that it is anchored in very solid institutional foundations. There will be no excuse if we squander the opportunity that has been given to us to reconstitute and reconfigure our nation, economy and security.

Samuel Edmond Nonie's recent piece on the Leonenet Discussion Forum, *The Road to Recovery and Reconstruction*, makes good and instructive reading. Underlying his arguments are what I perceive to be a strong will to succeed, and the defence of systems that are based on merit, openness and accountability. He raises a number of points on various aspects of Sierra Leone's development agenda, but I would like to address only the issue relating to military security. If we fail in the security field, it will be difficult for the productive sectors of the economy to pick up, for foreign investors to return or be attracted to the country, and for the very large number of professionals who fled the coup to return and help in the rebuilding process.

The professional standing army

There have been calls from various quarters for a restructuring, rather than dissolution, of the defeated Republic of Sierra Leone Military Force (RSLMF). Piecing together the various comments on the subject, one comes up with the following three arguments. The first seeks to differentiate among the soldiers that make up the RSLMF, and rescue the professions of those who are believed to be innocent, or not directly responsible for the mayhem of the last nine months, or indeed the last seven years. The point in this argument is that Sierra Leone still has a good crop of fine soldiers who could be relied upon to uphold their professional traditions and defend the territorial integrity of the nation. Given the fact that the country has spent a lot in training and building the careers of these soldiers, their retrenchment would amount to a waste of resources. Those who put forward this argument believe that some of these so-called well-trained soldiers could play leading roles in the restructuring of the armed forces and in providing valuable training to those who currently lack it.

The second argument relates to the social cost of disbanding the army. Sierra Leone has been at war for close to seven years during which period the army has grown from 3,000 to an estimated figure of 15,000. Soldiers often raise very large families, as visits to their sprawling barracks will demonstrate. On an average family size of six, we are talking about putting at risk the livelihoods of close to 100,000 people. Given the politics that has surrounded the formation of armies from colonial to independence periods, some ethnic groups have tended to be over-represented in the institution. For some, it has even become a family tradition to be enrolled in the army after school, college or some other work experience because father, uncle, grandfather, and in-laws have been, or are, military men. The dissolution of the RSLMF will obviously amount to the destruction of social and professional traditions for certain groups in the country.

There is likely, therefore, to be some backlash from these families, kin and ethnic groups. It is argued that a total dissolution of the RSLMF would create a big security problem for the country. The country is not only awash with arms, but the AFRC and RUF had about nine months to store large quantities of weapons in places that would be difficult for the government and ECOMOG to find. If the army believes that the current military order offers them no opportunities to practice their profession and feed their families, they will retrieve these weapons and engage in freelance banditry as a survival strategy. Some individuals contend, therefore, that it is only by offering the army a second chance to redeem itself in a restructured RSLMF that it is likely to collaborate in a full disarmament programme.

The third argument relates to the view that standing armies are the order of the day for most countries in the world. Sierra Leone cannot afford to disband what it already has. It should build on, not destroy, the expertise and infrastructure that it has in military defence. Besides, since the army knows that it has been thoroughly defeated, it will not want to stage another coup and cause such pain to itself and the nation. The leverage that it could have wielded under the Conakry Peace Plan has been weakened by its refusal to collaborate in its implementation. As a defeated army, it now has no alternative but to accept whatever the government proposes to offer it. The restored government has also learnt its lesson: it would keep a close eye on the army, ensure that it weeds out recalcitrant elements, and build a force that will be highly professional and disciplined. Furthermore, it is argued that there is simply no alternative to a standing army for a country that is threatened by a neighbour with strong links with the defeated RSLMF and RUF. Sierra Leone cannot rely on ECOMOG forever, and unprofessional militia forces cannot provide effective defence against well-armed and trained external forces. It is either these militia forces become the new professional standing army, or the RSLMF is thoroughly screened and restructured. But the country cannot be without a professional standing army.

My view is that we should not try to create another conventional standing army, however professional and disciplined we think it may become under the new political dispensation. We will only be laying the foundations for another coup in the long run. As the history of Latin America and Nigeria demonstrates, professional armies in underdeveloped countries, let alone those with unstable political cultures, are not immune from the disease of coup-making. For a long time after its political independence in 1965, Gambia had no national army, only a police force. The national army was created after the abortive coup of Kukoi Samba in 1981. The Senegalese government rushed troops to quell the coup, and Nigeria was invited to help establish a professional national army. This worked until 1994 when one of the students of that experiment, Yahaya Jammeh, decided to take over the reins of power from Dauda Jawara after an ECOMOG assignment in Liberia. Jammeh currently enjoys very cordial relations with Sani Abacha and top officers of the Nigerian army.

We should not bask in the illusion that the May 25 coup will be the last in the country. Sierra Leone will only become a coup-and-rebel-free zone if it succeeds in developing appropriate institutions to defend the gains of March 10, 1998. Four out of five of the leaders who witnessed the reinstatement of Tejan Kabbah--Sani Abacha of Nigeria, Lansana Conte of Guinea, Ibrahim Mainassara of Niger and Yahya Jammeh of Gambia--first came to power by military means. Mainassara and Jammeh overthrew democratically elected governments and organised flawed elections, which have won some support in the world community. Mainasara's coup was even as recent as 1996. Indeed, 21 out of 47 (or 42.5 percent) of Africa's current leaders first came to power by staging coups. An additional nine became presidents through armed struggles or civil wars. In effect, 63.8 percent of Africa's leaders have strong links with the military. We should note that military rulers have learnt to adjust their strategies of making coups or remaining in power by taking into account the new wave of democratisation: they legitimise their rule by organising flawed elections. Over the last three years, soldiers have mutinied repeatedly in Guinea, the Central African Republic, Congo and Niger over salaries and conditions of service. Given their location in the power structure and the monopoly they enjoy in the use of arms, the military will continue to pose a threat to the democratisation programmes and security of African countries.

Besides, Sierra Leone does not really have the resources to create a professional army that will not make unreasonable demands on the politics and resources of the country. National wages are seriously eroded, the basic physical infrastructure is badly battered, and the productive economy will need time to even reach its pre-coup level. What happened in Sierra Leone in the last seven years is, in a sense, not extraordinary. With collapsing institutions and depressed living standards all round, those in the army simply used the weapons at their disposal to extract rent from the state and private resources from the population. It is difficult to envisage a quick turn-around of the national economy and rapid growth of real national incomes to justify payment of reasonable salaries and incentives to a new standing army.

In war-torn Cambodia, the army was partly appeased by giving it concessions in the timber industry. This did not prevent the effective army leader and second prime minister in the coalition government, Hun Sen, from staging a coup and getting rid of the democratically elected first prime minister in 1997. The Colombian army is locked in struggles with drug cartels and guerrilla movements over territory and drugs, and seems to be able to sustain itself by access to drug money. Drugs have had a very corrupting influence on the military institution of that country. In Chile, the army sought and obtained, among other benefits, concessions in the copper industry, as part of the plan that led to the transfer of power to civil democratic rule. In Nigeria, retired and serving military officials are part of the rent-seeking class of business elites: they are heavily involved in the oil economy as middlemen; serve on boards of banks, transnational corporations and parastatals; and play leading roles in the arms procurement business. The lower ranks of the army are offered incentives such as above national average salaries; supply of basic commodities; health, education and housing subsidies; and opportunities for further training.

The question that arises from this review of country experiences is simple: would we like to give a professional standing army concessions in our diamond, gold, rutile or fishery resources? We should note the problems that were encountered even with the subsidised bags of rice that were given to the army before the coup. The army came to see these subsidies as a right, when the overwhelming majority of the population had problems with basic food security. Johnny Paul Koroma, the junta leader, cited the issue of rice procurement and other benefits as one of the causes of the coup of May 25. Do we want a new standing army to hold our country hostage again? Rushing to re-establish a standing army under current conditions of mass-scale poverty will only recreate the problems that we are trying to avoid. And giving such an army high incomes and other incentives -- which are really the material basis for professionalism -- when the rest of the population is mired in acute deprivation will not only be morally wrong, but can lead to widespread disaffection.

It is true that the dissolution of the RSLMF will pose real security problems, given the large size of the army and the people who are dependent upon it for livelihood. But this problem can be tackled without retaining or restructuring the army. If the army is retained or restructured on these grounds, it would, in a sense, toughen its resolve to make further demands on the state and society. It will continue to believe that it is a special interest group that needs to be pampered. Now that it has been defeated, the government should take the bold step to disband it, and set up a rehabilitation programme to avoid the social problems that always accompany post-war disarmament and demobilisation of combatants. There are lessons to be learnt from other countries that have carried out successful demobilisation programmes. The government should avail itself of those lessons to minimise the social and political costs of demobilisation. Under this scheme, the demobilised soldiers will become ordinary citizens and participate in the proposed national decentralised defence system.

A National Decentralised Defence Force

After what Sierra Leoneans have suffered in the hands of their standing army and the RUF, what the country needs is a popularly-based, highly mobilised, military security system. We can learn a lot from the *Kamajoi*

307

civil defence experience in the war against the RUF, and subsequently the CDF (Civil Defence Force) war against the AFRC junta and the RUF. Ordinary people took the initiative to defend themselves, their villages and towns. Villages, towns and districts need to be fully involved in the defence of their respective places and the nation at large. It will be very difficult to expect a standing army, which may be concentrated in the towns or a few isolated barracks, to be effective in defending the country if remote villages are under attack. Indeed, with the defeat of the junta and the RUF in the main towns, our efforts have to concentrate on how to secure the villages, which are likely to come under increasing pressure from the RUF and remnants of the defeated junta. Sierra Leone's villages are sparsely populated and widely dispersed, and have poor links with the main towns and the barracks. These villages can only be adequately defended if our new security system is sufficiently decentralised. The question is how to craft an effective decentralised military system. Four issues may need to be addressed.

The first concerns the issue of making the decentralised military national, not sectional. Defence should always be a national institution if we want to retain the country as a single unit. Because the classical standing army is centralised, one may be tempted to think that it is much easier to administer than a decentralised army. This, however, has not always been the case in much of Africa. National armies have tended to be drawn from ethnic groups that provide the support base of the ruling parties. Idi Amin packed the Ugandan army with the Kakwa; Samuel Doe favoured his clansmen from his ethnic group, the Krahn; Joseph Momoh recruited a lot of Limba into the Sierra Leone army at the expense of other groups; Jerry Rawlings has been accused of favouring the Ewe in sensitive posts in the Ghana army; Northerners hold the upper hand in the Nigerian military; Gnassigbe Eyadema's northern kinsmen are said to dominate the Togolese army; Arap Moi is said to have supported the Kalenjin in the army at the expense of the numerically strong Kikuyu and Luo; Milton Obote's Ugandan army was dominated by northern ethnic groups, especially the Acholi and Lange; the Tutsis dominate the armies of Rwanda and Burundi even though they are less than 15 percent of the population in both countries. However, a decentralised military system may have the additional problem of degenerating into competing ethnic armies, if its structure, rules and composition are not properly laid out, tightly regulated, and fully understood by the populace.

There have been suggestions about the need for two complementary armies: a standing army, patterned along the old RSLMF, and district-based militia forces. The argument here is that the reconstituted RSLMF will be responsible for national defence; and the militias will take care of local, or village-level, defence. This two sector model may prove to be expensive. It may also not be immune from the problems that often bedevil standing armies in poor countries -- isolation from communities and social responsibilities; and propensity to demand and enjoy rents from the state. Additionally, the two sector model may lead to factionalisation, rivalry, and accusations of ethnic favouritism or manipulation. The pre-coup rivalry between the RSLMF and the *Kamajoi* militia should be studied for appropriate lessons. My own preference would be for a single decentralised army, with appropriate checks and balances, and a clear national chain of command. How a national security system can be created, which at the same time respects the participation of local societies in the defence of their neighbourhoods, may require further reflection and debate.

The second issue concerns the need to make the military system autonomous of the designs of local cliques, powerful politicians, and political parties. Like all military forces world-wide, any military system that will eventually be adopted should be accountable to the government in power, and not to multiple centres of command, if we are to avoid local territorial conflicts and secessionist wars. But the decentralised army should be organised in a such a way that it can simultaneously see its mandate as the defence of the country, not the government. A society that has just come out of war is prone to capture by local chieftains or powerful national figures with influence in local politics. A decentralised military security system is likely to fall victim to such influences than a centralised one, although cases exist throughout Africa where powerful national and local figures sometimes mobilise friends, relations and resources in centralised national armies to settle local scores. For instance, in a few local government border conflicts in Nigeria in the 1980s, those with access to arms at the federal level were accused of using federal arms to tilt the local military balance in their favour. It is also well known that Francis Minnah collaborated with the Sierra Leone army and APC thugs to tilt the balance of power in Pujehun in his conflict with local elites during the 1982 elections. This led to the so-called *ndorgbryosoi* revolt that claimed the lives of many local residents, and refugee flights into Liberia. The question is how to ensure that the new decentralised army is insulated from these types of pressures.

The third issue concerns the management and security of armaments at local areas that will be free of leakage. Centralised armies experience arms leakage, especially when they are not properly supervised. Arms can also be lost to guerrilla or rebel groups during field battles. Indeed, before the May 25 coup, the RUF was known to have acquired a lot of its arms from the RSLMF -- many times through deliberate deals or special arrangements. However, the dangers of leakage may even be higher under decentralised systems. Even with very high levels of discipline and control, arms given to Swiss males -- who are allowed to keep official military gear at home as part of their citizen-based national military service -- have been found in the illicit arms market. Given the isolated character of Sierra Leone's villages and their relatively small population sizes, it may be possible for rebel groups with superior arms and men to overrun such villages and add to, or replenish, their stock of arms by taking the ones in the defeated villages. Methods of arms control, protection and supervision should, therefore, be properly studied to minimise leakage. Should arms be stored at the district, town, chiefdom, or village level? How do we ensure that these are not abused by those who have access to them, or do not fall under the control of rebels or thugs?

The fourth issue deals with the establishment of appropriate rules to determine when all or parts of the military force could be used. Sierra Leone currently faces two types of security problems. The first is internal aggression from the RUF and the remnants of the defeated junta, backed by politicians, businessmen and bureaucrats who collaborated, or sympathized, with the AFRC during its eight and half months in power. As the history of the RUF war and the rapid expansion of the RSLMF shows, unemployed youth are likely to be drawn into this group if nothing is done very quickly to address the phenomenal youth unemployment problem in the country. The lure of diamonds and other resources may prove to be too tempting for certain types of unemployed youth to refuse to collaborate with the RUF and defeated junta members if they feel that the latter can offer them alternatives and security in the mining areas. A second source of problem is likely to come from Liberia, whose leader has historic links with the RUF, and where the peace is still very fragile. National security may be threatened by sporadic attacks in small towns or villages; but it is also possible for relations with Charles Taylor to deteriorate to the point where he may want to launch a full scale attack on Sierra Leone. This means that the new military security system should have a flexible response strategy dealing with different types of threats, and different ways of combining aspects of the decentralised force to face the different threats.

The potentials and limitations of a decentralised military

I make the following preliminary suggestions on ways of instituting a decentralised national defence force. I also try to point out some of the dangers that we may have to keep in mind in efforts to establish such a force. We should always bear in mind that no military security system is risk-free.

Every adult person within certain age limits should be made to undergo military training. Sierra Leoneans should resolve, individually and collectively, that never again will they allow those with guns to terrorise them. The democratisation of military life will go a long way in demystifying the gun and the dangers of armed thuggery. It may also help to check the activities of local or powerful chieftains who may want to use the decentralised force for their own designs. Given what has happened to Sierra Leoneans in recent years, we should not entrust our security to armies that lack popular input or participation, even if they are village, chiefdom, town or district armies. For effectiveness, this new defence system requires individuals to be gainfully employed. This means that the new army should not be seen as a career army. Indeed, only those who are gainfully employed in other activities should be allowed to participate in it. The unemployed should be assisted with various training, credit and other schemes before they may be allowed to participate in the military system. The biggest problem with the RSLMF was its systematic "lumpenisation", especially under the NPRC regime. The army became an instrument for the pursuit of basic survival imperatives from marginal or underclass elements in society. What is being suggested as an alternative is not likely to face this problem.

To avoid the dangers of setting up permanent local armies that may simply repeat the problems of our defeated national army, local defence systems may need to be manned on a rotational basis in local areas. Indeed, since the entire able and working population will participate in the defence of the country, it follows that not everyone can do so at the same time. Countries such as Switzerland and Israel have national service schemes for their adult populations. The national scheme in Switzerland is restricted to men, and Israel's is open to both sexes. They operate on a rotational basis, as everyone gets to serve in the military field. These are known to disrupt normal work schedules, and employers sometimes complain, especially in Switzerland, about loss of man-days. The system also requires proper record keeping and good coordination. In a country that is highly decentralised and multiethnic, the popularly-based national defence system is, indeed, the strongest pillar of Swiss nationhood. Sierra Leone may, indeed, succeed in carving out an effective system of national consciousness and patriotism if it decides to embark on a defence programme that will entail the total mobilisation of the populace in all parts of the country.

An alternative will be for villages to set aside periods of the year when every able-bodied adult will undergo military training or retraining. It is quite possible to work out a system which does not require villagers to leave their localities to undergo training; and simple schemes could be set up which would assist those who seek to operate at higher levels of the defence system to do so. The system being envisaged will allow every able-bodied citizen in the locality to serve in the military at some point in the year, or some other appropriate time period; is familiar with the way the military system operates; and can be relied upon to take up arms when ordered to do so by the relevant authorities during times of danger.

If active service in the military system is run on a rotational basis, it will mean that at any given period, there will be a number of Sierra Leoneans who will be fully armed to defend the nation and localities; and the rest of the able-bodied population can serve as a reserve force at local and national levels. The system has the advantage of ensuring that potential aggressors are aware of the combat-readiness of the population, nationally and locally; while at the same time, it does not give those who are under arms a license to abuse the arms by attacking their compatriots. The fact that every able-bodied person will form part of the military system, which itself will be decentralised, should act as a serious constraint on potential coup-makers and rebels.

Civic-oriented, non-discriminatory, local government institutions may need to be established to make the decentralised military system effective. These need to be fully democratised to ensure non-partisan control and accountability of the decentralised force to the local population. They should also not discriminate in terms of who should participate in them locally. Residence, not ethnicity, should be the defining basis for participation. This means that the pre-coup decentralisation programme of the government should be reactivated and thoroughly reviewed. The transition from centralised to decentralised political systems are always fraught with difficulties -- tax-raising powers and revenue allocation; availability of competent local personnel; the regulation of local corruption and patronage; the extent and types of powers to be devolved; and relations between central and local institutions. These issues need to be properly scrutinised to ensure that the local government systems work, and do not simply become other havens for despotic and corrupt practices.

Military systems, by definition, are single, commandist, integrated machines. For effectiveness, they should not be exposed to serious internal disputes or the designs of politicians and external parochial interests. It is essential, therefore, for the decentralised military system to be above party politics at both local and national levels. Countries that have experimented with decentralised military systems have all been single party regimes--Nicaragua during the fight against the *Contras*; Uganda and its resistance councils, for instance. Under single party populist regimes, it is relatively easy for the population to follow national commands even when they are reacting to, or dealing with, defence issues at local levels. There is, thus, much synergy between the national and the local on issues relating to military security.

However, Sierra Leone is a multi-party, not a one party, state. The challenge, therefore, is how to ensure that the same military cohesion that is enjoyed in single party regimes in the defence of local and national societies, is also enjoyed in multi-party settings. The government should establish a workable framework with the opposition parties and the wider public that will make the military system non-partisan. Failure to do this may compromise the integrity and independence of the decentralised military system. It will encourage parties to seek control of sections of the decentralised force in parts of the country where they believe they enjoy much popular support. Political "pacts" among leaders and civic groups that keep military issues out of politics may need to be crafted from the national to the village or chiefdom levels if this problem is to be contained.

There is need for an organisation that would be responsible for the coordination and use of the force on a national scale. Those who run this organisation should be highly trained and disciplined, and should be fully knowledgeable about the way the decentralised military system operates in various parts of the country, and nationally. They should constitute a permanent core of military strategists and administrators, responsible for the running of the defence system, training of the population, protection of armaments, monitoring of security, and mobilisation of force against recognised threats. Members who serve at this level of the decentralised military system should be fully in touch with military developments world-wide and undergo periodic training overseas. Individuals, who should be first-rate military strategists, should serve at this level only after they have excelled themselves at local levels.

Promising young professionals from high schools and colleges could be targeted for recruitment at the initial stage of the formation of the force, but these should be made to serve at local levels before their employment at the national level is regularised. The idea is to ensure that those who run the system at the national level do not feel different from, or superior to, those who serve at local levels. The fact that this professional cadre of military administrators and strategists will be running a popular, citizen-based defence force should also make it difficult for them to abuse their powers by staging coups. This kind of professional organisation exists in countries like Switzerland and Israel that have citizen-based national defence systems. The national military organisation should be accountable to the government in power, but its rules should be clearly defined as obtains for normal professional standing armies. This should make the force a national or state army, rather than a government or party army.

National level officers within the decentralised military system would be responsible for the deployment of citizens/soldiers for national assignments. Given the current vulnerability of the country's eastern and southern borders, it should make much strategic sense to have military bases or frontier forces permanently stationed on those border areas. At present, there is only one military base or barrack, Daru, in this deeply forested and resource-rich area; whereas the Western area/Freetown, which is relatively safe, boasts of four military barracks – Benguema, Murray Town, Wilberforce, and Juba. There is also only one military barrack each at Makeni and Bo to take care of the whole of the Northern and Southern Provinces. Individuals should be posted on a rotational basis to these border military bases as part of their national service in the decentralised military system. The idea of retaining the rotational principle for these border forces is to prevent individuals who are sent to these areas from abusing their military status by turning on the local population and country at large. The same arrangement could be repeated for other border areas of the country that straddle Sierra Leone and neighbouring countries.

There should be a national youth service programme, which should be open to all youths -- students and non-students alike. Service could combine both military training and voluntary work in the communities. This should form part of an innovative scheme to address the appalling youth crisis in the country, which is largely responsible for the RUF war. Such a programme could make it difficult for the RUF and the defeated junta to mobilise this restless, vulnerable, alienated and impressionistic stratum of our population. Youths should undertake part of their service in areas of the country they do not normally reside. This should help to foster national unity and national understanding of our various problems. Nigeria has an experience of this service for its post-tertiary level students, which does not include military service. For effectiveness, we should make the youth programme open to all youths, and combine military service with voluntary work.

The bottom line is that we should not set out to recreate what has failed: a standing professional army. The latter may work in the short run, but the decision may come to haunt us decades later. A starting point is for the government and the public to use the opportunity created by the presence of ECOMOG to think through the national security issues properly. Conferences, workshops, and public debates may be helpful before we settle down on any model. We could even start with pilot schemes in a few areas to test the effectiveness and viability of the new system rather than set up an entirely new force all at once.

Conclusion

Sierra Leone's society, polity and security are at a crossroads. Our national institutions lay battered, and many of our citizens have suffered untold deprivation and terror in the hands of our national army and the RUF. What the situation demands is a major rethink in national defence policy and readiness to strike out in new directions to ensure permanent security for the populace and the country. A hands-on approach to institution building, not a tinkering with the defence system that has failed, is absolutely essential if we are to survive as a nation.

41

The Liberia Dilemma: A Comparative Perspective[41]

In this essay, I discuss the dangers of replicating the Sierra Leone model of conflict management in Liberia. The points raised by many commentators about the need for realism should make current leaders or negotiators who are concerned about peace in Liberia reflect further upon their plans. I am not even sure whether the time is ripe for us to celebrate Sierra Leone's model of conflict management. A lot still needs to be done before we can proudly tell the world that we have something to offer countries that are likely to find themselves in our current situation. It is true, of course, that we have made tremendous progress in positioning our country on the right path for peace and constitutional rule. And we should all be thankful for this.

Ironically, two years ago, many people felt that Liberia stood a better chance of solving its own crisis than Sierra Leone: the key groups in Liberia operated in public, whereas we did not know much about the RUF and whether there were other shadowy groups involved in our conflict. There was a time when the British and other European governments would not even discuss Sierra Leone independently of the Liberian war.

Although Sierra Leone and Liberia have a lot in common -- indeed, our war is, in a way, a spill-over from the Liberian conflict -- the dynamics of the two wars are radically different. It is useful to grasp these differences before we start telling Liberians about how to end their war.

The state system completely collapsed in Liberia. Despite the extremely fragile state of the NPRC government and the rebellious character of some of our soldiers, there was a functioning state system in Sierra Leone. The collapse of the Liberian state strengthened the position of the armed groups and undermined the authority of the leaders of the transitional governments that were set up to contain the conflict. Successive interim leaders -- Amos Sawyerr, Pa Tamba Tailor and Wilton

---

[41] An abridged version of this article was published in *West Africa* (London), 25 April-5 May, 1996.

Sankawulo -- carried no clout when pitched against rebel leaders Charles Taylor, Alhaji Kromah, Roosevelt Johnson and George Boley. Indeed, it was the utter lack of power demonstrated by Sawyerr's and Pa Tamba's interim governments that convinced Ghana's president Jerry Rawlings and ECOMOG to get the warring factions themselves to share power under the Accra and Abuja accords.

The point needs to be stressed that it is much easier to use existing political structures in striking deals with rebel groups than to experiment with new political systems in which armed factions would play dominant roles. Most of the successfully mediated wars have been based on models which seek to strike a balance between the competing interests of relatively entrenched governments and armed dissident groups: Mozambique, El Salvador, Nicaragua, Cambodia (to some extent), Zimbabwe. The alternative is all out victory and the imposition of a settlement on losers (Nigeria (Biafra), Eritrea, Uganda), but this is now a very rare outcome in Africa.

Efforts aimed at constructing peace under stateless conditions and multiple armed groups are new in world politics. The record so far is not encouraging. On this score, Liberia is much more comparable to Somalia and Afghanistan than to Sierra Leone. What we have been witnessing on our TV screens since last week are standard practices in Mogadishu and Kabul. Unfortunately for Liberia, there is no solution yet to the wars in Somalia and Afghanistan, so there is no useful lesson to be learnt from those countries as far as the building of central state organs is concerned. A comparative study of the three countries would be useful for countries that are likely to follow the path of stateless governments and proliferation of armed factions.

Right from its inception, the war in Liberia took on strong ethnic dimensions, whereas the war in Sierra Leone has been largely non-ethnic, even though its discourse among our elites has had some ethnic rumblings. Although the Sierra Leone war is heavily concentrated in the South and East, large parts of the North have not been spared of the carnage. The RUF may have recruited the bulk of its fighters from the South and East, but the leader is of Northern origin, and there are young people from the North and West who have been recruited into the organisation. The RUF itself does not espouse an ethnic agenda. Also, its brutalisation of Sierra Leoneans does not follow an ethnic pattern. Furthermore, for all the failings of the Momoh and NPRC regimes in

318

Sierra Leone, their governments represented rainbow coalitions of sorts, even though some colours in the rainbows were thicker and broader than others. This must have contributed to the faith which victims of the war continued to place on the unity of the country even when the government could not rescue them from RUF barbarism.

On the other hand, Samuel Doe's brutal style of rule set the stage for the "ethnocide" which ordinary Liberians have witnessed in the last six to seven years. His state-sponsored violence against the Mano and Gio, an ethno-linguistic group associated with his rival and former ally in government, Thomas Quiwonkpa, was short-sighted. The Gio and Mano became easy recruits for Charles Taylor's NPFL, which slaughtered a lot of Krahn and Madingo (seen as allies of Doe) when, in 1990, they fought their way into Monrovia from Nimba County, the base of their activities. Doe's execution by Prince Johnson's group (a breakaway faction of the NPFL) and the rapid spread of Taylor's power in the countryside and in parts of the capital city, weakened the grip of the Krahn military leadership in politics. Many fled to Sierra Leone. They were encouraged by the APC and NPRC governments (there were many reports which also implicated ECOMOG) to form ULIMO and fight alongside the Sierra Leone army against the RUF. The Krahn/Madingo alliance later broke up into Alhaji Kromah/Roosevelt Johnson factions -- ULIMO-K and ULIMO-J. Later, even the NPFL broke up when Tom Woewiyu, Laveli Supuwood and others accused Taylor of pursuing an Americo-Liberian agenda of destroying the resources and infrastructure of the countryside.

It is important to note, however, that ethnic fragmentation in Liberia is not the same as it is, for instance, in ex-Yugoslavia. In the latter, ethnic groups were fighting for self-determination. No armed group has made the issue of ethnic autonomy a major objective in Liberia. At least, this is likely to spare the country of the trauma of redrawing maps, relocating people along ethnic lines, and having permanently armed ethnic republics. Ethnic conflict in Liberia is largely about elite/individual and alienated youth control of power and resources within a united Liberia. All the "war lords" are rich, having turned Liberia's forests and mineral resources into their private property, which they control by force of arms. The richest and, therefore, most powerful is Taylor. His links extend deep into Cote d'Ivoire's power structure, France, and some of the transnational mining and timber

Yusuf Bangura

companies. However, the fact that the quest for material gain is intimately linked with elite-sponsored ethnic rivalry and brutal violence makes it difficult to end the war. Roosevelt Johnson's removal from his cabinet post in the agriculture ministry and the warrant of arrest that was issued by the transitional council (largely inspired by Taylor) was interpreted by the Krahn in what remains of the old government army (The Armed Forces of Liberia) as an unfriendly act against the Krahn. A thick cloud of mutual suspicion hangs over the so-called transitional council.

The density of militarisation -- measured in terms of the number of armed individuals per capita, with an intention to fight a war -- is also much higher in Liberia than in Sierra Leone. If we are to believe official figures about the military strength of the army and rebels, there are about 10,000 soldiers and 5,000 rebels in Sierra Leone for a population of four million people. In Liberia, we are told that the combined strength of all armed factions is about 60,000 out of a total of two and half million people. Thus, roughly 0.35 per cent of Sierra Leoneans are currently armed to fight a war, whereas for Liberia a much higher number of individuals, about 2.4 per cent, are armed. It is also well known that Liberia has a much higher number of armed factions than Sierra Leone. In the case of Liberia, there are four main armed groups and at least three minor ones, whereas only the RUF is known to exist in Sierra Leone. Fears of armed factions that are led or sponsored by exiled APC stalwarts in Guinea and the United Kingdom have so far not been borne out. Of course, Sierra Leone shares Liberia's misfortune of having "sobels" or "soldiers-turned-rebels" (AFL in the case of Liberia) and any number of bandits that may not be under the control of armed factions or bona fide government soldiers. On the basis of this analysis, it seems to me that controlling violence in Liberia is likely to be a much more difficult and costly enterprise than in Sierra Leone.

It is important also to take into account the calibre of leaders that the two countries have thrown up in their respective conflicts. Partly because of a functioning government in Sierra Leone, it was possible to attempt to hold leaders accountable for their behaviour. Even though NPRC functionaries and ordinary soldiers often took the law into their hands, it is well known that they loved to be praised for their attempts to steer the country towards a new path. Thus, there were always uneasy tensions between concerns for legality and illegality, thuggery and good

320

manners, and coercion and consent, in the behaviour of the NPRC leaders. Indeed, once Maada Bio and his government lost the initiative to the public in influencing the pace and direction of change after the Bintumani II Conference, Bio as leader decided to steer the transition to civil rule according to the rules. We were lucky also to have had a man of James Jonah's calibre to head the most important institution in the transition, the Interim National Elections Commission. Furthermore, the leaders of the two main parties, Tejan Kabbah and Karefa Smart, are people of integrity and wide-ranging public service experience. For now, these parties have mass support and are not beholden to armed groups.

Unfortunately, the picture in Liberia is not so rosy. The country has had its own share of honest and dedicated leaders -- Sawyerr, Pa Tamba Tailor and Sankawulo -- but these do not carry the same weight in Liberia as Tejan Kabbah and Karefa Smart do in Sierra Leone. The movers of events are those who have committed some of the worst atrocities in the sub-region. It is proper to question the morality of one faction "thief" trying to arrest another faction "thief" for crimes against the people. What we have in Liberia today is a classic case of the "prisoners' dilemma" -- or shall we say "thieves' dilemma"? All armed groups are keenly aware of the fact that each is capable of cheating and committing atrocities. Outside of their armed cocoons, none has operated under any formal system of rules that is based on trust, honesty, principles, and respect for law and order. Indeed, I suspect that the capture of Doe in 1990 right under the nose of ECOMOG commanders, and his subsequent torture and slaughter, may have played into the calculations of the warring factions, particularly Taylor's. Each leader has so much blood on his hands that none believes the other is capable of using power for the common good. Each is, therefore, likely to opt for the gun (which is surely a no-win situation since all will use it to deadly effect) in the "rational" belief that a first strike would give advantages to an armed faction, or in the "irrational" consolation that it is better to deny the prize to the enemy even if everybody and all factions die in the process. Events of the last week in Monrovia graphically illustrate the strength of this theoretical construct about human behaviour.

Options and questions for Liberia

The main questions we would like to ask are the following: First, why did ECOMOG and the world community allow the armed factions to enter Monrovia with their arms? Second, why was ECOMOG's role in the transition reduced to mere monitors, given our knowledge of the breakdown of countless number of settlements and the track record of the chief combatants? There are suggestions that Taylor may have deployed about two thirds of his arms into Monrovia. Reports from field officers suggest that the armed groups in Monrovia may now have only very tenuous hold on their rank and file fighters in the countryside. The latter are still engaged in random attacks, even deep into Cote d'Ivoire, in search of food and resources. It is true that the first stage of the military response and attack on civilians was started by the Armed Forces of Liberia. However, there are indications that other armed factions are engaged in the looting and killing of people. This madness is not just directed at Lebanese and ECOMOG troops. Ordinary Liberians are victims -- I suspect that they are likely to be in the majority. It is also difficult to share the view that the young fighters we have seen or heard about (or those described in the moving testimonies of victims in David Hecht's very useful posting) are "good fighters", unless if we have a different definition of "good". How good is a fighter if all he does is to terrorise defenceless and innocent civilians? Our alienated youth need rehabilitation and understanding, but they should not be glorified.

The main issue now is how to stop the chaos and restore some semblance of order in the capital. Like some commentators on Leonenet, I have also toyed with the suggestion of "trusteeship" or the need for a strong external power for Liberia. When we have a situation like the one I have just described -- lack of trust and non-adherence to rules and regulations by major actors -- only a disciplined superior body can maintain order and help actors to develop co-operative relationships. This is what the US and NATO are currently doing in Bosnia. The massive presence of NATO in Bosnia has brought the fighting there to an end. Our problem is that we do not have a NATO equivalent in Africa. ECOMOG has not been able to play this role. It is a major problem in Africa's troubled history.

As I have argued elsewhere, the UN is useful in helping to bring about peace and monitoring it, but I do not think a UN-sponsored trusteeship scheme is feasible in present day Africa. The last time the UN was given such a mandate in Africa to oversee the affairs of Congo when civil war broke out in that country at independence, cold war rivalry marred much of its work. A forward-looking and nationalist leader, Patrice Lumumba, was murdered by Tsombe and his mercenary supporters without the UN being able to do anything about it. After the UN pulled out, and following a series of events, Congo ended up with Mobutu.

The situation today is, of course, different. The cold war is over. But the UN is broke and over-stretched. The US is behind in its financial contributions to the world body. Besides, relations between the big powers and the UN are yet to be satisfactorily sorted out. The UN does not have the clout and resources to perform many of the tasks that the world seeks to throw upon it. The foreign policies of those who call the shots in world affairs are still driven by narrow self-interests and power calculations. Such powers do not want to subordinate their interests to the collective will of the UN. Indeed, the UN was humiliated in Bosnia, where NATO is now in charge. I also believe that a UN-administered trusteeship is not something to be recommended lightly by Africans, given the heavily skewed nature of the power structure within the organisation in favour of Westerners, and the so-called "Afro-pessimism" that currently prevails in Western societies. We should study the reckless way Americans behaved in Somalia, and compare it with their attitudes towards Bosnians.

What can be done now? First, I think ECOMOG will need to clean up its act and behave more professionally if it is to play a constructive role in Liberia. Despite the unquestioned commitment of many of the West African leaders to a successful resolution of the conflict, the operation remains very inefficient, and accusations of "sobel" types of behaviour by ECOMOG troops are rife. Second, given the "thieves' dilemma" that seems to prevail among armed groups in government, ECOMOG and the world community should consider the transitional government model of armed groups a failure. The next efforts to set up a government of national unity should give a newly reconstituted ECOMOG more powers to enforce peace and help Liberians to rediscover the path to constitutional government. Immediate elections under current conditions are likely to aggravate the problems of Liberia. More time would be needed to lay some credible structures and incentives that would allow groups to have confidence in the process and outcome. Indeed, a winner-takes-all constitution of the type that was used in organising the elections in Sierra Leone would spell disaster in Liberia. Any faction that loses would copy Jonas Savimbi's example in Angola and take to the bush. Sierra Leoneans were lucky to have organised their elections under a winner-takes-all constitution without RUF participation.

The work of ECOMOG would be made a lot easier if it were provided with sufficient resources to not only deal with the leaders of the warring factions but also carry out the disarmament programme and relate constructively with the fighters in the bush, who are still a menace to villagers. Massive funds for rehabilitation and resettlement are needed to convince the bandits in the bush that there are alternatives to terrorism. The problem with Liberia and Sierra Leone is that we do not have external donors that are willing to bank-roll a political settlement in the two countries. About US$ 2 billion was spent in Cambodia to get peace, mostly by Japan. Italy was largely responsible for footing the bill in El Salvador. And the Scandinavians in particular have played positive roles in Mozambique by providing funds for rehabilitation, resettlement and the reintegration of fighters into viable livelihood activities.

In the case of Sierra Leone, it has been suggested by UK Africanists that Sierra Leoneans should bombard the ODA in the UK with requests for assistance. Honestly, I find this suggestion very strange. I would have thought that it is people in the UK, with sympathetic links with Sierra Leone, who should pressure their governments to help. One would like to see the kinds of initiatives which Friends of Sierra Leone (FOSL) is undertaking in the US replicated in the UK. Please note that despite James Jonah's extensive foreign links, he was not able to raise all of the US$ 17 million that was needed for the elections in Sierra Leone. INEC has just put out advertisements in newspapers pleading with unpaid presiding officers and polling assistants to bear with the organisation until the shortfall of $ 1.3 million is provided by donors.

For our two countries, what we really need is short term support to re-integrate our alienated youth back into society. Sierra Leone has the resources to revive and sustain developments in the education and health sectors if our government can show strong commitment towards regaining control of our natural resources. Donors can help our new government to recover such control.

42

The Pitfalls of Recolonisation: A comment on the Mazrui-Mafeje Exchange[42]

The exchange between Ali Mazrui and Archie Mafeje (*CODESRIA Bulletin*, No. 2, 1995) on Africa's developmental condition raises important political and policy issues, which should not be clouded by the sub-texts on Mazrui's intellectual record and insinuations of competition or rivalry between the two scholars. In what follows, I will attempt to state what I believe to be Mazrui's diagnosis of the African condition, raise questions about whether his diagnosis, and Mafeje's critique of it, are well founded; and proceed to reconstruct Mazrui's recolonisation proposal, which he believes will cure the "cancer of chaos" that is currently afflicting much of the continent. I will then attempt a critique of his proposal, taking into account Mafeje's views on the subject. I will conclude by offering what I believe to be some of the critical options facing African countries in the quest for political stability and economic development.

The African condition

Central to Mazrui's call for recolonisation is an image of a continent that is in a state of decay: the gains of modernisation achieved under colonial rule are being reversed; state collapse has become an all too familiar picture of the African political landscape; war, famine and ruin have been the experiences of too many Africans since independence; Africans have been hopeless in uniting for economic development and political stability; and have not shown any capacity for "self-control and self-discipline" since colonial rule.

These are indeed stern comments, which are bound to deflate the pride of most African élites and those who have been directly responsible for shaping the continent's affairs. Except for the statements dealing with the reversal of the gains of colonial modernisation and loss of capacity for self-control, the overall thrust of the comments will be

---

[42] Published in *CODESRIA Bulletin* (Council for the Development of Social Science Research in Africa), No. 4. 1995.

very difficult to challenge even by a casual reading of Africa's recent experience. They are the sorts of comments that currently litter most Western newspapers and electronic media about Africa's socio-economic and political realities. They also feature in many discussions among Africans of all walks of life, frustrated by what they see as the wasting potentials of their lives, countries and continent.

Mafeje is right to question this one dimensional reading of the African condition. It is actually amazing that out of this continent of "chaos" also come popular demands for self-renewal, accountability and democratisation. Much of the latter is at an early stage of development and may not be of interest to outside commentators who are always keen to report quick results or dramatic events. Very rarely does one get good and sustained reports in the Western media on the positive steps Africans are taking in various countries to overturn decades of dictatorial and irresponsible rule. What we get instead are images of wars, violence, famine and disease. Dependence on such sources for an understanding of African problems, unfortunately, risks repeating the stereotypes, whether intentionally or not.

Mafeje's diagnosis of the "chaotic" part of the African experience is, however, less useful than that of Mazrui, who I think has a better grasp of the problem. It does not help the search for solutions to deny the fact that vital institutions in some parts of Africa are in a state of decay. Of course, one agrees with Mafeje that post-independence states have not been cohesive and self-sustaining and that the attempts to create "nation-states" in ethnically plural settings were ill-founded. But, surely, these problematic states were far more cohesive during the first two decades of independence than they are at present. The few instances of state collapse that we have experienced so far may well be a potent warning about the unviability of the nation-state experiment and the possibility of far worse crises engulfing the continent. In this regard, I question Mafeje's restriction of the concept of social or political decay to socially viable and old societies. The concept should equally apply to what we are witnessing at the moment.

It is also difficult to share Mafeje's convictions about the virtues of many of today's African wars. These wars have been very costly in terms of civilian casualties, their disorientation and militarisation of our youth, their large-scale destruction of physical infrastructure and resources, their displacement of very large numbers of people from their homes and livelihoods, and the high levels of social trauma and divisions they have created. How popular and useful are the wars in Somalia, Liberia, Sierra Leone, Rwanda, Burundi and Angola, for instance? What leadership qualities and visions do the warlords who lead these struggles resonate? 'Dominating structures' are obviously being 'deconstructed', but how confident can we be that something valuable and viable would come out of these wars?

I do not also think that we should suspend judgement on the ethnic dimensions of the conflict in Rwanda before we receive the results of CODESRIA's planned workshop on the social formations of the Great Lakes. While I will agree with Mafeje that most African conflicts cannot be reduced to ethnicity, it will be futile to deny an ethnic dimension in many of our conflicts, especially when they become protracted. What is more, even when conflicts are triggered by non-ethnic factors there is always a tendency for them to become ethnic when they turn into wars. This observation should not be surprising because of the weak foundations of the "nation-states" that Mafeje alludes to, and the uneasy tensions between secular forms of civic identity and those based on ethnic loyalties -- which all too often get manipulated in the difficult process of self-improvement. I think there is ample evidence on Rwanda and Burundi to support the view that ethnicity is a critical factor in understanding the genocidal carnage in those countries. Denying this will not help us get to the heart of the malaise.

Reconstructing Mazrui's recolonisation proposal

If Mazrui has put his finger on a vital aspect of the African condition, he has not been very helpful in stating what he means by recolonisation. Given the horrible track record of colonialism in Africa and the emotions which the concept of recolonisation is likely to generate among Africans, Mazrui should have been much more precise than he has been in his use of this concept. Unfortunately, many African scholars are likely to sympathise with Mafeje's vitriolic attacks on him because of this lapse. One could not help feeling that, perhaps, on this occasion Mazrui has gone overboard. Mazrui was given a second chance to make himself clear on the subject but, unfortunately, he chose instead to concentrate largely on the areas of Mafeje's criticisms that dealt with his academic record and the birth place and tortuous African journey of the contentious article.

Reference to his 1967 work, *Towards a Pax Africana* (a book I highly cherished during my student days), did not help matters much. One is not sure how much of the passion for African solutions still remains after 28 years of scholarship. The focus of the rejoinder is much more restrained than the original article -- in the former, he refrains from debating the issue of external recolonisation and opts instead to discuss the second dimension of his proposal: self-colonisation. However, he still feels it necessary to remind us of how far the original article and his ideas on recolonisation had travelled across the continent before they were picked up by the Western press. Is external recolonisation in or out?

In the rejoinder, Mazrui rejects European colonialism and Pax Britannica, and qualifies what he now calls "United Nations help" with the need to obtain African consent, but fails to point out whether some surrogate version of colonialism, albeit practised under the auspices of the United Nations, will be acceptable. In other words, Mazrui fails to make clear whether he has abandoned his trusteeship proposal, which occupied such a central position in the original article. There are just too many ambiguities in both the original text and the rejoinder for one to be absolutely sure about what Mazrui wants for Africa. I will, therefore, try as much as possible to sketch what I believe to be his position on recolonisation, hoping that my interpretation will, at least, not radically depart from what he actually has in mind.

The one thing that is unambiguously clear in Mazrui's two articles is the need for certain parts of Africa to re-submit to recolonisation. Illustrative examples are Somalia, Rwanda, Burundi, Liberia, Angola, Sudan and Zaire, although Mazrui strangely believes that the latter may sufficiently recover from recolonisation to colonise Rwanda and Burundi in the next century.

Two strands of recolonisation sit uneasily in his analysis. The first is what he calls a trusteeship system, akin to the responsibilities that were thrust upon the United Nations in 1960 to oversee the affairs of Congo when civil war broke out in that country, following the exit of the Belgian colonial power. Although such a trusteeship system will be "much more international and less Western", Mazrui is less than categorical about African participation in such an administering body: "administering powers for the trusteeship territories could come from

Africa *or* Asia, as well as from the rest of the United Nations membership". Based on this formulation, it might not be wrong to say that Mazrui envisages a truly colonial, even if multilateral, take-over of these countries as a distinct option.

The second strand of recolonisation is what Mazrui calls "self-colonisation". As I understand it, self-colonisation means allowing some regional African powers - South Africa, Egypt, Nigeria, Ethiopia and Zaire - to colonise countries that cannot govern themselves. These five countries will form an African Security Council and should be equipped with a Pan African Emergency Force, which can intervene in trouble spots to make and manage peace. Such a council will also liaise with the United Nations administering powers of the "trusteeship territories" as well as other UN agencies like those relating to refugees. Mazrui envisages some form of regional integration emerging from this form of colonisation, but it is the least clear of all the issues in his proposal. He prefers self-colonisation to external colonisation but one could safely assume that under current conditions he would not hesitate to recommend external colonisation because of what he believes to be Africa's incapacity for self-control and self-discipline since colonial rule.

The pitfalls of Mazrui's recolonisation proposal

I feel as outraged as I believe Mafeje and his Egyptian friends must have been by the recolonisation proposal, coming as it were from an African scholar of great repute. To start with, in his original article, Mazrui seems to support a long-standing Western view of colonialism, which most scholars in the continent and elsewhere will find abhorrent. He sees the colonial enterprise as a "white man's burden" which, under his recolonisation scheme, would become "humanity's shared burden". The reference in the opening paragraph to the reversal of 'dependent modernisation achieved under colonial rule' can be seen as a clever ploy to rehabilitate colonialism and offer respectability to his recolonisation proposal. In other words, if the socio-economic situation today can be presented as worse than what it was under colonialism then it will obviously make sense to many people to ask for the return of the colonialists. He ignores the more relevant issue of the weakening of the major advances made by these troubled countries in their post-independence history in expanding the modernisation project. By every available yardstick on social development—access to education and health facilities, number of schools and hospitals, number of doctors and nurses, number of teachers and graduates, access to water, etc.--more has been gained even in per capita terms under the limited rule of post-colonial regimes than under more than seventy years of colonial rule. What we should bemoan is the reversal of the post-independence gains, even though colonialism supplied part of the foundations for those gains -- one reason, as we shall see, why many of these states are dysfunctional today.

The point should also be stressed that the choice of the medium through which Africa's beleaguered states are to be revived is unfortunate. It may lend support to the interventionist plans of the multilateral agencies, particularly the World Bank and the IMF, who in the past 15 years have shown complete disregard for African expertise and capacities in the management of their economies. It is also likely to further whet the appetite of imperialist countries like France, whose drive for direct intervention in former colonies and associates is still very strong.

But let us get to the substance of the recolonisation proposal itself. We start with the notion of a trusteeship system to be administered by the United Nations. Mafeje is right to caution support for a UN system that will provide solutions to Africa's beleaguered states. Mazrui interprets Mafeje's criticisms as constituting a total rejection of the UN. This does not seem to me to reflect the dangers which Mafeje seeks to highlight. Given the rapid trends in globalisation and the wide-ranging problems which such trends generate, the United Nations is obviously the only multilateral forum available at the moment for addressing these problems. With all its imperfections, it is still not under the absolute control of any one state or group of states. And it is quite true as Mazrui states in his response to Mafeje that small and vulnerable countries like those in Africa need the UN more than the big powers. But do such states need to entrust their affairs with the UN under a trusteeship system?

Indeed, what is puzzling in this debate is Mazrui's apparent confidence in the UN to act as a trusteeship power in Africa. We should remember that trusteeship is a much higher form of governance or intervention than what the UN currently does in all of its projects around the world. The UN's record even in the limited field of peacekeeping or

330

reconciliation missions is very mixed. It has done fairly well in Mozambique and Namibia, but failed disastrously in Somalia and Angola (even though it is trying to redeem itself in the latter), and has not shown much interest in Liberia, Sierra Leone, Rwanda and Burundi.

Anyone who is seriously interested in engaging the UN as a trusteeship power in Africa should first think through the following fundamentals: how to ensure that sufficient African representation exists in the key organs of the UN body to influence the quality and content of the intervention; how to prevent the organisation from being used as an arm of the permanent members who are always willing to push through their own agendas and what they believe is good for Africa; how to improve understanding of African problems among operational staff; how to sustain interest on African issues and ensure confidence in local reconstruction efforts; and how to overcome the current very serious cash crisis within the organisation, which is affecting its capacity to intervene in crisis situations or address the numerous problems being thrown at it from all over the world. Simply recommending trusteeship without investigating its constraints, viability and acceptability, is a recipe for further chaos and irresponsibility, however humanitarian the plate is on which such trusteeship is served. Somalia should be a warning to whoever wants Africa to travel this road.

We encounter a different set of problems when we examine the recommendation on recolonisation from within or what Mazrui has called self-recolonisation. Let me state that I completely agree with Mazrui that African leaders need to set high standards of performance in governance and exert pressure on those who tend to stray off course. Such pressure does not necessarily have to result in military intervention, which can be very risky and, if prolonged, may become part of the problem itself -- although I very much agree with him that there might be extreme cases like in Rwanda, Burundi and Somalia where a properly organised and disciplined pan-African force with a clear mandate to restore order and help the contending groups to sort out their problems could make a difference. However, the overall aim is to create what Mazrui rightly calls "collective self-discipline", in which acts of blatant misrule or human rights violation will not be tolerated. There are various ways of maintaining such pressures, including exclusion from key international organisations, sustained advocacy, and selective sanctions that may hurt the leaders and supporters of such governments. This is what I understand by Mazrui's Pax Africana, and it is as valid in the 1960s, when he first advanced it, as it is today.

There have clearly been moments in Africa when one yearned for such collective self-regulatory mechanisms: Amin's brutal dictatorship, which was ended by Nyerere's Tanzania, cited by Mazrui. Other instances include Doe's terrible misdeeds in Liberia, Mobutu's in Zaire, Bokasa's in Central Africa Republic, Banda's in Malawi, and the long-running dictatorships that have spawned the horrors in Somalia, Rwanda, Burundi and Sierra Leone. The problem, of course, is that very few countries had the moral authority of Tanzania's leadership in the 1970s to set a threshold of human rights compliance that could be defended against wrong-doers. Doe was pampered by Nigeria's Babangida, who later tried to play the role of peacemaker when civil war broke out in Liberia. However, it was all too obvious that Babangida's hands were not only compromised by his previous acts in Liberia, but that his domestic record on human rights and governance were just as bad as those of other military dictators on the continent. In this vein, the military take-over of the Gambian government by Jammeh and his youthful colleagues should have been resisted in the same way the Southern African governments successfully resisted the coup in Lesotho. One should also cite the firmness with which the recent coup in Sao Tome and Principe was condemned by neighbouring countries like Angola and Gabon, which led to the reinstatement of constitutional rule in that country.

If the goal of collective self-discipline is laudable, the scheme which Mazrui has chosen to operationalise it, unfortunately, has serious limitations. Mazrui imagines a concert of African regional powers that will be strong enough to maintain not only continental peace but also the skills required to administer their newly acquired colonial territories -- the failed states. From a strategic point of view, there is nothing wrong with having core states that have a capacity to underwrite regional operations and activities. Mazrui's vision coincides with that of several African scholars whose choice of countries, incidentally, is exactly the same as those he has identified for his project on internal colonisation. The difference is that other scholars do not recommend colonisation since such a project is unlikely to succeed in any region of twentieth century Africa. All things being equal, Nigeria, South Africa, Egypt, Ethiopia and Zaire should have been able to play much more positive roles in their respective regions than they have done at present.

The question to ask is whether objective conditions permit these states to undertake the kinds of colonial responsibilities that Mazrui wants to thrust upon them. Let us start with Nigeria, home to one fifth of all Africans and 55 percent of West Africans; the largest African economy after South Africa; and blessed with numerous physical resources and educated manpower. Surely, its overwhelming presence in the sub-region cannot be ignored. Indeed, during the oil-boom period in the 1970s and early 1980s, Nigeria was already a magnet for a large pool of West Africans seeking to improve their livelihoods and professions. The country also had a very forward looking foreign policy - which unfortunately was undermined by the 1983/84 expulsion of Ghanaians - and prided itself, with justification, as the undisputed leader of Black Africa. Under Bolaji Akinyemi's tenure as Foreign Minister, when vision was still a valued commodity in that ministry, Nigeria had in fact put in place a pan-African force of professional volunteers to help other African countries with their problems of development. However, as Mazrui himself notes, Nigeria is currently going through very difficult times and it is unlikely that it can mount another major operation in the region after the fiasco in Liberia without reforming and democratising its state structures and system of governance, and launching a serious programme of moral rearmament. Indeed, it risks being put in the dock by Africans and the world community for its current unstable and deplorable behaviour.

It is true that Ethiopia was a major imperial power in the past -- indeed, the only country not to have been ruled by European imperialists. But it is precisely because of its imperial past that the country got itself in a big mess. It has already given Africa one new state (Eritrea) and it is not clear whether others are in the pipeline. I think Ethiopia's rulers seem to have drawn the correct lessons from the African predicament: colonisation can lead to costly wars and social disintegration; and there is no viable alternative to local or sub-regional autonomy if Africa's ethnic groups are to co-exist peacefully and develop their economies and rich cultural heritage. One may quarrel with the way Ethiopia has gone about restructuring its fractured polity, since the elements of open democracy and real autonomy have not taken firm roots in the society. But what this experiment points to, as Mafeje notes, is a new Ethiopia that has definitely shed its colonial past and seems ready to confront its internal problems. It seems unlikely that such a country will develop an appetite for new colonial responsibilities.

The case of Zaire should be obvious to everyone: a wasting giant in the middle of Africa. It is unlikely that it will be able to take Rwanda and Burundi under its wings in the next century, even if its leaders were to nourish such ambitions. Indeed, it has to be careful not to lose some of its own units if ever it were to conceive of such an adventure. Zaire is definitely going to be a key player in the search for peace in Rwanda and Burundi, which may involve some restructuring of boundaries and responsibilities, but not as a colonial power. This brings us to Egypt. The major problem there is Islamic fundamentalism. Egyptians may have to confront this problem in their own country before they start thinking about recolonising Sudan. If the fundamentalists over-run Egypt, it will definitely lead to closer ties between Egypt and the current leaders in Sudan, but this will only make matters worse in Southern Sudan and, indeed, in large parts of Egypt and Sudan. Even if fundamentalism is checked, Egypt's status as an Arabised country will disqualify it as a colonial power in Southern Sudan.

This leaves us with South Africa, clearly the only credible power in the continent at the moment. Even in its current form, South Africa is likely to exert great pressure on neighbouring countries in the sub-region, and it is definitely going to be a force for good behaviour in the future. If the current democratisation experiment holds, it might be difficult to envisage military or one party rule in Southern Africa for a very long time. But should South Africa play an imperial role? I believe that such a role will not only backfire in the long run, but that South Africa should entertain no interest in it, short of the very calculated moves the leadership has taken to raise the tone of moral responsibility in the region and farther afield, and exert pressure on leaders when this becomes necessary, as it has done in Mozambique, Angola and Lesotho. The greatest contribution South Africa can make to the rest of Africa is if it is able to resolve its enormous problems of racial inequalities and prepare Africans to assume the great tasks of running and owning a modern industrial state and economy. Any premature external adventure risks putting into service a largely unreconstructed racist war-making machine and system of administration, which may ultimately have negative repercussions in its own society.

Conclusion: Reforming the African State

It should be clear from this discussion that neither external recolonisation nor internal self-colonisation is a recipe for Africa's problems. Instead, Africa needs to look deeper into the way its current states allocate and administer power, and explore ways in which its social structures can be made to provide sustainable forms of political representation, accountability and good governance. To echo, in the form of a question, one of Mazrui's agonising, but pertinent, statements: why have Africans "utterly failed to unite for economic development and political stability"? The obvious place to start in answering this question is to examine the nature of the unity that African states have been trying to build since independence. What are the basic elements of this unity? And how realistic is it?

Central to the project on unity is an image of Africa that does not sufficiently recognise the relatively autonomous existence of the ethnic groups that make up the various countries. Individuals are expected to shed their ethnic identities or origins and embrace a new national identity in order to enjoy the fruits of modernisation. This image of centrally organised unity for modernisation was bequeathed by the colonial powers, which had practised relatively successful versions of it in their own continent, under the rubric of the "nation-state". The main difference, however, is that in Europe nation-state development for modernisation first meant the breakup of large units or empires into relatively self-contained ethnic units. In Africa, the nation-state project was to be promoted by suppressing the ethnic units and promoting larger national units. No wonder it has been a disaster, especially when we realise that many of the ethnic units, however small, had been relatively cohesive self-governing polities before the colonial intrusion. They had provided the cultural foundations for meaningful social life among their various peoples. What the new Africa tried to do can be likened to the drawing up of a programme which would tell the English to abandon their Englishness (however difficult it is to define) and embrace only a single British identity, or urging the Swiss Romand and Swiss Allemand to stop being French and German respectively and become only Swiss. What made matters worse is that in the case of Africa, the values and institutions that were identified for the construction of the new nation-states and identities were to be derived not even from the experiences of a dominant local culture but from the values of the departing colonial authorities and Western society in general.

This nation-state project has three important negative implications. First, it has meant the devaluation of all that has sustained the African in many millennia in the tropics: use of indigenous African institutions and values such as its languages, religions, collective social security arrangements, governance systems, health care provisioning cultures, training systems, military defence, etc. -- now confined to the non-formal sector, of value only to curious anthropologists. And yet, it is not that these institutions are fading away as in other continents that experienced far higher forms of Western domination, such as in Latin America, North America and Australia, for instance. In Africa, these institutions continue to define the lives of the vast majority of the people.

Two illustrations of the African's remarkable capacity to sustain and modernise indigenous culture can be drawn from the area of music and language, where it is obvious that the elitist modernisation project is clearly losing the battle. Even though Western languages remain official in all countries, the number of Africans sufficiently exposed to them for most periods of their daily lives are not only very small, but Western languages have failed to evolve as lingua franca even among élites. Mazrui's prediction of Zaire surpassing France as the "largest French-speaking nation in the world" seems misplaced -- unless we assume that if Zaire's population hits sixty or seventy million in the next century every Zairean will not only be fluent in French but that the language will be the key medium for conducting their social and working lives on any given day. This is a mistake which most people make when they describe African countries as Francophone or Anglophone. Anybody familiar with the social dynamics of Zaire will tell you that the most dynamic languages at the popular level are Lingala (which, incidentally has a glorious future, in part because of the national and continental reach of its rich music) and Swahili. The point is that every African country has one or a few languages that have emerged as lingua franca either at a national or regional level. In the area of music, even though traditional music is not adequately promoted by African leaders, ordinary Africans have modernised traditional African rhythms and sounds into a variety of music and dance forms, and have given African music a unique place in the world. Indeed, popular music represents the most successful project of modernisation carried out by Africans. It explains why, in this area, African musicians have been able to bridge the divide between élites and ordinary folk, something that cannot be said for our literary artists who use English, French and Portuguese in their works. Whereas both elites and ordinary folks enjoy African music without any interlocutors, only a few elites enjoy African literature.

A second problem associated with the nation-state project is its tendency to degenerate into authoritarianism. Since local culture and institutions are not engaged constructively, rulers may have no inhibition in extending conflicts developed at the national level to the assumed ethnic groups of their national opponents in local communities. Such targeted communities may be forced either to side with their "elite sons and daughters" and risk alienation and repression from central authority, or support the government and end up inviting deep divisions among their communities, especially if the estranged élites insist in putting up a fight. Either way, it makes it difficult to work out a system of checks and balances that will allow local communities to govern themselves without much central government intrusion or blind loyalty to their national élites.

Ordinarily, Africa's plural societies should have acted as an effective check on absolute power and repression, given the numerous hurdles an aspiring dictator will have to cross before he can impose his will on all of society. At least this is the great hope of classical democratic theory, which sees plurality - or polyarchy, in Dahl's formulation - as a fundamental necessity for sustainable democracy. However, in the African case, we have turned a natural sociological advantage into a political disadvantage: the tensions inherent in trying to get everybody to toe a single national line in a limited modern/western space easily led to military or one party dictatorships. We know the results of such dictatorships when one group or a coalition of ethnic groups ends up dominating them. Very often the national line became an ethnic line, which reflected the ethnic interests of those who controlled state power.

A third important problem of the nation-state in Africa is its tendency to encourage rent-seeking activities and difficulties in imposing penalties for wrongdoing. Once the euphoria of independence wears out and the national coalition that brought independence breaks down, it becomes difficult to identify a national group that will see its mission as that of the defence of the state qua state, and not just of government.

337

And yet, that is precisely the reality behind the nation-state revolutions in Europe: industrialists and middle class professionals were nationalists who fought for the creation of ethnically homogenous and effective states in order to support national industrial development.

The failure of such groups to emerge in Africa allows individuals who occupy or have access to such states to simply feed on public resources without any group holding them accountable. What is more, those who violate public resources often rely on their ethnic constituencies to shield them away from public scrutiny and punishment. It has also been very easy for disgraced politicians to get rehabilitated by their ethnic elite compatriots and deformed governments seeking new allies. Who would have thought that Umaru Dikko who was almost crated as cargo from London to Lagos by Nigeria Airways after the fall of the Shagari government in 1983, to answer charges of gross embezzlement of public funds, will today be a big player in Nigerian politics?

Where does all this lead us? The crisis of the nation-state in Africa cannot be solved by colonisation which, as we have seen, is responsible for the origins of the crisis in the first place. Should the affairs of Africa be handed back to pre-colonial governments? Even though there have been a few vocal voices in support of this position in recent years, I think it is an option that is clearly unviable, and is likely to lead to more blood, misery and pain than anything Africa has witnessed so far. A century or more of colonial and post-colonial rule has radically changed Africa's social and political landscape: there have been large scale population movements resulting in mixed settlements; mixed marriages are common place as was the practice even in pre-colonial societies; a high number of individuals may hate to be locked into ethnically homogenous states (remember ex-Yugoslavia and ethnic cleansing!); there have been changes in the structures and traditions of ethnic authority systems; and one should recognise the simple fact that a large number of these societies did not have state forms of government during pre-colonial times. It is indeed encouraging that with all the problems that one encounters with the current states, movements for self-determination are relatively few and hardly command consistent popular support even in the areas where they exist.

If the transfer of power to precolonial governments is out, a radical reform of the nation-state is an imperative for political stability and economic development. Mafeje recognises this imperative very well in his reference to the "demand for democratic pluralism and regional autonomy and decentralisation" as "indications of current trends in the continent". I can see such reforms being pursued in several dimensions: ensuring that the scourge of one party rule and military dictatorship is buried forever -- it does not allow for the necessary flexibility and respect for local autonomy that is required for managing multi-ethnic societies; devolving much real autonomy to local societies to cut out the ease with which authoritarian rule can be enthroned and economic rents collected at the central state level -- this should help to promote real intra-ethnic competitive politics and the growth of civic organisations in local societies, which are prime conditions for sustainable local democracy; protecting the full rights of ethnic minorities at all levels of society including in local areas in order to prevent "ethnic witch-hunting"; promoting a civic culture right through to the local level so that party politics does not become ethnic politics even though ethnic considerations may be an input to such politics; working out a scheme for managing power among the major political actors at local, regional and national levels -- such schemes should not be based on overtly ethnic formulae but the outcomes should ensure that ethnic groups feel sufficiently represented in the schemes; creating a system of electoral competition that allows for broad representation in legislative organs; developing appropriate accountability and transparency mechanisms for checking the actions of rulers and public officers at all levels of society; and strengthening the independence of the press, the judiciary, and trans-ethnic civil organisations.

Africa will not be able to form the viable regional integration systems that Mazrui alludes to, which are clearly necessary to enhance the continent's global competitiveness, if each state is not at ease with its local units. No programme of regional integration has succeeded anywhere in the world that is not based on solid foundations of local government. This is one lesson we should draw from Africa's failed attempts at regional and continental integration. Such organisations that exist tend to depend on the whims and caprices of a few leaders; since such leaders are not sufficiently committed to their states and constituent units, but only to their governments, they have often lacked the vision for, and commitments towards, a truly sustainable Pan-African integration system.

Reforming Africa's states under conditions of crisis and instability obviously harbours many inherent dangers. But Africans should not simply plod along as if nothing has changed, or proceed on the assumption that everything will be all right in the end. CODESRIA could assume the first task of getting African intellectuals, opinion leaders, national public figures, government officials, the press and non-governmental organisations to start a serious of discussion of these issues. I believe that this is likely to make the transitions less painful and more enlightened. It will certainly help us avoid becoming victims of Mazrui's recolonisation programme.

43
The Case for a Pan-African Intervention Force in the Great Lakes Region of Africa[43]

The current war between Rwandan-backed rebels in Eastern Zaire and the Zairean army threatens to further undermine political stability and human security in the countries that border the Great Lakes region -- Rwanda, Burundi, Zaire, Uganda and Tanzania. This region is host to over one million refugees. Two countries, Rwanda and Burundi, have the continent's highest population densities, and a recent record of state-sponsored and ethnically-inspired genocide. One country, Zaire, has Africa's second largest land mass and has been without effective political authority since 1991. Another country, Uganda, fought highly destructive civil wars in the late 1970s and much of the 1980s, and although it now has an effective government and a rapidly growing economy, the low-intensity war in the North has gained renewed momentum in recent months. Military rule has been restored in Burundi in which a minority group, the Tutsi, whose elites engineered the coup, feel threatened by the majority Hutu. That country also has the misfortune of having to deal with a range of sanctions which neighbouring countries slammed on it in July this year, following the military coup. Only Tanzania, which has recently organised multi-party elections that threw up much ethnic or racial hatred, appears to be an island of peace and stability. In short, we are dealing with a region that is likely to be plunged into large scale and protracted instability if immediate steps are not taken to reverse the current disorder and help the local populations rebuild their battered lives and institutions.

African leaders and the rest of the world have equivocated in the last three weeks as the fighting between the Zairean army and the rebels intensified. Large numbers of refugees and local people have been killed either directly by the warring groups or as a result of war-induced hunger and disease. For two years, the international community has been unable to find solutions to the problems of the refugees and the immediate crisis in Rwanda and Burundi. Bands of young men, the Hutu Interahamwe,

---

[43] Abridged version published in *West Africa* (London), 6-12 January, 1997.

who have committed some of the worst atrocities in post-independence Africa, were being fed by international relief agencies, and allowed to enjoy sanctuary among, as well as hold as hostages, a traumatised Hutu population in the camps at Goma and Bukavu. Events in the past few days have finally forced many of the refugees to return to Rwanda. Whether or not the war was planned by the Rwandan government and its Zairean-led rebels to force the refugees to return, the decision to return must rank as one of the great moments of refugee movements in our time. For now, the doomsday scenario of total anarchy that is being predicted and anxiously awaited by the purveyors of Afro-pessimism has been contained. The common sense of ordinary people has opened up new vistas of opportunity to bring peace and stability to the region. Africa and the world should seize the initiative now before a new dynamic unfolds.

Unfortunately, there is growing belief among African and world leaders that the situation will soon return to normal, that Rwanda would be at peace with itself again, and that the region would be spared of the conflagration that has threatened it in the last few weeks. Nothing could be further from the truth. More than ever before, what the situation requires is a disciplined, well-funded, and well-armed pan-African force to help stabilise the region, prevent further acts of opportunistic behaviour by contestants for power, and rebuild the institutions of the region. Africa should learn from the great efforts of NATO in helping to bring peace and create new all-inclusive political institutions in Bosnia. People who have been traumatised by war, genocide, and ethnic hatred are not likely on their own to show the maturity and discipline that is required to rebuild social lives, communities and political institutions. They need a sympathetic but firm external arbiter to help them do this. We believe that the initiative for creating such an arbiter should come from Africa and not from Western countries for the following reasons.

There is too much Afro-pessimism in Western countries at the moment for a Western-led intervention force in Africa to have much impact. Western soldiers do not understand African people, cultures and institutions, and probably hold many of the negative attitudes that are currently fashionable in their societies -- i.e. that Africans cannot govern themselves, are totally helpless like little children, and need to be dictated to if things are going to be done right. The disaster of the US mission in Somalia should provide a salutary lesson to both Africa and the West about how a mission that was meant to restore hope turned sour for both the US and Somalia. Americans went into Somalia without the foggiest idea about Somali traditions and institutions. They therefore resorted to high-handed tactics against the local population when what they thought was going to be an easy mission became difficult to manage. They later withdrew in shame to let the Somalis sort things out for themselves. As recent reports have shown, the behaviour of Canadian soldiers (it is being proposed that Canada is to lead the Western force) was also highly questionable. The world should not allow such acts of recklessness to be repeated on African soil under the banner of humanitarian assistance.

While Western forces may be able to explain the shedding of Western blood in Bosnia to their public, it seems unlikely that they would be able to do the same if they incur high body losses in Africa. In general, Africa is too remote to the everyday lives of Westerners, who would rather treat it as a basket case for the odd charity or relief work, and not as a place where strategic choices about Western lives and progress are to be made. Only companies and individuals that are currently making enormous amounts of money from the continent's rich mineral resources and arms markets would be interested in a strategy of long term engagement. But these, by definition, profit from state collapse and protracted civil war. The Great Lakes region is a difficult terrain, which would require long-term positive engagement, and perhaps readiness to absorb a certain level of human losses before the situation could be brought under control. Why start a mission that is likely to be aborted just when it would be needed most to defend local populations? Sending a Western-led force to the region would amount to misplaced priorities. What the region needs instead is Western logistics, finance, training and arms that would be controlled by an African-led force.

Besides, judging from pronouncements by political leaders in the US and Europe, the Western-led force would only be concerned with creating the conditions for the return of the refugees and to allow relief agencies to reach those who are still in the wilderness. They do not want to get involved in the difficult business of dealing with the Interahamwe and other armed groups, the ending of the armed conflict, and the rebuilding of institutions in the region. Why waste the political opportunity of positive long-term engagement with the region that has been created by the return of many of the refugees? What the region needs is much more than what the West is ready to commit itself to.

Two countries, France and Belgium, whose past activities contributed to the current problems in the region are strategically located in the Western power structure. Belgium was the colonial power in Zaire, Rwanda and Burundi. Its record of colonial rule stands out as the most barbaric even by Western standards. King Leopold's rule in Congo was a nightmare. And Belgian colonial officials helped shape and nurture the ethnic hatred between the Tutsi and Hutu by promoting the myth that the Tutsi were more intelligent than the Hutu. France was in very good terms with the previous Rwandan regime that committed the genocide of 1994, and has been accused of helping the fleeing killers in 1994, fearing that the new rulers of Rwanda, all of whom speak English by virtue of having lived in Uganda, are likely to take Rwanda out of the Francophone orbit. Despite the leadership role that has been given to Canada in the proposed force, Belgium and France are likely to play influential roles in any Western strategy of intervention. This will highly compromise the neutrality of such a force.

Africa and the world have no alternative but to support a pan-African led force in the region if the goal of long-term stability is to be attained. Recent pronouncements by the US show that it is already beginning to accept the wisdom of empowering pan-African institutions in the area of conflict resolution and peace building. It is helping the OAU to develop its conflict resolution department, and has provided support to the Economic Community of West African State's initiative in Liberia. These efforts are still not properly focused and there have been lags between external funding commitments and their disbursement. But they point in the right direction. The European Community should follow suit. Western comparative advantage lies in providing finance, logistics, armaments, and technical training to a pan-African force. There could even be technical links between this force and NATO, which has proved to be very effective in Bosnia.

Often, nothing gets easily done if initiatives for rapid intervention are left to international organisations alone. Without the intervention of the US, Bosnia would still be burning. In Liberia, it was Nigeria that took the initiative. The OAU was unable to do anything with the dictator, Idi Amin, until Tanzania took the initiative to oust him. The OAU is unlikely on its own to take the initiative for a pan-African force. The responsibility for setting up the force should fall on Tanzania, Ethiopia and Kenya, backed by South Africa. Uganda's neutrality is likely to be questioned because of its close links with the current Rwandan government. Zaire is in disarray. And Rwanda and Burundi need help. With the return of the refugees, these two countries are now ruled by regimes whose primary base of support comes from a very small fraction of the population. They would need to be assured that democratisation, when it eventually comes, would not lead to new massacres.

The pan-African-led force should have a long-term goal of deterring future acts of rebellion and genocide, allow people of that region to rethink the political systems of their countries from a regional as opposed to a purely national perspective, and helping local people to craft appropriate institutions for managing the conflicting claims of groups that have led to this terrible chapter of suffering, misery and pain. For all its current problems, there have been high levels of social interaction among groups in this region. The lingua franca in Eastern Zaire, Tanzania, and much of Uganda is Swahili. Contrary to current media stories, the Banyamulenge are not all Tutsi. Indeed, Banyamulenge translated literally means the people from the hill of Mulenge which, as is the case for the Kivu region as a whole, is rich in gold reserves, and therefore home to numerous ethnic groups in search of economic opportunities. All speak Swahili in addition to Mashi, Kinyarwanda and other languages in Kivu province. Many people in Rwanda also speak Swahili, Mashi and other languages in Eastern Zaire. There has been a lot of intermarriage over the centuries, and it is not always easy to differentiate groups on the basis of physical features alone.

44
Comments on Regional Security and the War in Congo[44]

The war in the Republic of Congo, which broke out on August 2 1998 in the eastern border town of Goma, threatens to become Africa's first modern regional war. Already five countries -- Rwanda, Uganda, Zimbabwe, Angola and Namibia -- have committed troops to the embattled country. Other countries in the region seem set to intervene or provide varying forms of support to those that are already in. Rebel groups in Angola, Uganda, Rwanda and Burundi have also been drawn into the war. And there have been reports that private security firms and mercenaries from South Africa may have been enlisted by both sides. Why did the situation deteriorate so rapidly in Congo, and what are the regional security implications of the war? These comments address three issues.

Rwanda and Uganda: A security blunder?

The first relates to the way Uganda and Rwanda have handled relations with Kabila's government and the security implications of the militarist orientation that seems to inform the foreign policies of the first two countries. One important question that needs to be asked is: why did Museveni and Kagame squander, in the space of a year, the goodwill and leverage they enjoyed in Congo, following the positive role they played in the overthrow of the corrupt and dictatorial Mobutu regime? In the views of many commentators, their support for the current rebel cause, whether covertly or openly, after just one year of installing Kabila in power, may stand out as one of the most extraordinary blunders in foreign and security policies in modern times.

---

[44] Published in M. Baregu (ed.), *Crisis in the Democratic Republic of Congo*. Harare: SARIPS. Series 3, pp. 10-17, 1999; I. Mandaza (ed.), *Reflections on the Crisis in the Democratic Republic of Congo*, SAPES Books. Harare. 1999.; Association of Concerned Africa Scholars *Special Bulletin: The 1998 Rebellion in the Democratic Republic of Congo,* October 1998, No. 53/54. Adapted version published in *The Monitor* (Kampala), 1 September 1998.

Kabila may well have acted in ways that were perceived by Kagame and Museveni to be contrary to the latter two leaders' national security interests -- defined broadly as the need to protect their national borders against threats from the Hutu Interahamwe and the Ugandan rebels, the so-called Allied Democratic Forces. Kabila's approach to governance issues, as has been pointed out by critics, has been clearly driven by nepotism and patronage. His governance policy has been narrow, repressive and distrustful of autonomous civic groups and political parties that had played major roles in weakening Mobutu's rule. However, allegations that his rule was worse than Mobutu's cannot be well founded. Nor are we dealing with an Idi Amin type of blood-thirsty rule that justified Tanzanian invasion of Ugandan territory on humanitarian grounds in 1979. It is debatable whether Kabila would have been able to police Congo's very long eastern border during his first year in office, and whether, in fact, he would have supported the Hutu and Ugandan rebels when he was so dependent on Rwanda and, to some extent, Uganda for his own security. The ease with which large segments of the armed forces of Congo collapsed or crossed over to the rebels suggests that the security situation may have been much more complicated than the story of official complicity in the use of Congolese territory by Hutu and Ugandan rebels. Is it the case that Kabila proved too independent for the designs of his former benefactors?

Whatever the reasons for the deterioration of relations between the three leaders, it seems that both Kagame and Museveni as well as their security advisers did not factor in the following issues when the decision was taken to destabilise Kabila's government and the country generally: the security fears of Southern African countries, which also have a legitimate stake in the stability of Congo; Kabila's historical ties with the leaders of these countries during their liberation struggles; Kabila's deft decision to seek membership of SADC, which effectively offered him the opportunity to reduce his dependence on Rwanda and Uganda; the unpopularity of the large presence of Rwandan troops in the country and ethnic Tutsi in the government; the fact that both Rwanda and Uganda are resource poor, when compared to the countries of Southern Africa; and the vulnerability of the very small population of the Banyamulenge Tutsi to Congolese nationalism.

In the long-term, landlocked Rwanda and Uganda face heightened tension and insecurity in eastern Congo, whether the government of Congo wins the war or not. With the presence of Angola, Zimbabwe and Namibia in the war, we can safely predict that western Congo is unlikely to be taken by rebel forces. If the east also falls to government hands, then Rwanda and Uganda will have a very large, resource rich, outspoken and hostile neighbour (a wounded lion?) to the west of their two countries. If, on the other hand, the east remains a contested zone, it is unlikely that Congo will accept the buffer that Uganda and Rwanda will ultimately seek to create on Congolese territory. Congo is likely to sustain the fight for the recovery of its land, using the kind of strident nationalism that it has demonstrated so far in this conflict.

The war could spill over into Rwanda and Uganda, and all parties in the conflict would be tempted to support their opponents' rebels. So, whatever the outcome, Rwanda and Uganda may come out of this war with higher levels of instability and threats to their security than they faced before the uprising of August 2. Whoever said that Kagame and Museveni are master regional strategists and visionaries? Rather than being a force for regional stability as was previously thought, their militarist policies risk plunging Central and East Africa into protracted chaos and a humanitarian disaster. In a context of ethnic divisions and social tensions, militarism may fan the flames of genocide as all parties to the conflict may be forced to calculate in terms of ethnic survival. The policy of exporting armed rebellions to foreign countries needs to be strongly queried and contained, especially in Africa where societies are ethnically fragmented, and political institutions and economies are very weak. In the Great Lakes region, this policy contributed to the Rwandan genocide of 1994 and, as the current war has shown, it has endangered the lives, security and livelihoods of the ethnic Tutsi in Congo. In the West African region, the export of armed rebellions by Libya, Burkina Faso and Liberia led to lumpen violence, untold atrocities, and widespread humanitarian disasters in Sierra Leone and Liberia.

South Africa, Zimbabwe and SADC

The second point I would like to address is the role of South Africa, Zimbabwe and SADC in the conflict. The question a lot of people have been asking is: how come it is small countries like Zimbabwe, Angola and Namibia that have taken the lead in the Congo crisis and not South

Africa, the real power in the region? Why is Mandela's government pushing the option of negotiation and cease fire, while his partners in SADC have opted for the military option? One explanation is that Mandela may not be fully in charge of the South African military, whereas Mugabe, the leader of the SADC military coalition in Congo, is in charge of his. Having just come out of apartheid, with an economy, public service and army that are still largely in the hands of white people associated with the previous apartheid regime, the last thing the ANC wants is to engage the SADF in external military activities.

Foreign and security policy in South Africa may also be constrained by inputs from "white or Western interests" in the bureaucracy in a way that they are not in Zimbabwe. These interests are not fully engaged in the African discourse north of the river Limpopo. Negotiation, compromise and tardy responses to African problems may seem, therefore, to be the defining features of South African policy until the real power balance shifts significantly in favour of Africans and Africa-focused individuals in that country. In a way, this crisis has exposed South Africa's limitations as the African country that is best placed to occupy a permanent seat in the UN's Security Council. Nigeria's leadership and decisive peace enforcement operations in West Africa under ECOMOG seem to put it in a much better position than South Africa to represent Africa in the Security Council if such types of UN reforms are to be implemented at this stage.

Through its defence industry, Zimbabwe obviously has military financial interests in Kabila's government, as has been widely reported in the media. A Southern African friend informs me that the Inga dam, the largest hydro-electric dam in the world, also produces about 10 percent of Zimbabwe's electricity needs, and is central to the operations of the copper belt in Zambia. It may also be supplying power to Congo-Brazzaville and Angola, and possibly even Rwanda. Does this explain why the rebels and their backers were able to reach an agreement with Angola not to blow the dam up, in exchange for a safe passage out of the area? On the Angolan side, Dos Santos's MPLA government is worried about the prospects of having an unfriendly government in Kinshasa that would make it difficult for it to have access to its Cabinda oil enclave, which is situated between Congo and the Angolan mainland. It is also concerned about its capacity to check the activities of the recalcitrant UNITA rebel movement.

An additional argument for Zimbabwean intervention is that Mugabe may, from his own experience in Zimbabwe, be sensitive to the dangers of allowing minority groups to lord it over majorities. It is, indeed, interesting to study how and why Mugabe was able to use his chairmanship of the military organ of SADC to isolate South Africa in the crucial meetings that led to the decision to give Kabila's government a helping hand: South Africa was not represented in the early meetings of 14 SADC countries on the crisis, and was also not part of the delegation that was sent to Goma to find out whether Rwanda and Uganda were truly violating the territory of Congo. Also worrying are the differences that developed between Mugabe, Mandela and the OAU on the strategies for the resolution of the crisis.

Given the fact that South Africa is a recent member of SADC, it may take some time before the former's neighbours begin to respect its natural claims of leadership in the region. These countries are used to running SADC without South Africa. There are closer official military ties among Zimbabwe, Angola, Namibia and Mozambique than between South Africa and these countries. These differences stem from the history of the liberation movements in Southern Africa and the fight against apartheid. Unlike South Africa, which had problems overhauling its apartheid army, the other Southern African countries relied substantially on their liberation armies in the formation of their post-colonial national defence forces. And since the latter have been independent for a much longer time than South Africa, they have a much more decolonised army than South Africa's. Military strategy in these early independence countries was also oriented against white rule and the need to contain the South African army. Angola, indeed, defeated the South African army in the 1970s at Cuito Cuanavale.

South Africa, it seems, may have lost the initiative to influence the situation in Congo. The Pretoria communiqué surely recognised Kabila as the legitimate ruler of Congo, but it failed to condemn the methods the rebels and their backers have used in their efforts to change the government. The 1997 OAU's Harare resolution -- passed after the military overthrow of the government of Sierra Leone --opposed the use of military means to change legitimate governments, and the organisation's charter itself is staunchly opposed to the violation of the territorial integrity of member states. The Pretoria communiqué should have upheld these two vital principles of African international relations.

It should be noted that there have been about 75 military coups in Africa since 1960, and about 18 civil wars in the 1990s, with the majority of the wars occurring under military governments.

What is more, current methods of armed rebellion harbour more dangers than traditional military coups in the dynamics of political change in the continent. Coups had, in the main, been swift and sharp, and had generally affected only the armed forces and resulted in minimum casualties. Armed rebellions on the other hand have brought untold harm on the civil population through indiscriminate mass killings, large scale population displacement, and destruction of economic assets and livelihoods. The latter have also exposed the African population to the power of armed factions and war lords who are not in any way committed to democracy and economic development.

It is interesting to note that the same forces that are now trying to overthrow Kabila collaborated with him in frustrating calls for the opening up of the political system to civic groups and opposition parties after the overthrow of Mobutu. The so-called political wing of the rebel movement, Rally for a Democratic Congo, has all the hallmarks of a hastily assembled front. The real power seems to be with the militarists as represented by Deogratias Bugera, Jean-Pierre Ondekane, and Sylvian Mbuki. Ernest Wamba dia Wamba, the leader of the political wing, is a fine scholar and pan-Africanist, but it is doubtful that he is in charge of the movement. In a recent CNN news report on the war, the military commander in Goma stated in Wamba's presence that he and his military colleagues would act against Wamba's political group if, on attaining power, they became dissatisfied with their rule. Wamba's recent interview with the Belgian newspaper, *De Standard*, is also revealing. He advanced the view that the political wing was formed after the military operation and, therefore, lagged behind the military system. He hoped that those whose views were in line with the political liberation of the people would eventually gain the advantage in the movement. But would they?

It is important to note that elements within the ranks of the militarists are among the forces that committed the genocide against Hutu refugees and rebuffed all efforts by the UN to investigate the crime. They are also associated with the corruption that has been levied against Kabila. Why should anyone believe that they will behave differently this time? Kabila's rule has surely not been inspiring, and there is an overwhelming and urgent case for internal political reforms, but these reforms cannot be brought about by military means. Militarism breeds a culture of violence and empowers those with guns at the expense of civic groups and pro-democracy political parties.

If the Pretoria communiqué had condemned the rebellion, it would have been much easier to work on its cease-fire provisions. Mandela would have been in a stronger position than now to bring pressure to bear on Kabila's ADFL to open up the political system to other civic groups and opposition parties, guarantee basic human and civic rights, and organise elections that will establish a truly representative government in the country. The prospects for a SADC peacekeeping force in eastern Congo, or the Great Lakes region itself, would have been much easier to push through than it is the case presently.

Instead, we have been left with a situation in which relatively small, underdeveloped, though resource rich, SADC countries with tenuous democratic credentials, have become the custodians of the OAU's resolutions and the territorial integrity of Congo. It would be difficult for Mandela's peace and reform option to prevail under these circumstances. And calling for a peacekeeping force now is likely to be interpreted as an attempt by South Africa to undermine Congo's independence and links with its military allies. Despite these problems, South Africa should still make the effort to condemn the rebel uprising, and stress the need to defend the territorial integrity of Congo. This may help to undo the damage that seems to have been created by the present policy of "neutrality." A policy of neutrality that does not uphold the principles of the OAU on the territorial integrity of member states and opposition to military methods in changing African governments is not likely to be effective. Upholding these principles may put South Africa in a formidable position to convince other SADC members and Congo of the need to place a peacekeeping force in the east to defend both the territorial integrity of that country and the security interests of the Banyamulenge Tutsi, Rwanda and Uganda. It will also make it relatively easier for South Africa and SADC to influence the political reforms that are badly needed in Congo.

The pitfalls of calls for US support for a Tutsi Republic

The third issue I want to talk about is Edward Marek's *New Congo News'* tired ethnocratic scenario, which expects the US to provide military support to the leaders of Rwanda and Uganda to do what the Jews have done in Israel -- create a Tutsi republic and defend it resolutely with armed methods. It is dangerous to draw a parallel between the Jews and the Tutsi. Until the last half of this century, no one seriously questioned the rights of the Tutsi in the places where they live. Despite the racial prism that has been used to explain the ethnic problems in the Great Lakes region, the Tutsi are an integral part of the African social and cultural formation. The vast majority of African countries are multi-ethnic non-nation-states, and are likely to be disturbed by calls for an independent Tutsi state. Others may well ask: Why not an Ewe republic? or a Zulu republic? or an Ndebele republic? or a Kikuyu republic? or a Buganda republic? or a Fulbe republic? or an Acholi republic? or, indeed, two thousand or more ethnic republics? The OAU saw the security dangers of such calls and decided, correctly, in its charter to freeze the colonially inherited borders.

The problem in Rwanda and Burundi has been the history of hierarchical structures that have governed relations between the Tutsi and Hutu, and the fact that both countries are in a way the only ethnic diarchies or bipolar polities in the continent. Social hierarchies breed feelings of superiority and hatred; and diarchies or bipolarity make it difficult to construct multiple alliances in the resolution of conflicts. One of the main reasons why Museveni's rule has been relatively accepted in Uganda is precisely because of the large number of ethnic groups in that country, which has made it possible for him to create a complex web of social and political alliances. If the elites of both groups in ethnic diarchies or bipolarities, such as in Burundi and Rwanda, do not recognise their limitations, their struggles for power can produce pogroms and genocide, because conflicts may be cast in zero-sum survivalist terms: one group's *gain* may be seen as the other group's *loss*. History suggests that minorities are unlikely to win such wars in the long run. The best long-term guarantee for minority rights is democracy and constitutional safeguards -- not ethnic hegemony, separatism or militarism.

It is true that Israel has survived as a Jewish polity in a hostile Arab environment largely because of US support. But that US support is grounded in concrete relations, not in emotions -- the large presence of Jews in the US, who not only have a high voter participation rate relative to their national size, but have been able systematically to influence and sustain US policy in the Middle East. Jews have a strong presence in the US executive, legislature, political parties, media, business and academy. Add to this the attractions which Congo, Angola, Namibia and other Southern African countries offer to US mining and business interests when compared to the economic value of Rwanda and Uganda. In short, encouraging the Tutsi to base a policy of survival on the US when the material basis for that policy does not exist is dangerous and silly. The Tutsi are better served by recognising the rule of the majority, and the crafting of institutions that will guarantee minority interests and civic rights. The key Hutu individuals who directed the genocide of 1994 surely need to be brought to justice, but the Tutsi rulers in Rwanda need to move away from the mind-set which tends to associate all Hutu with the genocide. The Tutsi leaders and their backers should learn from the whites in Zimbabwe and South Africa and, in a way, the experiences of the Ndebele in Zimbabwe who now have relatively cordial relations with the Shona after the brutal civil war of the 1980s.

Conclusion

A large multi-ethnic country like the Republic of Congo cannot be ruled by authoritarian, winner-takes-all methods. Nor can it be governed by foreign forces. The people of Congo need a pluralist democracy; and major state reforms that will produce equitable representation, accountability and efficient delivery of public services. They also need a civic order that will guarantee basic human rights.

354

45

Security Sector Reform Needs Inclusive Politics and Jobs for the Poor[45]

Security sector reform has gained prominence in recent years as the international community seeks solutions to seemingly intractable conflicts. However, in order to achieve sustainable peace, security sector reform needs to be grounded in inclusive government and growth strategies that deliver jobs to the poor.

Although development practitioners have embraced the notion of a security-development nexus, the development dimension in peacebuilding and post-war programming has been treated casually. It consists largely of ad hoc, poorly remunerated work schemes and micro credit that cover only a fraction of the population. Inclusive government has been reduced to quick fix power-sharing deals between warring factions without effective citizen participation, while the preference for standing armies – albeit better trained and incentivised than previous conflict-prone armies – makes it difficult to end the culture of militarism in post-conflict societies.

Security sector reform addresses two interconnected issues: disarmament, demobilisation and reintegration (DDR) of ex-combatants into society; and right-sizing and professionalisation of the military and police. Most wars today end with DDR programmes – by 2006, 51 countries had such programmes. However, results have been more positive in disarmament and demobilisation than in reintegration. There is often a funding gap and bias against reintegration. One estimate for programmes unfolding across 20 countries with a total of 1,129,000 ex-combatants suggests that disarming, demobilising and reintegrating one ex-combatant cost an average of US$ 1,686 in 2007.

A large part of DDR money is spent on short-term assistance, usually lasting a year. Ex-combatants often return to economies with few employment opportunities; some sell tool kits given through reintegration programmes to offset pressing problems; the vast majority join the ranks of under-employed youth in the informal economy. Some

---

[45] Published in *Open Democracy* (London), 19 March 2012; and UNRISD *eBulletin*. 19 March 2012.

are recruited into the security wings of political parties and may provoke violence during elections. In Sierra Leone, for instance, ex-combatants guard politicians and party offices, and often use violence during political rallies to demonstrate their relevance in the security field.

Professionalisation of the military is also beset with problems. In contexts where political parties draw their support from specific ethnic groups or regions, ethno-regional calculations may influence recruitment into the military, creating doubts about impartiality among groups that feel under-represented in the institution. In low income democracies where governments enjoy huge parliamentary majorities and parties lack strong ties with social movements, depoliticisation of the military can be challenging.

More fundamentally, since the military is the only legitimate group to carry weapons in defence of what is clearly a public good (national security), there are bound to be principal-agent problems. The military may demand rents – higher than average salaries, better perks, etc. – that may distort public finances; it may take over the state and fuse the roles of principal and agent; and it may be used by one of the principals – government – to repress the other principal – the public. These outcomes have informed civil-military relations in many poor countries. In much of Africa, soldiers enjoy superior provisioning to average citizens; militaries have staged more than 80 coups since 1960; and governments have repeatedly used the military to control popular dissent.

Professionalisation of the military under conditions of widespread poverty and weak civic institutions may not be a magic bullet for sustainable peace; indeed, it may empower professional armies to extract resources from the state. In Cambodia, the army was partly appeased in the peace settlement of 1991 by giving it concessions in the timber industry. Loggers paid between US$ 35 and US$ 90 per cubic metre of logs felled. This did not prevent the effective army leader and second prime minister in the coalition government, Hun Sen, from staging a coup and getting rid of the democratically elected first prime minister in 1997. In Nigeria, retired and serving military officers are heavily involved in the oil economy as middle men; serve on boards of banks, parastatals and transnational companies; and play leading roles in arms procurement, which takes up a large part of the government budget.

Participation, inclusion and development

Security sector reform that will lead to sustainable peace will require the democratisation of military security, involving the participation of citizens engaged in productive work. Under this alternate scheme, citizens need not carry arms at all times, but they will be required to participate in programmes on security education, methods of arms use and creative strategies of collective and self-defence. Switzerland's citizen-based military system, which combines work and military service, offers useful lessons. It is citizen involvement in national security, not professionalisation per se, that will check the chronic tendency of the military to threaten security and demand rents in poor countries. Furthermore, a citizen-based army may help to heal ethnic divisions, break rigidities in the political system, and serve as a basis for shared citizenship and nation-building.

A democratic security system cannot be built without inclusive government. Research suggests that the distribution of government jobs in countries with polarised ethnic structures often tend to be highly unequal, with ethnic groups associated with governing parties taking the lion's share of posts. This is often a source of tension that can threaten public peace. Until very recently, the response of the international community has been to impose power-sharing deals on contending parties. This happened, for instance, in Sierra Leone in 1999, and Zimbabwe and Kenya in 2008. Governments and opposition parties very quickly learned how to game the system by provoking violence when electoral outcomes are unfavourable, hoping to get a share of power through negotiations brokered by the international community. The UN-sanctioned military removal of Côte d'Ivoire's former president, Laurent Gbagbo, who refused to leave office after losing elections in 2010, suggests weariness by the international community for power sharing deals.

Except in a few cases such as in Bosnia, Iraq and Burundi, there have been limited efforts to craft long-term reforms for inclusive government in post-conflict societies. The constitutions of most countries are still based on winner-takes-all rules. It is critical to note that not all rules that promote inclusive outcomes are conducive to development. One of the limitations of power sharing arrangements that are devoid of institutionalised opposition is that elections may lose their bite by sanctioning poor performance. This is especially the case in poor countries where civic groups are weak, citizen engagement of public policy is difficult to sustain, and elections offer the only viable opportunity to hold leaders to account.

Governments tend to address popular concerns when electoral outcomes are uncertain. Indeed, it has been shown that new democracies tend to be associated with large political budget cycles as governments respond to voter pressures to satisfy basic needs during election periods. One study finds that the fiscal deficits of 44 African countries where competitive elections have been held increased by 1.2 percent of GDP during election years. This is not to suggest that all such expenditures are developmental; it is simply to highlight the tendency for governments to respond to popular demands under conditions of electoral competitiveness.

If the principle of organised opposition is to be retained in post-conflict societies, the challenge for governance reforms is to make all key political parties multi-ethnic. The political science literature is replete with rules that can be crafted to achieve such a goal. Politicians who wish to represent their parties in presidential elections can be subjected to primaries of the US type; threshold rules of vote shares across regions can be established for declaring winners of presidential elections; and the alternative or preference vote that ranks candidates and distributes the votes of losers to top candidates to achieve a majoritarian outcome can be adopted. These rules, which in essence represent pacts between elites, may encourage moderation, force candidates to appeal to voters outside of their ethnic homelands, and lead to the formation of inclusive governments. They can be backed up by a policy of power alternation among key ethno-regional clusters while still retaining the principle of organised opposition.

However, elite pacts are not enough for sustainable peace. A democratic security sector regime also needs an economy that grows and delivers jobs, so that the poor can have a stake in the social contract. One of the tragedies of international development policy in recent years is its failure to induce economic transformations that can generate jobs with decent incomes for individuals who eke a living in the informal sector. Despite the comprehensive nature of the World Bank's World Development Report of 2011, *Conflict, Security and Development*, it approached the employment challenge in post-conflict societies with less conviction for durable solutions, claiming that "...there is no consensus on the exact set of policies that can generate employment".

When employment policy is addressed in development policy, it tends to be detached from broader processes of structural change and restricted largely to ad hoc interventions, such as skills training, public works and micro finance that are poorly funded. Sierra Leone's youth employment programme, which is funded by the World Bank, German Technical Cooperation and the UN, costs US$ 46 million. It is expected to provide 106,000 jobs over a period of two years. This represents only 10 percent of the unemployed/underemployed youth population. The World Bank's youth employment programme for Côte d'Ivoire, which has a larger population than Sierra Leone's, is US$ 50 million.

Concerns for macroeconomic stabilisation often take precedence over development strategies that deliver jobs to the poor. This stabilisation approach has affected aid expenditure policy. A report by the IMF's Independent Evaluation Office of aid to Africa in 2007 found that countries with IMF programmes spent on average only 15 percent of aid receipts if their inflation rates were higher than 5 percent. Post-conflict countries tend to use aid to accumulate foreign reserves. They also engage in small-scale rehabilitation and resettlement programmes rather than support agricultural and industrial transformations that have a potential to improve employment opportunities on a massive scale.

There is no guarantee that current security sector reforms can lead to sustainable peace. The security sector needs to be democratised, governments made inclusive, and development that delivers jobs to the poor given priority in public policy. The good news is that the current global economic crisis has called into question the conventional stabilisation framework for managing economies. Many poor countries, including those affected by war, are beginning to demand policy space to stimulate their economies through extensive investments in infrastructure and adoption of agricultural and industrial policies that will generate positive changes in the real economy. High growth rates and improvements in revenues from minerals and taxation in recent years may serve to consolidate this trend. International development agencies would do well to support these initiatives, as it will require joined up planning to make security sector reform work.

Index

www.ingramcontent.com/pod-product-compliance
Lightning Source LLC
Chambersburg PA
CBHW072010270326
41928CB00009B/1610